The Life of
Sir Stanley Maude
Lieutenant General
K.C.B, C.M.G., D.S.O.

Gosling Press

ISBN: 978-1-874351-26-9 (Hardback)
ISBN: 978-1-874351-27-6 (Paperback)

Gosling Press

www.goslingpress.co.uk

Introduction

The life and achievements of General Sir Stanley Maude deserve to be better known, since today he is usually only known for his late arrival at the beach during the evacuation at Gallipoli and for the capture of Baghdad in 1917.

Born in Gibraltar on 24 June 1864, the son of General Sir Frederick Francis Maude V.C., he was educated at Eton and Sandhurst. He joined the Coldstream Guards in February 1884 and served with them in the Sudan. He subsequently served as a major in South Africa in 1899–1902 during which period he was awarded a D.S.O. In 1901 he was appointed Military Secretary to the Governor-General of Canada, remaining in post until the end of 1904. He then took up a series of general staff posts, reaching the rank of Colonel in 1911.

Maude's First World War career began in France on the staff of III Corps, and in October 1914 he was promoted to Brigadier General and given command of 14th Brigade. Seriously wounded in April 1915 he was sent home to England to recover, returning to France the following month. In June he was promoted to Major General and given command of 33rd Division, then training in England prior to being posted to France. However, following the sacking of a number of senior officers after the Suvla Bay landings, Maude was sent to command the 13th Division and successfully evacuated with them from Suvla to Helles to support the withdrawal from that place. From there the Division was sent to Egypt to reform and refit. From Egypt the Division was ordered to Mesopotamia to join the relief of Kut, although it arrived only in time for the final abortive relief effort.

In Mesopotamia, where he replaced General George Gorringe as commander of the Tigris Corps, Maude set about reorganising his British and Indian troops, and he was continually concerned to improve the conditions of the troops. No aspect of his men's welfare was unimportant for him – from medical support to food supplies and transport, this was especially so in Mesopotamia where issues with the administrative systems were so bad that a Parliamentary Commission was set up in 1916 to investigate the failings.

His greatest triumph was perhaps the capture of Baghdad in March 1917 although due to his untimely death in November 1917 from Cholera at the age of 53, it is perhaps eclipsed by General Allenby's capture of Jerusalem in December.

This study considers Maude's early postings in the Sudan and Boer Wars as well as his service in the opening phases of the Great War and his later triumphs, shedding light on a cautious and consistent, rather than a spectacular, commander.

The Life of
Sir Stanley Maude
Lieutenant General
K.C.B, C.M.G., D.S.O.

By Major General
Sir C. E. Callwell. K.C.B.

Edited by John Wilson

Sir Stanley Maude

CONTENTS

Illustrations

MAPS

CHAPTER I
Ancestry and Early Years

The Maude family trace their origin in this country back to an Italian warrior, Eustacius de Monte Alto, who came over at the Conquest, and who was in due course rewarded with the manors of Hawarden and Montalt – the latter presumably named after himself –for his services in the affrays during which the Welsh territories immediately beyond the Dee fell into Norman hands. He and his senior descendants in the male line became Barons de Montalt of Hawarden Castle and took the surname of Montalt, which has become corrupted into Maude; the name also occurs in another form in Mold, the town in Flint which has risen on the site of the ancient manor of Montalt. The barons who were heads of the family played an important part in the country for several generations in early Plantagenet days, acquiring great territorial possessions in the east and south to recompense them for their somewhat precarious hold upon their estates in the Welsh marches; and in the reign of Henry II, Andomar, the youngest son of the fourth baron, proved himself a doughty soldier, and is said to have been the capture of William the Lion of Scotland when that monarch was taken prisoner in the borderland. It was probably in recognition of this signal service that Andomar Maude became possessor of extensive lands in Yorkshire, enabling him to found the Yorkshire branch of the Maudes as territorial magnates. The Barony of Montalt died out during the minority of Edward II, when its estates under a special arrangement reverted to the acquisitive and unscrupulous Queen Mother, Isabella, and the family was thenceforward during Plantagenet days represented by the Yorkshire branch, of which there came to be several ramifications, all inheriting landed property. It was in 1640 that a Robert Maude of West Riddlesden and Ripon, head of the senior ramification, sold his estates, repaired to Ireland and there purchased valuable lands in Tipperary and Kilkenny. His descendants during the succeeding hundred and thirty years took a prominent share in the political activities of the Emerald Isle, and his grandson was given a baronetcy. The Barony de Montalt was revived in the Irish peerage in 1786 in favour of Sir Cornwallis Maude, third baronet, who was advanced to the dignity of Viscount Hawarden in 1791. His youngest son, John Charles, Rector of

Enniskillen, had six sons, of whom the second, George Ashley, joined the Royal Artillery, reached the rank of Colonel, was Crown Equerry to Queen Victoria, and died a K.C.B. The fourth, Frederick Francis, father of the Conqueror of Baghdad, likewise joined the army and rose to high rank, and a brief account of the career of a distinguished soldier, who was so closely related to the subject of this Memoir, will not be out of place.

General Sir F. F. Maude, V.C., G.C.B., was born in 1821, and in 1840 proceeded to India as an ensign to join the Buffs, then a single-battalion regiment. Within three years he had obtained the adjutancy of the regiment, in which capacity he served through the Gwalior campaign of 1843–44, having his horse shot at Punniar, and receiving the bronze star which was awarded for that memorable victory over the Mahrattas. The Buffs returned to England in 1845, but started on a fresh tour of foreign service in 1851, when they took ship to Malta. Here Maude, now a captain, became, first, aide-de-camp and afterwards Military Secretary to the Governor and Commander-in-Chief. This staff service lasted till 1855, but Captain Maude was at home for several months in 1853, and he then married Catherine Mary, daughter of the Very Rev. Sir G. Bisshopp; two sons, the elder of whom died in infancy, and three daughters were born to them in due course. The Buffs had proceeded to Greece in 1854, in the early part of the Crimean War, but they joined Lord Raglan's forces before Sevastopol early in the summer of 1855, and there Maude, now a major, rejoined them.

He was in command of the regiment for some weeks in August and September, and on the 8th of the latter month he led 260 of his men, who formed the ladder party of the 2nd Division, in the second assault on the Redan. The Buffs forced their way into the work and maintained themselves in the interior in spite of heavy losses for some time; but for want of support they were eventually driven out again, Major Maude being dangerously wounded, and his gallantry being subsequently rewarded with the Victoria Cross for services, described as follows in the Gazette:

For his conspicuous bravery during the final attack on the almost impregnable Redan on 8 September 1855, when he was in command of the ladder covering party of the 2nd Division. Placing himself well in front of all, exposed to round shot, shell, and death-dealing canister, he led his men right into the Redan. On looking round he only found nine or ten men there to support him, all the rest having fallen before the enemy's fire. Nothing daunted he dashed for a traverse, which he held although dangerously wounded, and only retired when all hope of support was at an end.

At the conclusion of the war, after the taking of Sevastopol, he was promoted brevet Lieutenant Colonel and given the C.B. in recognition of his brilliant record. He was furthermore nominated Knight of the Legion of Honour, was awarded the 5th Class of the Medjidieh, and received the Crimean medal with Sevastopol clasp and the Turkish medal.

A second battalion of the Buffs was raised in 1857 and Maude was given command, taking it out to Malta in the following year, and from thence on to Gibraltar. There he was given the appointment of Assistant Adjutant General which he held for five years, and it was while quartered on the Rock that, on 24 June 1864, was born his youngest child, Frederick Stanley, who, half a century later, was to help so materially in the extrication of the British forces from the Gallipoli Peninsula and was then to win such imperishable renown on the plains of Mesopotamia. From 1867 to 1873 Colonel Maude was stationed in Ireland, where he held the positions of Inspector General of Disembodied Militia and Inspector General of Auxiliary Forces, and in the following year he was promoted Major General. Then in 1875 he was offered a command in India, which he accepted, and on arrival he found himself in charge of the Allahabad District.

The outbreak of the Afghan War in 1878 afforded the general, who was now approaching his sixtieth year, an opportunity of adding to the laurels that he had won a quarter of a century before amid the outworks of Sevastopol, for he was selected to lead the 2nd Division of the Peshawar Valley Force. Shortly after taking up this command in the field he was promoted lieutenant general. 2nd Division moved into the enemy's territory in rear of 1st, commanded by General Sam Browne, and it was consequently engaged mainly in protecting the lengthy and exposed communications of the troops which had advanced to beyond Jellalabad; but General Maude took personal charge of two important punitive expeditions directed against the turbulent Zakka Khel Afridis, which effected their purpose; and after the Peace of Gandamak his services were recognised by the award of the K.C.B., and he received the thanks of both Houses of Parliament. During the later phase of the Afghan War, after the destruction of Cavagnari and his mission at Kabul, Sir F. Maude was in charge of the Rawal Pindi District, and there he completed his five years' tenure of Indian command. Lady

Maude and he returned to England in 1880, and they took up their abode first, for a year, in St George's Road, S.W.,[1] and then in Eccleston Square, so as to be near their son Stanley, now a lad at Eton intended for the Guards. Sir Frederick was not again actively employed, and he retired in 1885 with the rank of general, shortly afterwards receiving the G.C.B. Lady Maude died in 1892, and during the closing years of his life the general resided at Torquay. There he passed away in 1897, two days before the celebration of Queen Victoria's Diamond Jubilee.

Little Frederick Stanley arrived in England with his parents from Gibraltar in 1866, and the family then stayed for some months in London while his father, temporarily on half-pay, awaited fresh employment. On his getting the post in Ireland, Colonel Maude took a house in Upper Pembroke Street in Dublin, and the family lived there until 1873, Stanley in the interval developing from infancy into a sturdy little boy, who even at that early age took a precocious interest in all things military. Son of a distinguished warrior, and intended for the army, he used to astonish officers visiting the house by the eagerness and intelligence he displayed when manoeuvring the tin soldiers that were his especial delight. He was nine years old when Colonel Maude gave up the Irish appointment and returned with the family to England, to live for the following two years in Upper Cromwell Road. Then there came the great break in home life caused by his father accepting the Indian command in 1875. General Maude idolised his little son and had set his heart on sending the boy to Eton; he was however by no means well off, and he was to some extent influenced by the difficulties involved in keeping Stanley at an expensive school when he decided to proceed on a five years' tour of foreign service, leaving the boy at home. General and Mrs Maude took their two eldest girls with them to India, but the second returned home after a few months in the East. Before they sailed, Stanley had begun his school life, being sent to St Michael's School, Aldis House, the Rev. John Hawtrey's preparatory school at Slough, in September of that year.

During the absence of his parents in India, young Maude was latterly under charge of his sister Alice, and he generally spent his holidays at Debden Hall, Saffron Walden, with the Raymond Cely-Trevilians, cousins. But while at Hawtrey's he went abroad at Easter and in the summer of 1876 with his two sisters and their governess, going to Paris the first time and visiting Germany in summer. While there, they spent

---

[1] Wimbledon – Ed.

some time at Coblentz, the headquarters of the German VIII Army Corps and an important garrison town. There the little twelve-year-old lad enjoyed a rare opportunity of indulging his bent for things military. For he succeeded somehow in making friends with German officers stationed in the place, and these gave him special assistance and encouragement in respect to witnessing the summer exercises of the troops then in progress, enabled him to see what *Kriegspiel* – a pastime then almost unknown in England – looked like, and obtained for him access to the historic stronghold of Ehrenbreitstein, a fastness where foreigners were not in those days apt to meet with a cordial welcome. He had already contracted the habit of studying records of battles and wars; but he had enjoyed few opportunities when in Dublin and in London of seeing troops at work. So that the spectacle of considerable military forces, carrying out manoeuvres in the broken ground around the beautifully situated city at the meeting-place of the Moselle with the Rhine, no doubt remained a precious memory to him in the years to follow when the schoolboy was preparing for a soldier's career.

'I remember him as a thin, leggy boy with a high colour and a quiet smile,' the Hon. Gilbert Johnstone, who was at Hawtrey's and afterwards at Eton with him, describes Maude at this time. He joined eagerly in all games, and always received excellent reports, but he gave no great promise in respect to scholarship. During the holidays he learnt to fish and to shoot, and was quite a respectable shot at the age of fourteen when he went to Eton after the Easter holidays in 1878.

At Eton he was in Mr Cornish's House, where his first fagmaster was the Hon. M. B. Hawke, now Lord Hawke, who has played so prominent a part in the world of cricket and of sport ever since, and who describes him as 'one of the best little sportsmen ever entered at my Tutor's and a most attentive fag.' As fag he was associated with H. S. Rawlinson, now General Lord Rawlinson, with whom he was later to serve in the Coldstream, and was to be frequently associated in future years; and it is surely something of a coincidence that these two small boys, contemporaries in Cornish's House, should many years afterwards have come to be simultaneously commanding huge British armies in war, the one in France, the other far away in the Cradle of the World. 'Your brother is going on very well and seems in good spirits and to get on with everybody; his work also is satisfactory, and I am glad to have him in my House,' his tutor wrote to Miss Alice Maude a few weeks after her brother went to Eton. Another contemporary of Maude's at Cornish's was J. McNeile, who was somewhat older but, going to Oxford, joined the Coldstream after him; Major McNeile was recalled from retirement, and was killed while commanding a battalion of the K.O.S.B. in the Gallipoli Peninsula in 1915. Colonel Le Roy Lewis, who was Maude's fagmaster for some time, writes of him:

> I well remember Maude when he was my fag. He was one of the nicest small boys I ever had to deal with. The relations between a fagmaster and his fag may sometimes be difficult; but in our case our dealings were free from any unpleasant or disagreeable trait. I liked Maude and I think he liked me as we remained firm friends all our time. .... His was a sunny and cheerful disposition, which made for peace and comradeship amongst those with whom he was associated. At 'my Tutor's' he was popular with all hands, swells and scugs liked him, and as for his old fagmaster, all I can say is that the day on which I heard of his death was indeed a dreary one for me. If the world were only entirely peopled by men like Joe Maude it would be a charming place, for he had the rare gift of sympathy and kindness, which is not so often found as it might be.

He was already noted for his athletic prowess when at Hawtrey's, and at Eton he at once took to the river, although he played in the final at cricket for the Lower Boy Cup his first year. All his old schoolfellows testify to his popularity from the outset, to his infectious cheeriness, his good temper and his quiet determination in whatever he undertook. From a very early date he came to be known as 'Joe' Maude, which in reality speaks for itself – for when a boy or a man, whose name is not Joseph, is known as Joe it generally means that his company is sought for and his personality is attractive – and he carried the nickname on to Sandhurst with him, and from Sandhurst into the Guards. Although his scholastic achievements as a boy were merely respectable and never distinguished, he satisfied his masters; and when the time approached for him to go up for the Royal Military College he worked with a will. Still, it was as a runner and in the boats that he chiefly made his mark, although he was also in his House Football Eleven from 1880 onwards.

He ran third in the Junior Mile in 1879, and in the following year ran third in the Junior Steeplechase. In 1881 he was second in the School

F. S. MAUDE, Eton.

(1879.)

Mile, and that year he won the School Steeplechase. 'Maude deserves much credit for his careful training before and judgement in the race,' the Eton College Chronicle remarked in its report of the event – and his performances that year singled him out as a fine athlete. In 1882 he won the School Mile in the excellent time, for a schoolboy, of 4 minutes 45 seconds, when considerably handicapped in respect to special training for the distance owing to his being whip to the beagles. 'I have a vivid recollection of him finishing up the Dorney Road with a long stride and as fresh as could be,' writes Lieutenant General Sir C. Fergusson (with whom Maude was to be much associated in later life in peace and in war), adding that 'he kept up his running very late in life, and used to run at the Curragh in 1913, looking exactly as he did at Eton thirty-one years before. All his Eton contemporaries testify to his extreme modesty about his performances.'

He also became a fine oarsman and he took part successfully in many exciting events, rowing and as a sculler, from an early stage in his school career. Then in his last year he was reserve man in the Eight and was for a time included in it, and he fully expected to be one of the crew entered for the Ladies' Plate. His not rowing at Henley was a bitter disappointment, as he had looked forward to representing Eton from the time when he first went on the river; his losing his place at the end was due to the return of one of the crew shortly before the race, who had met with an accident and had not been expected to be fit. 'The incident most fresh in my memory with regard to him,' writes the Hon. G. Johnstone, 'was the wonderful quiet pluck with which he accepted losing his place within a fortnight of Henley.' It was my misfortune to tell him, 'You are not down to row tonight,' and he took it with a quiet smile and no sort of complaint. Eton had not won the Ladies Plate for a dozen years, their triumph on this occasion naturally aroused great enthusiasm in the school, and it was Maude who sent off the telegram from the riverside announcing the success of the Eight. Mr F. I. Pitman, who was a contemporary of his in Cornish's, who stroked Cambridge home to victory in 1885 in one of the most exciting races ever rowed from Putney to Mortlake, who won the Diamond Sculls in the following year, and who is accepted as one of the finest oarsmen of his time, draws a very attractive picture of the great soldier as a schoolboy sportsman:

> At this length of time it is not easy to record with any great accuracy one's recollections of old school friends, but Stanley Maude was so boyish in spirit right up to the end that one's memory seems to take one back to Lower Boy days.

I remember him very well in 'my Tutor's' Lower Boy Football Eleven, and later in the House Football Eleven, with great long legs which never seemed to be quite under control but which got over the ground at a rare pace. His great length won him the School Mile, and I have a painful recollection of running, more or less untrained, in the House Handicap Mile with Maude at scratch; he was just beaten after a great race by my younger brother.

As an oar he was very nearly first class, and I always thought him rather unlucky not to get into the Eight. Probably the greatest race he ever rowed was House Fours in 1882. Our four had two 'Lower Boats' in the bows, with Maude at three and myself stroke. In the final we were up against Carter's, with three in the Eight and one in the 'Victory.' They rowed over forty all the way. We with our 'Lower Boats' never got over thirty-five. We were behind a few hundred yards from the end, but managed to get our nose in front at Windsor Bridge, and won by a yard. Even in those days you could depend on Maude to keep his head.

Like most of us, I don't think he ever bothered himself too much with books – he certainly was not a 'sap.' He always had a cheery, jolly laugh, and was generally singing about the House the songs from comic operas of the day. There are few of whom one has more pleasant memories.'

As was only to be expected in view of the passion for soldiering which he had been displaying ever since he had been able to toddle about, Maude joined the Volunteer Corps and did his utmost to excel at drill and on the range. Those were before the days of the Officers' Training Corps, and the cadet system was not taken so seriously at Eton, nor at other educational establishments, as it is now. Many of the most prominent members of the school – those whom the Lower Boy naturally looks up to – were not enrolled on the books of the Eton Volunteers, although the corps enjoyed certain especial advantages, notably in respect to having a regular officer as adjutant; but Maude took this early soldiering very seriously from the start, and he was promoted sergeant in 1881. It was towards the end of the Christmas holidays at the beginning of that year that Sir Frederick and Lady Maude, whom young Stanley had not seen for more than five years, came home from India, to their son's great joy. Many of the family had entered the army at different times, but not one had gained such a reputation as had the leader of the Buffs on the occasion of the second attack on the Redan, and the Etonian was justly proud of this distinguished father of his, come back from the Afghan War. It may be mentioned here that, very soon after this pleasant family reunion, a cousin, Captain the Hon. Cornwallis Maude, who was heir to the Hawarden peerage, was killed on Majuba Hill by the side of Sir G. Colley. The then Lord Hawarden, after this and for some years subsequently, often asked Maude to stay for shooting at the family place, Dundrum in Tipperary, visits which Maude always greatly enjoyed.

The future army commander in Mesopotamia was now a tall, slim lad, rising seventeen, and the time for his competing for Sandhurst was already coming into sight. If he was to pass, it was indispensable for him to take up seriously certain subjects not included in the ordinary school curriculum. 'We were in the Army Class together in 1881–82, up to Walter Durnford,' writes Sir C. Fergusson. 'Maude worked hard and very earnestly, and he never took advantage (as most of us did) of easy-going French and German masters.' Although possessing marked ability and plenty of determination, he would not seem to have possessed the knack of propitiating examiners or of shining at bookwork in its schoolroom sense, resembling in this respect many other youths who have come to the front in after life. Neither passing in, nor passing out of, Sandhurst did he, so to speak, run quite up to his form; and it was the same at a later date when he went up for the Staff College.

The year 1882 was his last at Eton and he was elected to 'Pop' – the College debating society and an exclusive body. After a short period of special tuition at Mr Northcote's establishment, Rochester House, at Ealing, he passed for Sandhurst that autumn and he left the school, which to the end of his life he always loved even more possibly than the majority of Etonians, in December. His name is carved in Upper School, among a small batch of 1882 names, at the end of the desks on the left-hand side leading from Upper School into College Chapel. In the triumphs that were to come to him in later life, at moments when his name was in every mouth throughout the British Empire, when he was figuring at once as a conqueror and a liberator of the land that claims the most ancient of histories, Maude's first thought after each new achievement ever was that it would please them at Eton and in the Regiment.

He joined the Royal Military College early in 1883. The Governor of Sandhurst at this time was General Sir Richard Taylor, a veteran who had held many important posts in the army, and had acted as locum tenens for Sir G. Wolseley as Adjutant General while Sir Garnet was absent from the War Office at the time of Tel-el-Kebir, and who was uncle, as it happened, of the lady whom Maude was to marry some years later. The place was run on genuine military lines, the instruction, although necessarily partly theoretical, was also very largely thoroughly practical, and to a youngster bent on fitting himself in every respect for the soldier's career there was much in the year's course that particularly appealed. Maude speedily made his mark amongst his fellow-cadets. He became under-officer of No.1 Division, and is described by one of his contemporaries as 'one of the show cadets of the year, first rate on parade, in gymnasium and in the riding school.' Sir R. Taylor particularly noted him at the time and predicted a great career for him. The intimate association with officers who formed the staff, and the strict military discipline that was maintained during official hours, delighted him. Quite apart from the ordinary studies that were necessary, he managed to read works on the art and history of war at hours which his fellows were disposed to devote to other indoor pursuits.

At the same time he bore his full share in all outdoor sports. He played Association Football hard during the season, and when the date came for the Annual Sports he fully sustained the reputation which he had brought with him from the Eton playing fields as a long-distance runner. He moreover proved a terror to the Woolwich cadets on the occasion of the usual yearly competition between the two great military institutions; for he won every event that he started for with comparative ease. As had been the case at school, he was extremely popular with his brother-cadets, who appreciated his blithe disposition and good fellowship while they respected his grit and admired his feats as a sportsman.

He passed out of Sandhurst 38th on the list at the end of the year. H. S. Rawlinson was just a little way ahead. Another cadet, now Major General Sir H. T. Brooking, who was a few places in front of him and who in due course went into the Indian Army, was, later on, to gain high distinction under his command at the head of a division in Mesopotamia. Three other cadets passing out at the same time had, as will be seen in the next chapter, received nominations for the Coldstream Guards besides himself. His early days were at an end.

CHAPTER II
From 1884 to 1889

Four young officers from the Royal Military College joined the Coldstream Guards on 6 February 1884. Of these J. A. G. (now Colonel) Drummond-Hay, R. Grenfell, and F. S. Maude went to the 1st Battalion, stationed at Chelsea Barracks, while the Hon. W. (now Major General Sir W.) Lambton joined the 2nd Battalion. The Coldstream at this time, it should be mentioned, only consisted of two battalions. Owing to their respective positions on the Sandhurst list, Maude was junior to both Lambton and Drummond-Hay – a circumstance which in years to come was to affect his regimental promotion somewhat adversely, especially in respect to his prospects of obtaining a battalion command, although, as it turned out, he might not have been able to accept this. The 1st Battalion was at this time commanded by Colonel A. Lambton, who had Lieutenant the Hon. H. (now Sir Henry) Legge for adjutant. Amongst officers then belonging to it that have since come markedly to the front in the service were Captain and Lieutenant Colonel (now Lieutenant General Sir R.) Pole-Carew[2] and Lieutenant (now Lieutenant General Sir A. E.) Codrington. Two brother subalterns of Maude's then quartered at Chelsea were also to enjoy distinguished careers in future life outside of the army; these were Lieutenant (now Colonel Sir J.) Ross of Bladensburg, the historian of the regiment and for many years Chief Commissioner of the Dublin Metropolitan Police, and Lieutenant George Wyndham, who after a few years in the army turned his attention to politics and literature, and who was to win a great place for himself in the public life of his country before his premature death in 1913. Joining his regiment with an enviable reputation as an athlete and oarsman, Maude at once became extremely popular with all ranks, and he showed indefatigable zeal in perfecting himself in the

---

[2] The arrangement under which officers of the Brigade of Guards held special army rank, superior to their regimental rank, was drawing to a close at this time.

duties which a regimental officer has to perform. He speedily came to be known throughout the Brigade of Guards, as he had been known at Eton and Sandhurst, as 'Joe' Maude. 'I remember looking upon him as a ' good recruit,' over six feet high,' writes Sir H. Legge, 'having won ' school' races at Eton and been first choice out of the 'Eight.' I can recollect no occasion on which fault could be found with him or his duty, for he was from the first a keen smart soldier thoroughly to be trusted, and with a love of the regiment.'

Whenever he was quartered in London during the opening years of his service Maude had his home with his parents in Ecceleston Square. The battalion moved to Aldershot for a couple of months to undergo musketry a few weeks after he joined, and he then made his first acquaintance with a station where he always found himself in his element in later years. The 1st Coldstream returned to Chelsea in May and moved into Wellington Barracks in July. This was practically his first experience of a London season, and although he had little taste for society entertainments he enjoyed the life, attending closely to his duties and always keeping himself in the pink of condition by lawn tennis and going on the river when possible. He was a favourite wherever he went, but he never cared much about dancing, and he was not a particularly good performer at it; as quite a young man he was however noted for his good nature in coming to the rescue of girls who were not getting their fair share of partners; he had no liking for turning night into day, and all his life long was an early riser. It was probably largely due to his determination always to keep thoroughly fit and to his predilection for rowing that he never smoked, either as a youngster or later on in his career. Lieutenant General Sir W. Pulteney, with whom he was to be closely associated years afterwards in South Africa, and again in France in 1914, writes: 'The first time I came against Maude as an athlete was at Burton's Court at the Brigade of Guards Sports. It was in the Quarter Mile, which I remember he won very easily although many of us fancied ourselves on the start he had to give us.'

The year 1884 was signalised by the formidable spreading of the Mahdist movement throughout the Sudan and the investment of Gordon in Khartoum. An expedition despatched to Suakin early in the year gained some successes in the field, but it exerted no appreciable influence over the situation as a whole. Mr Gladstone's Government vacillated for a season, but eventually they decided that an expedition should advance up the Nile to succour Gordon, and in September Lord Wolseley proceeded to Egypt to take up command. Shortly after assuming charge of the operations he requested that detachments from the Guards and from the cavalry regiments stationed at home should be sent out to him to be formed into camel corps, and it was thereupon decided to form a composite Guards Camel Regiment under command of Lieutenant Colonel the Hon. E. Boscawen (afterwards Lord Falmouth) of the Coldstream, to which the Coldstream contributed four officers and its quota of other ranks. There was naturally much competition for the very few places available, and a recently joined officer like Maude had no chance of being selected; amongst those chosen was Lieutenant (now Major General) Vesey Dawson, then in the 2nd Battalion, on whose staff he was to serve in a Territorial Division a quarter of a century afterwards. But the expedition up the Nile started too late, the sands were running out in Khartoum by the closing weeks of the year, and the original plan of following the great river right up to the beleaguered city with the entire force had to be abandoned. The Camel troops had to be thrust across the Bayuda Desert from Korti to Metemmeh. They started on 30 December, more or less as a forlorn hope, and they were late. For a few weeks the eyes of the world were upon the slender column, hard beset in a region where the existence of the force depended upon a few scattered wells, and then the news arrived that Khartoum had fallen and that Gordon was dead.

This catastrophe aroused the nation. The Government realised that something must be done, without their having any very clear idea as to what course it was best to pursue, nor what was to be the objective of such further operations as should be undertaken. But they came to the conclusion that a force ought to be sent to Suakin, and that a railway from that place to Berber ought to be constructed under its wing; and, amongst the troops whom it was decided to gather together on the Red Sea littoral, a Guards Brigade was detailed and orders for its mobilisation and embarkation for the scene of action were issued. This brigade, which was to be under command of Major General Lyon Fremantle, who was already on the spot, was composed of the 3rd Grenadiers, the 1st Coldstream and the 2nd Scots Guards, so that Maude within a year of his obtaining his commission found himself, to his great delight, under orders to proceed on active service. He and the other two subalterns of the battalion of only a year's service were very nearly left behind as being too young; but Colonel Lambton insisted on their going, saying that the boys would be bitterly disappointed were they to be excluded, and would regret missing the campaign all their lives.

The battalion marched out of Wellington Barracks early on the morning of 19 February, getting an enthusiastic send-off from the public, and embarked on river steamers at Westminster Steps for Gravesend, where it was transferred to the Manorah. The transport reached Suakin on 8 March, when the Coldstream straightway disembarked and went into camp hard by, the Grenadiers and Scots Guards arriving on the following day. Even so early as March the climate of the Red Sea littoral is trying to Europeans who are unaccustomed to the tropics, and the troops speedily discovered that campaigning in this theatre of war involved drawbacks, quite apart from such inconveniences as the Dervishes might cause by their combatant activities. The Hadendowa of this region proved themselves doughty and vexatious opponents from the outset, particularly during the night watches. Cut-throats would succeed in evading the sentries in the darkness and would create havoc, killing and wounding quite an appreciable number of soldiers during their nocturnal forays. The firing that took place on such occasions moreover disturbed the rest of the troops who were not immediately concerned. There were constant alarms; and the searchlights of the warships did not prove an unmixed blessing, seeing that they illuminated the encampments as well as the ground in their neighbourhood where the enemy were supposed to be lurking. It is interesting to note in this connection that Maude, who was at this time junior subaltern in the late Lieutenant-Colonel C. Fortescue's company, retained a vivid recollection of this form of naval enterprise many years afterwards when he was concerned in the evacuation of Helles in the Gallipoli Peninsula; for his diary indicates that he felt somewhat nervous lest the sister service should start employing its projectors at an inappropriate juncture. Although the nocturnal scares were a serious nuisance to the Guards, as they were to the rest of the force, their encampments suffered scarcely at all from the hostile depredations. Their camps were nevertheless moved back into a safer position after a few days, and zeribas were constructed to render them more secure against Arab intrusion. Sir Gerald Graham, who was to command the Expeditionary Force, arrived on 13 March, and he at once prepared to set in motion the offensive operations which the situation demanded.

This was in some respects a perplexing one. The bulk of the enemy forces were known to be mustered in a direction south-westerly from Suakin, about Tamai, some dozen miles or so from the port; that place had been the scene of a Homeric encounter during the campaign of the previous year. There was also a lesser hostile gathering in the direction of Hashin, situated about six miles to the north-west of the port, and it was the Hadendowa assembled in that vicinity who, it was believed, produced the nocturnal marauders who kept prowling about the encampments of the Expeditionary Force. The country was covered in many places with extensive areas of thick scrub, which must necessarily impede the movements of any considerable body of troops, and which at the same time provided admirable cover for the type of foemen with whom the army was about to deal. Everything in a measure hinged upon water. On the one hand, the enemy's dispositions were to a large extent governed by the siting of the groups of wells. On the other hand, Sir G. Graham's force was obliged to carry its water with it as soon as it quitted its base, an obligation which greatly added to the difficulties of the transport problem and which tended to transform the army, when on the move, into a mere escort for its own impedimenta. Finally, the strategic objective to be aimed at was that of protecting the construction of a railway through the heart of the enemy's country, a railway which, for some reason that has always been a puzzle to those concerned in the campaign, was to be a broad-gauge one involving very heavy labour.

General Graham started his combinations with a reconnaissance made on the 19th in the direction of Hashin, in which the Guards Brigade took part; the enemy's presence was detected, but there was only some little skirmishing on the part of the advanced troops. Next day he moved out again at the head of two brigades, the Guards in reserve, leaving Suakin about 6 a.m. and he advanced to Hashin. A prominent hill beyond that place was carried by troops of the leading brigade, and it was then decided to withdraw to the base, leaving one battalion in a zeriba to be constructed on a hillock dominating Hashin. It was then that Maude underwent his first experience of an engagement. The Guards covered the retirement when the prominent hill had been evacuated, and – as is usual in a fight with antagonists such as the Hadendowa – the retirement of the troops served as a signal for the enemy to follow up promptly and to act with vigour. Falling back, formed as a big square, the Guards Brigade provided an excellent target for the not very efficient marksmen to be found in the Dervish ranks, and some little loss was sustained. But the steady volleys from the square kept the tribesmen at a distance, and they did not venture upon the charge of spearmen which was generally delivered by these daring fanatics when they saw the slightest prospect of achieving a success. After retiring slowly a mile or two, the force ceased to be troubled by hostile activity and it got back to Suakin before dark, after a very fatiguing twelve hours. One result of the day's work was that from that time forward nocturnal annoyance practically ceased in the immediate neighbourhood of the base. The establishment of a strong post at Hashin moreover relieved General Graham of anxiety with regard to his right flank when embarking on his next operation, that of trying conclusions with the main body of the enemy in a south-westerly direction.

The other brigade, under Sir J. McNeill, moved out on the 22nd with the purpose of establishing an advanced post and supply magazine about half way to Tamai. It reached its destination, a spot known as Tofrek, without incident, and the troops were for the most part busily engaged in constructing an extensive zeriba, when they were very suddenly assailed by a large force of Dervishes that advanced rapidly through the surrounding scrub, and a desperate fight ensued. The position of affairs was for a short time critical enough; but the enemy was eventually beaten off, although not until after many casualties had occurred amongst the British and Indian troops engaged in the furious affray, and not without very serious confusion having been occasioned amongst the camel transport with the force. The zeriba was then completed.

The Guards moved out from Suakin next day in charge of a convoy for Tofrek, which got through without difficulty; the Coldstream remained at the zeriba while the other two battalions returned to the port. Then, on the 24th, the Coldstream and a battalion of Marines marched back half way from Tofrek to meet a convoy coming out from Suakin, which they were to shepherd on to the zeriba. After taking charge they formed a square round the camels, and on the way they were assailed boldly by considerable bodies of the enemy; it was the severest encounter which the Coldstream experienced during the campaign, for the Hadendowa delivered their onset with unmistakable resolution. 'They came on in line, guided by flags on each flank, in a most gallant manner,' writes Sir J. Ross of Bladensburg in his history of the regiment, 'and directed their attack mainly at the left face of the square. But, unable to stand our fire, they were soon defeated and most of them killed, though one or two did actually succeed in getting as far as our bayonets before they fell. After this event they left us alone, and we got back to the zeriba without further trouble.' The escort of the convoy on this occasion could fairly claim to have gained a substantial success which was earned cheaply, although the Coldstream had about twenty casualties. The Dervishes indeed never showed much stomach for fight during the few weeks that the campaign was still to last, after the very rough handling they had met with in their assault on the troops when they were constructing the zeriba, and after the rebuff they met with on the 24th.

The Coldstream marched back to Suakin on the 26th, and Maude was glad to resume the habit of ablutions after being out in the desert for several days with no water available except for drinking. One of his first acts after getting back to the base indeed was to expend half a crown on a bottle of soda water for tooth-brushing purposes. Owing to being at Suakin for a few days, the Coldstream were on the spot when a New South Wales contingent landed on the 29th – a historic event which heralded the support that the Overseas Dominions were to afford the Mother Country on an incomparably greater scale in wars which were unthought of at the time.

All was ready for an advance to Tamai by the beginning of April, abundant supplies and a goodly store of water having been got together at Tofrek, so the bulk of Sir G. Graham's forces moved out from Suakin on the 2nd under his personal command and, having halted for the night at the zeriba, advanced next day to Tamai which was occupied with little trouble. It was evident that the Hadendowa were to a great extent cowed, that the first phase of the campaign was at an end, and that the railway, the terminus portion of which had already been begun, could now be extended beyond the immediate environs of Suakin. The weather, it should be mentioned, had grown much hotter since the date of the landing of the Coldstream three weeks earlier and there was already some sickness amongst the troops. The bulk of the force returned to the base from the Tamai direction on the 4th; and from that time forward the operations as long as they lasted were practically confined to pushing forward slowly along the line which the railway was to follow, and to establishing and holding a string of posts.

A force in which the Coldstream were included moved out some distance along the line on the 6th, and two days later the regiment occupied Handub in company with the New South Wales contingent, without fighting. Maude's battalion was distributed between that place and a post a few miles on named Otao for more than a month, and it was not an altogether pleasurable experience. The troops were mainly engaged on fatigue work during these weeks, clearing away scrub, improving communications, constructing zeribas for animals, and so on. The enemy seldom showed up by day, but there was a certain liveliness by night owing to small parties of Dervishes creeping up, tearing up the sleepers and burning them, and causing as much mischief as they could. The heat grew greater from day to day, and the proportion of officers and men on the sick list or sent home invalided began to mount up somewhat ominously; it is generally the younger members of a force who break down when campaigning in a torrid climate, but Maude contrived to keep fit throughout. As will be readily understood he as a junior subaltern had few opportunities of making his mark during these somewhat drab days; but he won golden opinions from his seniors, as always being dependable under all circumstances, and Colonel Follett, who commanded one of the companies and who at a later date commanded the battalion for part of the time that Maude was adjutant, remembers their agreeing that the regiment had acquired two uncommonly clever young officers in George Wyndham and Joe Maude.

The Government had in the meantime gradually been making up its mind that the attempt to reconquer the Sudan was not to be proceeded with, and that the force which had advanced up the Nile before the fall of Khartoum was to be withdrawn to the neighbourhood of the Second Cataract. The decision had to some extent been accelerated by events on the Afghan frontier, where a somewhat awkward encounter between detachments of the Ameer's and of Russian troops had taken place. Under the circumstances, the project of constructing a railway from Suakin to Berber naturally fell to the ground, just at the moment when the line was beginning to make some way. Early in May Lord Wolseley arrived at Suakin and paid a visit to the front, where it soon transpired that the operations on the Red Sea littoral were to be wound up.

The Coldstream moved back from Handub to the base on the 14th and they embarked on the Deccan two days later. The vessel arrived at Alexandria on the 23rd, and the regiment then spent nearly a fortnight on board ship in the harbour before landing and encamping on the beach at Ramleh, a pleasant enough place at that time of the year in spite of the heat. It was however decided after a good deal of delay that the Guards Brigade was to be transferred to Cyprus, and that it was to remain in that island for the present. So the Coldstream took ship afresh, this time on board the Orontes, and proceeded to Limasol, from which place they marched up to Troodos and encamped there with the rest of the brigade for some six weeks. Then, orders having come that the Guards were to be brought home, the Coldstream marched down to Limasol and embarked on the Orontes on 26 August, and Maude arrived in London on 11 September after an absence of nearly eight months. He in due course received the Egyptian medal for the campaign with the Suakin clasp, as well as the Khedive's Star.

On their return from the Mediterranean, the 1st Coldstream found themselves allotted to Chelsea Barracks, and Maude resumed the life that he had been leading when the battalion had been suddenly ordered on active service, making his father's house his headquarters. The usual period of musketry was passed at Pirbright in the early summer of 1886, and in the autumn the battalion, now under command of the late Colonel R. S. Hall, moved to Windsor. During this summer Maude began to take an interest in racing, and he soon became a particularly good judge. His remarkable memory helped him in this; but he also possessed a natural gift for noting the points of a racehorse, and this he developed by a careful study of the subject and by attending many of the more important meetings when his military duties permitted of it. He had excellent eyesight, and although he never carried race-glasses he could tell the colours at the furthest off point of any course. It remained a hobby of his for many years, and his attendance at racing centres often represented practically the only leave that he would take in a year; they occupied only short periods, and he was always uneasy if away from his regimental duties for any length of time. His reputation as a particularly smart and efficient officer was spreading through the Brigade of Guards, in which he was becoming a well known figure. In July of this year, 1886, his eldest sister, married to Major (now Major General) F. W. Hemming, who had been his father's aide-de-camp, died in India.

With the facilities which it provided him for the exercise for which he always craved, Windsor was in many respects more agreeable to him as a station than had been the Metropolis. To an oarsman such as he was, the proximity of the Thames was naturally a great attraction, and he also liked being near to his old school. It may be mentioned here that he stroked the Coldstream Eight in brigade regattas for a period covering, with intervals, seventeen years, and he always got every ounce that was available out of his colleagues behind him. 'I well remember,' writes Sir W. Lambton, 'how the rest of us used to groan when he began one of his spurts at a very quick rate – usually at the beginning of the race.' He also generally rowed and sculled in other events on the occasion of the annual regatta. He was naturally often at the Guards Club at Maidenhead during the summer of 1887, and it may be mentioned that it was on the river in that year that he first met Miss Taylor, whom he married some time later. He was unable to afford to keep a horse at this time, so used to run regularly with the Eton and Stoke beagles during the winter of 1886–87.

The 1st Coldstream returned to town in the autumn of 1887 to be stationed in Wellington Barracks, and while the battalion was there he was, in March 1888, appointed to fill the adjutancy. Battalion adjutants at that time, it should be remarked, were subalterns, alike in the Guards and in the Line. It should moreover be added that an adjutant in those days was in many respects a more important figure, in spite of his junior rank, than he is at the present time; and this was perhaps even more the case in the Guards than in the Line. Company commanders were allowed far less independence than came to be the practice a few years later, even before the introduction of the 'double company' system. Maude ever since he joined had singled himself out by his intense keenness in respect to matters regimental and matters military, by his assiduity at company duties, by his smartness as a parade soldier, by the familiarity with administrative detail which he had managed to acquire, and by his study of the art of war in its more theoretical aspects. His selection for the post of adjutant when he had only four years' service was a recognition of this.

He did not take long to win a, in some respects, very enviable reputation throughout the Brigade of Guards, thanks to the manner in which he was filling the place. By nature disposed to grasp control into his own hands in any work he had to do in concert with others, the 1st Coldstream while he held the appointment was perhaps even more of an 'adjutant's regiment' than most battalions were. All brother officers who were in touch with him in those days testify to his devotion to his task. He was strict to the extent of being something of a martinet, and he may not at first have been popular with the rank and file – he would naturally be disliked by the few indifferent characters that are to be found in every unit. But all ranks gradually came to acknowledge his zeal and efficiency, his perfect knowledge of drill in all its forms, and his invariable fairness. The non-commissioned officers and men appreciated his kindliness when off duty, they were aware of his deep interest in the regiment, they admired his prowess as an athlete, and they took to him in the end.

'We were both adjutants, he of the 1st and I of the 2nd Battalion from 1888 to 1892,' writes Sir W. Lambton, 'and I had many dealings with him. As an adjutant he was a great disciplinarian, but very popular with all. Even in those days he showed rare aptitude for administration and was a great writer of memos; we used to have friendly passages of arms over his fondness for paper and for initiating reforms which were not much favoured at the time.'

Sir W. Lambton's reference to Maude's addiction to paperwork calls for some further observations. All through his service he was a little inclined to expand office labours. He spent long hours in the orderly room when adjutant, and he may possibly have sometimes made work unnecessarily. During the four years that he held the appointment he took no leave, except for a day or two at a time, and he was always up and busy by 6 a.m. As has been observed above, the adjutant of a battalion in those days was a more important person than he is now, and had more to occupy himself with; still one can imagine that battalions in excellent order existed at that time whose adjutants did not find it imperative to spend such long hours at their official duties as Maude did.

But for the usual trip to Pirbright, the 1st Coldstream spent the whole of 1889 at Wellington Barracks; after that they were stationed for some months at the Tower. In July 1890 they moved to Chelsea, and Colonel Follett shortly afterwards succeeded to the command. Then, in the autumn of the following year, the battalion was transferred to Dublin, which in those days was a station of the Guards, and Maude renewed his acquaintance with a country of which, but for occasional short visits, he had seen very little since he was a small boy. He hunted from Dublin during the winter and went well. Had he not been so wrapped up in his work as adjutant he would probably have paid visits to his many relatives dwelling in different parts of the Emerald Isle. But during the winter he suffered a great bereavement, for his mother, Lady Maude, died in January 1892, and his appointment was moreover now drawing to a close. On its expiration in March he found himself posted to the 2nd Battalion under command of Colonel the Hon. H. W. Corry, stationed at Wellington Barracks. The late Lord Falmouth succeeded to the command in the autumn, Maude continuing, as previously when quartered in London, to make his home in Eccleston Square.

He had made up his mind to go up for the Staff College on giving up the adjutancy, and he set himself to work hard for the examination to be held in the coming summer. Before the time for it came, however, a very important event in his life took place, for he became engaged in May to Miss Cecil Taylor, daughter of the Right Hon. Colonel Thomas Edward Taylor of Ardgillan Castle in County Dublin, who had died in 1883; her twin sister had married Lieutenant Skeffington Smyth of the Coldstream four years before. Her father, elder brother of Sir R. Taylor who had been Governor of Sandhurst when Maude was there, had been a very prominent figure in the Carlton Club and in the ranks of the Conservative Party in his day. He had represented County Dublin for over forty years, defeating Parnell in 1865 and 1868, had been Conservative Whip for seventeen years, and at the time of his death was Chancellor of the Duchy of Lancaster. Disraeli had in 1868 declared him to be the real author of household suffrage, the measure introducing that extension of the franchise having been passed mainly owing to Colonel Taylor's energy as a Whip.

The marriage took place on 1 November 1893 at St Paul's, Knightsbridge, from Sir R. Taylor's house. Events of this kind were not unfamiliar to Maude, although this was the first occasion on which he took the title role. He had been best man to a number of his brother officers during the past few years, his popularity in the regiment making his selection for the post almost a foregone conclusion, and his handsome presence sustaining the bridegroom during a ceremonial to which the principal actor generally looks forward to with apprehension. Maude had not been in the habit of taking long leave in the past and had taken no leave at all while adjutant; but on this occasion he was away from his military duties for nearly three months. The honeymoon was spent, first at Amport, Lord Winchester's (a Coldstreamer's) place, and afterwards abroad. The newly-married pair afterwards went visiting relatives in Ireland, after which they settled down in Sloane Street in February 1894.

Maude had gone up for the Staff College in the previous summer; but although he had passed he had not been high enough on the list to obtain one of the vacancies. This had been a great disappointment; but shortly after being notified of his ill-success he was given a special nomination by the Duke of Cambridge, then Commander-in-Chief, under the rule introduced shortly before which made special provision for successful adjutants. The nomination could not however take effect for a year owing to lack of room at Camberley – that is to say, he was not to join the institution until the beginning of 1895.

The 2nd Coldstream remained at Chelsea till the summer, when they took part in manoeuvres about Aldershot, and the Maudes then had a house for a short time at Frensham. The battalion moved to Dublin in the autumn, and Maude spent a few weeks with it in Ireland before proceeding to the Staff College; his elder daughter, Stella, was born in October. Seeing that his going to Camberley interrupted his regimental service for a period which was to last nine years, Lord Rawlinson's opinion of him during his early days in the Coldstream may be appropriately quoted here: 'As a boy and young man Maude was a particularly attractive fellow and deservedly popular with all who met him – a very keen soldier, a first rate adjutant and, good at all games, he made his personality strongly felt in the regiment and always for good.' Rawlinson when he left Sandhurst had in the first place joined the King's Royal Rifle Corps; but on promotion he had exchanged into the Coldstream, coming in just above Maude on the list; and they were for some months in the same company. General Sir George Higginson, who

Lieutenant F. S. MAUDE.

Coldstream Guards, (1894.)

24

was in charge of the Home District during part of the time that Maude was serving as a regimental officer in the Coldstream, pays the following tribute to the memory of an old Guardsman friend:

> My acquaintance with his early career was necessarily slight as I was a long way his senior, and although we were both Guardsmen we were not in the same regiment. But I often heard from his brother officers, and subsequently from officers of my staff when I was General Officer in Command of the Home District, of Maude's high promise both as a company officer and as adjutant. His marriage to a dear friend of my wife's afforded me more frequent opportunities for observation, and I then foresaw that, given the chance, a brilliant career was likely to follow. To the historian is reserved the duty of recording his merits as a soldier. To me there remains a memory of him which I shall always cherish.

The Staff College was at this time under charge of Brigadier General (the late General Sir H. J. T.) Hildyard. Since assuming control, the Commandant had striven to modernise the course of study, to render it a thoroughly practical one from the point of view of furnishing the military forces of the Crown with a corps of officers who could be trusted to acquit themselves creditably on the staff in peace and in war, and to devise means for testing the students under his orders exhaustively in respect to their fitness for the work which they would in future be called upon to carry out. The batches who passed through the institution about the time that Maude was at Camberley enjoyed moreover the privilege of finding, amongst those set over them to watch their progress and to instruct them in their future duties, the famous author of Stonewall Jackson, Colonel George Henderson.

The Maudes settled down for the two years to be spent at Camberley in Osnaburgh House. Several of the officers who joined the Staff College with Maude at the beginning of 1895 were to become well known in the service in later years. Captain (now General the Hon. Sir H. A.) Lawrence became a particular friend of his, and they were to be closely associated many years afterwards at the time of the evacuation of Helles in the Gallipoli Peninsula. Captain (now Lieutenant General Sir G. M.) Kirkpatrick, Maude also came frequently into contact with in later years – in South Africa, in Canada, and during a visit which General Kirkpatrick, as Chief of the General Staff in India, paid to Baghdad in 1917. Another of this year at the college who has since made his mark was Captain (now Major General Sir E. E.) Carter. Maude also saw a great deal of Captain (the late Brigadier General H. J.) 'Sandy' Du Cane, both at Camberley and afterwards. Amongst the officers who were already in their second year of the course in 1895 was Captain (now Lieutenant General Sir D.) Henderson, who was to perform such valuable service during the South African War on the Intelligence Staff under Sir R. Buller and Lord Kitchener, and who later on played so great a part in developing the military air service before, and during, the Great War. Captain (now Lieutenant General Sir K. A.) Alderson also belonged to that year.

From the outset Maude was immensely interested in the course. He appreciated the lectures delivered by the staff – although anybody who did not appreciate a lecture from Colonel Henderson would have been hard to please. The outdoor work suited him down to the ground, both on account of its practical nature and from the fact of its being carried on in the open, while from his point of view it had the additional advantage of affording plenty of exercise. The country life suited him, and when not at work he was always walking and riding about, or playing hard at lawn tennis, or out with the drag-hounds. As had been his way before joining the institution (except just at the time of his marriage) he took no leave of any length of time while at Camberley, except in September 1895, when Mrs Maude and he were away for a short time paying visits in Scotland – this although the regulations provided for certain definite periods annually. He preferred to remain at Osnaburgh House, studying and entering into the local life of his place of residence. He was promoted captain in his regiment in August, having then over eleven years' service; his contemporaries at Eton and Sandhurst, Rawlinson and Lambton, had gone up long before him – Rawlinson had been promoted (in the K.R.R.C.) in 1891 and Lambton in 1892.

The batch of new officers who joined the college at the beginning of 1896 included some aspirants for staff honours who were to go far in years to come – the names of two of them have indeed become household words throughout the British Empire. Captain (the late Major General Sir T.) Capper, for whom Maude's diary shows him to have entertained a great admiration, was killed when commanding a division at Loos. Captain R. C. Haking is now a Lieutenant General and K.C.B. and proved himself a most successful divisional and army corps commander on the Western Front from 1915 to 1918. Then there were also included in the score or so of new arrivals Captain Edmund Allenby and Captain Douglas Haig. The work of this second year was even more to Maude's taste than had been that of 1895, involving as it did more outdoor operations and a good deal of making acquaintance with new scenes in Hants, Surrey and Berkshire. Reconnaissance, bivouac schemes, staff rides, was the order of the day. Framing an appreciation of a military situation, real or imaginary, always had a fascination for him, and he developed a great aptitude in the art. When on the warpath in later years, the attention which he had given to this subject at the Staff College indeed frequently stood him in good stead; while campaigning in France, at the Dardanelles, and later on in Mesopotamia, he made it a habit frequently to draw up an appreciation of the situation in the theatre where his command was operating, as it presented itself to him at the moment. This practice made it the easier for him to produce one at short notice if called upon by superior authority, and it enabled him when in responsible charge to envisage the position of affairs at any moment himself. His second daughter, Beryl, was born at Osnaburgh House in July of this year.

'My recollection of Stanley Maude takes me back to the time when we were fellow-students at the Staff College in 1895–96,' writes Sir E. Carter, 'It was at that period that I saw most of him, although we met frequently at intervals afterwards. He was my senior by some years, but our individual work often threw us together when working in 'syndicates.' I remember even in those days having an admiration for his keenness and for his extraordinary capacity for work, backed as it always was by soundness of judgement and by fertility of resource. One realised that these would show themselves fully whenever a real opportunity should offer. But behind it all was his distinctive and outstanding personality. In the highest sense of the word he was a British officer and gentleman, invariably courteous and at the same time gifted with a sense of humour which kept him cheerful and made him attractive to those with whom he was thrown in contact.

'When I heard of his earlier personal successes in the late war I felt strongly that none would deserve advancement to a position of prime responsibility better than he did. To sum up his personal characteristics in a word, Stanley Maude was essentially 'human.''

The appointment of brigade-major to the Brigade of Guards in the Home District happened to fall vacant at the end of 1896, just as Maude completed the course at the Staff College. He was given the post – always a coveted one amongst comparatively junior officers of the Guards who are qualified for staff service – and he took up his duties from 1 January 1897. The commander of the Home District at this time was Lord Methuen, the Assistant Adjutant General and chief staff officer was Colonel (now General Sir Henry) Mackinnon of the Grenadier Guards, and amongst others on the District staff was Major the Hon. A. Henniker-Major of the Coldstream. They formed a happy family. Lord Methuen's period of command properly expired in April; but he was given a special extension in view of the military responsibilities that would be thrown upon the Horse Guards establishment by the celebration of Queen Victoria's Diamond Jubilee, which was to take place in June.

The Maudes took up their residence in Lower Sloane Street, in a house of which Maude had bought the lease, and they lived there during the three years that he held his appointment. The work of the brigade-major of the Brigade of Guards was in the nature of things largely concerned with office routine; but matters in connection with the Diamond Jubilee caused Maude much extra anxiety and extra labour during the first few months of his stay in the Horse Guards. All arrangements for this had to be drawn up with forethought and with the utmost exactitude, and the brigade-major's mastery of detail and his diligence were of the utmost assistance to Lord Methuen – outside of the army it is scarcely realised what elaborate organisation is required to ensure that some great ceremonial in which troops are involved shall be carried into execution without a hitch. The programme was to be on a considerably more ambitious scale in 1897 than it had been ten years before on the occasion of the Queen's Jubilee. Detachments from overseas which represented the fighting forces of Dominions and Colonies, placed especially under the command of Lord Roberts, were to participate. The route which the Royal Procession was to follow extended through a considerable area of the East End, and it traversed portions of the Metropolis situated south of the Thames. Lining the streets, marshalling the procession, calculating the time at which every incident in the programme would take place – problems such as these only represented a fraction of the preparations that had to be thought out. Troops drawn from various quarters were to assemble in and about London, and arrangements had to be made for their accommodation and for their comfort. Close touch had to be kept with the railway companies in connection with the military movements. Negotiations had to be carried out with various municipal authorities. It is not suggested that all, or even most of, this work fell to the lot of Maude; but Lord Methuen and his chief staff officer, Colonel Mackinnon, had reason to congratulate themselves upon having so efficient and hardworking a brigade-major to help them in their troublesome task.

The actual celebration of the Diamond Jubilee on 22 June proved a triumph of masterly organisation and of felicitous stage-management, but Maude played his part in the great pageant under circumstances somewhat distressing to himself. For his father, who had been in declining health for some time before and who was now seventy-six years of age, fell ill and died on the morning of 20 June at 'Sutherland Towers,' the house where he had been living at Torquay for the previous five years. Maude had therefore to hurry off to the funeral as soon as the great day of thanks-giving was at an end. He had always been not merely very fond, but had also been very proud, of this father of his, who years before had fought in the Mahratta War and who had been one of the first to win the Victoria Cross, and he felt the old man's loss keenly. In his diary many years afterwards on 20 June there appears an entry noting the anniversary, with the remark, 'I shall never cease to think of him as the best of fathers and as a brave, loyal, retiring Englishman.'

A great parade was held at Aldershot in honour of the Queen on 1 July, at which Lord Methuen commanded the 1st Division composed of the Guards, with Maude on his staff; all seven Guards battalions were present on this occasion, and it appears to have been the first instance of the whole brigade appearing on parade as one body for a great number of years. Shortly afterwards Lord Methuen vacated command of the Home District and was succeeded by the late Major General H. Trotter, and events in the military world in London then gradually settled down into their usual groove after the upheaval caused by the Diamond Jubilee. To Maude's great joy a son was born to him in October, and was baptised as Edward Frederick, after his two grandfathers of whom he was then the only grandson; but he has always been called 'Eric' as standing for both names. A change of considerable personal interest to the brigade-major took place in the Coldstream shortly afterwards, for a 3rd Battalion was formed, although its completion took several months. This necessarily accelerated promotion throughout the regiment, and Maude, in common with a number of his brother officers, benefited considerably – so much so indeed that, although he had been behind-hand in arriving at the rank of captain, he reached field rank quite as soon as is usual in the army.

The work that he had to perform as brigade-major was not of a character to be especially interesting to the average staff officer. But he always took pleasure in detail, and he was always ready to immerse himself in the most trivial questions if they increased the very remarkable knowledge of things military which he had already acquired. He had displayed an unusual addiction to paperwork when holding the position of adjutant, and he displayed this at least equally as brigade-major, his methods not meeting by any means with the unqualified approval of commanding officers in the Brigade of Guards. They noted a disposition on his part to get control into his own grip, besides being unable to regard some of the lengthy memoranda emanating from the Horse Guards with gratification. The practice of quartering a Guards battalion in Dublin had ceased, and at this time there always was a battalion at Gibraltar instead. Maude endeavoured to maintain a control over this isolated unit in respect to furnishing returns, and so forth, which was quite contrary to the spirit of army regulations, even allowing for the somewhat abnormal organisation of the Brigade of Guards; and this brought him to loggerheads with the commanding officer. In such a matter he was bound to have the War Office and the superior military authorities on the Rock against him, and the incident shows that his two years' course at the Staff College had not influenced, much less eradicated, a proclivity for centralisation which, speaking in a military sense, was Maude's besetting sin. He still loved parade work, it should be added, and he still loved ceremonial for their own sakes, as he had loved them when a young adjutant ten years before. The term 'parade soldier' has sometimes been used as a term of reproach, but only by those who do not realise that, whereas a parade soldier does not necessarily make an efficient commander in the field, an efficient commander in the field has generally been a parade soldier in his day – as was the case with Maude.

In connection with his private affairs the year 1898 was an untoward one for him. Never a wealthy man, and by no means so well off as the majority of his brother officers in the Brigade of Guards, he sustained serious financial losses which caused him grave anxiety at the time, and which hampered him in his military career for several years afterwards, as will be seen in later chapters. Colonel Mackinnon's time at the Horse Guards came to an end during the summer, and he was succeeded by Colonel Ivor Herbert (now Lord Treowen), a Grenadier. This year, 1898, it should be noted, was the year of Lord Kitchener's conquest of Khartoum and of the downfall of Mahdism in the Sudan, and several of Maude's contemporaries at the Staff College and in the Guards gained advancement for their services during that eminently successful campaign – Rawlinson, Douglas Haig, and Capper amongst their number. He was however himself promoted major in the Coldstream early in 1899.

That year will ever be rendered memorable throughout the British Empire by the outbreak of hostilities between this country and the Boer Republics. From a comparatively early date in the year most military men perceived that a campaign was certain to take place sooner or later, and during the ordinary summer trainings the news from Cape Town and Pretoria was being eagerly scanned in every officers' mess throughout the service. It was an open secret that if the disputes of long-standing between the Home Government and that of the Transvaal were to lead to actual war, very large forces would be placed in the field for the purpose of settling the question of supremacy in South Africa for good and all. That a Guards Brigade would form part of the expeditionary army was assumed almost as a matter of course. It therefore evoked no surprise in the Home District when, on events reaching a climax early in October and orders for mobilisation being issued, such a brigade was included in the 1st Division under orders of Lord Methuen.

Command of the brigade was allotted to Major General Sir H. E. Colvile, and it was made up of the 3rd Grenadiers from Chelsea Barracks, the 2nd Coldstream from Wellington Barracks, the 1st Scots Guards from Chelsea Barracks, and the 1st Coldstream from Gibraltar, the latter battalion proceeding straight from the Rock to the Cape. Maude had fully expected to go out as brigade-major, and he was bitterly disappointed to find himself excluded. His existing appointment would seem to have given him a good claim to be chosen – the more so seeing that it expired in any case within three months. He had necessarily enjoyed particularly close association with the three battalions that were going from England as they were all stationed actually in London, and his being passed over amounted almost to a slight. The fact that two of the four battalions happened to belong to his own regiment made the blow all the more painful to him personally, and he probably underwent few more trying experiences in his career than when he had to go down one October morning to Nine Elms to see the 2nd Coldstream off, and when as the train steamed out the rank and file expressed their regret vociferously that he was not coming with them.

Amongst the many officers who proceeded to South Africa on special service was Colonel Herbert, who was succeeded temporarily by Colonel Mackinnon. As it turned out, Maude was not long in following. He sent in an official application asking to be permitted to resign the post of brigade-major, with a view to his rejoining his regiment, and a letter came to hand from the War Office on 8 December assenting to this. He found on inquiry in Pall Mall that he was to proceed to South Africa as soon as possible. He vacated the brigade-majorship on 12th, and a few days later left for Southampton to take part in his second campaign.

CHAPTER III
The South African War

Maude sailed for Cape Town in the S.S. *Avoca* on 16 December in command of the troops, which consisted of drafts for various regiments, spent Christmas at St Vincent where the ship coaled, and arrived, after a somewhat stormy voyage, in Table Bay on 7 January. He landed next day and arranged with Lieutenant Colonel 'Sandy' Du Cane of the staff at the base, who had been in his year at the Staff College, that he should go straight up and join his regiment at Modder River – it had at first been intended that he should continue the voyage to Natal in the Avoca in charge of drafts that were proceeding to join Sir R. Buller's army. He proceeded up country with a small draft and, arriving at the front late on the evening of the 11th, joined the 2nd Battalion. The Guards Brigade consisted of the 3rd Grenadiers, the 1st and 2nd Coldstream and the 1st Scots Guards, under command of General Colvile, and formed part of 1st Division under Lord Methuen. The maps on page 34 illustrate the operations in South Africa in which Maude was concerned.

Since its disembarkation in South Africa three months before, Lord Methuen's Division had experienced a somewhat strenuous time. Its task had been to attempt the relief of Kimberley, which was closely blockaded by the Boers, and in its advance along the railway that ran from De Aar across the Orange and Modder Rivers to the diamond city, and on from thence to Mafeking and Bulawayo, it had met with determined resistance at several points. In the first struggle with the burghers, at Belmont, the Guards Brigade had played a prominent part in the capture of what was a very strong position. The brigade had been practically in reserve on the occasion of the next encounter, the combat of Enslin; but it had been fully engaged in the well-contested action of the Modder River, where the troops had suffered much from heat and thirst during a protracted day of conflict. The Guards had been in reserve during the critical opening hours of the unsuccessful attack upon the hostile position at Magersfontein on 10 December, and had consequently only been very partially engaged on that day of

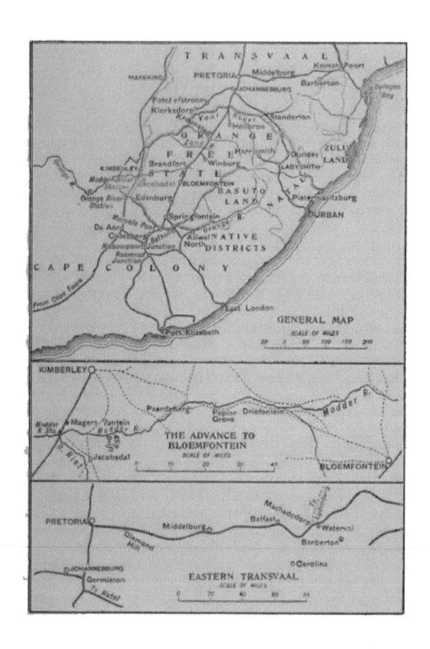

GENERAL MAP

SCALE OF MILES

THE ADVANCE TO
BLOEMFONTEIN

SCALE OF MILES

EASTERN TRANSVAAL

SCALE OF MILES

discomfiture. During the month which had elapsed since that reverse, Lord Methuen's troops had remained virtually inactive, facing General Cronje's well-entrenched line, which presented a most formidable barrier athwart the road leading from Modder River to Kimberley at a point about six miles from the former. They had confined themselves to occupying the attention of the enemy by means of occasional feints and bombardments.

Maude found himself in charge of a company for the first few days, the battalion being under command of Lieutenant Colonel the Hon. A. Henniker-Major; but owing to the second in command having to go to hospital on the 17th he assumed that position. In common with several of his brother officers, his health suffered somewhat from the trying condition of heat, damp and indifferent water under sedentary conditions; but he was not obliged to report himself ill and did not allow sickness to interfere with his duties. He was from time to time in charge of the outpost line. The operations on the Modder remained for two or three weeks virtually at a standstill; news however arrived on the 31st that large British forces were about to assemble in this area, and the enemy began to show greater signs of life about the same time.

'Went on outpost duty at 3 a.m.,' he noted in his diary of 5 February, 'turning out divisional, brigade and battalion guards before doing so. Very dark morning and, so, difficult to find one's way about. Rode round the remaining outposts at 10 a.m. Spent some time at 2 A, whence I could see great activity among the Boers. They were busy making a work between Magersfontein and the River Modder. Also they were patrolling the river bank in large numbers. As I left the work snipers landed two bullets within twenty yards of me, but they were almost spent. There are about 30,000 men in camp here now. The 6th Division, 10th Hussars, 12th Lancers, 16th Lancers, and 7 batteries R.H.A. having come, besides the Household Cavalry.'

The battalion was for two days busily engaged in pitching Lord Roberts' headquarters camp, and the Commander-in-Chief and Lord Kitchener arrived on the 8th. Two days later a new division, the 9th, was formed under command of General Colvile, whose place at the head of the Guards Brigade was taken by Major General Pole-Carew; and, as the brigade-major of the brigade went with Colvile on the new divisional staff, Maude to his great delight was nominated to fill the place. These arrangements came into force on the 11th. The Coldstream were now very strongly represented in the Guards Brigade, for, besides two of the four battalions belonging to the regiment, the brigade commander and brigade-major were Coldstreamers, and the general had moreover taken another of the regiment, Lieutenant F. Farquhar (who was killed in Flanders in the winter of 1914–15 in command of Princess Patricia's Canadian Regiment) as A.D.C.

Lord Roberts' great offensive against the Orange Free State from behind the Riet River was about to materialise. The army which was destined to carry into execution this memorable combination of war had been silently gathering for some days past, concealed by Lord Methuen's troops. Part of it had been moved round from about Colesberg on the other line of railway that connected Port Elizabeth with Norval's Pont on the Orange River, and ran on thence from Bloemfontein and Pretoria (the general map above shows the railways). Other contingents had come from intermediate positions. Some of the army, composed of the newest arrivals in the theatre of war, had been railed up straight from Cape Town. The Commander-in-Chief had gathered together the Cavalry Division under General French, 6th Division under General Kelly-Kenny, Colvile's newly formed 9th Division, and 7th Division under General Tucker, besides various mounted corps and special units, preparatory to launching them on a boldly conceived plan of campaign which hinged upon mobility. The design was that French's mounted force should make a wide detour, should pass by the left of Cronje's position and should make for Kimberley, while the infantry divisions would move in a generally easterly direction along the line of the Modder valley, cutting – or at all events threatening – the communications of the Boer force which was barring the way to Kimberley, with Bloemfontein and the main line of railway connecting the Free State and the Transvaal. That railway was Lord Roberts' ultimate objective, and he hoped to make it his main line of communication in due course when advancing on Pretoria. Methuen was to remain for the time being facing Cronje, his force acting as a curtain to conceal the development of the opening phases of the plan of offensive campaign. The Cavalry Division started at 3 a.m. on the 11th, the same day as Maude took up the appointment of brigade-major to the Guards Brigade, and headed at first south-eastwards and therefore away from Kimberley, previous to wheeling round to the north and making for Klip Drift (see the map 'Advance to Bloemfontein' above). The 6th and 7th Divisions moved off on the next day passing near Jacobsdal. The 9th Division followed suit on the 18th. A careful watch was kept on Cronje's lines by the Guards and the rest of the force under Methuen; as far as could be observed, however, all remained as usual in the Boer position, and there was no sign that the enemy realised the nature of Lord Roberts' scheme of operations. The news that French had that afternoon arrived at Kimberley with part of his cavalry, that the siege was raised, and that the first act of the drama had thereby been brought to a highly successful conclusion, reached the troops on the Modder shortly after nightfall on the 15th.

At a very early hour next morning Maude repaired to the outposts and remained for an hour at a coign of vantage, closely watching the position which the Boers had been occupying for the previous two months. There was no sign of movements nor of smoke, and it became apparent to him that the enemy lines were deserted. He reported this at once, and news to the same effect was brought in by a native scout. So a force under General Pole-Carew, Maude accompanying it as staff officer, moved out to make a reconnaissance in force in case the Boers should be preparing a trap, as they had done on former occasions; but the trenches were found to be vacated, and there were unmistakable signs moreover of Cronje's retreat having been an extremely hurried one. That commander had been very slow in detecting the nature of his formidable antagonist's plan. Only after French had passed by his left flank and was already practically in Kimberley, had the Boer leader begun to realise that a great hostile movement was in progress, designed to cut him off from Bloemfontein and to intercept his line of retreat, and that British mounted troops were already behind him. But he had at last become aware of his critical situation on the afternoon of the 15th, had thereupon decided to retreat up the Modder valley towards Bloemfontein, and so the huge caravan created by his burghers and his ox-wagons and other vehicles got under way at sundown and were streaming eastwards all that night.

The Guards Brigade remained in front of the vacated Magersfontein position with Methuen for two days longer, while the rest of the army with its impedimenta was surging after Cronje, and while French's troopers, making heavy calls upon their weary horses, succeeded at last on the 17th in cutting across the Boer line of retreat beyond Paardeberg. That night however orders came to hand from Army Headquarters directing the brigade to follow the rest of the force immediately. It marched off at 2 a.m. on the 18th and halted at Klip Drift, fifteen miles forward. A warning had come from Lord Roberts that it might have to hurry on in support of the troops ahead, but this proved a false alarm and eventually half the brigade remained at Klip Drift while the other half moved on six miles; the Guards then for some days constituted a detached force occupying an important point on the line of communications, while the bulk of the army was encircling Cronje in his laager. They consequently took no part in the sharp fighting that took place at Paardeberg before the trapped Boers surrendered. There was however plenty of work to be done in the matter of pushing food convoys forward and in regulating the convoys of wounded which passed through on their way to the railway in rear. Maude especially busied himself with the problems of sanitation of the encampments, as the brigade was occupying ground which had been traversed by successive divisions, leaving dead and dying transport animals and the jetsam that is shuffled off in course of rapid progress, behind them. Regimental officers at that time were hardly so well acquainted with this subject as they have come to be since; but it was one to which he always paid great attention, not only then but also in later days – in Flanders, on the shores of the Augean, and in Mesopotamia. On the 27th, Majuba day, news arrived that Cronje had surrendered. That evening the vanquished general and his party arrived; they were put up for the night and were sent on next day, on which the captured force passed through on the way to the internment camps, the 3rd Grenadiers furnishing the necessary escort as far as Modder River Station.

Although the enemy force which so long had kept Lord Methuen at bay, and which had so effectually protected the commandos that were beleaguering Kimberley against interference from the south, had now been disposed of, the position of the army was by no means without anxiety. The active and resolute Boer leader, De Wet, had, on discovering – too late –how critical was the situation of Cronje, made great efforts to come to that commander's rescue with forces gathered from various quarters. He had failed in this object, but he was now drawn up about Poplar Grove, facing the victorious British and with his troops extended athwart the route that they must follow in advancing to Bloemfontein and in gaining possession of the railway which Lord Roberts proposed to depend upon as his main line of supply. Considerable disappointment had already been experienced in bringing up ammunition and supplies by ox-wagon from the railway in rear – one very important convoy had indeed been captured by the enemy – and the further east the army moved the longer would be its line of communications, the greater would grow the perplexities of protecting it against the raiding of mobile antagonists, and the worse would become the difficulty of getting the transport along at all. The Commander-in-Chief therefore decided to cast the army adrift from its previous communications, and to move on Bloemfontein, carrying sufficient supplies with him to cover the time that would elapse in reaching the Free State capital and in opening up the railway line back from there to Cape Colony. This involved defeating De Wet and any other hostile forces that might endeavour to bar the way, it necessitated cutting down rations for men and animals, and it was bound to throw a great strain upon cavalry and artillery horses which had already been highly tried, and upon transport animals which were already in poor condition. In pursuance of the plan, the Guards were summoned to join the main army. They marched on 5 March and, arriving at the front on the evening of the 6th after considerable difficulties in connection with their transport, became part of the 'Corps Troops' attached to headquarters, and they found that the advance was to begin next morning.

As De Wet's force was in position facing Lord Roberts only a very few miles off, the advance on the morning of 7 March meant a general action, and an elaborate plan, designed with the idea of surrounding the bulk of the hostile army, had been drawn up. It miscarried however, for the Boers effected their retreat from Poplar Grove without suffering a disaster, and the Guards Brigade took no active part in the somewhat desultory engagements. A halt of three days followed, while arrangements in connection with supplies, transport, and so forth, were perfected. Then the army advanced afresh on the 10th, to find itself somewhat unexpectedly opposed by a considerable force of Boers under De la Rey, who was holding a strong position at Driefontein. The action that followed was fought almost entirely by the mounted troops and by the 6th Division, which was in advance. The Guards coming up in the afternoon were ordered to support that division in its attack on some high ground that the enemy was still clinging to, but it achieved its purpose after some sharp encounters without their assistance.

'As we approached Driefontein in the evening,' Maude wrote in his diary for that day, 'we could see shells bursting everywhere, Kelly-Kenny being heavily engaged. Got into camp about 5.30 p.m., having ridden forward to ascertain from Grierson where brigade was to bivouac. Soon after the brigade were settled down a message came from Lord Roberts to say that we were to attack a kopje about three miles off. I was galloping to find the general when my horse came down, turning a complete somersault. He landed with his hindquarters on my spine, crushing me severely. Great pain all night in hospital. Nothing broken.'

He got a very bad fall, spectators fearing that his neck had been broken, and as a consequence of this accident he was obliged to travel for the next four days by ambulance on the sick list, and he suffered greatly from the jolting on the rough roads, remaining however with the Guards Brigade. The advance was continued on the 11th, and that evening news reached Lord Roberts that the Boers who were gathered together to defend the capital were about to be strongly reinforced by commandos coming from the north, and by others which had been in Cape Colony between Colesberg and Norval's Pont that were expected from the south. He therefore decided that a dash must be made by the mounted troops, with the twofold object of gaining possession of the town before these additional enemy forces should arrive, and of cutting the railway so as to secure possession of such locomotives and other forms of rolling stock as might be left south of the point of severance. General French consequently pushed on on the 12th, and portions of his force reached the railway both north and south of Bloemfontein before nightfall. The Guards had been led to hope that the Commander-in-Chief would march into the Free State capital at their head, and with that in view they started off on the afternoon of the 12th, reached bivouacs at 2.30 a.m., and started off again three hours later and marched nearly all day. They arrived that evening at the town, but learnt that the enemy had evacuated it during the previous night and that Lord Roberts had made his entry into the captured city about midday. They had covered thirty-six miles in the last twenty-six hours.

'Returned to my work as brigade-major this morning,' wrote Maude in his diary on the 14th. 'Arm still bound in a sling, rather painful, but could not stand being on the sick list any longer. Lord Roberts inspected the brigade at 1 p.m. and made a nice speech, after which we marched past him in column on our way back to camp. He said that he regretted that through a mistake he had not been able to lead the brigade through the streets of Bloemfontein, but that he hoped to lead them through Pretoria instead.'

After twenty-four hours' rest a portion of the Guards Brigade was called upon for a fresh effort, which however turned out to be merely an easy and interesting excursion. The Commander-in-Chief was determined to open up communication without delay with General Gatacre's force, which was moving up from the south, and to secure possession of the railway line back to Cape Colony. So a force composed of the Grenadiers and Scots Guards, with four guns and details, under General Pole-Carew, Maude acting as staff officer, was despatched early on the 15th in four trains which were made up of rolling stock intercepted three days before by the cavalry, with orders to proceed southwards towards the Norval's Pont bridge over the Orange River. This operation, it may be observed, in certain respects constituted a somewhat daring move, for it involved the movement of troops by rail through a district that had not yet been otherwise occupied. But Lord Roberts calculated upon the moral effect which his victorious march across the Free State and his capture of Bloemfontein was bound to exert, and his confidence was fully justified by the event. For Pole-Carew met with no opposition. On the contrary, the Commandant of the district, the field cornets and the leading inhabitants met him at various stations along the line to tender their submission and to promise the yielding up of arms in due course. Information came to hand during the move that some 3,000 Boers, with a train of wagons, in retreat before the British troops that were moving up from the south, had crossed the line, going north-eastwards, late on the 14th; so the general sent a message to headquarters suggesting that a force should be sent out to try and intercept this hostile contingent. This was not however considered feasible at Army Headquarters.

The staff, travelling in the leading train, did not meet General Gatacre next morning until they were within a very few miles of Norval's Pont. After a discussion it was then decided to turn the force from Bloemfontein back, while Gatacre continued his advance; but Pole-Carew and Maude went on in a breakdown train to the bridge to see the position.

'3.25 p.m. Reached Norval's Pont,' Maude writes in the staff diary. 'Three large girders broken down and one pier blown down. Fine broad river, about eighty yards wide with steep banks thickly covered with trees. Commanding ground on both sides of the river.'

Pole-Carew's force remained at Eden berg, situated about half way between Norval's Pont and Bloemfontein, that night, and returned to headquarters next day, having in reality placed the coping-stone on the strategic structure designed by Lord Roberts six weeks earlier. The mobile army which under the Commander-in-Chief's personal orders had advanced from the other railway, and which had cast itself entirely loose from its communications after Paardeberg, was now definitely linked up again with Cape Colony by the line of railway that connected the Free State capital with East London, with Port Elizabeth, and with Cape Town, the three maritime bases of the British forces apart from the divisions in Natal under Sir R. Buller. The main army was placed in a position to reorganise its administrative services after the month of hard campaigning that it had gone through, and to prepare under comparatively favourable conditions for a resumption of the offensive should the enemy, in spite of the discomfitures recently met with, decide to continue the struggle.

A somewhat prolonged pause in respect to vertebrate offensive operations nevertheless took place, although the attitude of the Boers soon made it apparent that they had no desire to abandon resistance. This lull in the proceedings was mainly due to the imperative necessity of amassing great stores of food, of forage, and of munitions before starting upon the march to Pretoria which the Commander-in-Chief contemplated. Time was however also required to bring up the drafts intended to fill up gaps in units at the front, and to rail forward the substantial reinforcements that were now arriving from home at the southern ports. Then there was furthermore the question of making good the hospital requirements, which for some little time gave grounds for disquiet. The expediency of placing the medical service on a thoroughly satisfactory footing was indeed clearly demonstrated by the outbreak of an epidemic of sickness amongst the troops almost as soon as they came to a halt at Bloemfontein – an epidemic traceable to drinking tainted water and to halting under insanitary surroundings during the operations which had carried them across the Free State during the previous few weeks. Moreover, the assembling of troops, of supplies, and of war material of all kinds was seriously retarded by the awkward break in the railway line where this crossed the Orange River; the necessary deviation and temporary bridge at Norval's Pont were not completed until the end of March.

In the meantime the headquarters of the Guards Brigade remained in Bloemfontein, a comfortable house on high ground having been secured. Maude still suffered much from his shoulder owing to his accident at Driefontein; it indeed never fully recovered, and it gave him trouble throughout the campaign. It may be mentioned here that he was in due course awarded a pension of £100 for the year owing to the injury, that this was repeated during the following five years, and that it was eventually granted him for life. Had he taken greater care of the injured shoulder at first, and had he made greater efforts to recover full use of it by constant exercises, in accordance with medical advice, it might possibly have been completely restored; but he was hard worked and he never spared himself. As will be seen, he had to undergo an operation on getting home a year later, and he suffered from a stiff shoulder for life.

The Boers lost little time in indicating that they had no intention whatever of abandoning the struggle, and so early as the 19th a bridge on the railway a short way north of the town was blown up at night. The consequence was that two battalions of the Guards had to be sent out to guard this point, and another was sent south to Eden berg for the same purpose, leaving only one in Bloemfontein. Other troops moved in a northerly direction later, and on the 29th Pole-Carew and Maude rode out to see an attack carried out by 7th Division and a cavalry brigade upon a position which the enemy had taken up at Karee Siding, about twenty-five miles north of Bloemfontein, returning by train in the evening. The enemy was also beginning to show a great deal of activity to the east, and on 1 April there occurred the unfortunate affair of Hannah's Post; the two Guards battalions which had been out protecting the railway to the north returned to the capital that day. On the 8th the brigade moved south by rail to protect the line at a point about twenty-five miles from Bloemfontein, and that day General Pole-Carew heard that he was to command the 11th Division which was about to be formed, including the Guards Brigade. He asked that Maude should be appointed his A.A.G.; but this Army Headquarters would not approve, much to Maude's disappointment. Major-General Inigo Jones arrived to take over command of the brigade on the 12th.

There was much rain during the next few days and the troops bivouacking in the open had a very unpleasant time. On the night of 20/21 the brigade was moved back nearer to Bloemfontein, and two days later it started off eastwards with the rest of the 11th Division (which included 18th Brigade, besides artillery and the usual divisional troops). The enemy had been giving a good deal of trouble to the south-east of the capital, and had succeeded in surrounding a British force at Wepener on the Basuto border; and they were gathering in considerable force at Dewetsdorp, on the way from Bloemfontein to Wepener. During the next few days the 11th Division cooperated with General French and General Ian Hamilton in an endeavour to trap the burgher contingents. These however were under the ever-active and wary De Wet, and the project failed; for they slipped off to the north, and Wepener was relieved easily enough. Such fighting as there was fell almost entirely upon the mounted troops, and the Guards were never engaged although they had to cover a considerable amount of ground. The 11th Division returned to Bloemfontein on the 29th, bringing in large captures of sheep, cattle, and horses, which the mounted troops had managed to round up during the preceding days. The general result of these operations was that the country to the south and south-east of the capital was to a great extent cleared of the roving bands of Boers which had been infesting it latterly, and that, as abundant supplies had now been collected and the administrative services were ready, the Commander-in-Chief was able to fix a date for the great move northwards to begin. The Guards marched to Karee Siding with the rest of the 11th Division on 1 May, as a preliminary.

In his contemplated advance Lord Roberts proposed to keep 11th Division with himself in the centre, following the line of railway by Kroonstad to the Vaal, and thence to Pretoria. As it turned out, the centre force, which included 7th Division and certain contingents representing Overseas Dominions and Colonies, had little excitement during the triumphant progress through the Orange Free State. Its experience was mostly that of a succession of long marches followed by halts. To belong to it had, however, been intended as a privilege.

'Here then,' says *the Times History of the War in South Africa*, 'was the place of honour in the soldier's eye, and here Lord Roberts took care to have every part of the Empire and almost every branch of the service represented. To the backbone of infantry, composed of Guards, battalions from the North Country, the East Coast, the South and the Midlands of England, from Wales and from the Highlands and Lowlands of Scotland, he added the battalion of Militia from Canada and London's picked Volunteers. The New South Wales Lancers and the Australian Horse shared in the dangers of the cavalry, where Ireland, unrepresented in the infantry, found her place. In the mounted infantry the regular companies, drawn from English, Welsh, Scottish, and Irish regiments, were brigaded with representatives from Canada, New South Wales, Queensland, Victoria, South Australia, West Australia, and Tasmania, from New Zealand, from South Africa, from India, Burmah and Ceylon; three companies of the Imperial Yeomanry and a company of the City Imperial Mounted Volunteers were attached to headquarters. The Navy also sent guns with their complement of bluejackets to take their share in the advance.'

Although some of the troops that were destined to advance well away on the flanks were on the move a day or two earlier, it was on 8 May that the central force started from Karee Siding, and the small town of Brandfort was occupied that evening after a little skirmishing. The enemy had been reported to be gathered in some force and prepared to offer resistance, so the Guards had anticipated an action, but in this they were disappointed, as the burgher forces withdrew as soon as the mounted troops approached.

'Among the lasting impressions made upon me by Joe Maude was on the advance from Bloemfontein in May 1900,' writes Lieutenant General Sir W. Pulteney, who was commanding the 3rd Scots Guards at the time; 'the Boers were reported to be holding Brandfort in strength, and Pole-Carew, preceded by Pilkington's mounted detachments, was the central column marching on that place. Orders for the attack were issued and dictated to us commanding officers by Maude. They were the most lucid orders that we had had up to that time. Perhaps his orders sometimes had a little too much detail, but I well remember they were far in front of anything we had had before, and reflected the greatest credit on his own and on his Staff College training. Although the Boers did not wait for our attack to develop at Brandfort, the confidence in his staff work remained until 11th Division reached Komati Poort.'

11th Division halted next day, but advanced again on the 5th, reaching the neighbourhood of the Vet River, where the Boers offered some opposition. There were affrays on the flanks that day, and Pole-Carew got his guns into action, but the Guards were not engaged, and the enemy withdrew during the night, falling back to take up a strong position on the Zand River some twenty miles further north. Considerable enemy reinforcements congregated there to help their comrades who had retreated along the railway, and on the 10th, when the infantry of the central column drew near, there appeared to be every prospect of a stiff fight. But the cavalry forces which were pressing forward steadily well away to the left, managed to swing right round the burgher's right flank and compelled these to evacuate their position, although they left a few snipers to impede the advance of the British centre. The 11th Division were to have assailed the enemy's centre had the Boers stood, and owing to the outflanking operations of the mounted troops the Guards were disappointed of what at one time looked like the prospect of a serious trial of strength.

'Brigade marched at 6.15 a.m., crossing in rear of 18th Brigade which had started at 3.15 a.m.,' wrote Maude in his diary. 'Tucker's division heavily engaged on our right, and our cavalry and mounted infantry in front. After crossing the drift the brigade deployed for attack, 1st Coldstream and 1st Scots in first and second line, and 2nd Coldstream and 3rd Grenadiers in third line; 1st North Stafford (attached to brigade) in reserve. Fighting all afternoon till we bivouacked at about 3 p.m. just beyond Riet Spruit. Cavalry and mounted infantry still pursuing the retreating Boers. Transport, guns, et cetera, much delayed by drift over Zand River.'

For some little time next day it still looked as if Lord Roberts would be called upon to fight a general action before he got to Kroonstad, because the hostile commandos had occupied and had prepared elaborately a position in a broken region which barred the way to the town. But, just as had been the case on the Zand River, the outflanking operations of the British horse decided the enemy chiefs to hurry their men away north out of harm's way, and on the 12th the Commander-in-Chief made his entry into the place, riding at the head of the Guards Brigade. The centre force had covered 130 miles in ten days' marching; but it was now autumn in South Africa, and although the troops were much inconvenienced by the dust they no longer suffered much from heat.

It may be mentioned appropriately here that Maude makes frequent uncomplimentary references in his diary to the character of the staff work which came to his notice from time to time. This according to him often caused the troops unnecessary fatigue and inconvenience. The fact of the matter was that, with the exception of a comparatively few officers – who had studied the subject, who had practised themselves in the issuing of full and intelligible orders, and who realised the importance of method and system in this matter, the staff of the British Army in South Africa did not know how to translate the intentions of the Commander-in-Chief and of his superior subordinates into the words that would convey their intentions to the troops who had to carry those intentions out. The fault in this respect lay rather in a misapprehension of their duties and responsibilities on the part of the superior staff officers than of the juniors, who had been properly trained of very late years at the Staff College. Some contemporaries of Maude at Camberley, like Major D. Haig with the Cavalry Division, and Major T. Capper who was with the 5th Division in Natal, had practically nothing to learn in this respect; but many of their seniors were versed in the theory of staff work rather than in its practice, and the results were most unsatisfactory. The whole staff organisation was moreover wrong from the point of view of carrying on operations in the field, as there was no General Staff.

Lord Roberts halted for ten days at Kroonstad, while the various breaks that had been effected by the Boers on the railway were overcome by making low-level deviations at the river crossings, and while mounted troops, working forward by wide sweeps on the flanks, cleared the country to a great extent on either side of the line that was to be followed by the central force when it moved forward again. This advanced afresh on the 22nd, and in five days, marching about sixteen miles a day, reached the Vaal, which was crossed on the morrow practically unopposed. The main Boer force, which was now under command of General Louis Botha, had fallen back to a strong position along a line of hills thirty miles north of the river covering Johannesburg from the south. Lord Roberts advanced on the 28th with his main infantry force, and on the 29th, 11th Division reached Germiston, the junction eight miles east of Johannesburg where the branch line to that city turns off from the main line of railway.

'Brigade marched at 6.45 a.m.,' Maude notes in his diary. 'The railway bridge over the Klip River delayed our crossing for some time as the head of the column had to be halted. The 1st Line Transport started, luckily enough, at 6.30, as most of it got over the main bridge before the naval guns broke through it, causing a long delay. Brigade pushed forward, as the cavalry, mounted infantry and Hamilton were fighting in front and on the left flank. Reached Germiston at 3.30 p.m. As I rode forward to find camping place, found the Boers in occupation of the town and was fired at. Saw three trains start for Pretoria filled with Boers. Selected camping ground. Brigade deployed for attack but Boers bolted.'

Some sharp fighting had been taking place on the 28th and 29th on the left of the central army. Generals French and Hamilton attacked and outflanked Botha in the rugged high ground to the south-west of Johannesburg and by their determined action obliged him, after offering a stout resistance, to abandon his position. This greatly facilitated the forward movement of 11th and 7th Divisions from the Vaal to Germiston (see map 'Eastern Transvaal' on p.34). The Guards halted at Germiston on the 30th, and Maude that day rode into Johannesburg. The Commander-in-Chief made his triumphant entry into the gold reef city on the morrow, and, after the Union Jack had been run up at the court-house in place of the Vierkleur, 11th and 7th Divisions marched past him, the Guards later proceeding to a camp six miles outside.

Lord Roberts only halted two days at Johannesburg. On 3 June he moved northwards, heading for Pretoria. Two despatch riders from Botha came in that day, whom Maude personally conducted to Lord Kitchener. For a short time next day it looked as if the Boers might try seriously to contest the approach of the invaders to the Transvaal capital; but they were not in strong force, and, although 11th and 7th Divisions had partially to deploy for attack, the burghers quietly abandoned the strong position which they occupied to the south of the place. Some of the mounted troops reached the outskirts in the evening and the victorious field marshal made his solemn entry on the 5th at the head of contingents of his troops, a fitting climax to what in many respects had been a signally successful operation of war.

'At 2 p.m. the brigade arrived in rear of the naval guns in action,' Maude wrote in his diary for the 4th. 'General and I rode forward and came under fairly heavy fire on the reverse side of the slope from bullets just clearing the crest. Orderly's horse shot within five or six yards of me. Brigade formed for attack, 1st Coldstream in first and second line, 2nd Coldstream and 3rd Grenadiers in third line; 2nd Coldstream ultimately pushed up into firing line to take a couple of small kopjes. Under fire till dark, 5.30 p.m., when troops bivouacked where they stood...' Next day he writes: 'Brigade advanced on Pretoria at 6.30 a.m. At 8.30 a.m. the 2nd Coldstream rushed the station after an inter-change of a few shots, capturing a good deal of rolling stock, and prisoners with arms and ammunition. I pushed on into the town with Skeff's (Captain Skeffington Smyth) company and Gwynne (Reuter's correspondent), and placed guards on the Raadzaal, law courts, government offices and stores, post and telegraph offices and banks, and then went to the Presidency where I found Mrs Kruger. Made Eloff a prisoner, disarmed the guard, picketed the streets and mounted an English guard. We received a great reception from the townspeople. Made arrangements for the march past on the market square. Grenadiers lined the square and furnished the guard of honour. Guards Brigade led the march past. Prisoners all safe. Brigade bivouacked west of the town.'

But the advance from Bloemfontein to Pretoria had been a somewhat disappointing experience for the Guards and for their brigade-major. There had seemed to be promise of an infantry engagement in the centre of the moving front on more than one occasion; but, either under pressure of outflanking movement of horse, or else owing to a not unreasonable indisposition to accept combat on the part of the Boers, the enemy had invariably slipped away at the last moment. The brigade had marched 299 miles in thirty-four days, ten of them spent at Kroonstad during the long halt in that town; but not once had it been really in action. Imbued with those instincts of the fighter which he was so often to display as a commander some years afterwards, Maude was not wholly content with the course that the operations had taken, quite apart from his natural regret at taking no part personally in a serious combat. The Boers had never once been brought to book – they had been outmanoeuvred, not outfought except in a few petty affairs. They had been defeated in no determinate conflict, as they had been defeated at Belmont – mainly by the Guards – and as they had been defeated in the end on the Tugela. Most educated soldiers subscribe in theory to the principle that the destruction of the opposing forces in combat is the true objective to be sought after in war, and not the occupation of territories and of places, but not all of them act up to that principle in practice, or try to act up to it, so unyieldingly as did Maude.

A pause in active movements, in so far as the 11th Division was concerned, ensued for a few days after the entry into Pretoria. The Boer Executive of the Transvaal had a few days before moved off by the railway which led eastwards from the capital to Delagoa Bay, and had established Machadodorp, half way to the Portuguese frontier, as the seat of government (see map 'Eastern Transvaal' above). Botha, after abandoning the attempt to save Pretoria, had withdrawn his burghers in the same direction, and he was now in position some twenty miles from the capital. Negotiations were proceeding with the enemy Commander-in-Chief with a view to a settlement, although Lord Roberts in the meantime was in no way relaxing preparations for actively continuing his operations. Reorganisation of the supply and transport services was proceeding after the heavy strain of the great advance from Bloemfontein – a work that was complicated by the energetic action of the Free State Boers, for De Wet just at this time actually cut the communications for a few hours by seizing three points on the railway between Kroonstad and the Vaal. However, on 8 June the 11th Division, together with large part of the troops assembled round Pretoria, moved out eastwards with the object of operating against Botha, who was now holding a long line of hills athwart the line to Machadodorp and Delagoa Bay. Maude's horse came down with him on the 9th and rolled on him, injuring his chest. On the following evening Lord Roberts issued his instructions for certain highly important operations to be undertaken next day with the object of compelling the Boer commander to abandon his position.

His plan followed the lines that had been adopted in similar cases on the way up from Bloemfontein. His desire was to turn both hostile flanks and to hold his centre back till these eccentric operations should have affected their purpose. French was to make a wide sweeping movement north of the railway, mounted troops supported by infantry under Jan Hamilton were to act similarly south of the railway, Pole-Carew's division, with most of the artillery, was in the centre to await the success of the flanking forces. But, as it turned out, Botha had foreseen that his opponent was likely to pursue his accustomed plan of battle, and had made dispositions accordingly. 'The Boer position covered some thirty miles and extended beyond the lines of advance on either hand which had been indicated to French and Hamilton. The burghers also were on this occasion in comparatively strong force on the two flanks and relatively weak in the centre. The consequence was that Lord

Roberts' tactical scheme in the first instance practically miscarried. French was entirely unable to carry out the task allotted to his comparatively small force; he indeed found his troops in a somewhat uncomfortable position at nightfall. Hamilton was somewhat more successful, but was also brought to a standstill without carrying out the task assigned to him. The 11th Division in the centre was not engaged. Such was the position on the evening of the first day of the affair of Diamond Hill.

Lord Roberts decided during the night that the 11th Division should deliver a more or less frontal attack upon the Boer left centre next day in conjunction with part of Hamilton's force, and he issued orders to that effect which reached divisional headquarters at 8 a.m. Pole-Carew at once set the Guards Brigade, with some of his artillery, in motion to move to their right front towards Hamilton's left; but he retained 18th Brigade in the centre, in accordance with the Commander-in-Chief's explicit instructions. The task of the Guards and of Hamilton's infantry was to be the capture of some seven miles of ridge known as Diamond Hill, of which the northern end was about five miles south of the railway. The Guards had a troublesome march through boggy country before they reached their rendezvous.

Maude's account of the day's fighting in his diary runs as follows:

> Brigade marched at 8 a.m. to support Ian Hamilton's division. Moved due east at first, but at 10.15 a.m. orders were issued to move in attack formation against Kleinfontein; 1st and 2nd Coldstream in first and second line, and 3rd Grenadiers in third line. First Scots remained stationary with the 5-inch guns at first. The naval guns and a battery accompanied our advance. At 1 p.m. I saw Balfour, late 11th Hussars, galloping past and asked what he wanted. He said that Ian Hamilton wanted reinforcements. As my general had remained behind with the 5-inch guns about two miles away, I took upon myself the responsibility to act and told Surtees to take the 1st Coldstream and reinforce Hamilton.
>
> Second Coldstream occupied Kleinfontein Kopje at 1.30 p.m. and enemy opened shell fire upon us. Got up naval guns and field battery, who replied. At 2.30 p.m. the 2nd Coldstream under cover of artillery fire moved against the main Donkerhoek ridge (Diamond Hill) and occupied the same at 3.15 p.m. I went up with the firing line, as Arthur Henniker had

just hurt his thumb and Shute was with the hospital. Under very heavy fire until 5.30 p.m., but luckily under good cover. I saw that we could not advance further as we were on the edge of a big ravine commanded from the other side by the Boers. Two guns of 83rd Battery came up into our firing line and engaged the Boers at 800 yards with good effect.

At dusk, in the absence of the general who had not come up, I arranged to take up outpost line on the line we held, making our left secure and communicating with Hamilton's force on our right. Second Coldstream bivouacked on the ridge and the remaining battalions below it. First Scots and baggage did not come up till very late. First Coldstream bivouacked with Hamilton's force. Went over to see Hamilton who had been hit by a spent shrapnel. Four companies on outpost duty. Fine, cool day. South wind. Casualties in brigade one officer and eleven men. Very seedy all day from the severe crushing I had had, and felt quite helpless.

It is clear from the above extract from his private diary that on this day Maude was carrying out his duties under very serious disabilities. On the previous day it had taken two men to get him into his saddle at all, he was so stiff and bruised from his accident on the 9th. Nevertheless he went through an exhausting day in the field, accepted considerable responsibility in diverting one battalion to the right in the absence of his chief, and, when it came to the actual advance against the formidable ridge, moved forward with the firing line of the leading battalion. Actually the Guards only captured part of the long ridge of Diamond Hill, portions of the heights more to the right being won by contingents of General Ian Hamilton's troops. The end of the heights on the extreme right of the assailants, furthest from the railway, was moreover not taken until late, for the Boers were still holding on grimly in that quarter, and they showed no disposition to abandon the position altogether; just before dusk, however, an attack delivered by some of the mounted troops secured the end of the ridge, and Botha quietly withdrew his forces during the night, uninterrupted by his opponents. In this action of Diamond Hill the Guards had contributed largely to such success as had been achieved; they had not suffered many casualties, in spite of the difficulties involved in delivering what was virtually a frontal attack upon a strong position; their lightly purchased success had been largely due to skilful handling coupled with effective artillery support.

They were withdrawn towards Pretoria two days later, but eventually passed most of the next six weeks in the neighbourhood of the position they had helped to win. Lord Roberts' intention was to move eastwards and to gain possession of the Railway line down to Komati Poort on the Portuguese frontier; but the accomplishment of this design had for various reasons to be deferred for a considerable time, during which a number of sets of operations were carried out in different parts of the theatre of war in which the Guards took no part. These operations involved the advance of the leading troops of the Natal army along the railway coming up from the Natal frontier to Germiston so as to establish a fresh line of railway communications between Pretoria and the coast. They included some very successful work in the Orange Free State in which a large Boer force was eventually to be surrounded and captured. There was also a good deal of marching and fighting in the Western Transvaal during the month of June and the early part of July.

From 15 to 21 June the Guards Brigade was outside Pretoria, and the brigade staff occupied a house. Maude disliked the plan of living under cover while the troops bivouacked, but it enabled him to have his shoulder massaged daily, as this had been giving him a good deal of trouble; the effects of the fall on the day before the opening of the Diamond Hill fight he soon got over, but the old trouble from the accident at Driefontein was ever-present, causing him pain and annoyance besides making writing difficult. The brigade then moved back to near Diamond Hill, and for some time to come the brigade staff occupied a farm in that neighbourhood. Operations further to the front were constantly in progress, but were carried out mainly by mounted troops. There were occasional scares of Boer attacks however, constant vigilance was required at the outposts, and parties of the enemy were seen from time to time not far from the section under charge of the Guards. In the meantime Maude and the staff had come to be on quite friendly terms with the farmer and his family; but, after nearly a month's stay under their roof, his suspicions were aroused and he had the garden of the house searched, when £8,000 in gold was found buried, together with twenty-two rifles and a number of incriminating papers. So the family were sent into Pretoria; they had been in communication with the Boers out on commando the whole time.

Three days after making this haul, on 20 July, Maude received a telegraphic message from Lord Minto, the Governor-General of Canada, offering him the position of Military Secretary. He telegraphed home to consult Mrs Maude, and in due course he accepted the offer, subject to his being permitted by the military authorities to take the appointment up when the operations then imminent for clearing the railway to Komati Poort should be concluded, which, it was hoped, would bring the war to an end. Further reference to his decision in this matter will be made at a later stage, but it may be observed here that the general impression throughout the army in South Africa at the time was that the campaign was drawing to a conclusion, and that there consequently appeared to be every reason to suppose that the Guards would shortly be proceeding home.

Lord Roberts' preparations for a further advance towards Middelburg and Machadodorp were now completed, and on 23 July the 11th Division moved forward eastwards from the position that it had occupied for some weeks near Diamond Hill. Pole-Carew's troops were to form part of the army which Lord Roberts proposed in due course to unite with portions of the Natal forces that were to move north under Sir R. Buller, and then to use for clearing the railway as far as the Portuguese frontier. The advanced troops coming from the west, under Generals French and Hutton, occupied the town of Middelburg on the railway on the 27th, and then there occurred a fresh pause to permit of several important railway crossings being repaired between Diamond Hill and Middelburg, and to allow the necessary time for Buller's anticipated movement up from the south. The general situation in the theatre of war as a whole was greatly improved on the 29th by the surrender of upwards of 4,000 Boers and three guns, together with much ammunition, to General Hunter in the Brandwater Basin in the Orange River Colony, as the Free State now was called, the most important victory that had been won since the capitulation of Cronje at Paardeberg.

For nearly a month, during which the mounted troops were kept active on the front and the flanks, the 11th Division was occupied in guarding the railway and constructing local de-fences at important points, so that the Guards had an experience of a class of work which the infantry were largely to be engaged upon during the later stages of the war. During the first half of August, however, they were gradually pushed forward towards Middelburg, as troops came up from the rear to relieve them, and then, on the 21st, the 11th Division began moving eastwards from that place. Buller was now approaching and renewed active operations, which promised to achieve decisive results, were well in sight.

General Botha was now occupying an extensive stretch of country athwart the railway, with his centre posted near the small town of

Belfast. His front more or less coincided with the general line where the very rugged, broken country of which the extreme eastern regions of the Transvaal consist may be said to commence as one moves eastwards from about Middelburg. General French with most of the cavalry was operating to the south of the railway and in touch with General Buller. The 11th Division now came up on their left, and on the 25th Pole-Carew occupied Belfast after encountering a certain amount of opposition, while some of his troops also worked off to the north.

'The division marched at 6.45 a.m.,' Maude records in his diary, 'the Guards moving on the south side of the railway with one battery. At noon we came in sight of Belfast, and, reinforced by the siege guns, advanced to the attack. We secured the hill south of Belfast without difficulty, but further advance was difficult owing to our coming under a hot shell and musketry fire. So we held on while Henry (General St G. Henry, commanding a brigade of mounted infantry) turned the Boer right. Bivouacked at 4.30 p.m. just south of the railway station. Eighteenth Brigade held Monument Hill. Quiet night. Casualties fourteen. Boers began shelling 18th Brigade bivouacs at 7 a.m.,' he writes in his diary of the following day, 'and shelled all our bivouacs with high velocity shells at intervals during the day. Not much damage done.'

On that day Lord Roberts, who had been back at Pretoria for some time superintending the general course of operations all over the vast theatre of war, arrived to take personal command. He soon satisfied himself that the Boers were covering a wide stretch of difficult country on both sides of the railway and were at many points holding prepared positions in terrain that was generally very suitable for defence. He moreover found that the three main groups constituting his own army, under command respectively of Buller, French, and Pole-Carew, were in a cramped situation and by no means satisfactorily placed for dealing effectively with so elastic, so mobile and so elusive an enemy as the burgher forces opposed to them. He therefore arranged to take French out of his present central position next day and to transfer him to the extreme left, north of the railway, his troops making a detour to the rear. He further ordered Pole-Carew to move the Guards Brigade to the north so as to link up with French's mounted troops when these should come up into line. This left only Buller south of the railway line, which as it happens, turns south-eastwards for about five miles beyond Belfast. But the troops from the Natal side represented a strong infantry force and they were well supplied with guns, besides including an adequate proportion of mounted men, so that they could be depended upon to give a good account of themselves. The consequence of these new dispositions was that the Guards had on the 26th to make an uncomfortable flank march, more or less along the front of part of the Boer general position and well within artillery range of it.

'Brigade marched at 6.30 a.m.,' Maude wrote in his diary on the 26th, 'with orders to make a reconnaissance in force, in conjunction with French, towards Dullstroom. Orders changed twice, and although we were in position to start at 7.30 a.m. we did not advance till 2.30 p.m., as French was busy on the left. His advance was very pretty and rapid as he drove the Boers from kopje to kopje. Henry covered our advance and did splendidly. I had the working of siege guns, naval 12-pdrs and a field battery and had rather fun. Terrific fire during our advance and after dark. Brigade fired 32,000 rounds and drove the Boers back splendidly. Three men killed and twenty-two wounded. Two battalions on outpost.'

The general result of the movements of French's mounted troops and the Guards, however, was to press back the extreme right of the enemy to some extent, and to pave the way for the action of the morrow. The 27th was to prove a day of victory, but neither French nor Pole-Carew were for practical purposes employed in making the most of it. Only a comparatively small portion even of the Natal force was indeed actually engaged. General Buller delivered an attack with two battalions supported by many guns upon the ground about the farm of Bergendal which lay near the railway some four miles beyond Belfast, and the troops employed gained a complete local success. This threatened the whole of Botha's left wing, which hurried from the ground, and the Boers north of the railway who were facing Pole-Carew and French followed suit late in the day. The burghers made off through difficult hilly country, proceeding in various directions; but the bulk of them under Botha himself took the route that leads north-eastwards to Lydenburg.

This combat of Bergendal marked one of the turning points of the war, not merely in that it opened the way along the railway to Komati Poort and the Portuguese frontier, but because from that day forward the Boer Commander-in-Chief showed more and more disinclination to keep any large part of the burgher forces together as an army, and began to devote his attention rather to the guerrilla form of warfare which De Wet and other Free State commandants were already employing to excellent advantage for their side. President Steyne of the Free State had joined Mr Kruger, the Transvaal President, at Machadodorp (which is about twenty miles by rail beyond Belfast) two days before the fight of Bergendal after an adventurous journey. The two Presidents then proceeded east by rail for some distance, and after the defeat of Botha's army it was decided that Kruger should repair to Europe, for it had become apparent that the Transvaal Executive would henceforward have to pursue a nomadic career.

It may not be out of place here to comment on Maude's description of the flank march of the Guards on the 26th, as illustrating military opinion in the British Army at that date. A particularly level-headed soldier, who had studied his profession assiduously ever since he joined and who was in close touch with the ablest officers in the service, we find him using the expression 'terrific fire' with reference to the shelling and the musketry experienced by a whole brigade of infantry, moving under somewhat disadvantageous circumstances, which only suffered twenty-five casualties during several hours spent in comparatively close touch with the enemy. Describing that same day's work, or a similar day's work, the majority of British staff officers would have probably used a similar expression. The numerous campaigns which had been undertaken against irregular warriors in various parts of the world during the last quarter of the nineteenth century had taught the military forces of the Crown numbers of lessons calculated to be of use in warfare of any form. But they had not tended to impress upon those who had taken part in them that serious fighting is a sanguinary business, and that, when opposed to a resolute and well-armed enemy, you cannot make omelettes without breaking eggs.

On ascertaining that the burgher forces were retreating eccentrically through the mountainous region in front of him, Lord Roberts decided to dispose his troops for the pursuit on corresponding lines. Buller was to go off north-eastwards to Lydenburg and beyond. French was directed to take a wide sweep south and then east, heading for Barberton, an important place with a branch line leading to it from a junction on the main railway at a point forty miles short of Komati Poort. Pole-Carew was to take a central line, moving more or less along the railway, but he was to allow the two forces on the flanks to get well ahead. In pursuance of these instructions the Guards Brigade was moved forward to a place called Waterval Onder, about ten miles beyond Machadodorp, on 30 August, and it remained there until 12 September. At Machadodorp, it should be observed, the railway begins descending what soon becomes a deep valley which leads right down to the low veldt bordering Portuguese territory. Any advance down this valley must be somewhat hazardous so long as the high ground on either flank was not cleared of the enemy, and it was partly owing to these conditions that Pole-Carew's force was to wait until Buller's and French's operations had developed satisfactorily on either hand.

Barberton was captured by surprise by some of French's mounted troops on 18 September, great quantities of stores being secured as well as much invaluable rolling stock. Buller also had made good progress beyond Lydenburg in very difficult country. The consequence was that when Pole-Carew, with the Guards and some mounted troops, advanced from Waterval Onder on the 12th they were troubled only by topographical difficulties. After proceeding along the line for about fifteen miles, the force on the 14th turned off by a little used track across the hills. The route taken involved an ascent of 2,400 feet, and the Guards that day had to cut a path for a long distance through a tangled wilderness. 'Roads terrible and ascent very steep,' Maude wrote in the brigade staff diary. Next day there was a descent, and on the 16th and 17th the troops were obliged to traverse nearly twenty miles of waterless waste before they hit off the branch line to Barberton and established connection with French's force. After that Pole-Carew followed the railway with the Mounted Infantry, the Guards and some artillery, making for Komati Poort, which involved some hard marching in hot weather, the force being now down on the low veldt. Then, on the 20th, a special request came from Lord Roberts for an effort to reach the frontier as soon as possible.

'Force marched for Broken Bridge at 5 a.m.,' Maude wrote in his diary for the 21st, 'Divisional staff could not tell us which road to take, so we had to find it ourselves. Merely a track and very much up and down hill. Engineers had to work hard all day assisted by our men. Also large fatigue parties required to push the wagons along. Made most of Guards Brigade march on the railway line, as the marching was easier there. Arrived at our bivouac at 5 p.m. No water reported nearer than two miles off, so went to look for some. Found some at last and arranged bivouac accordingly. Baggage got in very late.

'Of the arrival at Komati Poort on the 24th,' he writes: 'Force marched at 5 a.m. for Komati Poort. Mounted Infantry in front, followed by Guards Brigade, guns, et cetera Boers reported to be in position ahead. At 6.30 a.m. we had a long halt while the M.I. reconnoitred Komati Poort. Kruger and 1,000 men reported to be waiting at bridge to surrender, but this was only a story as usual. Brigade reached Komati Poort station at 9.45 a.m. where it halted and watered. At noon, brigade moved into bivouac at the junction of the Crocodile and Komati Rivers. Charming bivouac, excellent bathing, good water and plenty of wood. No outposts. Immense masses of rolling stock on Selati-Delagoa railways. Boers had tried to burn most of it. A Long Tom and some ammunition found. Plenty of stores.'

His staff work during this advance into the extreme east of the Transvaal was invaluable to the brigade, his inexhaustible vigour and physical strength helping him to overcome obstacles of all kinds in defiance of the heat. General Pulteney pays the following fine tribute to his services at the time: 'Maude never spared himself, and if he had a fault it was expecting his clerks to display the same energy and lasting power, without sleep, as he possessed himself. The way he looked after the interior economy of the troops on this very trying march from Waterval Onder to Komati Poort in September 1900 was superb, and all who took part in it owe him a debt of gratitude.' The attempt to give a coup de grace to the Boer forces in this region had failed, even if most valuable captures had been made at both Barberton and Komati Poort, especially in respect to railway material. Although broken up as an army since the combat of Bergendal, large bodies of the enemy had retreated to the Portuguese border; but they had dispersed outwards as the forces under Buller, French and Pole-Carew worked eastwards through the mountain country, the greater part eventually proceeding north and evading Buller. There was consequently no object in keeping any large force at Komati Poort, and two battalions of the Guards were sent off to Pretoria by rail on the 27th. On the 28th there was a ceremonial parade in honour of the King of Portugal's birthday; next day the other two Guards battalions entrained; and the brigade staff followed on the 30th. Owing to the steep gradients leading up to Machadodorp and to congestion on the line, it took the staff three days to reach that place, and they only arrived at Pretoria on 4 October. Tents were now available, so that the Guards, after many months of bivouacking, found themselves temporarily under canvas, and it was generally understood that they would shortly embark for home.

Maude had a quiet time at Pretoria for several days awaiting developments, considerable doubt prevailing as to the future. A telegram arrived from the War Office on 17th to say that he was to go home as soon as he could be spared, as Lord Minto had need of his services; but General Inigo Jones was unwilling to release him, although Lord Roberts was quite ready to assent to his departure. He had recently been suffering a good deal from his shoulder and arm, and Colonel Magill, the medical officer of the Guards Brigade, was anxious that he should go into hospital for a time and have them properly attended to. 'So am I,' he wrote in his diary, 'but duty comes first, and I don't see that I can have it done yet as we are not sure that we shall not have to move.' This indeed happened almost immediately afterwards, as two Guards battalions with cavalry and guns were sent out hurriedly to the west of Pretoria on the 20th, in view of an alarm that Boers were going to break through from the south on that side. Maude acted as staff officer to the force. Nothing happened however, and the column returned to the capital on the 24th. 'A good deal of talk about our going home,' he wrote in the diary on the 27th, 'but I fear that it is all talk. We have heard so much of this sort of thing that we do not believe in it much.' In the meantime the divisional organisation was being broken up generally throughout the theatre of war, as it was no longer suitable to the conditions as these were understood at Army Headquarters. This affected 11th Division, and it will not be out of place to quote here an appreciation of Maude's work from his old brigade and divisional commander in South Africa:

I have known Joe Maude ever since he joined the Coldstream,' writes Lieutenant General Sir R. Pole-Carew. 'To know him was to love him and respect him. He was a first rate adjutant of the 1st Battalion. When I commanded the Guards Brigade in South Africa he was my brigade-major, and when I afterwards was given command of the 11th Division I tried hard to get him appointed chief staff officer of the division. This however was not permitted, but, as the Guards formed a brigade of the 11th Division, Maude was with me in the advance from Modder to Bloemfontein and to Komati Poort and back to Pretoria. I do not think it would be easy to find a better staff officer – active, energetic, full of common sense, and beloved by officers and men.

On the 29th news came that the 3rd Grenadiers were to go home, but this proved to be a false alarm. Prince Christian Victor died that day at Pretoria, and he was buried there on 1 November, Maude making the arrangements for the funeral parade of the troops. That afternoon orders came which definitely put an end to any idea of the Grenadiers or any of the Guards shortly proceeding to England, for the staff, with two battalions, were directed to entrain for Bloemfontein with the object of forming a flying column to act in that vicinity. The fact was that it was already becoming apparent that the war was by no means over. It was taking a purely guerrilla character, a character which it however had been maintaining in the Orange River Colony for the previous seven months. They arrived at Bloemfontein on 5th, where General Hunter took up general command a day or two later. It speedily transpired that there was but little prospect of the Guards being formed into a flying column – it was indeed already becoming apparent that the proper functions of infantry in the guerrilla warfare that was now in progress consisted in guarding railways, in securing communications, watching important strategic points such as drifts over big rivers, and in forming pivots to act as bases for really mobile columns composed of guns and mounted troops to hinge themselves upon. Under the circumstances, Maude became very anxious to go home with a view to having his shoulder seen to and to then proceeding to Canada, and he communicated with the staff at Pretoria on the subject. 'I have nothing to do here,' he wrote in his diary on the 6th. On 15th, however, news arrived that the Boers were certainly going to invade Cape Colony, and this at once threw important responsibilities on his shoulders; for it was decided that the Guards should be distributed along the Orange River to hold the drifts, and their disposition for this purpose, and the administrative arrangements connected therewith, practically devolved upon him. It took a few days to make the necessary arrangements and to get the detachments into position, General Jones' headquarters being at Springfontein on 16th and moving on to Norval's Pont on the 20th. The other two Guards battalions were in due course brought down from the Transvaal.

A somewhat anxious time followed. The force available to hold the long line of the Orange River between Aliwal North and the railway bridge over the river between De Aar and Kimberley was manifestly insufficient for the purpose. Maude not unnaturally felt anxious, as a hostile irruption into Cape Colony was bound to create an awkward military situation and might prove a signal for a rebellion. 'Applied to Hunter for two more battalions to hold this line; posts are terribly weak and must be cut off if Boers cross in any force; river is very low and fordable almost anywhere,' Maude wrote in his diary on the 28th. 'Great talk of a rising in Cape Colony, but I rather doubt it; martial law should be proclaimed everywhere,' is an entry on 2 December. Lord Roberts, it should be mentioned, had handed over command to Lord Kitchener at Pretoria on 29 November preparatory to going home.

A fortnight of considerable suspense ensued for the wardens of the marches of the 'Old Colony,' small bodies of the enemy being seen from time to time on the north side of the Orange River, and the ever-active De Wet manifesting a threatening activity in the south-eastern regions of the Orange River Colony. At last intelligence reached Norval's Pont to the effect that 700 Boers had crossed between Bethulie and Aliwal North on the previous night, and on the morrow tidings came to hand that another hostile force was over the river at a point considerably to the west of Norval's Pont. Cape Colony had in fact been invaded by two hostile forces, which were respectively under Kritzinger and Hertzog, operating a long way apart. The effort to prevent the anticipated offensive stroke on the part of the Boers by holding the drifts – or several of them – had failed, as Maude had indeed fully foreseen would happen if the enemy really meant business. A new situation had arisen calling for prompt and vigorous measures. Mobile columns had to be created without a moment's delay to grapple with the hostile commandos which had overflowed the barrier. Instructions had to be sent in all directions. And an immense amount of organising work was imposed upon Maude, as he was for the moment virtually in the position of chief staff officer on the Cape Colony frontier, called upon to make proposals to Lord Kitchener and General Hunter as to how this new situation was to be met. His proposals were approved. Then on 19th, Northern Cape Colony was broken up into 'command areas'; all its western part was placed under the orders of General Inigo Jones, and the organisation and spheres of responsibility were thereby regularised.

During the next two days troops which were hurried down from the north by rail came pouring through Norval's Pont, and on the 24th General Jones' headquarters moved to Naauwpoort and lived in a train. A number of mobile columns were already in full cry after the intruders and within a few days were hunting Kritzinger and Hertzog hither and thither through the difficult hilly country of which northern Cape Colony for the most part consists. The districts involved were all placed under martial law, all the troops whether sedentary or nomadic in the western area were controlled from Naauwpoort, and the general management and the switching about of the columns was for all practical purposes in the hands of Maude. Although his personal inclinations were for active work in the field such as the numerous column commanders were carrying on, rather than for the duty of pulling the strings from an office, he certainly could not now complain of having nothing to do. But the work, if not in all respects congenial, was remarkably interesting and of the highest importance. Endeavouring to outwit the extremely agile Boer commandants working under Kritzinger and Hertzog by following up their movements and those of the pursuing force on the map, gave ample scope alike for ingenuity and for foresight. Dealing with the innumerable administrative problems that were involved, and sending the requisite orders by telegram to large numbers of different military authorities scattered about the area, many of them perpetually on the move, taxed

Maude's memory, involved heavy labour and demanded constant concentration of thought. But in spite of all efforts of the staff and of the active and energetic column commanders, the enemy detachments could never be brought properly to book. They raided townships and farms, they turned up at unexpected points, and, worst of all, they were ever managing to work further and further southwards into the heart of Cape Colony. 'Went for a short walk,' Maude notes in his diary on 4 January; 'first time I have stirred out of the railway carriage for four days.' To a man of his exceptionally active habits such a life must have been particularly trying. Colonel D. Haig however arrived a day or two later to take over general charge of the mobile columns in this part of the theatre of war, and this lightened Maude's responsibilities. Thenceforward General Inigo Jones was in command only of the sedentary troops, although for practical purposes it was impossible sometimes to draw a hard and fast line between what were mobile troops and what were sedentary troops.

During the next three weeks the hunting of Kritzinger's and Hertzog's commandos continued without any very satisfactory results; but the work was considerably less exacting for Maude than it had been during recent weeks, owing to the mobile columns that were pursuing and trying to destroy the roving hostile bands being now under an independent command. The nomadic parties of Boers that were wandering about in Cape Colony at this time were, however, merely the forerunners of what was intended to be a much more serious invasion, an invasion for which they were preparing the way by drawing the British mounted forces in the colony away to the south. At an important Boer gathering that took place in the centre of the Orange River Colony on the 25th, it was decided that De Wet should undertake this, and he at once gathered forces together and proceeded southwards. Lord Kitchener speedily heard of what was brewing. He immediately set all the forces that could be spared from the Orange River Colony and from the Transvaal in motion to try and head De Wet off. They poured towards the Orange River by rail, some of them moved on into Cape Colony, and General N. G. Lyttelton was given a general superintendence over the operations.

General Lyttelton arrived at Naauwpoort on 4 February, and his forces assembled rapidly from various quarters. But in spite of their efforts they were unable to prevent De Wet either from reaching the Orange River, or from crossing it – which he did on 10 February about forty miles west of Norval's Pont. There followed what has come to be called the 'Great De Wet Hunt.' The invaders were headed off from the east and south and were herded across the De Aar-Kimberley railway into north-western Cape Colony, and they thus moved out of the area for which General Inigo Jones was especially responsible, while Lyttelton moved to De Aar. A special letter had been addressed to Pretoria with regard to Maude's going to Canada on the day before De Wet's incursion, but the situation created by the invasion prevented Lord Kitchener from entertaining the request for the moment. For although the activities of De Wet's force hardly increased the responsibilities of the staff at Naauwpoort after he had once been turned away westwards, the commandos which had crossed the border some weeks before were still in the field and giving a great deal of trouble. Armoured trains were proving of considerable use at times in dealing with these, and that there was plenty to think about at Naauwpoort is shown by the following entries in Maude's diary at this time:

'22.2.1. Wire between Hanover and Richmond cut. Rosmead heard heavy firing towards Cephanjespoort, and so Donald with his mounted men moved out from Rosmead to Middelburg at 2p.m. Firing had ceased by then. No.3 train sent to watch line near Bangor and to go on to Cradock if all clear in the morning...

'23.2.1. Fish River attacked at 4 a.m. Sent armoured train from Rosmead which soon scattered Boers. Roodehoogte occupied by Boers at 9 a.m. and station burnt. Sent 150 of 7th Fusiliers to occupy it. Gorringe and Herbert drove Boers towards Spitzkop. Henniker's armoured train engaged, but gun broke down.

'28.3.1. Heard at 11.38 a.m. that 800 Boers were at Blauwkrans. As these were practically outside the mobile columns, directed Norval's Pont and Colesberg to send at once every available man to try and drive them back from heading south or east....'

(Most of the names do not appear on the general map; the passages are merely quoted in illustration.)

De Wet was in due course hunted back again from the north-western region over the De Aar-Kimberley railway and, under pressure of Colonel Plumer and other active column commanders, was driven eastwards along the south side of the Orange River trying to escape into the Orange River Colony, having been very roughly handled. The river was in flood in the early days of March and his position a very anxious one, but he succeeded at last in getting across not far from Norval's Pont on the night of 28 February. This greatly eased Lord Kitchener's anxieties as regards Cape Colony, and on 6 February he telegraphed to intimate that Maude might now go home. Maude consequently left Naauwpoort for Cape Town on 9th, sailed in the Dunvegan Castle on 18th, and landed at Southampton on 30th, a little more than fifteen months after quitting England.

His record during the South African War was a good one, and he was perhaps somewhat unfortunate in not getting better opportunities of displaying his merits in responsible positions. As brigade-major he made a reputation for himself; but the scope was necessarily somewhat limited, and he missed the severest fighting that the Guards Brigade was engaged in, owing to not arriving at the front until January 1900. Had Army Headquarters assented to his taking up the post of chief staff officer with 11th Division, as General Pole-Carew wished, it might well have made a considerable difference in his career in the immediately succeeding years. Perhaps the most valuable service that he performed during the campaign was at the time when the Boers crossed the Orange River into Cape Colony in December 1900 and during the immediately succeeding weeks, work for which he got little credit and gained no reward, because Lord Kitchener could hardly be expected to help an officer whom the War Office were at the time trying to withdraw from him. From the point of view of his prospects in the service, his leaving the theatre of war at the very time when there was such an opening for a man of his capacity, his vigour and his standing in the army, could hardly be otherwise than detrimental to his interests. But, having once accepted the appointment on Lord Minto's staff, he had no option in the matter. He received the D.S.O. for his services under Lord Roberts, and he appears to have preferred this to receiving a brevet lieutenant colonelcy which, considering that he was a comparatively junior major in the army would have been of great help to him in future years.

CHAPTER IV
The Time in Canada

A day or two after arriving in London and reporting himself Maude went to Miss Keyser's Hospital to have his shoulder attended to, and he remained there under treatment during the early part of April. After this there were various arrangements to make before he could proceed to assume his new post. But he sailed with Mrs Maude and his three children and household on 16 May in the Lusitania of the Allan Line, reached Montreal on the 27th, where Lord Minto's private railway car was ready to meet them, and they went on to Ottawa that night, settling shortly afterwards at Rideau Cottage, two miles from that pleasant city, in the grounds of Government House. During the voyage home from Cape Town and the interval before arriving at the Dominion capital, he had read all books about Canada that he could lay hands on.

The appointment which Maude was taking up was a military one in name rather than in reality. The Military Secretary of a Viceroy, be the Viceroy the Sovereign's representative in a self-governing Dominion or in the East Indies, holds what is virtually a household position and is concerned only in very limited degree with questions affecting fighting forces. He is responsible for many matters in connection with vice-regal ceremonial and with vice-regal exercise of hospitality, and the management and administration of vice-regal tours falls mainly to his lot. The post is one which calls for organising powers, for the exercise of tact not uncombined with uncompromising firmness at times, and for the possession of engaging social qualifications. But the occupant of the appointment has no executive military responsibilities, although questions may from time to time arise in connection with the local army or with the local militia, as the case may be, in regard to which his chief may be glad of the counsel of a soldier with whom he is in intimate personal relations. Quitting South Africa to take up a post such as this, at a time when young and active officers of nerve and experience were badly wanted for commanding columns and for carrying on staff work in connection with the puzzling situations that arise in partisan warfare, could not be expected to forward Maude's prospects in the service. But he had committed himself to the post many months before, at a juncture when no one foresaw that the struggle with the Boers would last so long or would take such a peculiar form as it eventually did.

As Viceroy of the Dominion of Canada, Lord Minto was in a position on all fours with that of a constitutional monarch. He was Head of the State, but he was ruler merely in name. Executive power rested for all practical purposes absolutely in the hands of the representatively chosen Government, and whatever might be his own opinion as to the expediency or otherwise of the proceedings and decisions of that body, he was virtually bound to endorse them.

In so far as the military position in Canada at this time was concerned, a somewhat divided form of responsibility in the matter of defence existed. A small Imperial Force of British
Regular Troops, under command of a British General Officer and administered and controlled by the War Office, provided the garrisons for the naval stations of Halifax and Esquimault.

There was also a local force, comprising an exiguous nucleus of permanent troops maintained mainly for instructional purposes, and a considerable body of very loosely organised and almost wholly untrained non-permanent troops or militia, the whole usually under command of a British General Officer lent to the local Government by the War Office. This latter post was held in 1901 by Major-General R. H. O'Grady Haly, who was no longer on the active list, largely as a consequence of the abnormal condition which had been created throughout the Empire by the South African War.

The new Military Secretary speedily discovered that there was a task before him which would tax his capabilities of methodical organisation. Their Royal Highnesses the Duke and Duchess of York (now Their Majesties King George and Queen Mary) were to make a progress in state through Canada in the autumn, arriving in September. The programme for the visit had to be drawn up, all the multifarious arrangements involved in connection with it had to be elaborated, and Maude's experience of Queen Victoria's Diamond Jubilee in 1897 had taught him – had his own keen perception of the fitness of things not assured him of it in any case – that this prospective Royal Tour must be prepared for systematically, presciently, and with meticulous care. The whole business was in practice handed over to him to deal with, and the effect upon local opinion of his attitude in regard to the matter and of his methods of proceeding, and particularly their effect upon local opinion as this was reflected in the columns of the local press, afforded him an interesting and an instructive insight into the habits of mind that are apt to prevail in a State of somewhat recent origin.

The painstaking care with which details of the programme were being formulated, the systematic manner in which seeming trifles were being provided for, the exhaustive instructions which were being issued to everybody who was in any way connected with the ceremonial that was to be observed under various conditions and in different localities, furnished the Fourth Estate with material for uninformed criticism and derisive comment, which was directed at the vice-regal entourage as a whole, but of which Maude was the principal butt. Nor did the invariable courtesy shown by the Military Secretary to young and enterprising journalists, combined as it was with an obvious capacity for keeping them in their place, make these penmen any the less disposed to exercise their wits at his expense in the newspapers whose staffs they adorned. The very fact that he completely ignored all attacks made upon him, and that he took the pleasantries of which he was the object in disconcerting and even irritating good part, served as a stimulus to their literary activities.

'Maude, Minto and Co., with their fuss, feathers and red tape,' was quite a common heading in the newspapers; the better-class Canadians deplored such conduct and they could not understand his being amused instead of feeling hurt by such attacks. Still, it is but just to place on record that when the progress of Their Royal Highnesses through the wide expanse of the great Dominion had become an accomplished fact, when it had become patent to all and sundry that the whole programme had been gone through without the slightest hitch, when the people of Canada (including the journalistic world) realised that the unqualified success of the entire proceedings was reflecting credit on their country and themselves – whoever it might be who had pulled the strings – the Press admitted in a most sportsmanlike manner that it had made a mistake, and praises were showered by it directly and indirectly upon Maude. The Military Secretary had taught this new country that the practices of the old were not wholly without merit. Even the youngest amongst us at times has something to learn.

An untoward event, the murder of Mr McKinley the President of the United States, occurred two or three days before the eagerly awaited visitors arrived in Canada. The Ottawa Government were with good reason seriously perturbed; it was even debated whether the tour ought not to be abandoned, or at all events be much abridged, so as to reduce any risks that might be run by the distinguished guests. Maude was much concerned when he heard of this, realising what an unfortunate effect the adoption of counsels of excessive prudence might have upon public opinion; but the Government speedily came to the conclusion that the proper course was to carry out the programme as already drawn up. Special steps were however taken to safeguard the Duke and Duchess and to keep watch on the huge stretches of railroad which were to be traversed, and the police authorities of the Dominion spent some weeks of great anxiety.

The Royal Party arrived at Quebec in the specially commissioned *Ophir* on 16 September; two days were spent in the historic capital of the French Canadians, and a full programme was carried out, after which the Royal Train proceeded to Montreal. In addition to the suite of the Duke and Duchess of York, Their Royal Highnesses were accompanied during their tour by the Governor-General and Lady Minto, with representatives of their household and staff, the party requiring two trains, one besides the actual Royal Train for the Viceroy's household, the press, et cetera. Two more days were passed at Montreal and the distinguished visitors reached Ottawa on the 20th, where four days were spent. Then the Royal Train proceeded westwards by the Canadian Pacific Railway to Vancouver, where it arrived on 30th, a stay of some hours having been made at the three principal places on the route, Winnipeg, Regina, and Calgary. From Vancouver the tour was continued by the S.S. *Empress of India* to Victoria in Vancouver's Island, and back. On the return journey eastwards a special halt was made at Banff in the Rockies, to permit the Duke, with Lord Minto and portions of the suites, to proceed on a shooting trip, while the Duchess with Lady Minto and the ladies remained at Banff. The Royal Train arrived at Toronto on 10 October, and a four days' stay was made there, admitting of a visit to Niagara. On the way from Toronto to Halifax the Royal Party paid visits of a few hours to Hamilton, Kingston, Sherbrook and St John's, arriving at the port of departure on 19 October, and H.M.S. *Ophir* sailed east at daybreak on the 21st.

In connection with every place where a stay was made during this Royal Progress – except at Banff where the halt partook of an unofficial character – a programme had been drawn up in advance, fixing the exact hour when presentations of addresses, military reviews, special processions, acceptances of honorary degrees by His Royal Highness at abodes of learning, presentations of colours to regiments and of decorations and medals to individuals for the South African War, social functions, visits to places of particular interest, and so forth, were to take place. Full instructions concerning salutes and escorts had been issued well in advance. Everybody concerned in the ceremonies and receptions, and in the movement by railway and by road and by ship, knew exactly what they had to do. Nothing had been overlooked, the whole transaction amounted to a triumph of foresight and of organisation, and practically all this was the work of Maude. From the point of view of control and management, it was in fact a one man show. Lord Minto's staff sometimes wondered what would happen if the Military Secretary were by some mischance to become hors de combat. 'On the principle of 'if you want a thing well done, do it yourself'? Joe worked out everything personally and kept the details in his own hands,' writes Major A. C. Morrison-Bell, who was one of the A.D.C.'s.

In connection with this Royal Tour Maude incurred a certain amount of personal unpopularity in localities which time did not permit of the Duke and Duchess visiting, and amongst individuals who for various reasons could not be presented or who were not taken quite so seriously as they took themselves. This was inevitable, as the Military Secretary well knew. He remained undisturbed, satisfied that he had done his best and that the conduct and management of the Progress had met the requirements of the case. The journey to Victoria and back had moreover made him acquainted with a region previously unknown to him, and in this respect Mrs Maude, who had accompanied Lady Minto, had enjoyed a like experience. He received the C.M.G. in recognition of his services.

The whole question of Canadian defence and of the possible development of the fighting resources of the Dominion in the interests of the Empire as a whole, was beginning to engage the attention of the Home Government and of the War Office in the latter part of 1901, although interest in military matters was naturally in the main riveted upon the progress of the South African War. Maude had however been asked by the War Office to take note of the position of affairs in the part of the Empire that he was going to, and to communicate his views on the subject privately from time to time.

'Ever since I landed in Canada,' he wrote to Colonel (now Lieutenant General Sir E. A.) Altham on 31 October, 'I have had my hands absolutely full with the organisation of the preparations for the Royal Visit. Knowing as you do the extent of this country, you will readily realise that it has been almost more than one person could do, and of course the fact that I have never been in Canada before made it all the more difficult for me. However, owing to the great assistance and the hearty cooperation of the various officials throughout the country, we have managed to make a fairly good job of it, and now that H.M.S. *Ophir* has sailed for England, I hope that I shall have a little more time to give to other matters.

'...At present owing to the short time I have been in the country and to the causes above mentioned, I can scarcely say that I have grasped fully the details of the whole system; and, as you know, it is difficult in this country to pick up information quickly, owing to the fact that if Imperial officers are too eager in trying to find out about such matters, their action is liable to be misunderstood and resented as unnecessary interference.'

The attitude of the Dominion Government in connection with projects for common defence within the Empire was not marked by much enthusiasm for the cause at this time. Sir W. Laurier, the Premier, maintained reserve, and he had given but scanty encouragement to the desire of large portions of the community to provide contingents of troops for the operations against the Boers on a scale analogous to that adopted by Australia, New Zealand, and some of the Crown Colonies. The Canadian Executive moreover was not prepared to make any contribution to the Imperial Navy, although willing to enjoy the benefit of its protection. Maude however was not unduly discouraged, he continued to communicate his views from time to time privately to the War Office, and he studied the problems connected with the local military organisation with assiduity. He speedily discovered that a special committee of military experts had been sent out from home at the request of the Canadian Government so far back as 1898, and that this body had submitted a full and illuminating report on the subject. But, as is not unusual in like cases in the United Kingdom, the document had been pigeon-holed, and it did not take the Military Secretary long to perceive that, for a country with some five and a half million inhabitants, a vast land frontier, and a lengthy coastline, the means existing for self-defence were deplorably backward. However, in July of 1902, the South African War being at an end, Major General the Earl of Dundonald arrived to take up the appointment of Commandant of the Militia.

Lord Dundonald had interested himself in the problems involved in the constitution of a citizen army, had commanded mounted forces under Sir R. Buller in South Africa that were largely composed of contingents from Dominions and Colonies, and had been specially chosen by Lord Roberts as an officer who, owing to his varied experience and to his reputation as a leader in the field, as also owing to the attention that he had devoted to the subject of making the most of the martial instincts of a population indisposed to undergo military training of an exacting kind, seemed particularly well fitted for the post. This appointment, it may be observed, had never proved to be a bed of roses for any soldier bent on improving the system in the past, although there were plenty of officers and men within the Militia itself who were fully alive to the shortcomings of the organisation to which they belonged. The fact that certain improvised units had proved themselves under the peculiar conditions attending hostilities on the veldt as efficient combatants as had British regular regiments during the South African War, was moreover at this time fostering the notion that the importance attributed by professional soldiers to training was the mere outcome of prejudice. The Dominion Government also was, excusably enough, very jealous of Imperial interference in any shape, a circumstance for which the uninformed condition of public opinion in the United Kingdom concerning States that were then and indeed sometimes are still characterised as 'colonies', was in no small degree to blame. The incoming Commandant of the Militia was in fact taking up an appointment which was, in the nature of things, hedged around with pitfalls. This Maude, who had made himself thoroughly acquainted with the Militia organisation, such as it was, by the summer of 1902, realised from the first.

Still, the arrival of the new commandant was greeted with unmistakable satisfaction by the country and by the Militia, and marked progress was made during the remainder of 1902 and during 1903 in respect to the training, and also to certain points in connection with the organisation of the local forces. Public opinion in Canada was a good deal concerned with regard to the subject as a whole in 1903. The progressive action of Australia and New Zealand in respect to accepting a reasonable share of responsibility for their own security, was not without its effect in bringing home to the people of the Dominion the somewhat ignominious position in which they stood, and the question of defence was taken up with an interest that had not previously been displayed in Government circles. A new Canadian Militia Act was drafted; in his endeavours to improve the training and to develop the fighting efficiency of the local forces, Lord Dundonald for the time being received a gratifying support from the Ministry; the completion of a local rifle factory at Quebec just about this time gave promise that the crying need of an adequate reserve of small arms would shortly diminish; and contracts were entered into for the supply of a number of the 18pdr guns which the Home Government had decided to adopt.

Maude watched these proceedings with interest, from time to time he gave the War Office the benefit of his views privately, and he kept the Intelligence Department in London well acquainted with any changes worth noting that were taking place. Sir F. Borden, the Minister of Militia, proceeded to England in the autumn of 1903 with the draft of the new Militia Act for discussion with the home authorities, and Lord Minto's Military Secretary then wrote a letter on the subject to the private secretary of Mr Arnold-Forster, the Secretary of State for War, some passages from which deserve quoting:

'I do not believe that it would be necessary or even advisable to have a number of Imperial officers on the headquarters staff in Canada, provided that there were Canadian officers fit to undertake such duties. There are many excellent officers in the Canadian Militia, some of whom, such as are well known in England. The drawback is that they have had no opportunity of getting a thorough staff training, and I cannot help thinking that if some system could be introduced offering inducements to a certain number of the smartest Canadian officers to attend the Staff College annually in England, Canada would soon produce staff officers fitted in every way for the important duties of the headquarters staff .... I have mentioned the headquarters staff primarily as being of first importance, but the lack of staff training of course permeates the whole of the Militia district staffs throughout Canada.

'As regard the new Militia Act, I should like to mention three points: (a) The position of the Governor-General as Commander-in-Chief, representing His Majesty; (b) The command of the Canadian Militia; (c) The relative rank of Imperial officers serving in Canada.

'As regards the first point, it is most important that the Governor-General, as His Majesty's representative, should be recognised as the Commander-in-Chief. In the draft of the Act which I saw some time ago, this was not clearly brought out and I feel sure that occasions may arise in the future, as they have done in the past, where the knowledge that he holds this position may be of great value to the Governor-General. I have never understood why it is that, whereas the Governor-General of Australia is shown in the Army List as Governor-General and Commander-in-Chief, the Governor-General of Canada is shown as the Governor-General of the Dominion of Canada, and Commander-in-Chief in Prince Edward Island only; but I suppose that there is some reason for this.

'The second point, namely the command of the Militia, is one that I know will be raised, Sir F. Borden holding that the chief command of the same should be thrown open to Canadian officers. There is a certain strong feeling that this should be done, but I do not believe that this extends to the more thoughtful and best officers of the Militia. Personally I think that there are many reasons which would make such a scheme undesirable. I know that Sir F. Borden's idea is that the appointment of a Canadian should only be made permissible, and he by no means intends to appoint a Canadian himself forthwith; but if the Militia Act made such a thing possible a situation might easily arise where a weak Ministry or a weak Minister of Militia might be unwillingly forced into appointing a Canadian. Not only is there at present no officer fitted by staff training to assume chief command, but, even if there were, such an officer would find himself in a position embracing many difficulties from which an Imperial officer would be free. The chief of these is the question of political patronage, which permeates public life here and which does much to stunt the growth and efficiency of the Militia. An Imperial officer has no ties with Canada and can resist this to a certain extent, but a Canadian officer in chief command would find the pressure brought to bear on him politically from without absolutely irresistible.'

Maude went on to discuss the question of uniting the appointment of Commandant of the Militia with that of General Officer commanding the Imperial troops; but as the Imperial troops were withdrawn about two years later, this matter is of no interest now.

The third point was one of detail. It may be mentioned that under the Militia Act, as finally passed, the Governor-General was given the position of Commander-in-Chief, that Maude's suggestion as to Canadian officers going to the Staff College was adopted some little time afterwards, and that the creation of a Militia Council in the following year put an end to the appointment of Commandant of the Militia.

It will thus be seen that although Maude's position was in the main not a military one, he contrived to keep himself closely in touch with military matters in the part of the world where he now found himself, and was able to afford useful assistance to his military superiors at home. Still, questions of this kind only represented a small part of the subjects which he was called upon to deal with in his official capacity, secretarial duties being his main concern. One of the most important and the most exacting functions which the entourage of a Governor-

General is called upon to fulfil is that of acting, so to speak, as a buffer between the Sovereign's Representative and politicians or others who, if accorded interviews or audiences, may be placed in a position to quote some opinion expressed by His Excellency when off his guard, the publication of which would be inappropriate. For a duty of this kind Maude, having girded on his armour of breeding, discrimination, candour, and firmness, was particularly well fitted. 'If he was at all open to criticism,' writes Sir Joseph Pope, who was Under Secretary of State at the time, 'it was for a quality in which I specially delighted, that is, his spirit of sincerity and frankness.' He made some enemies, no doubt, from time to time, but by his management of matters of this kind he contributed to no small degree towards ensuring the success of Lord Minto's viceroyalty.

He also had to figure prominently in the social gatherings at Government House, and although he had no special liking for such entertainments he played his part so conscientiously and effectively that he conveyed to His Excellency's guests the impression that he delighted in the occupation. At the balls he always made a point of dancing with those who seemed not to be enjoying their fair share, just as he had done thirty years before as a youngster in London. All the arrangements when his chief was performing some State ceremonial or some public act he kept in his hands. In accordance with his bent for centralisation he managed all the most trivial details in respect to the Viceroy's numerous tours through different portions of the Dominion himself. Everything on such occasions invariably went like clockwork, thanks to his genius for organisation and to his mastery of detail. He could always carry the programmes for several different transactions of this kind in his head at one time. 'Just send this wire to Winnipeg about detraining the horses and carriages tomorrow night,' he would say to one of the A.D.C.'s while he was in the act of putting the finishing touch to, say, a medal presentation at Toronto.

'I was always immensely attracted by his great personal charm,' writes Captain Harry Graham, an old Coldstreamer who was A.D.C. to Lord Minto for some part of the time that Maude was in Canada, 'by the constant unselfishness he displayed in little everyday matters which greatly endeared him to his colleagues, by his wonderful industry and devotion to his work, and by his unfailing cheerfulness and good humour. He was rather quiet and reserved, but this did not conceal the strength and self-confidence that underlay a somewhat shy and diffident manner. Even in those days he had opportunities of displaying the remarkable talents as an organiser which were afterwards to stand him in such good stead, and that swiftness of decision which made him an ideal leader. I never met so conscientious a worker. No detail was too unimportant for him to trouble himself about; and he possessed a capacity for taking pains which certainly amounted to genius. Besides all this, his strong sense of humour, his love of children, and his keenness as a sportsman made him an ideal companion, while his devotion and loyalty to his chief and his subordinates never failed.'

The mode of life obtaining in the country afforded him plenty of opportunity for exercise and for keeping himself in training, as was his wont. In the winter time he made a practice of running with the Ottawa Harriers once a week, which meant a paper-chase. Sometimes he ran as hare and sometimes with the pack, and when acting as hare he constantly gave evidence of possessing a wonderful eye for country, seeming to know by instinct where he would run risk of being viewed and where he was sure to travel concealed. Ice sports he enjoyed and took part in, but especially in their more active forms of skiing and tobogganing – circling in a posture of rigid discomfort around an orange according to the tenets of the English school of skating did not appeal to him.

'Joe used to turn out regularly for the hockey matches played on the private rink between the House and the Stables,' Major Morrison-Bell writes, 'and he certainly pulled his full weight in a team of amateurs more noticeable for their zeal than for their science. Some of the stable lads – Canadian boys brought up on the ice from their cradles – could make rings round us all, and a thrilling rush down the rink by the Military Secretary generally ended in two of these little mosquitoes sailing in and taking away the 'puck' out of the very mouth of the goal.'

In the summer he spent many spare hours on the Ottawa River and, being an old 'wet bob,' he could manage a canoe on its water like a native. Moreover, Mrs Maude and he often went on prolonged trips in a small naphtha launch through the network of channels and lakes which form such a feature of Eastern Ontario, cooking on the banks and putting up for the night at village inns. In this pleasant fashion they were able to traverse the Rideau Lakes and the Rideau Canal, to pass in and out amongst the Thousand Islands where the lowest of the great inland seas merges gradually into the channel of the St Lawrence, and to make a voyage down the artificial channels with their chain of locks by which great vessels from the west find their way down to Montreal. In their last year in the country they were accompanied on some of these excursions by Mrs Maude's sister, who was with them on a visit from England, and by their eldest daughter Stella, now ten years old. In connection with the children it may be mentioned that while in Canada Maude instituted a plan, which he continued for years after, of drilling the trio for a quarter of an hour before breakfast every morning, out of doors if possible, and that he was just as strict during the observance as if they had been soldiers, although 'off parade' the most affectionate of fathers. Members of the local social clubs did not for a long time altogether appreciate his disinclination to make free use of those institutions; they were somewhat disposed to attribute this attitude to an aloofness which was altogether foreign to Maude's character. But when they learnt that the reason for it was that he disliked the constant whiskies and sodas, and that he hesitated to hurt the feelings of hospitable members by refusing it, as a difficulty which others from the Old Country also feel at times when visiting the Empire overseas they were perfectly satisfied.

He found time in the summer of 1903 to make a trip to the United States, in the course of which he visited a number of the more important of the battlefields of the War of Secession, in the annals of which he was greatly interested and with the story of which he was familiar. He likewise explored the earlier history of the States, especially in connection with the War of Independence. The time devoted to these studies did not however prevent his mastering available literature concerning the Dominion itself. Thanks to his application, to his excellent memory, and to the facility with which he could absorb the contents of unexhilarating official documents, his knowledge of the country that was his temporary home was almost encyclopaedic before he left it. They used to say of him that he must in some former state have been a dweller in Canada, so fully was he acquainted with its past, its physical features, its products and its forms of administration.

When he took up his appointment Lord Minto had already been two and a half years at Ottawa, and the Governor-General was due to give way to a successor in the latter part of 1903; but he was asked to remain on another year, and his staff naturally remained on with him. As it happened, some awkward questions arose during the last year of his extended viceroyalty. It had been agreed early in the year 1903 that a difference of opinion which had developed between the Canadian Government and the United States concerning the boundary of Alaska should be referred to a specially constituted tribunal in London composed of representatives of the Empire and of the United States, and on this the Lord Chief Justice of England was the principal Commissioner on the side of the Empire, having two Canadian representatives associated with him. The verdict was given against Canada on some of the more important points, owing to the Lord Chief Justice concurring in the American point of view. This caused some commotion in the Dominion, and Sir W. Laurier publicly hinted that Ottawa ought to possess treaty-making powers – overlooking the obvious connection that exists between treaty-making powers and the power to enforce treaties when made. The matter blew over in due course; but a more serious trouble came about in connection with Lord Dundonald in the summer of 1904.

On 7th June the Commandant of the Militia, in the course of a speech made at a private gathering of officers, uttered some caustic criticisms of the action of the Minister who happened to be acting at the moment for the Minister of Militia, in allowing political considerations to govern the giving of commissions in a newly formed unit of horse. The speech was however reported in a newspaper, and the result was that Lord Dundonald was dismissed from his appointment by a local Order in Council. The affair aroused strong feeling throughout the Dominion. After his dismissal he repeated his charges in a public speech at Toronto, and much sympathy was felt for him, particularly so in the Militia itself. On the occasion of his departure from Ottawa for home he was made the subject of a remarkable ovation in the streets.

Whatever the private views on the subject of the Governor-General may have been, he had no power to interfere with the action of the Executive; and, the Executive having decided to support the Minister especially concerned, it was clearly impossible that the Commandant should retain his position. As it happened, it was already practically decided to institute a Militia Council, on lines analogous to those of the Army Council in London. Under this reconstitution of the central military administration, an Imperial officer (Brigadier General P. Lake, whom Maude was to be closely associated with a dozen years later in Mesopotamia) became Chief of the General Staff, the appointment of Commandant was abolished, and an Inspector General was set up; the arrangement however only came into force just about the time that Lord Minto quitted the country.

'I saw a good deal of Major Maude, as he then was, when I commanded the Canadian Militia;' writes Lord Dundonald. 'I was always impressed with his devotion to duty, the soundness of his judgement, and his high standard of honour.

Major F. S. MAUDE, C.M.G., D.S.O.

Military Secretary, Ottawa, (1904.)

'In 1904 I felt it my duty to warn the people of Canada publicly of the danger of political interference in the selection of soldiers, in other words of a system which gave to officers with what was called a 'political pull,' advantages over those who had no such backing, necessarily to the destruction of military efficiency and of the preparation of Canada for the world war, the imminence of which was apparent to the well-informed.

'It was at this time, when I was summarily dismissed by the Laurier Government for my utterance, that I fully realised the manner of man that Maude was. For, while some of the officers who were really friendly to me came to bid me good-bye but after dark; in order, as they told me openly, not to be black-marked Maude came in the day, and several times, and what appealed to me most was his solicitude for my future career in the Army, for he understood the power of those whom I had offended, with their press and their many allies in Great Britain.

'Major Maude of the Coldstream Guards was of the type that has made the British officer respected and loved by men alien to him in race, and by others differing from him in social degree and in political ideals. I have met in the course of my life more than the average of such men in the Coldstream Guards, and I do not attribute it to chance.'

Lord Minto carried out an extensive farewell tour during the last summer of his viceroyalty in what, but a few years before, had been aptly described as the Great Lone Land of the west. All the arrangements were as usual made by Maude: the large party dwelt for a time under canvas on the prairies, they covered wide stretches of country in the course of their wanderings, and the Governor-General, with his Military Secretary and one or two others, at one time travelled five hundred miles on horseback. As the time for departure approached, later on, the outgoing Viceroy received assurances of popular good-will by every form of demonstration on the part of those amongst whom he had for six years represented the Sovereign. A succession of banquets, of presentations of addresses from municipalities and other public bodies, of gatherings in which great crowds took part, testified to the esteem in which he and his staff were held throughout the Dominion. Lord and Lady Minto, with their household, which included the Maude family, sailed on 19 November on board the Tunisian from Quebec after two days there of farewell festivities, arriving in London, via Liverpool, on 28 November.

CHAPTER V
From 1905 to 1914

On arrival in England, Maude found himself second in command of the 1st Battalion of his regiment, stationed at the moment in Wellington Barracks under Colonel Pleydell-Bouverie. After an absence from regimental work ever since the end of 1894, he was very glad to take up afresh duties which had always greatly interested him. He thoroughly enjoyed direct contact with the rank and file, and he maintained his enthusiasm for drill while at the same time fully alive to the importance of more advanced forms of military training for an infantry unit. His family spent much of the winter at a house lent to them at Henley, and on visits, and for a time he made Henley his personal headquarters, going up and down daily; he was for several weeks in command of the battalion during the first two or three months, while the Colonel was away on leave.

Returning home and reverting to regimental duty in the Guards, with the expenses of a family to meet, he however found his financial position somewhat difficult, and he was obliged to look around for other military employment. Hearing that the command of the Transvaal Volunteers was vacant he tried to obtain the appointment, but learnt that he was ineligible owing to not being a cavalry officer. His prolonged absence from regimental duty, and the fact of his having held a virtually non-military appointment in Canada, no doubt stood in the way of his obtaining a staff appointment for the time being, in spite of his excellent record in South Africa. The popularity which the Maudes enjoyed, coupled with the anxiety of the Coldstream to keep one of their foremost members with the regiment, helped to some extent to smooth over troubles in respect to money matters, accommodation being lent at a time when the family had no house of their own vacant. But insufficient means were for several years to handicap a soldier whose exceptional gifts for command were not recognised even by his most intimate friends till the opportunity provided by a great Continental war enabled him to make apparent to them and to his country the stuff that he was made of.

His family were at Oakham for a long time in the summer of 1905, and he frequently managed to spend weekends there. He astonished neighbours in that country district at this time by the knowledge which he contrived to absorb of the minutest topographical details of the region. They found that he knew more about it than they did after having lived there all their lives. It was a species of instinct with him, when bicycling about the highways and byways, to note such matters. Just as he made it a habit, as it were, instinctively to draw up appreciations of the situation when he was on the warpath, so also was he ever carrying out reconnaissance work in his head when walking, or riding, or bicycling, or motoring about any region with which he was not previously acquainted; and thanks to his remarkable memory he kept all the details in his mind. This habit was due no doubt in great measure to a recognition that it was his duty to be ever preparing himself for the duties of a staff officer in the field, but he was also naturally of a very observant character and was gifted with a particularly good eye for country.

He conducted a regimental tour about Basingstoke in Hampshire early in the year. Apart from this his experiences in the Coldstream were necessarily of a somewhat humdrum character, and he did not take long to make himself thoroughly conversant with the various changes which had been introduced into the training and the organisation of the army while he had been on the further side of the Atlantic, as a result of the teachings of the Boer War. But when the battalion moved to Pirbright in July regimental work took on a more interesting form than was possible in London, and he often managed during the weeks spent under canvas there to pass some hours watching the advanced exercises of other troops around Aldershot.

While he was at Pirbright he heard that his late chief, Lord Minto, was to be the new Governor-General of India; so he asked to be taken as Military Secretary. Somewhat to his disappointment, he was not however chosen. He proceeded to North Wales shortly after the return to Wellington Barracks to take part in a special staff ride that was conducted under the aegis of the War Office, with General Sir N. Lyttelton as Director. It was to be an exercise in hill warfare as practised against warriors of the Pathan type, to be carried out amongst the crags and ravines of the Snowdon region, and the work was after Maude's own heart, involving as it did plenty of walking amidst glorious scenery, and participation in a form of military training which was quite new to him. Three parties, of which he was with the centre one under Colonel (now Major General Sir Colin) Mackenzie, advanced into the heart of the mountains, and the staff duties were carried out on the assumption that the columns were operating against Afridi tribesmen swarming in the hills.[3] 'It has been a most interesting staff ride,' he wrote in his diary on the day after it came to an end, 'and I feel that I have learnt a tremendous lot about frontier fighting.' It was a few weeks after this, just at the time when the battalion was about to move to Aldershot for a year, that he received a letter from Mr Arnold-Forster, the Secretary of State for War, offering him the appointment of private secretary in place of (the late) Major Marker of the Coldstream, who was about to proceed to India on Lord Kitchener's staff.

Maude accepted the appointment gladly and he took up the duties at once, although he contrived to combine them to a certain extent with those of second in command of his battalion. The family was moving to Aldershot to occupy the Commanding Officer's quarters in Ramillies Barracks, and he was living there while at work under Mr Arnold-Forster, although he often had to remain in London. This was his first experience of the War Office, and it initiated him to some extent into the routine of that institution, with which he was to become better acquainted a few years later. He does not find fault with this in his diary which is interesting seeing that he was an acute critic in respect to questions of administration, and never hesitated in his own private record to reprobate what he considered unsatisfactory. He was particularly delighted at finding so voluminous and so well managed a library in Whitehall, of which he made free use during the few weeks that he held the appointment for his association with Mr Arnold-Forster was of short duration. On 4 December the following entry appears in the diary: 'Mr A. F. said good-bye to me, as he is off to Ireland and will not return to the War Office. Mr Balfour resigns tomorrow.' The outgoing Secretary of State had not been seeing eye to eye with the Military Members of the Army Council, and the situation had not been an altogether comfortable one. Maude hoped to have been taken on by his successor; but Mr Haldane (as he then was) did not at the moment wish to be associated closely with his predecessor's entourage. For the next few days Maude was busy clearing up papers in the late Secretary of State's office – no light task – and he then settled down again to regimental life at Aldershot. In his diary while on leave for a few days after Christmas he made an entry which well deserves quoting, for it has almost a prophetic ring:

---

[3] The author, who was in charge of the right party, met Maude for the first time on this occasion,

I work about six or seven hours a day at military subjects, although I am on leave. Some day this may be of use not only to my small self but I hope, perhaps only in a minor way, to England. At all events it is right to try to do the very best one can.

Early in January he for a time had under consideration the question of applying for the command of the Macedonian Gendarmerie, which carried good pay with it and offered prospects of active duties owing to the disturbances which were perpetually breaking out in the Balkan storm-centre in those days; but he gave up the idea. He conducted a regimental tour about Winchester in March, and was greatly pleased with the style in which the work was carried out; he had the gift of making such exercises interesting, he always took the utmost trouble to make them a success and he enjoyed the full confidence of those under him; for they realised that he knew what he was about, that his criticisms were thoroughly to the point, and that his expositions were well worth listening to. Then in May he was on the directing staff of a brigade staff ride conducted about Cirencester by Brigadier General (now Lieutenant General Sir Francis) Lloyd, who was in command of the 1st Brigade to which Maude's battalion belonged and who was much struck with his aptitude at exercises of this kind. All this time he was, when at Aldershot, constantly occupied with regimental duties, supervising training and busy with the interior economy of the battalion. In June he motored down to Okehampton and spent some days at the artillery camp, which greatly interested him. In view of his experiences at a later date, it is worthy of note that, while sensible of the efficiency of the batteries and of the excellence of the arrangements for conducting the firing on the ranges on Dartmoor, he was not greatly impressed with the resultant effects of gunfire. 'Watched artillery practice from the target end,' he wrote in his diary on the last day. 'Very interesting, but my respect for artillery fire is in no way increased although excellent practice was made. Its effect is, as I have always thought, mostly noise.'

In July he acted as chief umpire at the brigade training under General Lloyd which took place in the Longmoor direction, and later on he commanded a skeleton force, found by the 1st Division, during Sir J. French's inspection of the 2nd Division in the field about Frensham. The 1st Division training followed. He was keeping himself thoroughly fit as usual by riding and bicycling whenever any pause in the drill season took place, and he rowed in two races at Windsor towards the end of the month. At the end of August he on one occasion rode from Aldershot to see cavalry exercises on the Berkshire Downs, starting at 4 a.m. one day and getting back at 10 p.m. on the next. 'Very dark the latter part of the ride,' he wrote in his diary, 'but horse quite fresh, although we must have done nearly ninety miles in the two days.' But all this time he was doubtful about his future, for he recognised that he would hardly be able to afford to take command of a battalion of the regiment when his turn came, and he was becoming very anxious to obtain staff employment, with a half-pay lieutenant colonelcy; he was much encouraged by finding himself selected to act on Sir J. French's staff during the extensive command exercises which took place in the latter part of September, covering a wide tract of country reaching from Sussex to Dorsetshire. He arrived home from this outing late on the day on which his son Eric, now nine years old, had gone off to Cordwalles, a private school near Maidenhead, for the first time.

A few days later he received an offer of the appointment of D.A.A. and Q.M.G. of Coast Defences at Plymouth, a post which was about to fall vacant. It was not a particularly attractive position for a soldier of his standing and experience; but, after consulting with a number of friends who all advised him to go, he wrote an acceptance. 'On the whole it seems best, although it is difficult to say,' he wrote in the diary. 'The only way is to do one's level best, and perhaps then I may become a useful soldier some day.' He evidently was disappointed and hurt at not having been chosen for work of a somewhat higher class; he had indeed been anxious to get a place on the General Staff at the War Office, and had entertained some hope of being selected for something of the kind.

'We never served in the same battalion together until he became second in command to me when I had the 1st Battalion,' writes Sir W. Lambton of him; 'in that position he was of the utmost value, organising regimental funds, institutes, and so forth; but there was not in reality sufficient scope for his activities in such a position, and he reluctantly went on the staff, thus foregoing his prospects of command. I know that he felt this very deeply, for he consulted me. But his financial position, added to the fact that he would have to wait a couple of years or so before a battalion command would be vacant, decided the question.'

The 1st Coldstream moved from Aldershot to Chelsea Barracks in October; but Maude remained on for a few days at Aldershot, as he was to take up the Plymouth appointment in the middle of November, when he proceeded to his new station. 'Work not very interesting, I fear,' he wrote after a couple of days taking stock, 'but must make the best of it and perhaps something will turn up later; but I feel I am rather wasting my best days when I could do so much more. Naval things will however be interesting.' He was on the other hand very glad to find himself so near Sir R. Pole-Carew, and during his stay in the West Country, and particularly during the first months while he was still looking out for a house, he spent many pleasant weekends at Antony, his former chief's and brother-officer's place on the further side of the Hamoaze.

The general in command of the coast defences, which included the fortress of Falmouth as well as that of Plymouth, was Sir J. Leach, an artillery officer, and Maude found much to interest him in connection with the armaments and training, although, as his work was that of administrative staff, his duties were concerned mainly with other matters. For the first three months of his term in the appointment he lived in the Rifle Brigade barracks and he made great friends with the regiment. It took some time to find a house that was suitable, seeing that he was anxious to have some little ground and a garden, and that he wished to be in a quiet neighbourhood if possible. Military conditions at Plymouth struck him as dull and the tone somewhat apathetic, after Aldershot. 'I never saw a more sleepy and dead-alive command,' he wrote. The amount of correspondence passing daily through the office seemed to him to be out of all proportion to the results which it brought about, and he set himself to work to introduce more life into the proceedings and to reduce mere ineffectual paperwork as far as was practicable, although addicted to paperwork himself. He was, on the other hand, greatly impressed with what he saw from day to day of the Senior Service in and about the great naval station; its vigorous methods and the zest with which its operations were conducted appealed to him. 'It is a pleasure to see them and to see everything so well done,' he commented in his diary; his boy was intended for the Royal Navy. He covered a great deal of ground on his bicycle in the afternoons, both for the sake of the exercise, and also with the object of familiarising himself with the country around Plymouth and Devonport, meeting with an accident on one occasion which incapacitated him for some days, although not sufficiently to oblige him to go on the sick list. He directed a staff ride near Sherborne in March, and shortly afterwards settled down with his family at 'Stone Hall,' a house in the Stonehouse area of the Three Towns, belonging to Lord Mount Edgcumbe, with a garden in which he found plenty of occupation in spare times, assisted enthusiastically if not very effectually by his small girls.

It was now more than a year since the fall of Mr Balfour's Government, and, as it was known that Mr Haldane had ever since been maturing a new organisation for the second line, his statement in the House of Commons when introducing the Army Estimates was awaited with some impatience in military circles. Maude's comment in his diary on the day when he read the War Minister's speech is of particular interest, seeing how closely he was to be identified with the Territorial Forces before long. It runs as follows:

> Mr Haldane brought out his new scheme, and it is of course much criticised. Its worst point seems to be that it contemplates drill and training for six months after the outbreak of war before the troops can take the field. This time no enemy worthy of the name will give us. Tomorrow there is to be a great debate in the House of Lords on the subject; but they are apparently only going to treat it from a 'militia' point of view, instead of taking up the broader question of the defence of the Empire, and considering whether the scheme will give us an adequate force for that purpose.
>
> It looks as if Mr Haldane was convinced that Conscription was necessary, and as if he was riding for a fall in that direction. It certainly seems almost impossible to go on as we are now, and if something is not done soon we may be beaten by Germany or some other Continental Power, and then it will be too late to set our house in order. We are as a nation too sanguine and cocksure of our own abilities. It has always been the same story since the days of the American rebellion.

Soon after this Maude made up his mind to apply for a half-pay lieutenant colonelcy, being satisfied that he could not well for financial reasons command a battalion of the Coldstream; he would have to wait some time before obtaining command in any case, owing to his position on the list of the regiment, and he could not but remember that, under the bad old system of the adjutant being all powerful, he had virtually commanded a battalion more than a dozen years earlier. His Staff College contemporaries with a good record were moreover all going ahead of him in respect to army promotion, on which the prospects of his ever rising high in the military world seemed to depend. He consulted many military friends of experience before doing so, and they one and all recommended him to take a step which was likely to help him on in the service, however much he might regret severing ties with his regiment. In due course he therefore sent forward the request officially.

In the meantime he was busying himself with re-drafting the Plymouth Defence Scheme, a work to which he devoted great attention for several months, and which his liking for detail made him especially well fitted to carry out. He flattered himself that he had considerably improved office procedure; but he found it hard to make any effectual impression on the inertia existing in what he regarded as a backwater station. Moreover, although this was his first experience of an administrative staff appointment, he was so well acquainted with army regulations and departmental procedure that the duties which he was performing from day to day could not teach him much that he did not know before.

The West Country is almost proverbial for hospitality, and the Maudes were during their stay in this part of the world made welcome on all hands; but although the girls throve exceedingly, the enervating climate of South Devon did not suit Mrs Maude, who was not at the time in very good health. This made Maude all the more anxious to get employment which would at once be more in consonance with his abilities and experience, and would be more congenial to an enthusiast for field training than an administrative office job ever could be. He heard privately from the War Office on 16 June that he had been chosen for a half-pay lieutenant colonelcy by the Selection Board and received the tidings with mixed feelings. 'Delighted with the step, for there were only four vacancies in the whole army,' he wrote in his diary, 'but more sad than I can say at the prospect of leaving the regiment. Ever since I have left school, for twenty-three years in fair and foul weather, the regiment has been my home, and I cannot help feeling the parting sorely.'

He was enabled to pay a visit to the artillery practice camp on Salisbury Plain in July, and he went on to witness some siege manoeuvres at Chatham which greatly interested him, while next month he was for two days at the cavalry manoeuvres about Marlborough. 'I run a half to three-quarters of a mile every morning directly I get up, and this does me a lot of good and keeps me fit,' he wrote one day in August. Then in September he was selected for the umpire staff at the Southern Command manoeuvres about Salisbury. He was afterwards on the directing staff of the Aldershot Command exercises in the Aylesbury country, and was much encouraged as regards his chances of getting a more suitable appointment before long, rather expecting to go to Aldershot. 'I am so keen about soldiering,' he wrote in his diary in

November, 'and feel that I could do something big if I had the chance.' He occasionally went out with the harriers during the autumn and winter, was invited to several shoots, and, as the Defence Scheme had been got into shape and the office work for which he was responsible had been revolutionised, he felt more at liberty at the end of the year to devote time to private pursuits than, with his strong sense of duty and his bent for counsels of perfection, he had felt twelve months before.

Early in January Maude went to hear a series of lectures by Mr Julian Corbett at the Naval Barracks on 'Invasions,' and a comment in his diary is worthy of note: 'Very good and interesting, as they always are; but I think he is a little too sure that England cannot be invaded without the sea being permanently in the hands of the enemy.' A few weeks later he learnt privately from General Mackinnon at the War Office that he was to receive the offer of a General Staff appointment in one of the Territorial Divisions about to be constituted. He was somewhat sorry to leave his house, as Mrs Maude had latterly been in much better health there, and he also felt doubt as to whether the appointment was in itself a good one from the professional point of view and likely to help him on in the service; but on this latter point he received most satisfactory assurances from Headquarters. Therefore, when formally offered the post with the Midland Division and headquarters at Warwick, he accepted. 'I think it best to see soldiering under every form and condition,' he wrote in the diary, 'and the work ought to be interesting if I have a good general and a keen County Association.' Shortly afterwards, however, he was asked whether he would accept the same appointment in one of the London divisions instead – an arrangement which he accepted gladly – and at the end of March he bid good-bye to his many friends at Plymouth and went up to London so as to start work on 1 April, when the new Territorial organisation came into force. His division was the 2nd London, under command of his old brother-officer in the Coldstream, Major-General Vesey Dawson, and he must have regarded the date of taking up his new post as somewhat appropriate, for he records in his diary that there were 'no office, no stationery, no pens, ink or paper, and no clerks.

> Personally I am very keen on the scheme, and mean to work my best to make it a success. I do not in the least see why it should not succeed. But its success or failure of course depends largely upon the keenness and exertions of those composing the force. I go up every morning to 28 Lancaster Gate (General Dawson's house), and there we have a temporary office, but everything is

very difficult, for we have veritably to make bricks without straw. It is nice to be with old Vesey again.

Maude was however the sort of man who does make bricks without straw, and in a very short space of time had succeeded in getting the Territorial Association to agree to the hire of an office in Craig's Court, and was installed in it and working at high pressure. He had to think of a home for himself as well as of accommodation for divisional headquarters and, after seeing two or three houses, Mrs Maude and he chose 'Greengates' at Carshalton, where the number of rooms was limited, but where this drawback was compensated for by an extensive garden. He resided there with his family for four years, longer than in any other house that he occupied during his married life.

'We are settling down gradually into our office,' he wrote on 21 April, 'and are very comfortable. But one has to do everything for oneself and organise all from the very start.

'No doubt the scheme is a great advance on anything we have had previously, for at least the divisions will be properly organised and on a sound military footing; but the questions as to the number of men that will come forward and as to the amount of training are critical ones for the Empire, and time alone will prove what will be the result. Possibly we may work up to the full numbers ultimately, but only at the expense of training; for the tendency now very clearly is to sacrifice the amount of training to be done in order that more men may be attracted to the colours.'

Although there was an immense amount of office work to be got through in the early days, Maude and his chief had also to carry out a certain amount of inspection work from the start, and early in May he was already preparing for an officers' tactical exercise. Towards the end of that month he definitely settled down at Carshalton, going up to town usually by the 8.28 train and getting back in the evening. Always looking ahead, he was already pressing upon the Territorial Association the need for making all arrangements for the annual camps to take place at the end of July and beginning of August, and he found some difficulty in getting that body to move in the matter. His tactical exercises for officers were a great success from the outset, and they were highly appreciated by those attending them. Maude was particularly expert in conducting work of this kind; he did not look for, nor expect, to find knowledge, but he did look for keenness on the part of those participating, and there was no lack of this. That being so he was always prepared to take an infinite amount of pains, as was apparent to the officers of his division, and they therefore invariably worked their very best when in contact with him on such occasions. He was by nature somewhat intolerant of ignorance; but, competent craftsman as he was, he could always bring himself down to the level of his audience so long as this clearly showed that it was following his expositions with intelligence and interest, and his lectures were much valued by those under instruction.

His general and he had a very busy time, involving a great deal of travelling, towards the end of July. The division, as it happened, when out for this, its first annual training under the new organisation, was a good deal scattered. They were twice at Lydd and twice on Salisbury Plain. Maude was much pleased with the progress noticed amongst the artillery on the second visit to Lydd. The work of the infantry on Salisbury Plain was perhaps a little too far advanced, because after some nocturnal work he writes in his diary: 'Very poor, and I have learnt this week never to embark on night operations with Territorials if we go to war. The troops were very fortunate in their weather this first year, for it was hot and sunny throughout – Vesey's face quite raw and mine beginning to peel – and the period on the plain ended with a big field day on 12 August in which Regulars took part.

'Our division, which was only 1,700 strong, charged by the whole Cavalry Division and the fight given against us. It is doubtful what would have happened on service. Territorials looked at charging cavalry but never fired!'

In September this year Maude joined the directing staff of the Aldershot Command, which was now under Sir H. Smith-Dorrien, for the manoeuvres; they took place about Winchester, although they included an elaborate strategic scheme beforehand. Brigadier General (now General Sir W. R.) Robertson was Smith-Dorrien's Chief of the General Staff at Aldershot at this time, and it was the first occasion that Maude had much to do with two officers with whom he was to be closely connected in later and more stirring times. 'I enjoyed the manoeuvres immensely,' he wrote; 'they were very instructive.' After this Maude settled down to the usual office routine in town in connection with the 2nd London Division. He always seems at this time to have had an inordinate amount of paperwork to dispose of; General Vesey Dawson indeed declares that he never at this time succeeded in getting to Craig's Court before his General Staff Officer or in outstaying him there. It is however somewhat significant that when Maude came to compare notes at conferences and meetings with officers holding the same appointment as he did in other Territorial Divisions, he was puzzled to find that they did not complain of their office duties being very onerous. It has to be remembered that these officers were, like Maude himself, experienced in staff work and that they had been especially selected for their appointments, to which much importance was attached at the War Office. Is it to be supposed that they neglected their responsibilities? Surely not. One gets the impression, although it may be quite a mistaken one, that Maude was – to borrow a sailor's expression – a little disposed to make heavy weather of office transactions.

The routine at Craig's Court was however frequently interrupted by the carrying out of special exercises with officers of the division. One particular set of these which had Hatfield for its scene lasted nearly a week in the month of October. Soon after completing it Maude passed a time of great anxiety for several weeks owing to Mrs Maude becoming dangerously ill and having to undergo a serious operation; the operation proved quite successful, but for some months afterwards she was in delicate health which caused him alarm at times. He attended the General Staff Conference held by General Sir W. Nicholson, Chief of the Imperial General Staff, at the Staff College in January – a gathering which came to be an annual institution from about that time. 'I had five days' leave at Christmas, which is all I usually have now as work is incessant,' he wrote in his diary at this time; 'there is no limit to the amount of work that one can do with the Territorials with a little exertion' – evidently referring to their training and to special exercises of officers. Mrs Maude started off for a two months tour in the Mediterranean for the sake of her health in February; and, very shortly after she had left, he was asked by General Mackinnon to take up the appointment of Assistant Director of the Territorial Forces from 1 April, an offer which he gladly accepted, as it carried with it the rank of Colonel, with a rise in pay. Still, when the time of parting arrived he wrote: 'Very sorry to leave old Vesey and the 2nd Division, where I have made many friends.'

'I knew Maude as well as most people,' writes General Vesey Dawson, 'for we served together for many years in the Coldstream, and he was afterwards on the staff of the 2nd London Division T.F. when I commanded it.

'His chief characteristic was devotion to duty, but he was extraordinarily energetic, and he never thought of, or spared, himself when there was work to be done. He was also exceptionally modest. By nature very impatient of ignorance or slowness in others, he managed to conquer this feeling when dealing with the Territorial officers, and nothing could have exceeded the trouble that he took to educate them, although many were completely ignorant of military duties.'

He was not favourably impressed with War Office methods on joining the staff of that institution definitely for the first time. In connection with the administration of the Territorials much of the correspondence was necessarily with the civil side; he found their ways unduly deliberate, and he wrote in his diary that 'people seem to think nothing of keeping papers for days at a time, and doing nothing with them.' The office hours proved even longer than he had found them when on the staff of the 2nd Division, and there were few of those breaks caused by inspections, tactical exercises, and so forth which he had always enjoyed; but he felt that much could be accomplished to effect improvements in the force which Mr Haldane had done so much to develop. Still, he lost heart somewhat at times. 'The War Office gives one the idea of a building in which all the officials have gone to sleep for twenty years, and then wake up and carry on their work on lines which have been long out of date,' he wrote. Although General Mackinnon had agreed to his dividing the branch up into three sub-sections, each with its particular functions clearly laid down, his tendency to centralise made itself felt very plainly now that he had several junior staff officers under him. This tendency remained with him to the end of his career, and when he had risen very high in the service. Outspoken references to the matter will have to be made later in the volume, seeing that it at times created a certain amount of difficulty and that it was criticised even by those under him and those over him who had the greatest admiration for his qualities of heart and head.

A pleasant interlude came for him in July at the time of the annual camps of the Territorial Forces. He visited the divisions at work on Salisbury Plain, in Wales, and in Lancashire, covering a great deal of country and travelling considerable distances, and on his return he wrote full reports for the information of his chief. He was disposed to think that in some cases the training was too far advanced, and that these non-permanent troops were being taught to run before they could walk. Sir C. Fergusson, who was Inspector of Infantry at this time, mentions having had many dealings with him in connection with the training of the Territorials and always finding him 'most helpful and accessible.' In September he went on the umpire staff to the Army Manoeuvres held under Sir J. French, an outing which he greatly enjoyed; he was attached to the Royal Irish Fusiliers, to whose efficiency and good fellowship he pays a handsome tribute in his diary, and returned full of zest to the office routine of Whitehall.

But there he found much to deplore. 'The Finance Branch are doing the Territorial Scheme grave damage by their grinding economy,' he wrote in his diary. 'They save little by it and are putting up the backs of all the County Associations and of leading men connected with business who will not stand such interference; they will be compelled to give way ultimately, which will only make us look foolish after the harm has been done.' Still, it is only fair to the Finance Department officials of the War Office to observe in this connection that they are not exactly free agents in such matters as are here referred to. Only a certain amount of money is available in any case, and the Treasury at all events in peace time keeps a very tight hold over disbursements, besides being by no means precipitate in arriving at its conclusions. The result is that, if war supervenes, the country suffers grievously from the point of view of economy and from every other point of view, the Finance Department is shouldered out of the way by other War Office departments under dire stress of circumstances, and the Treasury, swept off its legs by the flood of urgent expenditure on imperative naval and military requirements, fails to recover financial control until long after hostilities have been brought to a conclusion.

The Maude family had in the meantime settled down very comfortably at Carshalton and Maude liked the place, taking much trouble with his garden and interesting himself unobtrusively, in so far as his limited leisure from military duties permitted, in local affairs. In the winter of 1909–10 he made a practice of going out on Saturday afternoons with the
Worcester Park beagles, and he continued to do so during succeeding winters; they generally met within five miles of 'Greengates,' and he used to bicycle or walk out to the rendezvous according to the state of the weather, although he sometimes used the railway. His friend and medical attendant, Doctor A. T. Peatling, in a letter regarding him at this time throws an illuminating sidelight upon Maude's invariable practice of keeping himself in good condition; it shows that he had an object in all this, quite apart from the healthy instincts of an active man who happens by force of circumstances to spend much time at the office desk.

> One Saturday he came to me just before dinner complaining of a discomfort in his chest. I found that he had been running with

the beagles hard all the afternoon, and then had a three or four miles walk to the station. He had overdone it, and his heart was 'jibbing' at the extra strain. I expostulated with him and told him I thought a man of his age was too old to run for any length of time. 'But I must keep fit,' he said. 'But why on earth do you want to keep in the condition of a prize-fighter?' was my reply. I remember so well how he leant forward towards me and said impressively: 'Because any day we soldiers may be wanted badly; any day we may be plunged into a huge war which one can't grasp the extent of. I shall see it, and you will live to see it. That is why I feel it my duty to keep myself in top-hole condition.' This occurred four or five years before the Great War. It made a great impression upon my mind at the time, and I have often recalled his words since.

He was churchwarden here and I met him at several parish and church meetings; he always took a very commonsense view of things, entirely free from sentiment. I envied very much his temerity in wearing white ducks at church during the summer. I have never, before nor since, seen a churchwarden taking the bag round dressed so coolly. He was one of the most courteous men I ever met; I should think that it took a little time to gain his confidence, but when once obtained he would give his trust freely.

As will also be seen from the Rev. G. Vaux's appreciation which is quoted further on, Maude took a somewhat prominent part in questions connected with the parish and with Carshalton Church, this in spite of the long hours which he passed daily in London and of generally carrying papers home with him to deal with after dinner. He was in fact spending a somewhat strenuous existence. All through his military career, however, he seemed to thrive upon hard work, nor did he ever grudge time and labour if he saw the slightest prospect of his efforts leading to some tangible result. But with regard to the newly formed category of the fighting forces with which he was so closely concerned, he sometimes almost lost heart.

'Delays and procrastination still rife at the War Office,' he wrote in March 1910, 'incalculable damage being consequently done to the Territorial Scheme. We have however got some improvements through. Instead of ex-regular officers, we are to have regular officers in the higher commands and a certain proportion of staff officers, but it has been a fierce struggle to get it through. Still it is a great triumph and I feel amply repaid, for the consequences will be far-reaching.'

He had attended the General Staff Conference at Camberley in January, and Mrs Maude again went abroad for two months in the spring of 1910. King Edward died in May, and at the
funeral Maude was in attendance on Queen Mary and Queen Alexandra, going from place to place in a motor to meet them, first at Westminster Hall, then at Paddington, and finally at
Windsor. During the summer he spent a considerable time visiting Territorial camps and manoeuvres. He was on Salisbury Plain in June, he went to the exercises in Scotland in the following month, and in August he attended the Eastern Command manoeuvres in which Territorials took part with Regulars. He was fairly well satisfied with what he saw, noticing considerable advance since the early days. 'Territorial troops did fairly well, and no blame attaches to the men themselves who are wonderfully good considering the experience that they get,' he wrote in his diary; but he was troubled with regard to their numbers and to their discipline in the field. 'The great trouble is that we do not sufficiently formulate our military requirements and then work on those lines,' he remarked. He was shortly afterwards offered the Assistant Controllership in the Lord Chamberlain's office. This meant a settled business practically for life and an improved financial outlook; but he decided to refuse. 'I am not a courtier,' he wrote in his diary, 'but wish to give my life and best days to the military service of my country. Some day I may be of use to her if I keep pegging away at the humdrum work and drudgery of peace soldiering as I mean to do.' At the end of October General Mackinnon, to Maude's great regret on personal grounds and as it meant a break in old associations, gave up the appointment of Director General of the Territorial Forces, taking up charge of the Western Command at Chester. He was succeeded by Major-General Cowans.

Writing of his old subordinate in the Home District and in the War Office, in 1919, General Sir H. Mackinnon pays the following tribute to his memory:

> I was a very intimate friend of Maude's almost from the time he joined the brigade in 1884. He showed signs of his future powers – when he became adjutant, which was in a surprisingly short time of his first appointment to the Coldstream. But my closest intimacy with him was when we worked together for six years, firstly on Lord Methuen's staff in the Home District, and

then under Lord Haldane in the War Office during the preparation and the launching of the Territorial Force.

Although one cannot say that Maude laid himself out to make life easy and comfortable for himself or for those he worked with, and although I have frequently known him refuse to join in sport or amusement when work was waiting, still I look back on him as the very best of colleagues, and for two reasons firstly, because of his great knowledge of the army and of its regulations and customs, and, secondly, owing to his untiring energy. The six years we had together were pretty strenuous ones, especially those connected with the Territorial Force, and I can never remember his leaving work undone which he could finish. The heavy bag that he always took home with him testified to a great deal of night work to be got through. His judgement too was very sound, and one knew that any opinion that he gave was founded on the deep-down knowledge he possessed of all arms of the service. He had a great love of exercise, and even in his hardest periods of work he would always have a morning run to keep himself fit.

His regiment and the whole Brigade of Guards mourn his loss, and I am confident that all who knew him in the army will benefit by the splendid example he set as an officer and a gentleman.

The subject of this Memoir was now to serve under a chief who brought with him to the War Office a genius for organisation that was unvitiated by any overpowering enthusiasm for the desk. To a man like Maude, whose bent for punctuality and for the systematic conduct of office duties amounted almost to a passion, the somewhat mercurial exits and entrances of the new Director General of the Territorial Forces in connection with the buildings in Whitehall were anathema for a time. But, as he became familiar with his superior's ways and was able to judge of the results, he had to acknowledge to himself – and it is characteristic of him that he should do so freely in his diary – that General Cowans did somehow get things done. Nor is it wholly unlikely that association with a successful administrator, who arrived at the same goal as he did but by a wholly different route, may have been an illuminating experience for a keen and zealous staff officer who, in spite of having subordinates with their duties definitely told off to them at his beck and call, always seemed to have almost more paperwork to get through than he could dispose of within the time at his disposal.

All this time Maude practically never took any leave, except for a day or two, although each year he allowed himself a holiday of five days at Christmas; these latterly were generally spent at Carshalton and not at Henley. He was often on visits to Territorial centres with Mr Haldane (who was raised to the peerage in 1911), but, except during the season of the annual trainings in the summer, he enjoyed little relaxation from indoor work such as he had experienced at tactical exercises when on the staff of the 2nd London Division. He attended the General Staff Conference as usual in January 1911, and on this occasion questions in connection with the Territorials were particularly brought forward and discussed.

Little of interest is recorded in the diary during the early part of 1911. Maude and Mrs Maude were present in Westminster Abbey at the Coronation, which he describes as a most interesting and beautiful sight. 'Directly the Abbey ceremony was over, I changed my things and went down for two days to the Boat Club at Maidenhead, where I had two delightful days' rest.' He was shortly afterwards asked if he would like his name considered for the appointment of Military Secretary in India, Military Secretary to the Commander-in-Chief, that is to say, not a virtually civilian appointment like that of Military Secretary to a Viceroy and he replied hoping that his name would be put forward, as it was; but the post went to a considerably senior officer. In August he visited General Byng's Territorial Division in Norfolk at their annual training, and afterwards the two Yorkshire Divisions under Generals Bullock and Hubert Hamilton. He was not much impressed with what he saw on this occasion, and he wrote in his diary, 'It makes me shudder to think how these troops would fare in a European war.' Major Morrison-Bell mentions having once about this time discussed the Territorial Force with him, and his saying that in the event of war they would all have to go abroad, and that they ought to be told so.

'This was in the hey-day of Haldanism,' writes Major Morrison-Bell, 'and I replied that they were only enlisted for home service. Maude's reply was very forcible and to the point; for he was one of that comparatively small band who really did clearly foresee what was coming to pass.'

Like the majority of soldiers he had never been able to reconcile himself to the idea that the Territorial Forces were to have six months grace after mobilisation before they were to be actively employed; he pictured them to himself as meeting Continental Regulars on the outbreak of war. He observed that the 'real criminals' were those who would not realise that 'you can both support the Territorial movement till we got something better, and yet advocate compulsory training.' He afterwards went on an official visit to the Swiss manoeuvres.

'Had a delightful time in Switzerland,' he wrote in his diary. 'Went first to Berne, but we were accommodated most of the time at a charming hotel in Lausanne. There were about thirty foreign officers and we were most hospitably entertained. Start out usually about 8 a.m., and most officers got home by noon; but I liked to stay out later, and generally got home only about six or seven in time for dinner. We were beautifully mounted and the weather was lovely, if a little hot.

'Not much to learn from the manoeuvres (as the troops are practically untrained like our Territorials), except the wonderful patriotism of the people and the popularity of the military service, their system of billeting, and the use made of cooking wagons generally throughout the force.'

In a letter written about this time he expressed the opinion that it was perfectly feasible to devise a system of compulsory training which would not be incompatible with voluntary recruiting for the regular army, and which would not appreciably dislocate economic conditions. He always realised the advantages of the Territorial Forces organisation in so far as its furnishing a framework was concerned; but he entertained no illusions as to its efficiency on the outbreak of war, and it was obvious to him as to all other experienced soldiers that the numbers on the rolls were entirely inadequate for the purpose of immediate mobilisation in the event of a national emergency arising. He was moreover convinced that far larger numbers would have to be placed in the field in the event of a European war, than were contemplated under the scheme of organisation for the military forces of the country which held good. He thought much with regard to these subjects. He clearly foresaw the coming of a great international crisis, in which his country would have to play a prominent part if it was to retain its position in the world.

His son Eric, who had been for five years at school near Maidenhead, and who was now fourteen, was sent to Lancing College (where he had obtained a scholarship) after the summer holidays; after passing satisfactorily for Osborne, the lad had been rejected on account of colour blindness. In the winter the family spent some time at Klosters in Switzerland enjoying winter sports, and after the General Staff

Conference Maude took a very short period of leave and went out to join his eldest girl there while the others came home. Shortly after his return from abroad he received the offer of the appointment of General Staff Officer, 1st Grade, with the 5th Division in Ireland, headquarters at the Curragh. This he accepted at once, overjoyed to find himself once more identified with regular troops and after three years at the War Office to be employed again on thoroughly congenial tasks involving much work in the open air. The appointment fell vacant at the beginning of April, and his departure from, the War Office to take it up brought his close and especial connection with the Territorial Forces to an end, although he was destined to have units belonging to this category of the army under his command in the field in later years. Under the circumstances it will not be inappropriate to quote here the tribute paid by Lord Haldane, in the House of Lords on 6 March 1918, to Maude's services in connection with the Territorial Scheme, on the occasion of the discussion with regard to the special grant made by Parliament to Lady Maude.

After a reference to Lord Curzon's remark that war is a supreme discoverer of merit, Lord Haldane proceeded: 'To me I can scarcely say he was a discovery, because I had an opportunity of seeing those qualities very early in his career. At the time when the Territorial Forces Act passed, and when it was very doubtful whether officers and men could be got to come forward, it was necessary to make personal efforts, and night after night, afternoon after afternoon, General Maude – who was the General Staff Officer attached to the Territorial Forces organisation at the War Office – used to set off with me, sometimes to distant parts, to stir up enthusiasm. Mine was the ornamental part; but his was the difficult business of explaining away all difficulties and of showing how the things could be accomplished. This he did with supreme ability. He then showed the great quality, which I think was distinctive of him afterwards, of visualising clearly and distinctly what was the object which he had in view, and at the same time of being conscious almost by intuition of the means by which to attain that object. That was a distinctive characteristic of him and the secret of his success in those much humbler days of his life.

'Later when he became the commander of a brigade, and again of a division, and again of a corps, and finally when he became Commander-in-Chief, he always visualised with the utmost distinctness what he was aiming at, and he always knew how to get at his object. Shortly before his death I had a long letter from him, in which he told me that he had turned himself completely into an administrator. He knew what he meant to do, and was concentrating upon that the very necessary grasp of the material facts and resources which a great general always has and always insists upon in himself before he sets out to the attainment of a new object. From the personal experience and intimacy which I was privileged at one time to have, I am able to testify, as noble Lords who have already spoken have done, to General Maude's great qualities, to his personal charm, and to his supreme combination of the two kinds of military gifts.'

This staff appointment at the Curragh meant leaving Carshalton and seeking a residence on the further side of St George's Channel, and, apart from considerations affecting his professional duties, Maude was inclined to regret leaving 'Greengates,' where he had made himself very comfortable and had greatly enjoyed developing the garden with the assistance of his children. He was sorry to bid good-bye to a place with which he had identified himself during a stay of four years, and where he had made many friends in all classes of society. Nor was the regret entirely on his side. That he was liked and honoured by those amongst whom he lived in this temporary Surrey home of his is shown by the following striking appreciation of him, written by his friend and neighbour of those days, the Rev. G. Vaux:

> Like the 'daily breaders' of these suburban districts who only dine and sleep and breakfast, watch in hand, in their homes, Colonel Maude, as we then knew him, started each morning by an early train and only returned late in the afternoon. But Carshalton was to him no mere dormitory. He threw himself with characteristic energy into the social life and the church life of the place. An agreeable companion, a courteous gentleman, he was to all of us an excellent neighbour and to many a valued friend. Those who knew him best discerned the great qualities which found scope in larger fields. With a handsome and dignified presence he coupled entire simplicity of character. He put on no 'side,' and he was at home with all sorts and conditions of people but no one ever thought of taking liberties with him. He was a welcome guest at any parish function a supper to choir-men or altar-servers was incomplete without him. When he was wanted to give the prizes to the Church Lads Brigade he would appear in his war paint, and this in no spirit of vainglory but just to show respect to those who, in their small way, were aspiring to some measure of military discipline.

His industry never flagged. After a hard day's work in town, when most men claim the indulgence of a novel or a rubber of bridge, one would find Maude buried in arrears of papers or deep in a volume of military history. And this was only part of that rigid self-discipline which kept him alert and fit in mind and body. When offered a cigarette he would say, 'No, since I rowed in the boats at Eton I have always been in training.' Hard worker as he was, he made time for necessary exercise. In summer he was up betimes, playing a set of lawn tennis with his children, and in winter striding across country as fast as his long legs would carry him; and on Saturday afternoons, the half holiday of the British working man, he would run with the beagles.

A tender and affectionate father, his children were devoted to him, and when the life of his wife was hanging in the balance, those who were admitted to share his anxiety admired the Christian fortitude and forgetfulness of self which mastered his grief. For, above all things, Stanley Maude was a man of God, a practising Christian. He never missed the early celebration on a Sunday, and he was rarely absent from the other services. To him a 'layman' was no mere negative title – one not in holy orders, an individual who may be relied on for an occasional sovereign or half-crown; on the contrary, he realised the true meaning of that honourable word. A layman was to his thinking one of the Aaos, the people of God, and he acted on that conviction.

Colonel Maude accepted office as churchwarden, not without misgivings. He doubted if he would have time to do justice to the task. As a matter-of-fact he did thorough justice to it, and this thoroughness was the hallmark of everything that he undertook. After attending the three hours' service on Good Friday, he would take his part bareheaded in a perambulation of clergy, choir and people round the poorer districts, and listen to some poor singing and indifferent preaching. This is not a thing which a distinguished officer would do just for fun. He would take infinite trouble to help young men in their plans and prospects. So it was that we greatly missed him when he left Carshalton for the Curragh in 1912. We followed with keen interest the steps of his great career. We rejoiced over each distinction conferred upon him. And when the news came of his untimely death, we assembled in large numbers at the parish altar to remember before God in solemn requiem the soul of his servant.

Maude's new chief was Major General W. P. Campbell, who had already been in command of the 5th Division for more than three years. The division was distributed to some extent over Central and Northern Ireland, although the greater part of it was collected fairly near to the headquarters. The 13th Infantry Brigade, which was at this time under the late Brigadier General T. Capper, was quartered in Dublin, the 14th Infantry Brigade was quartered at the Curragh, the 15th Infantry Brigade, which was under Brigadier General Count Gleichen, was stationed at Belfast and in the north of Ireland. The artillery was for the most part gathered together in County Kildare; but one of its brigades was at Dundalk. In the nature of things, the fact that the troops were somewhat scattered inevitably involved a certain amount of travelling about the country for the divisional commander and his chief staff officer, especially during the long days and fine weather.

On joining at the Curragh, Maude in the first instance lived for some time with the 4th Hussars, who were quartered there forming part of Brigadier General Hubert Gough's 3rd Cavalry Brigade. He made great friends with the Hussars, although a good deal older and much senior in the service to the majority of the members of the mess; his keenness in respect to all matters of sport naturally commended itself to the younger officers of the regiment, even if they stood somewhat in awe of a full colonel. The Curragh delighted him; and even if he was necessarily much occupied in his office, his habit of early rising enabled him to be about, looking on with the utmost interest at units of the various arms at their drills and exercises, before the hour came for settling down to paperwork. He had always taken the utmost pleasure in all questions connected with the training of troops, and his position as Chief of the General Staff of a regular division afforded him ample scope for turning his bent for such subjects, and the knowledge which he had acquired by study and experience in connection with them, to good account. The quarters attached to his appointment were small and inconvenient, and eventually, in October, the Maudes settled down at Moorefield Lodge, just outside Newbridge.

Inter-divisional manoeuvres between 5th Division and 6th Division, which was quartered in the south of Ireland, were in contemplation this year, but Maude's preparations for annual training had rather to do with the purely divisional programme. He paid a visit with General Campbell to the north of Ireland early in the summer to inspect 15th

Brigade, and they covered a great deal of ground by motor, proceeding as far as Rosapena in Donegal, as one of the battalions was quartered in Londonderry; they returned by way of Mullingar, where another battalion was stationed. Later on they were present at the brigade training of 13th Brigade, which took place on the Boyne. Unfortunately, the inter-divisional manoeuvres, which were to have taken place in Carlow, had to be abandoned at the last moment owing to an outbreak of foot-and-mouth disease, and a proposal to shift the venue to Glen Imaal had to be given up owing to objections raised by local farmers. However in the autumn a divisional staff ride was held at Clonmel in which Maude acted as assistant director under his general, and on this occasion he greatly impressed the officers taking part in it by his masterly summing-up of different situations, holding his own in this respect with so accomplished and practised a manager of staff rides as General Capper, who had been on the staff of the Camberley Staff College and had afterwards been commandant of the rival establishment at Quetta.

Nevertheless, in spite of much hard work which was often interrupted by travelling on inspection duty with his chief, Maude played much lawn tennis, and he bicycled and rode all over County Kildare. Sir W. Pitcairn Campbell describes him as the best general staff officer he ever came across, and he won a great reputation for himself amongst the many zealous officers in 5th Division by his thorough knowledge of his profession, by the lucidity of his expositions, and by the skill he displayed in the framing of all orders in connection with training that were issued from divisional headquarters. General Campbell's period in command came to an end early in February 1913, and he was succeeded by Sir C. Fergusson, whom Maude had known intimately since early days at Eton.

During the winter time Maude hunted occasionally with the Kildare, but as the drill season approached he became wrapped up in the preparations for the various trainings, and in issuing detailed instructions concerning them. As in the previous year he covered a good deal of ground with his chief, inspecting the units included in the division at different times. The brigade trainings took place in three separate localities; but towards the end of August the division assembled complete for a week of divisional training about Nenagh, which lasted from 1 to 6 September. This was followed by inter-divisional manoeuvres between 5th Division and 6th Division, which were carried out in the country lying to the south of the Sleve Bloom mountains not far from the Shannon, and which were attended by

General Sir C. Douglas, the Inspector General of the Forces, although under the direction of Sir A. Paget, the Commander-in-Chief in Ireland. The operations passed off very successfully.

Towards the end of the year Maude received a communication offering him the position of General Staff Officer, 1st Grade, in the Training Directorate of the War Office. He was in the first instance much disposed to decline the offer. He had already laboured long in Whitehall. He had no love for service in the War Office, whereas he was thoroughly content with his work in the 5th Division, work that was most congenial, and he moreover liked the life near the Curragh. But he realised that his selection for an appointment in the training branch at Headquarters was a compliment, and that a refusal to take it up would not be welcome in high places; he moreover had always entertained the view strongly that it was an officer's business to go where he was sent and to fall in with the wishes of superiors, whatever these might be. He therefore wrote an acceptance, and his connection with the 5th Division in peacetime came to an end early in 1914. Of his work with the Division, Sir C. Fergusson writes as follows:

> In February 1913 I went to command the 5th Division in Ireland, where I found Maude G.S.O.1 of the division, and we were together until January 1914 when he went again to the War Office. During this year we were of course intimately associated, and it is difficult to describe his work without appearing to exaggerate. To say he was thorough is not enough, he was a very highly trained staff officer who had mastered his profession and every detail of it. His capacity for work was unlimited. His judgement was very sound. He never would give an opinion in a hurry, and would lapse into silence when turning a matter over in his mind; when he did speak he put the pros and cons clearly and concisely and gave a decided opinion, from which nothing would turn him.
>
> He was most helpful to everyone, but may have seemed to those who did not know him well somewhat stiff and reserved in manner when discussing official details. I have at least heard that said – but it does not describe him. His preoccupied manner was not in the least due to boredom or to want of sympathy no man was more sympathetic but to intense concentration on the business in hand. When at work he was entirely absorbed, and he wasted no time. He was strict and unbending in working hours, and was very severe on any

departure from the rules and customs in office work or routine which he laid down. Once work was over, he threw off every care, was as bright and sunny as any boy, and enjoyed life to the full. He was a delightful companion to everyone, entering wholeheartedly into games and sports and the interests of the moment. He was very active and athletic, a fine rider and always in the very pink of condition.

As an instructor and a staff officer in the field he was at his very best. In staff and regimental exercises his schemes were always clear, interesting, and instructive, and his criticisms sound and helpful. He took an immense amount of trouble with them. A little intolerant of stupidity, he was sympathetic and painstaking to a degree with those whom he was instructing, and he spared no trouble to make the work interesting to officers taking part. He had a wonderful capacity for drafting clear and good orders. Given the scheme or plan, he would in a few moments call a clerk and dictate without hesitation the longest and most complicated orders, in which not a word had to be changed and which could hardly have been improved. He was impatient of interruption or interference on these occasions.

A more pleasant or loyal staff officer never existed. He was the life and soul of the division, and no one who served with him could fail to appreciate his qualities.

On joining at the War Office at the beginning of February Maude found himself for the first time associated for a season with Sir W. Robertson, although, as already mentioned, he had been for a few days in close touch with his new chief during the manoeuvres of the Aldershot Command in 1908. He at once devoted himself wholeheartedly to a task which greatly interested him too wholeheartedly some of his subordinates were disposed to think. His tendency to centralise has already been touched upon, and in this case he was coming in from outside to take up charge of a section of the General Staff in Whitehall which was a going concern, a section administered by an existing staff of specially selected officers, most of whom had already been serving in it for some time and who consequently were well acquainted with the scope and the details of their duties. These found it somewhat trying to be to a great extent deprived of the responsibilities that had been entrusted to them as a matter of course by Maude's predecessor, responsibilities which corresponded more or less in respect to importance to those undertaken by staff officers of analogous grading in the various other War Office departments and branches. Still, all speedily recognised the striking ability, the heartening enthusiasm, and the exhaustive knowledge of the subjects to be dealt with, which their new section chief brought with him, and as they got to know him better they became to a great extent propitiated by his unfailing kindliness and courtesy.

The annual Army Manoeuvres were to have been held this year on the borders of South Wales, the area chosen being the intersected and hilly country beyond the lower Severn. It was a part of the country that, in so far as troops were concerned, was almost virgin soil, although it had been a field for numerous staff rides in recent years, and Maude was a good deal concerned in the preparations necessary for the contemplated exercises from an early date after taking up his appointment at the War Office. That question of residence, which is generally so troublesome a one for married officers whenever they change their military station, had also to be considered; but after some house-hunting a suitable abode, 'Mardale,' was found at Watford, within easy distance of Whitehall. There the family settled down in the spring. It may be mentioned here that owing to his departure from Ireland at the end of January, Maude was saved from the unpleasantness involved in being at the Curragh on the occasion of the acute problem connected with Ulster that arose soon after he left, in which the 4th Hussars, with whom he had lived when first he went to Kildare, as well as General Gough and the 16th Lancers, figured somewhat prominently events which aroused strong feeling throughout the 5th Division and its 15th Brigade quartered in the north. The month of April in 1914 was, on the other hand, also a somewhat ruffled one at the headquarters of the army, as a consequence of that remarkable Hibernian imbroglio; nor was the Directorate of Military Training wholly unconcerned in the matter. The sequel was that the Chief of the Imperial General Staff, Sir J. French, resigned, together with the Secretary of State and the Adjutant General, and he was succeeded by Sir C. Douglas. Mr Asquith became War Minister.

During the remainder of the spring and the early summer Maude spent long hours daily at the War Office, going up and down from Watford by train. Everything in connection with the September Army Manoeuvres was already in train, and he had thoroughly settled down to his work in the Training Directorate at Headquarters when this country and Europe in general were startled by the news of the assassination of the Archduke Ferdinand at Serajevo. There is no need to tell the story here of the gradual development of the acute international differences that followed. By the end of July the Continent was in a blaze, a few days later the British Empire was at war, and, as the great conflict which followed was to afford Maude the opportunity that he needed to prove himself the great soldier that he was, this will be an appropriate place in a record of his life to indicate what was his position in the military forces at the time, and what were his prospects of mounting the ladder, before he proceeded to France on the staff of the Expeditionary Force in August 1914.

'His career as a staff officer may be said to have commenced when he graduated at the Staff College in 1895–96,' writes Lord Rawlinson. 'Though I never served in really close touch with him on the staff, he was well known for his clearness of vision and for his indefatigable energy. The vigour with which he attacked every problem that was presented to him was quite remarkable, and, whether as a brigade-major at Horse Guards or, later on, holding that position during the South African War, he proved himself to be possessed of outstanding abilities as a staff officer. Except in charge of a company, he held no executive command until in October 1914 he was given a brigade in France. Had he been able to accept the command of a battalion of the Coldstream (which for financial reasons he was unable to do) I think that he would have risen more rapidly. His enforced service on the staff failed to bring to light those great qualities as a commander in the field which became so conspicuous in his case in his last years. One is seldom as a staff officer called upon to accept heavy responsibilities, it is the commander of the formation on whom all responsibility rests, so that long continued service on the staff is liable to dim, if not to stultify, the powers of a born leader of men such as Maude undoubtedly was.'

When the army mobilised for war Maude was just over fifty years of age and he figured as a full colonel, about a quarter of the way up the roll of officers holding that rank. A glance at the statistics given in the Official *Army List* of that time shows him to have been rather ahead of the majority of men of his own length of service, but not very much ahead. Many who had joined after him had moreover passed him by. In the ordinary course of things he might fairly have counted upon finding himself a Major-General by the time he was fifty-two or fifty-three years of age. If his prospects, in a word, might be regarded as satisfactory, they could not have been called brilliant. Had he remained on active service in South Africa, instead of going to Canada at a time when he was doing very important work on the staff in Cape Colony, and when he would very likely before long have been chosen after Lord

Kitchener assumed control for the command of an independent column operating against the scattered burgher forces, he might well have secured by brevet so early as 1902 that promotion which he actually only secured on the half-pay list five years later. He might then already have been a general officer in the summer of 1914 when the Great War came. But, as we have seen, he had been handicapped by lack of means throughout; and the consequence was that, even if his merits were realised throughout the Brigade of Guards, and if they had latterly become at least partially known to the highest military authorities, he was to the army at large to all intents and purposes an unknown quantity. That he suffered from disappointment himself during those somewhat lean years which intervened between his return from Ottawa and his transfer from London to the Curragh, is apparent from his diaries. Some passages from them have been quoted. But he never showed discouragement outwardly; nor did he ever permit any mortification that he may have felt to abate his ardour in carrying out such military duties as fell to his lot, to weaken his love for the profession that he had chosen, or to deprive him of that confidence of possessing a capacity for great things which he carried with him from the days of boyhood till he had accomplished his task in Mesopotamia.

CHAPTER VI
On The Staff of III Corps in France

As a member of the General Staff at the War Office and holding a responsible position on it, Maude was naturally much better informed as to the critical development of affairs on the Continent during July than the general public. As soon as it became apparent that Austria-Hungary in her outrageous demands upon Serbia was acting with the full support of Germany, it was obvious to well-informed soldiers that a European war was in sight. The General Staff entertained no illusions as to the intention of the Central Powers to enter upon an aggressive campaign should it suit them to strike. The military preparations of Germany were too exhaustive, the elaborate extension of her railway systems towards the Belgian and French frontiers for purely strategic purposes too flagrant, to justify any doubt on the subject. All such steps as it had been possible to obtain sanction for had been taken by the War Office months before, and Maude was in due course informed that the organisation of the Expeditionary Force, should it be sent to the Continent, would be in three 'Armies' – the more appropriate title 'Army Corps' was substituted after hostilities had actually broken out – and that he was to be General Staff Officer, 1st Grade, of the 3rd Army. This was to be under General Pulteney, with Brigadier General J. P. Du Cane as chief of the staff. Pulteney was an old Guardsman friend with whom he had already once been associated on active service at the time of the South African War, as has been mentioned in the chapter dealing with that campaign. The 1st and 2nd Armies were respectively to be under Sir D. Haig and Sir J. Grierson.

'Normally,' he wrote in his diary, 'I ought, in virtue of the appointment which I am holding in the Training Directorate at the War Office, to remain there.' He was too level-headed and clear-sighted not to realise that his absorption into the Expeditionary Force under the circumstances was inappropriate. He could not but perceive that the plan of withdrawing a considerable number of the officers who were holding the most important posts in Whitehall, just at the moment when the country was about to embark upon a great Continental war, was open to many objections; but he was naturally pleased that he should be one of those selected to go. By 1 August all hopes of an accommodation as between the Central Powers and the Franco-Russian Allies was at an end, and during the next four days he, in common with a good many other soldiers who were more or less behind the scenes, was in a state of acute irritation at the attitude of the Cabinet.

'It looks tonight as if we were going to stand aside and not to help France,' he wrote on the 1st, 'What a disgrace! No wonder we are called a nation of shopkeepers, perfidious Albion, et cetera, on the Continent. I believe that many such as say openly that we ought not to fight. I could understand their point of view if there had been no *Entente Cordiale*, but surely as it is we have a debt of honour to France to pay. And, apart from the present, what of the future? Surely no nation will trust an Englishman's word again, and we shall revert to our position of isolation which existed at the time of the Boer War. That will scarcely do nowadays, and we shall be an easy prey to any Continental combination that chooses to attack us. Still our preparations at the War Office are going forward .... I have started getting our staff together, which, as it consists of nineteen officers, takes some gathering together.'

'Every moment's delay on our part seems criminal,' he wrote next day, 'and yet the Cabinet appear to do nothing but procrastinate. .... The Cabinet meeting lasted this morning from two to three hours, but the only points so far apparent are the stopping of some Territorial trainings and the establishment of the censorship, both of which ought to have been done before.'

However, Germany's deliberate violation of her pledges in regard to Belgian neutrality, coupled with the unmistakable feeling of the nation and the attitude taken up by the Opposition leaders, decided the Government to send the ultimatum to Berlin which made a rupture practically certain, and war was declared on the night of 4/5.

Mobilisation began on the 5th, the rank and file of 3 Army Headquarters staff assembling at Southampton; but General Pulteney and most of the staff officers remained in London. The comprehensive plans for the transfer of the Expeditionary Force to France, which had been prepared in the fullest detail many months before, together with the timetables and schedules in connection with transportation by land and sea, contemplated the immediate departure of 1 and 2 Armies. They were to be closely followed by 6th Division, which was stationed (all but one of its brigades) in Ireland, and which was to embark for the most part at Queenstown, following 5th Division of 2 Army from that country. 4th Division was to await events. But the plans were upset by an absurd scare about an impending German invasion – which incidentally very nearly caused portions of the 1st Army to be switched off to the North Country and the whole transportation scheme to be upset. This delayed the start of the Expeditionary Force for two days, and it caused 6th Division to be brought over to England from Ireland, creating great inconvenience. 4th Division under General Snow, stationed in peace time in the south-east of England, concentrated after mobilisation at Harrow. 6th Division under General Keir, as it arrived in England, gradually concentrated at Cambridge, and eventually 4th Division was allowed to follow 1st and 2nd Armies without any delay, while 6th Division, which took several days to arrive at its destination, remained where it was.

Maude accompanied Generals Pulteney and Du Cane to Harrow on the 20th to see 4th Division, which was to begin moving over to France on the next day, and on the 24th orders arrived for the corps staff to follow. They embarked at Southampton on the 26th in the Braemar Castle, which also carried some 2,500 troops, and proceeded to Havre, where they stayed until the 29th. That night they proceeded via Paris to General Headquarters at Compiégne, arriving on the following day, and General Pulteney then definitely took up command of his corps. This at the time only consisted of 4th Division, which had been heavily engaged at Le Cateau and while falling back, and the 19th Brigade, a new formation composed of four battalions which under the original scheme had been told off as 'line of communication troops.' It must be understood that at this time the Expeditionary Force was still in full retreat, with the enemy pressing after it. III Corps was on the left (facing the enemy) with II Corps (which was under Sir H. Smith-Dorrien, who had taken the place of General Grierson on his death) next on its right, and I Corps beyond that again. All the next day General Pulteney's troops were withdrawing through the Forest of Compiégne, and the retirement continued again on 1 September and during the following night.

'Exciting times sometimes,' Maude wrote home on the 2nd, 'as we have no protective troops for our headquarters, and uhlans are plentiful and strong on the wing! Yesterday they were all round us, and we had to get together any stragglers we could find to help us. We accounted for three out of one lot of five.'

Continuing the retirement on the 2nd and 3rd, after a rearguard action on the 2nd which somewhat delayed 4th Division, the corps reached and crossed the Marne by the 4th, and that day it enjoyed a welcome rest. Maude wrote home that the men were in excellent spirits although tired, and that the German prisoners that were being taken were quite worn out. In his diary at this time he expressed some doubts as to the expediency of blowing up all the bridges during the retreat, as he foresaw that there must shortly be an advance; he presumed that the French plan of falling back was the right one, but greatly disliked it. While the corps was resting on the Marne on the 4th the gradual movement of the enemy in a south-easterly direction across the front was observed. On the following day this became still more noticeable, and Maude learnt that the French VI Army had formed up in the country to the north-west of where III Corps was halted, and was preparing to move against the enemy's outer flank. That evening the welcome orders arrived for advance to take the place of retreat.

The order to advance was not confined to Pulteney's Corps, nor to the British forces under Sir J. French. The entire Allied host was turning upon its pursuers, and was about to inflict upon them a very serious defeat. Now that formidable reserves called up from the extreme right of his far-flung line were ready to play their part, that 6th Army under Maunoury was driving its attack home against Von Kluck on the German right, and that the enemy was manifestly exhausted by a tremendous effort, General Joffre was ready for the counter-stroke which created what by common consent of victors and vanquished has come to be called the Battle of the Marne. Pulteney's Corps on the British left was at the moment placed almost at the elbow which was created by Maunoury striking in as he did, practically across the front of the Allies' forces, from the left. Consequent on Maunoury's general line of advance and on the movement south-eastwards of the German right under Von Kluck which had been proceeding on the 4th and 5th, the direction taken by Sir J. French's army for the first three days was not northwards but almost eastwards, with a little north in it; the III Corps was practically following II Corps, but with its left flank somewhat exposed to hostile shell fire. During those days Maude first received reliable tidings of the casualties that had occurred in other corps than his own during the great retreat from Mons; news of that kind had previously been arriving rather in the form of vague rumours, some of which fortunately turned out to be incorrect. He learnt that he had lost many friends, that the Coldstream had suffered like most other regiments, and that amongst their killed was his cousin, Viscount Hawarden.

'After our long retirement it is delightful to be once more advancing,' he wrote from La Ferté Sous Jouarre on the Marne on the 9th, 'and this we have been doing for some days now. Yesterday we drove the Germans opposed to us across the River Marne, and shelled them till late at night as they were trying to get away. One of our brigades got across the Petit Morin River just before dark, and I went down to see how they were getting on. They were in a very difficult bit of country, for the Germans were above them in some woods and were firing down on them. At the end of the village thirty Germans had been cut off, but they would not surrender and prepared to resist till dark. They were most resolute and killed a very good officer .... It was late when I got back, and long after dark.'

Pulteney's troops had not found it by any means easy to force a passage over the Marne on the 9th, in face of the skilfully emplaced machine guns which the enemy brought to bear upon the points of passage. Lord French, who visited the corps headquarters early in the morning, refers particularly to its fight at La Ferté sous Jouarre in his book 1914. Maude was anxious to find some place on the river where advance would be unopposed and to try and get a few men across by surprise, but the project was not entertained. All attempts by 4th Division to win a way over the channel direct at La Ferté during the daytime were brought to a standstill by the machine gun and artillery fire from the further side, and it was not until after dark that 11th Brigade found it possible actually to reach the near bank. There they managed to seize a number of boats. In these a battalion of 11th Brigade and three battalions of 12th Brigade succeeded in effecting a crossing, whereupon the engineers constructed a pontoon bridge under very heavy fire 'R. E. did excellently,' Maude notes in his diary of the 10th – and the greater part of III Corps passed over the river by this bridge at a very early hour on the 10th.

When Pulteney's troops resumed advance on that day it at once became manifest that the Germans were in full retreat. Many prisoners were taken, wounded were discovered in a number of houses, and the roads were found to be littered with abandoned vehicles of all kinds, with munitions and with impedimenta. The infantry were jubilant, realising that the British regular had proved himself the superior of the vaunted foot soldier from the Fatherland at all points, and they made light of long marches that followed routes which were in indifferent condition, for heavy rains had set in. During the next day or two, III Corps was moreover uncomfortably sandwiched in between the French and II

Corps, there were misunderstandings as to the allotment of the communications, and Pulteney's force rather suffered in consequence. Although the staff enjoyed the advantage of horses and motor cars, and also of usually passing the night in comfortable quarters, they were very hard worked during these strenuous days. On the 11th Maude notes in his diary that, owing to orders generally not coming to hand before 11 p.m., to being called up frequently during the night, and to moving off daily between 4 a.m. and 5 a.m., they did not on the average get more than three hours' sleep in the twenty-four.

The advanced troops of the corps reached the River Aisne at a point a little to the east of Soissons late on the 12th, to find all the bridges along their front demolished and the enemy on the further side, well posted and ready to contest the passage. The 11th Brigade however managed to work its way across the remains of a broken down girder bridge during the night and to make good some important high ground beyond, a feat which prepared the way for pontoon bridges to be thrown and for other troops of the corps to pass the formidable obstacle. The arrival of the Franco-British forces on the Aisne, it may be observed, for practical purposes brought the prolonged Battle of the Marne and the ensuing pursuit to an end. The Germans had been worsted all along the front. They had suffered heavy losses in men and material; and they had suffered even more in morale, for they had encountered no such defeat as this for a hundred years. The distance which III Corps had covered between the Marne and the Aisne at their heels had been upwards of thirty miles.

The passage of the river by 11th Brigade on the night of the 12/13 may be said to have inaugurated, in so far as III Corps was concerned, that long-drawn-out combat, which eventually merged into stagnant, unprofitable, trench warfare and which has come to be known as the Battle of the Aisne. Pulteney's infantry, his gunners and his sappers performed a valuable service to the rest of the British Expeditionary Force on their right, as also to the French on their left, because, by securing a footing on the far side of the formidable obstacle, they in a measure paved the way for comrades on either hand to force a passage likewise. Some doubt existed for a day or two as to whether the opposition put up by the Germans on the line of the river merely meant delaying action in a naturally favourable position, while the bulk of the hostile legions pursued their way north-eastwards, or whether the enemy had resolved to make a definite stand. But it soon became apparent that the hostile retreat was at an end. II and III British Corps had a severe struggle to get across the Aisne, and the French likewise only advanced on the left of III Corps under considerable difficulty. III Corps itself was brought to a standstill almost on the ground won within the first few hours, and it spent the next three weeks in that situation, 'hanging on by our eyelids to the edge of the plateau, with a river with broken bridges behind us,' as Maude expressed it.

The 6th Division from England arrived near the front on the 16th, and should have completed General Pulteney's Corps, to which it properly belonged; Sir J. French however felt himself obliged to keep it as a general reserve for the time being. The troops in contact with the enemy gradually dug themselves in. But this did not prevent them from suffering somewhat heavy losses daily owing to the German shell fire, which was accurate and almost incessant, and the heavy howitzers which had been brought up by the opposing side caused many casualties. Maude comments in his diary and in his letters on the tremendous expenditure of artillery ammunition that was taking place, and on the great advantage enjoyed by the enemy in being much the better supplied.

'They (the enemy) are very strongly entrenched,' he wrote home on the 19th, 'and we are unable to make much impression against them; so we are just holding on to our positions, and the French are collecting a fresh army to outmanoeuvre them and turn their flank. It has been a hard week for the troops, for they have had to be in the trenches practically day and night, and it has been pelting rain almost without cessation. The shell fire has been stupendous all the week, for the Germans have 8-inch guns which throw an enormous shell, the explosion of which is almost deafening if you are anywhere near.... We are getting lots of reinforcements, so can keep merrily at it. One thousand five hundred men arrived today to reinforce the corps, so that replaces our casualties of the week, and leaves something to spare...

'The Germans are evidently very nervous, for last night they opened a fusillade at apparently nothing! I am very keen to get them to move forward by night attacks, for the Germans hate that sort of warfare, and we have practised it thoroughly. The other night an officer's patrol got right into the enemy's trenches and found them all asleep! So I feel that we could do a big thing that way; but I cannot quite get them to accept my suggestion, as it is thought too risky. Still, one cannot make war without taking some risks. I expect that we shall be here for another week or so, till the French movement develops. We have got a charming chateau for our headquarters, and I feel rather mean when it rains, thinking of all the troops who have got to be out in the wet; but I suppose we must be under cover to get our work done.

'Their infantry are not much good, except for discipline,' he wrote two days later, 'and not a patch on ours. Their artillery is excellent and very effective, but their cavalry are not very redoubtable, and we have seen little of the latter since we began to advance.'

The trials undergone by the troops on the Aisne were, as it was to turn out, merely a foretaste of experiences which would last for months and months to come. It is doubtful if many of the tacticians on the German side had foreseen that the campaign on the Western Front – and indeed on all fronts – was to degenerate into a stalemate form of trench warfare. The British Army at all events was wholly unprepared for such a development. Maude's hopes that the intervention of a new French army, coming up into line on the left and turning the enemy's flank, would compel the hostile legions to give way, were destined to be disappointed; for the Germans were able to meet and to neutralise this combination, of which great things were for a time expected both by General Joffre and by Sir J. French. The army was under command of General Castelnau and it assembled on the left of 6th French Army under General Maunoury, which like the British Expeditionary Force had been definitely brought to a standstill. Although Castelnau failed to roll up the German right as had been hoped, and thus to enable the Allies' forces on the Aisne to advance, his intervention had within a short space of time in reality the effect of changing the main line of battle from one running east and west to one running north and south.

This influence on the general situation was however gradual. Heavy fighting continued from time to time along the front that was in occupation of the British Expeditionary Force during the next ten days. The brunt of this however fell rather upon Sir D. Haig's and Sir H. Smith-Dorrien's troops than upon those of Pulteney, and in consequence of this the 6th Division, instead of remaining under the orders of its own corps commander, had to be distributed with the object of relieving or of assisting such units in the other two corps as had especially suffered or as were particularly heavily engaged. During the sedentary operations on the Aisne, Maude kept himself fit, in spite of heavy office work and of moving about chiefly by motor, by a run of a mile or so every morning.

'This continued inaction is very unsatisfactory,' he wrote home on 2 October, 'for one feels that it is opposed to the true spirit in which war must be made, in order to bring about decisive results. Wide turning movements as in South Africa are useful to manoeuvre an enemy out of a position, but they will never bring us nearer to the end of a campaign, which can only be effected by sledge-hammer blows against the enemy's field army. As it is, we seem to be losing our grip on the enemy here, while he is moving away available men to meet the French turning movement.

'There is still hard fighting all along the front daily; but we are merely on the passive defensive, and though we repel every attack handsomely we do not prevent them from detaching troops to the north. However there are indications that we may be on the move again before long, which is splendid. I should much like to get further forward, and feel one was doing more active work in connection with the fighting.'

The move very vaguely hinted at in the above quoted letter had in the case of II Corps actually begun on the previous night. Maude was careful to give no indications as to the nature of the delicate operation to which Sir J. French's army was being committed. The two commanders-in-chief had agreed that the British forces were to be extracted from their present position on the Aisne in the middle of the French host and were, together with some French troops, to be transported round to the north, so as to extend the front in the direction of Lille and beyond. This very important transfer of fighting resources was being undertaken, partly with the idea of outflanking the enemy, and partly with the object of establishing an army in an entirely new area which would be in a position to forestall and to confront any hostile effort that might be made to advance towards Calais and Boulogne, menacing the Straits of Dover. Both sides were, as a matter-of-fact, turning their attention simultaneously to the same point without either of them realising what the other was contemplating. But the result was to transfer the centre of strategic interest from the undulating, wooded country about the Aisne, to Flanders and to the low-lying country bordering on the western fringes of the French industrial and mining area of which Lille is the centre.

In pursuance of the project, II Corps, which had been fighting in the middle of the British front, was quietly picked up out of the line by night, and its place was taken partly by troops of I Corps on its right and partly by troops of III Corps on its left, these extending their flanks inwards so as to fill up the gap. 2 Corps moved off to the south-west, and in due course it entrained for the north. Most of the cavalry started off on the 2nd and 3rd, moving by march route in the same direction behind the French front. Then, on the night of the 6/7, the III Corps was deftly withdrawn out of front line and relieved by French troops. It moved south-westwards by road to the neighbourhood of Compiégne and began entraining in that neighbourhood on the afternoon of the 8th. This operation, which was executed most successfully and without the enemy learning for some time what was actually afoot, threw very heavy work upon General Pulteney's staff. The orders necessarily dealt with a very complicated problem, the more so as during the struggle on the Aisne some units of the corps had become inconveniently intermingled with those of I and II Corps.

'After being a month here all but four days,' Maude wrote on the 8th, 'we are off this afternoon to give the Germans a surprise in another direction, and as we shall be constantly on the move now you must not expect many letters. The troops, although the time has been a trying one in the trenches owing to constant shell fire, sniping and persistent attacks by the Germans, are in splendid fettle and capital spirits, and ready and anxious to take on the Germans in another direction .... The French did well yesterday and are very pleased with themselves today in consequence, so we start on the new phase under the best auspices.'

Maude himself motored on ahead to St Omer on the 10th. Most of III Corps were to detrain there and were to move up outside (i.e. on the left) of II Corps, which had already arrived in the new area and was pushing eastwards. Arrangements had to be made for the immediate distribution of III Corps on its detraining and for its subsequent advance.

'All the people seem to be delighted at our arrival,' he wrote on the 11th, 'and I have had some very complimentary remarks made to me about the men and their behaviour. One old lady said to me, 'How can you possibly be anything except on the winning side with such troops as yours!' .... Antwerp, as you will see, has fallen and the Belgian Army has evacuated it. They did not try to defend it. Our IV Corps, recently formed under Harry Rawlinson, is covering their retirement, and we hope to get them away. I am glad in a way, although sorry for the Belgians, for there was great danger that some of our troops might have got locked up in the town, and that would have been the worst thing that could happen. It is of the greatest importance that all our field troops should keep the field and be available to manoeuvre and to fight according to circumstances. If they were to be shut up in a garrison it would probably be only a matter of time before they were captured and destroyed.'

The view here expressed as to Antwerp would assuredly be endorsed by most soldiers. Maude would not seem to have been aware at the time that some British troops had actually been sent to the city, that a somewhat half-hearted attempt to defend it had been made instead of evacuating it in good time, and that the Anglo-Belgian troops concerned had suffered appreciable losses and were perhaps fortunate in escaping at all. The infantry of the III Corps began arriving at St Omer by train on the 11th. II Corps, which had already moved a considerable distance in the direction of Lille, was in the meantime finding itself more and more strongly opposed, and it was making but slow progress; the enemy forces in this northern area were apparently growing in numbers. The fall of Antwerp moreover seemed likely to liberate formidable German contingents which, it could safely be assumed, would hurry westwards and either try to prevent the junction of the retreating Belgian Army with the newly arrived IV Corps, or else endeavour to intervene between the Allied forces that were now coming up from the south, and the IV Corps and Belgian troops who were trying to form a junction with these. Orders for the infantry of III Corps to hurry forward and to come up in line with II Corps were therefore issued by Sir J. French, and arrangements were made to transport them from St Omer by motor-bus, a plan which on this occasion did not prove an unqualified success.

'Motor-buses rather a fiasco,' Maude wrote in his diary on the 18th. 'It was only a short march, that we could have done easily, but we waited for the buses according to orders and they were five to seven hours late, and consequently the advanced guard and mounted troops and first line transport moved at daybreak, but the two brigades of infantry moving by motors were not able to get there till 4 p.m., instead of 10 a.m. The first two brigades and the last two brigades had to start marching at 4 p.m. and were only picked up en route, except 1,200 of the 10th and 900 of the 11th Brigades who were able to get away in motor-buses at 6 p.m. They all got scattered in the darkness, and were not able to rejoin the division until next morning. Luckily the enemy did not interfere.'

This move was to near Hazebrouck, which Pulteney made his headquarters for the moment; its position relative to St Omer and to the region which was about to form the battleground of III Corps is shown on the inset map above. Beyond Hazebrouck the corps was advancing on to the low-lying plains of Flanders, and it was to begin operating over a terrain very different to the chalk uplands which overlook the Aisne. There was sharp fighting on the 18th with somewhat inferior German forces, composed

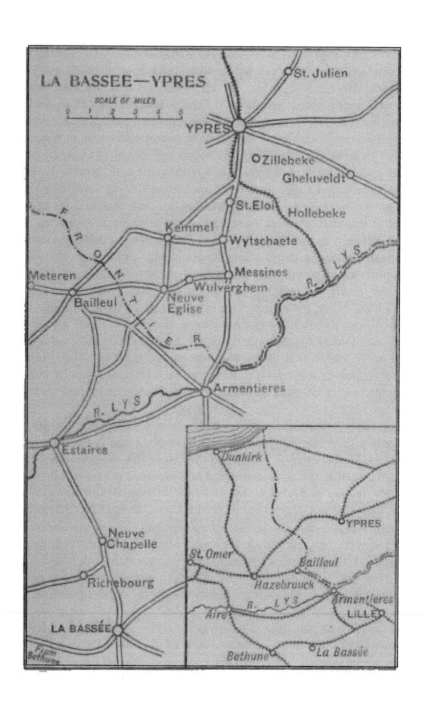

LA BASSEE—YPRES

SCALE OF MILES

St. Julien

YPRES

Zillebeke

Gheluveldt

St. Eloi

Hollebeke

Kemmel

Wytschaete

Meteren

Messines

Wulverghem

Bailleul

Neuve
Eglise

Armentieres

R. LYS

Estaires

Dunkirk

YPRES

Neuve
Chapelle

St. Omer

Bailleul

Richebourg

Hazebrouck

Armentieres

R. LYS

Aire

LILLE

LA BASSÉE

From
Bethune

Bethune

La Bassée

mainly of mounted troops but with infantry support; these stuck obstinately to their ground, as mist and fog interfered with the use of artillery and made offensive operations difficult. But Meteren – a name to become very familiar to the British Army during the next three years – was occupied, the combat continuing far into the night. Pulteney's divisions were constantly moving forward during the next two days, Bailleul being taken on the 14th; but progress was slow owing to the nature of the country and to the stubborn opposition offered by the hostile detachments, which were as usual well supplied with machine guns, and Maude chafed at the deliberation of the advance across the flats towards the Lys, realising the importance of securing the passage of that sluggish stream. He felt sure that the enemy would not be striving so hard to maintain a hold of this ground with inferior forces, unless there was some definite object in view. The left of the corps reached the river near Estaires late at night on the 15th, and the engineers at once started throwing bridges across. Some of I Corps were passing through Hazebrouck at this time, and Maude had opportunities of meeting the 2nd and 33rd Coldstream and of exchanging notes with them.

Part of 4th Division and 6th Division crossed the Lys during the 16th, and Armentiéres was occupied on the 17th; the greater part of 4th Division however worked along the left bank of the river, that being intended as its general line in the contemplated advance. Corps headquarters had remained at Hazebrouck till the Tuesday, but were now pushed on to the little town of Bailleul, which, having been in German occupation, was in a semi-ruinous condition – pillaged according to the usual practice of the brutal enemy. II Corps was advancing simultaneously on the right of 3 Corps, but was separated from it by a gap which was partially filled up by French detachments. I Corps was gradually detraining in rear and prepared to come up on the left, while communication had been established by the cavalry on the left with General Rawlinson's IV Corps that was moving southwards from about Ostend and Bruges, beyond which again were the Belgians. But the whole of the front that was more or less in occupation of the British was much extended, and as they moved eastwards they were constantly meeting with more and more determined resistance; for strong bodies of infantry were being hurried up to support the German mounted troops.

III Corps continued to press slowly forward beyond the Lys from the 17th to the 20th, but by the latter day it found itself confronted by at least equal hostile forces and almost thrown on the defensive. 'Our line is very much strung out and we have no reserves, which reacts on the nerves of the troops,' Maude wrote in his diary. That day the 19th Brigade, which was helping to fill the interval between III and II Corps, was driven back by a resolute hostile attack, and a somewhat awkward gap was created; but the situation was to a great extent retrieved during the night. Corps headquarters had been pushed forward from Bailleul to Armentiéres on the 19th; but that town was constantly under shell fire, two of the staff were wounded on the 20th, and, somewhat to Maude's disappointment, Pulteney consequently decided to withdraw headquarters to Bailleul.

The position, in so far as III Corps was concerned, had become for the time being one of stalemate, and all along the British front the enemy was showing up in strong force. Lord French states in his book that he abandoned all hope of an immediate offensive on the 21st.

'We have been having hard fighting for the last few days,' Maude wrote home on the 23rd, 'and we are still hard at it. The Germans are making a determined effort to roll us back, and have brought up every man that they can scrape together; consequently we have our hands pretty full, but we are doing well and giving the enemy plenty of punishment whenever he attacks. But we have for the time to suspend the forward movement. The 18th, 20th and 21st were particularly heavy days for us and we had in our corps about 4,000 casualties on the three days. Today our 6th Division is being strongly attacked, but all is going well.

'An officer from General Headquarters has just come in, 3 p.m., and has brought the news that I am to command the 14th Infantry Brigade. This will give me the rank of Brigadier General. Of course I am delighted at getting so good a command and think myself very lucky, though naturally I wish it could have been one of the Guards Brigades.

'The Indian troops arrived up here yesterday, and will probably be in action in a day or two. They look very fit and well, but the infantry do not like the paved roads; they hurt their feet.'

Maude left to take command of 14th Brigade that evening, and his connection with Pulteney's Corps thus came to an end, for 14th Brigade formed part of the 5th Division in II Corps. 'His greatest asset in South Africa and afterwards in the European war,' writes Sir W. Pulteney, 'was the way he would see everything for himself where any doubt existed; in fact he gave one so much confidence in this respect that it prevented one as a commander from going oneself on some occasions.'

Although he had spent less than two months as a prominent member of the corps staff in the field, he had acquired much valuable experience during that strenuous period. The very fact that III Corps had been somewhat unlucky, first of all in being the last to take the field and afterwards in being so long shorn of one of its divisions, had perhaps made actual staff work all the more difficult to carry out, and had caused the lessons to be learnt from it in some respects all the more valuable. In studying Maude's diaries and letters of these few weeks, certain of his qualities as a staff officer and as a soldier are made very apparent. As a staff officer he had the well-being of the inferior staffs and of the troops constantly in mind. He frequently complains of the late arrival of orders from above, not because of the inconvenience which this caused to himself and to his immediate associates, but because of the still greater inconvenience that it necessarily caused to divisional and brigade staffs to whom, after some unavoidable further delay, these orders had to be communicated. He attached great importance to orders being issued with the utmost possible promptitude on all occasions, and was by no means tolerant of laxity in this respect. Still, in these matters he was merely voicing what are generally accepted principles (even if those principles are not always followed by their advocates in practice); he was giving expression to views that are not unusual in a highly trained officer of wide and very varied experience, such as Maude was when he went to the front in 1914.

But what is even more noticeable, alike in his diary and in the numerous letters that he managed to write home during this anxious time, is the unmistakable evidence that they afford of the qualities which make the natural leader of men, concealed though these were behind the mask of the genial, courteous, well-informed, capable, methodical administrator and office man. Maude's delight when orders came to hand that the army, which had day after day for nearly a fortnight been falling back before the rising tide of German invasion, was to turn upon his pursuers, was shared by the whole force. But few belonging to it were perhaps more thoroughly discontented than he when that force, after being brought up short on the Aisne, found the situation developing almost imperceptibly into sedentary warfare after its short sharp spell of exceedingly mobile operations. Then, when the British contingent came to be transported round to fresh fields and pastures new in the north, he was straining at the leash, impatient to press restlessly forward, bent on brushing the not very formidable opposition met with during the first two or three days unceremoniously aside if possible; he realised that even if fighting meant losses at the moment, it would probably effect an important purpose and might peradventure save lives in the end.

Even that small matter of the retirement of corps headquarters from Armentiéres to Bailleul illustrates the character of the man as a soldier in the field. From Bailleul to Armentiéres does not mean more than a quarter of an hour's run by motor. Dealing with delicate operations, solving problems on paper and wrestling with complicated administrative questions, can never be so easy a task when carried out under shell fire as when dealt with in quieter conditions. But the instincts of the fighter induced this member of an army corps staff to ignore the inconvenience involved, in his eagerness to be as near as possible to the thick of the fray. There are few officers whose hearts when the enemy is in the gate will not be gladdened by an intimation that they are to take up an active command, but, of the many gallant British soldiers who found themselves called upon to assume charge of brigades
in the field between 1914 and 1918, not one probably received the news with greater pleasure than did Stanley Maude.

CHAPTER VII
In Command of the 14th Infantry Brigade

Tue 14th Brigade to which Maude had been appointed was, as it happened, one with which he was already familiar, for it formed part of the 5th Division which he had only left a few months before. It moreover happened to be the brigade that had been quartered at the Curragh when he was there. Sir C. Fergusson no longer commanded the division, although he had brought it out to France in August; he had been promoted lieutenant general in the meantime, and had been replaced by Major General T. L. N. Morland. The division still formed part of II Corps under Sir H. Smith-Dorrien, and it was placed at the moment on the right of the British line, with the 3rd Division on its left. 14th Brigade was the left brigade of the division, so that Maude's command was next to the 3rd Division, and it was at the time of his joining occupying trenches about Richebourg, a little to the north-west of La Bassée. The map 'La Bassée-Ypres' above illustrates the movements of the brigade while he was its chief.

Maude motored over to take up command on the afternoon of the 23rd, and he reported himself on the way to Generals Smith-Dorrien and Morland at their respective headquarters, arriving at his own near Richebourg long after dark, and finding Lieutenant Colonel J. R. Longley of the East Surreys temporarily in charge. The brigade at the moment consisted of the 2nd K.O.S.B., the 3rd Worcester, the 1st East Surrey, the 1st D.C.L.I., and the 2nd K.O.Y.L.I. Of these only the East Surreys and the D.C.L.I. properly formed part of it as it had originally arrived in France; the 2nd Manchesters were temporarily detached. During his eight months in command Maude often had outside battalions temporarily under his orders, and was from time to time called upon to send off his own to be attached for the moment to other brigades; but the battalions properly forming his brigade throughout were the 1st Devons, besides the East Surreys, D.C.L.I., and Manchesters; the 5th Cheshire was added in February 1915. He found that the strength of the five battalions under him when he joined was 78 officers and 3,209 other ranks; so that his force was considerably below war establishment. Besides the five battalions, he had for the time being under his orders a brigade of field artillery, a field howitzer battery, a company of field engineers, and a field ambulance. Captain Dick-Cunyngham of the Gordons was brigade-major.

'Dirty headquarters in an estaminet,' he wrote in his diary next day, 'but there seems to be nothing better available, and it was under continuous shell fire all day, though luckily they never quite got the range. Plenty of Black Marias falling, and the road we walked up in the afternoon was strewed with fragments. Heavy attack in the morning on the 13th Brigade on our right, and in the evening and during the night on the 7th Infantry Brigade on our left, but both repulsed.'

The general situation at the Flanders end of the Western Front was at this time a singularly interesting one. The Allies under Sir J. French and General Foch had been making a great effort to outflank their opponents, simultaneously with joining up with the Belgian Army coming from Antwerp; but the associated chiefs had only just begun to realise the formidable strength of the forces gathering against them. Nor would the Germans appear to have been well posted in the disposition of the armies that were opposed to them in Flanders. In so far as the British Expeditionary Force was concerned, I Corps, IV Corps (it only included at the moment 7th Division), and the bulk of the cavalry, were still being pushed forward on the left; but II and III Corps further to the south had already been brought to a standstill and they were holding entrenched positions along most of their front. The Indian Corps was coming up from the centre of France, and the (3rd) Lahore Division began to arrive at Estaires in the rear of the II and III Corps on the 22nd.

The Germans were about to make a determined effort to roll up the Allies' forces north of the Lys, while keeping those that were south of that river fully occupied. The position indeed was that either high command had made plans for turning the flank of the other, but that the Germans were in the stronger force of the two on the flank and that this had only been just discovered by Sir J. French and General Foch. The result was to bring about a great battle of encounter north of the Lys, in which I Corps, 7th Division and the cavalry, together with the French operating alongside of them, found themselves opposed to almost desperate odds while covering an unduly extended front. The furious affrays that ensued have by common consent been given the name of the First Battle of Ypres; but determined combats were at the same time in progress south of the Lys, where the enemy also succeeded in gradually bringing somewhat superior forces to bear against II and III Corps. Maude on taking over 14th Brigade found himself involved in this struggle, his troops occupying awkward ground and under heavy artillery fire.

On taking stock of his brigade and of its position, he found that it was suffering somewhat severe losses from the enemy's shell, and that his men were very tired after nearly a fortnight of almost continuous fighting. They had been obliged to do a great deal of digging and had enjoyed very little sleep; commanding officers, regimental officers, and rank and file were nevertheless all alike in good spirits and full of confidence. Realising that stationary operations were likely to be the order of the day in this region, he at once set to work to have obstacles developed covering his front, to construct communication trenches (the importance of which he was one of the first to perceive), and to establish a system of supporting trenches with the object of permitting a larger proportion of the infantry to be withdrawn from the actual front line. The character of the ground favoured concealment of small parties and sniping operations, and he found it difficult to reach the headquarters of his different battalions on his first day with the brigade, as the roads were under continuous rifle fire.

'Tried twice but unsuccessfully,' he wrote in his diary, and this experience confirmed him in his view that communication trenches were an absolute necessity in this kind of warfare;
it was a point that he always paid great attention to, not only as a brigadier but also later on as a divisional commander in the Gallipoli Peninsula and in Mesopotamia.

The Germans kept delivering partial attacks for the next day or two against portions of the front occupied by the 3rd and 5th Divisions; these were, however, generally repulsed with no great difficulty and with loss to the enemy. But on the 27th 3rd Division was heavily assailed by strong hostile forces, and was obliged to fall back at some points, the situation becoming so threatening that towards evening Maude was ordered to deliver a counterattack with such troops of his own as he could employ, reinforced by other battalions from the 5th Division placed especially under his command for the purpose. As this was practically the first occasion on which he had found himself in charge of a mixed body of troops undertaking a special operation of importance, his account of the action, which was written home four days later, may appropriately be quoted. The record in his diary goes into considerable detail, and it could not easily be followed without a plan:

> On 27th the brigade on our left were driven out of a place called Neuve Chapelle. I was given three and a half battalions additional to my own, and Sir Horace suggested that I should personally direct the attack, so I sent off one battalion at once to cover some ground, and hurried off the remaining two and a half battalions as soon as I could collect them. By the time however that we were all assembled and ready to commence the attack it was pitch dark, and no moon. The ground over which we were to attack was unknown to me and to the battalions with me. We had not been able to reconnoitre the positions of our troops and of the Germans beforehand, and the battalions that I had with me had been badly shaken by their losses during the last few days. Consequently I thought it would be more prudent to delay action till daylight.
>
> I therefore motored in to see General Morland, 5th Division, and General Mackenzie, 3rd Division, to represent the state of affairs, feeling that there was still time to deliver the attack before daylight if they still so wished. However, they thoroughly agreed with my view, and Sir Horace told me next day that he was much relieved to hear that I had decided not to attack by night.
>
> The next day the attack was delivered and failed, so I don't know what would have happened if we had gone forward by night. I commanded my mixed lot of battalions during the fight that day, in addition to my own regular command, and we had a very exciting day. For when the Indians were driven back I sent forward two battalions to stop the gap, and we successfully slackened the German advance. It was an interesting day. The shell fire was terrific all the time.

'Only once did I see Joe Maude really rattled,' writes Lieutenant Colonel Dick-Cunyngham, the then brigade-major of 14th Brigade, with regard to this affair, 'and that was soon after he took over command of the brigade, when we were fighting round Richebourg-l'Avoue at the end of October 1914. Our lines had been heavily attacked and shelled for many hours, and the Germans had captured Neuve Chapelle on our left during the evening. About 7 p.m. we got orders to make a counterattack and retake the village, and certain troops were sent us from another brigade to carry out the counterattack. When they arrived, one could see at once that they were not in a fit state to make the attack, and the circumstances under which the counterattack had been ordered were moreover now completely altered. But Maude considered that an order was an order and had to be carried out. Finally he was persuaded to postpone the counterattack and to make a personal report to the divisional commander.'

Actually Maude with his special force was on the 28th attacking on the right, while other troops were endeavouring to retake Neuve Chapelle from in front. But the effort failed, and that village remained in the enemy's hands until it was captured in an important action four months later. On the night of the 29/30 14th Brigade was relieved in front line by the Garwhal Brigade of the (7th) Meerut Division which had been coming up from the south during the past two or three days. Its new commander was delighted with the behaviour and bearing of the officers and men over whom he had assumed command. The brigade had suffered heavily at Le Cateau and had been fighting hard in difficult country ever since arriving in the northern area from the Aisne; but all ranks were in good heart. 'Troops very fit and cheery,' he wrote on the 31st, 'in spite of the severe work they have had. All four regiments have done splendidly and never budged an inch in the most trying circumstances.' 31 October and 1 November, it will be remembered, were especially critical days further to the north, where an attenuated line of British infantry and cavalry, opposed to vastly superior numbers in front and to the south-west of Ypres, could barely hold their own. Only the rare grit and heroism of the troops, confidently handled under untoward conditions, prevented a disaster there which must have had far-reaching effects on the whole course of the war. The sound of incessant cannonade from that direction was heard where 14th Brigade was, and all were aware that a desperate struggle must be in progress.

The brigade now nominally formed a reserve to the Indian troops, and it was placed for the time being under their corps commander, Sir J. Willcocks; it had however to be constantly on the quivive, as the enemy was particularly active just during those days, and the Indian Corps was at times hard pressed. Most of the rest of the 5th Division had gone some distance further back, and was resting in billets. The difference in staff methods between those in vogue in the Indian forces and those to which Maude had been accustomed at home and with the original Expeditionary Force, gave rise to some inconvenience during the period that he found himself attached to General Willcocks' Corps, and, as it turned out, his battalions although they were supposed to be resting got very little rest. There was marching and counter-marching, and eventually the brigade had to go back into the trenches as early as the night of 7/8 November in relief of the 8th Infantry Brigade. This was at a point somewhat further to the north than the old position which it had occupied south of Neuve Chapelle. It consisted now of the 1st Devons and 2nd Manchesters, besides the East Surreys and D.C.L.I.

'The part of the line that we are holding now is as flat as the palm of one's hand,' Maude wrote home on 10 November, 'and so constantly fire swept, and it requires some skill (and luck) to get up to the firing line, especially as one does not know quite when the outbursts of firing are going to begin. I like to go up occasionally, as one learns exactly what commanding officers have got to say, and one gets into closer touch with the feelings and the wants of the troops. I went up and saw all the battalions last night, but had to pick my time as the enemy had been shelling us very hard all day, and they had got the exact range of the road that I wanted to go by. But we managed to dodge them all right, and as a matter-of-fact the musketry up there was not so severe as usual last night. There is always a lot of sniping going on however, and we are bothered to a certain extent by German snipers who have crept behind our lines and who are behind our lines of trenches; but I am having steps to have them stalked and shot and all the battalions are on the qui vive for them.'

Although the nature of the country rendered the construction of deep trenches very difficult where the Indians were, moderately good cover had been created by strenuous labour, and the line was fairly well protected by barbed wire. On the night of 14/15 Maude's battalions were relieved by the newly arrived 8th Division, which properly belonged to IV Corps. The brigade was thereupon taken back into the 5th Division, and it again came under the orders of Sir H. Smith-Dorrien and General Morland.

'I think I am very lucky in getting such good regiments in my brigade,' Maude wrote on the 14th. 'They are all first rate, and I have every confidence in them. They are still weak – especially two of the battalions, 500 and 600 respectively – and the other two are each about 800 strong. This is owing to the heavy casualties we had about a fortnight ago, but I hope we shall soon get drafts to fill up with. We have already had one or two, as a matter-of-fact, but expect more. Officers are a difficulty, but this is common to the whole army, for we have all lost heavily in officers; and, with the best intentions in the world, it is impossible to produce trained officers (or men for the matter of that) with a few months' training.

'Discipline is everything in a war like this, and it is the regiments that have most discipline that shine out above the others. But discipline, equally with training, cannot be acquired in a day, but must be the result of continuous gradual military education. But what we have lacked in peace time, owing to those who thought that they knew better than soldiers, has been compensated for as far as possible by the splendid work of the regimental officers and their men. Speaking mainly from what I have seen of my own brigade, no praise is too high for their conduct, tenacity, endurance and devotion to duty, and to my mind no reasonable amount of force brought against them will beat them.'

His brigade only enjoyed one complete day's rest after quitting the Indian Corps and rejoining its own division, for on the night of 16/17 it was called upon to take over a stretch of front line about Wulverghem, between Bailleul and Messines, from the 156th Regiment of the 39th French Division, which division had been holding the line between the Indian Corps and the III Corps. The relief proved a lengthy and difficult business, as the advanced works were only about thirty yards from the German ones. The trenches were found to be shallow and imperfect, and much work had to be got through by night under close and harassing musketry fire before they could be considered as giving adequate security. The brigade was joined on the 17th by the 1st Norfolks, which brought it up to a strength of five battalions. Maude also had under his orders for the time being a French battalion on the left, three British field batteries and one horse battery, also a French field battery.

Wulverghem was in Belgian territory, and the roads on that side of the border were found to be much inferior to those on the French side. There was moreover a dearth of buildings and farms, which made adequate billeting a great difficulty. The weather had turned much colder, and the troops were suffering serious discomfort in the trenches as the full supplies of warm winter clothing for them had not yet arrived. Maude however set himself to overcome these difficulties by energetic action. Coke was available, and large quantities of this form of fuel were sent up to the troops in front line, who succeeded in making braziers by various devices and thus turning it to account. Buildings were moreover transformed into bath-houses with the assistance of the Royal Engineers, and arrangements for warm water set on foot. That no time was to be lost in making full preparations for winter had indeed been shown by one or two cases of frostbite; but almost a superabundance of warm clothing came to hand after a few days.

The Germans were mainly on the defensive in front of the brigade, and they contented themselves with shelling the lines very heavily at times. The Prince of Wales, who had recently joined Sir J. French's staff and who was staying at Sir H. Smith-Dorrien's headquarters, paid brigade headquarters a visit on 20th and again on 25th. 'He was very anxious to go up with me to the front trenches,' Maude wrote home, 'but I told him it was impossible, His Royal Highness' eagerness to penetrate into zones where shells were dropping and bullets were flying, if he could manage it, caused senior officers frequent qualms at this time. Some additional battalions were attached to Maude's command at this juncture, so that he had altogether eight under his orders when the time came for his brigade to be relieved on the night of 28/29. It moved back some four miles across the Franco-Belgian border and went into billets north of Bailleul.

'The men are in splendid spirits,' Maude wrote on the 30th, 'and very healthy considering all they have gone through. In fact in my brigade the 'normal' sick as opposed to casualties are only about the same as on manoeuvres. I have been round two battalions today talking to the men and hearing their experiences; they are all very keen to get on and to have another go at the Germans. The fighting has been spasmodic during the last few days. Everyone is refitting and replacing casualties. But there has still been a good deal of shelling and sniping, and in this brigade we have lost 150 killed and wounded, including five officers killed, during the week. There is a westerly wind blowing today, and for the first time for three months one is out of earshot of the cannonade; it seems quite strange without it.'

The King was paying the first of his many visits to his troops on the Western Front while 14th Brigade was back in billets on this occasion, resting, and on 3 December His Majesty inspected Maude's force.

'Parade for King at 2.40 p.m.,' Maude wrote in his diary. All went well. Received him with Royal Salute, troops on parade and keeping ground taking the word from me. Gave them a short practice beforehand just to brush them up. King asked me how long I had been out and what I had been doing previous to getting brigade. Said he was so glad I had got one. Asked for my arm and took me on box of his motor car till we got to end of my command. Gave three cheers for King after parade and another Royal Salute, all by my word of command. Prince of Wales also present, and D.C.L.I. gave three cheers for Duke of Cornwall.'

Although 14th Brigade was performing excellent service and had full confidence in its leader, Maude would not seem to have in all respects shown himself to be an easy man for his staff to work with at this time, or to have quite carried the commanding officers serving under him with him in all that he did. He had a wonderful insight into every kind of administrative detail, and he went most carefully into the minutest points connected with the feeding and the comfort of the troops, greatly to their advantage in many cases. But he had his own ideas of what a man could do in a day's work – and they were large ideas. Most of his commanding officers were of opinion that the men were being overworked; but he never changed his mind, and he gradually trained the rank and file to get accustomed to very long hours. Always fit himself and a strong man of fine physique, he perhaps hardly made sufficient allowances for others not possessing to the full those advantages.

'He was about the most systematic man I have ever met, and was known in the brigade as 'Systematic Joe',' writes Lieutenant-Colonel Dick-Cunyngham; 'he got up at the same hour and did everything at the same time every day of the week, and hated doing anything that upset his usual daily routine.

'Before he took over the brigade I was doing staff officer's work– writing all orders, etc., thinking ahead, and putting the tactical situation before my brigadier. But when Joe Maude arrived I was no longer allowed to do this, and I naturally at first resented it.

'On one occasion indeed I had a row with him and told him I was not his staff officer, but merely his clerk. His dictation of orders and messages every day was a tiresome business; they were long, often contained repetitions, and entailed an enormous amount of work on the Signal Section. It took me over two months to get him to condense his daily order into fewer lines, with a 'working-party table.' It used to be quite a joke in the brigade when I was found fast asleep at my desk, trying to write at his dictation. Yet, although there may have been times when one felt that to serve on Maude's staff was not altogether pleasant, we got by degrees to know his ways, and I think that I am right in saying that when he left the brigade for home every one was sorry to lose him.'

As has been mentioned at the end of the previous chapter, Maude attached great importance to the early issue of orders, in the interests of inferior staffs and of the units concerned. In that respect he was considerate and the troops affected benefited thereby. But promptitude in this respect is not the only point to be borne in mind. Conciseness is of almost equal importance. On active service orders and messages have to be transmitted by various means to their destination, the transaction necessarily involving labour in some quarter; they have then to be copied by officers or clerks, working often under great difficulties; and then every superfluous word becomes a nuisance. It is much easier for a person dictating to dictate a long message, than it is to dictate a short message which says the same thing. It is those who have to take the message down, those who have to transmit it, and those who may have to copy it, or parts of it, away out in the dug-outs, who suffer from any redundancy.

14th Brigade went back to the front during 4 and 5 December, changing places with the 13th Brigade which had relieved it less than a week before, and occupying nearly the same ground as before, with headquarters at Neuve Eglise. A Territorial battalion, the Queen Victoria's Rifles, one of the first of such units to arrive in the theatre of war, joined the brigade, mainly for training purposes and as a temporary measure, on the 4th. The return to the trenches on this occasion took place in particularly inclement and trying weather. There were torrents of rain and sleet, the cold was extreme, and as a result of the deluge the trenches were flooded and afterwards proved most difficult to drain. Their sides moreover kept falling in. Maude started working parties to cut up brushwood and to make fascines for flooring the excavations and for revetting them where necessary, and the situation was gradually improved; but life in the trenches was becoming very trying. He moreover insisted upon a great development in respect to elaborating communication trenches and supporting trenches, as he realised the importance of being in a position to mass considerable bodies of infantry close up to the firing line in case of emergency, alike for purposes of defence and for purposes of offence. The enemy in front of 14th Brigade, as also of the 3rd Division on its left, enjoyed, it should be observed, all the advantage of ground; all the higher portions of the Messines-Wytschaete-Hollebeke ridge were in hostile possession, so that the British were more or less dominated and overlooked by the opposing side. The Germans moreover were very strongly entrenched, their whole front was well protected by elaborate wire entanglements, and the high ground provided them with good artillery observation stations. It was also easier for them to drain their trenches than it was for the British troops to do so, owing to the general lie of the ground.

'Last night too the weather was very bad,' Maude wrote home on the 8th; 'floods of rain, and you would have laughed to see me coming back from the trenches, slipping and sliding about in the slush – which was nearly up to one's knees in some places – tumbling into ditches and shell holes filled with water, for it was pitch black and one could not see five yards ahead. I took one header into a ditch and came out in a state somewhat similar to that after my bath when I was out with the Kildares last year, though not quite so bad; and the excitement was intensified at one point by a sniper putting a bullet between my brigade-major, who was walking just in front of me, and myself. Of course it was only a chance shot, as he could not possibly see us.'

The enemy was comparatively quiescent during the first few days that the brigade was back at the front, and on the 14th somewhat important offensive operations were started on our side. It had been arranged with the French that an attack should be delivered by 3rd Division, acting in close cooperation with the 32 and 16 French Corps on its left, against the uplands about Wytschaete and Hollebeke. The result of the heavy fighting of the latter part of October and the early days of November in the region to the north of where 14th Brigade now was, had been to give the enemy possession of the highest ground round practically three sides of Ypres. Wytschaete, due south of the place and less than five miles from it, enabled the Germans to command the approaches to the town with artillery fire very effectively, and the capture of that village was therefore particularly desirable. The project was that, so soon as the 3rd Division and the French should have accomplished their purpose, Maude on their right would advance against Messines, which lay two miles south of Wytschaete; but in the first instance he was merely to demonstrate and to keep the enemy immediately in front of him occupied. Suggestions were made that some of his troops should attempt minor local attacks on particular stretches of hostile trench, besides demonstrating; but he was opposed to such spasmodic ventures.

The offensive actually began on the 14th, and on that day and the following three days Maude and his staff proceeded before daybreak to a small farm well forward, from which a good view was obtainable. The operation however only produced minor successes, and merely enabled the line held by the 3rd Division to be slightly advanced. The high ground was not captured, and the French on the left of 3rd Division made scarcely any way at all. Fighting went on for four days and then gradually petered out, the German entrenchments and entanglements proving too strong to be broken through without a much heavier artillery bombardment than was practicable. Maude's share in the proceedings was therefore confined to maintaining a vigorous artillery fire, while his battalions expended a large amount of ammunition with their rifles and machine guns – about half a million rounds on the first two days; he did not altogether like these tactical methods; they taught the infantry to fire without aiming, seeing that their task was merely to keep sweeping the ground in front of them with bullets. 14th Brigade was relieved on the 17th, and it went back into billets in rear for a rest.

'One of the saddest parts of my day is my daily visit to hospital,' Maude wrote on the 20th. 'I have just been to see a very sad case. One of my officers was wounded three days ago, being shot through the neck and spinal cord, so he was paralysed below the neck. He was however wonderfully cheery, although he could scarcely speak, and seemed such a nice fellow. He cannot live long, they tell me.

'We have wounded varying from ten to fifty a day, and in addition twenty sick. I cannot bear seeing the wounded, I don't know why; but they always seem glad to see one and to be spoken to.

'The men are wonderfully cheery in spite of their hardships. The other day I met a man in the Manchesters being carried to hospital with his foot bound up, so asked him what was the matter. He said 'Rheumatism.' I said 'Nonsense, you've got gout. You've been drinking too much in the trenches.' 'Yes,' he replied, 'there was plenty of water there,' and roared with laughter. They are most amusing, and I like talking to them quietly at times. Then there is the other side of the picture, when I have to jump down their throats for being slack. I have got some footballs for them, and we are having great games while here during these four days. They are playing league matches, which should last a long time judging by the few occasions we have for playing.'

Maude not only made it a practice to visit hospital daily if he possibly could manage it, but he also invariably attended the funeral of any one of his officers who was killed or died of wounds within reach; he moreover often attended the funerals of non-commissioned officers and men when he was not too occupied. The brigade went back into the trenches again on the 23rd, and was therefore in them during Christmas time, the line taken up being somewhat further to the south than the section which had been in its occupation a few days before. The trenches were found to be in very bad condition owing to the wet, and, as it proved almost impossible to improve them, Maude decided to have entirely new trenches dug along certain stretches of the front by night in advance of the previous firing line. This work was skilfully and successfully carried out at most points, and without the enemy being aware of what was in progress till it was completed.

Some very noteworthy changes in the organisation of the British troops were carried out at the end of the year, and ought to be recorded. The Expeditionary Force was reconstituted as two armies, the First Army under Sir Douglas Haig, and the Second Army under Sir H. Smith-Dorrien; Sir Horace was succeeded in command of the II Corps by the late head of the 5th Division, Sir C. Fergusson, so that Maude found himself again under his old chief of the Curragh period. The intention was that the Second Army, which was constituted out of the II, III, and V Corps, should be on the left, and the First Army should be on the right. V Corps was being formed from 27th and 28th Divisions, which had been organised in England out of battalions and batteries brought home from far distant foreign garrisons. Major-General J. R. Longley, who had been commanding officer of the East Surrey since the beginning, left 14th Brigade about this time to take up command of a brigade himself, and his views with regard to Maude as a chief may be recorded here:

> I was only about two months in 14th Brigade after he took it over before passing on to a brigade command, but that was more than long enough to realise his powers of leadership. He was not altogether a stranger to us, having been previously G.S.O. to the 5th Division when my battalion first joined it in 1912.

> We all appreciated our good fortune in having a man like him as our brigade commander. All ranks had the utmost confidence in him, and felt that all would be well in the brigade with 'Joey' at their head. Time only served to strengthen the esteem and confidence in which he was held by his brigade, and I am sure that there was a general feeling of personal loss when he left it on promotion.

Maude's brigade went back out of the line to rest for a few days at Bailleul immediately after the New Year, and returned to the trenches on the 10th in a somewhat different sector from that left a week earlier. They were in very bad order owing to the wet, and much labour was necessary to make them more habitable and reasonably secure. General

Morland, who used to visit brigade headquarters daily, suggested shortly afterwards that it might be better if Maude were to take over his present position in the front permanently, and if the plan of frequent reliefs were to come to an end – a proposal entirely to Maude's taste, as he felt sure that his battalions would work even better than they had been doing under such conditions. The troops were having a trying time owing to the incessant wet weather and were suffering considerable hardship in consequence, and this somewhat increased the numbers on the sick list, which was a matter that always caused the brigadier concern. The enemy, on the other hand, was showing little activity except with artillery; but the German guns and howitzers were very lively from time to time, and caused appreciable losses; the village of Neuve Eglise where the brigade headquarters was fixed was often ' shelled violently.

'Shelling greatly due to stupidity of men who will stand and gape at aeroplanes,' Maude wrote in his diary in some irritation on 29 January. 'On the last two occasions when we have been shelled I warned every one that in consequence of this stupidity we were certain to be shelled, and on each occasion my prophecy came true.'

A week later, on 6 February, occurs this entry: 'Thirty-one years' service, but don't feel like it. What an eventful life to look back upon, and how interesting.'

Writing home on the 7th, he remarked: 'Nothing very exciting going on here. They have taken to shelling us pretty regularly two or three times a day in our headquarters, but for so far they have not done any very good shooting, and it is only occasionally that they get a lucky shell in. However, directly they begin to shell us, I turn all my guns on to Messines, which is the corresponding village opposite, so I suspect we do them much more harm than they do us. Our trenches are getting on splendidly. I have about 1400 or 1500 men working at them each night, building up and repairing traverses, shoring and revetting them, baling them out, and draining and making shelters for the men. They work splendidly, all four battalions, and it is so satisfactory to see the progress each time one goes round. The whole line is three or four times as strong as it was when we took it over, and we have no fears if we are attacked in anything like reasonable numbers. I don't think much of the lot we have got opposite to us, as it is impossible to stir them into any sort of activity. A few days ago we bombarded them from trench mortars, then for two nights we turned machine guns on to their working parties, and last night we pelted them with rifle grenades from our nearest trenches. But none of these 'insults' seemed to stir them up to any response. In fact, they seemed to be afraid to take any sort of aggressive action.'

In respect to the shelling of Maude's headquarters, it may be observed that both the corps commander and the divisional commander considered its position to be somewhat unduly exposed, and that they made representations to him on the subject. But he was unwilling to make a change, and he was a man who was not easily influenced in a matter of this kind once he had made up his mind. 'It is scarcely right for a brigadier to be always moving about from place to place, when the men have to stop where they are,' he remarks in his diary. But under instructions from the corps commander, General Morland early in March insisted on the headquarters being moved out of Neuve Eglise.[4] The early days of the month of February passed quietly in the region where 14th Brigade was located. In the middle of the month Maude heard privately from his friend General Lambton, who was Sir J. French's Military Secretary, that it was proposed to appoint him Brigadier General on the General Staff in VI Corps, which was about to be formed, and he was greatly put out by the news. 'Terrible blow,' he wrote in his diary, 'as I love my brigade, and the work is astonishingly interesting. Besides, one feels that one is doing some fighting here, whereas back with a corps one might as well be in England.' A few days later he heard that he had been mentioned a second time in despatches and that he had been awarded the C.B. The project of transferring him from his brigade to the staff eventually fell through – possibly because he did not conceal his preference for remaining where he was from Lambton, and also because Generals Fergusson and Morland were both very anxious to keep him.

It had been decided at General Headquarters that an important offensive was to be carried out by the First Army in the region of Neuve Chapelle (where 14th Brigade had been located when Maude took it over in October), and with the object of assisting this operation indirectly II Corps had been instructed to be aggressive for the time being. Maude gave his brigade directions accordingly on the 9th, explaining that the action of battalions was to be limited to organised sniping, machine gun fire, rifle and hand grenade activity, sapping, and trying to capture enemy patrols and to destroy the German wire entanglements. He was particularly pleased with the work done in these directions on the

---

[4] He scored off me by moving up nearly a mile closer to the front,' writes Sir C. Fergusson.

following night, and especially mentions the skill and dash of two young officers in his diary. He was always very careful to recognise good service and to send his congratulations to those concerned when any small success was achieved; when writing home on the 3rd he had expressed unbounded pleasure at seeing that his battalions had received a fair share of rewards in a recent Honours Gazette. The assistance afforded to the First Army by II Corps took a more active form on the 12th, for on that day 3rd Division, alongside 5th, delivered an attack, and Maude's guns gave what support they could; the operation was not successful in itself, but it no doubt served the purpose of holding the enemy and of preventing any hostile reinforcements being sent south towards Neuve Chapelle. The attack of the First Army, although it had achieved a considerable measure of success, had not led to the complete rupture of the German front which had been hoped for, although a dent had been made in it; and the latter part of February was unmarked by any incident worthy of note.

Rumours reached Maude several times during the early part of March that his brigade was going to be moved north nearer to Ypres, and these reports proved to be true in a measure; but as it turned out the move, which was made on the 24th, was only to about Kemmel, situated six miles north of Neuve Eglise.

'Very sad that we shall lose our trenches on which we have spent so much trouble and labour, and had hoped that, till the advance came, we might retain them,' Maude had written in his diary on the 19th. 'But it is the fortune of war and we must take the rough with the smooth. I fancy that those we are going to are not nearly as good as these, but luckily I have made a private hoard of sandbags, as I know that stores will be the difficulty, and I have from 15,000 to 20,000 ready to hand. The only difficulty will be to transport them.'

He was much gratified after the change at receiving a message from General Pulteney, commanding III Corps (one of whose brigades had taken over 14th Brigade trenches), that for the first time in the campaign the corps had no complaint to make on taking over other people's trenches. On the other hand, he found much work to be necessary in the sector taken over, and as the sniping at night was heavy it made any development and improvement of the trenches difficult at first. He always paid great attention to the work of the batteries that happened to be from time to. time attached to his brigade, so as to ensure immediate cooperation between the guns and the infantry in case of emergency, and so as to counter hostile shell fire promptly should

140

this suddenly become troublesome. The shortage of artillery ammunition was however making itself much felt at this time, and the gunners were consequently working under considerable difficulties. Maude had seven batteries under him in his new position, but they were all field or horse artillery units, and as they were only provided with shrapnel they were of little use for battering the enemy trenches; he however occasionally succeeded in getting some of the heavy guns which were not under his orders turned on to these.

Another move was however in prospect, for Maude was told on 1 April that his brigade was to be transferred to a position still further to the north, near St Eloi, and a day or two later he learnt that he was to occupy this new sector more or less permanently, as had been the case at Neuve Eglise an arrangement that he entirely approved of. The brigade in the meantime went back for a few days into billets; but it moved into its new trenches on the night of 8/9. These Maude regarded as very far from perfect, and he immediately concerted means for substantially strengthening and elaborating them with the engineers. Then, in his diary for the 12th, the following entry occurs:

> Back for a hurried dinner and then down to trenches again with brigade-major and Fleming. Started at 28 and went along to 23, which is the right of my line. Wanted especially to see machinegun positions. Twenty-eight is a curious trench, a series of bastions with nothing between. All trenches were badly deficient of parados, and many of traverses. Bullets seemed to come from every direction and we have quite a few casualties, However the men are working splendidly and we shall soon make the trenches better.

> On the way back got hit by a stray bullet, which went through my right arm and into my right side, finally lodging close to my spine, pointing upwards. Walked on as far as the East Surrey's dressing station, whence I was carried down on a stretcher to Lankhof Chateau. Here an ambulance met me and I was taken to 14th Field Ambulance at Ypres. Inoculated against tetanus and put to bed, having first sent a note to Charlie Fergusson asking him to wire to Eric to let him know that I had been hit. Could not sleep.

He was anxious to remain in the war area and not go home, and next day he had visits from Generals Fergusson and Morland, who were extremely sorry to lose his services even for a short time. He also received a note by special messenger from General Smith-Dorrien, scribbled in pencil and running as follows:

> I am indeed most deeply distressed to hear you have been wounded. I am told it is not serious, but even comparatively slight wounds take a long time to heal, and all that time you, than whom there isn't a more valuable brigade commander in the army, are lost to the cause. B will tell you how a heavy one day cold prevents my coming to see you personally. I cannot thank you sufficiently for all you have done and for the grand example you have set others. May you soon recover.

He was strongly advised by the many friends who came to see him to go back to England; there was doubt as to whether the bullet was still in his body (as he believed himself), and the first attempt with the X-rays at Ypres was a failure. His diary suggests that he was not in all respects a very amenable patient on the subject of whether he was to be sent home or not. It had been the same when he met with the accident on the day of Driefontein in South Africa, at which time the medical officers had failed to keep him as long in hospital as they thought desirable in view of the serious injuries he had received with the result that his shoulder was a trouble to him ever afterwards. Holding the strong views that he did on the subject of discipline, his attitude in this matter is worthy of note, for it illustrates one side of his character. He knew that his services at the head of his brigade were of real value to the country, and that the regret expressed on all hands at his mishap was very genuine. He would have been more than human had he not been influenced to some extent by fear of losing his command if he quitted the war zone. Still, he was too experienced a soldier not to be well aware that an officer on the sick list is under the orders of the doctors, and he eventually saw himself that it would be better for him to proceed home. He was moved to Boulogne first, where he was again X-rayed and where the exact position of the bullet was ascertained. On the 17th he crossed the Channel, and on reaching London he found himself noted to go to Lady Ridley's Hospital in Carlton House Terrace, where his family at once came to see him. There never was any question of an attempt to extract the bullet, which in the future did not cause him much annoyance; but the wound took more than three weeks to heal, although within a very few days he was able to walk about a little and to do business in London. He was in a state of considerable anxiety lest he should lose his brigade, and he wrote to Sir H. Smith-Dorrien and to Generals Fergusson and Morland on the subject, undertaking that he would be back on 2 May.

It should be recorded here that while Maude was away from his brigade in England, the distinguished leader of the Second Army, who had been associated with the 5th Division and the14th Brigade from the beginning, first in the capacity of their corps commander during the critical days of the great retreat from Mons, during the advance across the Marne and the struggle on the Aisne, and during the anxious November and December period on the Flanders border, and who had then remained associated with them as their Army Chief since the opening days of 1915, relinquished charge of the northern half of the British line and returned to England. The high opinion which Sir H. Smith-Dorrien had formed of the capacity of the brigadier of 14th Brigade, as displayed during the previous six months, is expressed as follows in a letter written by him from Gibraltar in April 1919:

He took over command of a brigade in October 1914, and I soon discovered that I had got a brigadier of exceptional grasp, energy, and personality. He joined his brigade at a time when prospects were far from bright. The brigade had been fighting incessantly from the commencement of the campaign, at Mons, Le Cateau, the Aisne, and on the La Bassée-Ypres front, their casualties had been enormous, they were far below strength, and in them were few representatives of the original units which had started from England. The weather was past description torrents of rain daily – and to construct habitable trenches was almost impossible; and yet, excepting a few days behind the line occasionally owing to lack of reserves, he found his battalions day after day and night after night in close contact with the enemy.

Maude's untiring, cheerful nature and soldierly intuition at once infused new life into the brigade, and the latter, realising that he was a born commander who never thought of sparing himself, quickly gave him their whole confidence and affection. The last entry in my diary when I was commanding the Second Army in France, referring to Maude, sums up fairly well my appreciation of him:

'18 April 1915. One of my best brigadiers was wounded in the trenches last night Brigadier General Maude. He makes light of his wound, as anyone who knows him would expect. He has gone off to Boulogne today, and I have just heard that the bullet is still in and that they are sending him to England. I hope that he may soon recover and come back to us, as he is an extraordinarily valuable man.'

As it happened, there was severe fighting about Ypres in the latter half of April. The famous 'Hill 60,' near St Eloi, was captured on the 18th, and it was two or three days after this that the Germans delivered their great gas attack further north about St Julien, drove the Entente forces back some distance, and created a critical situation for the moment. On the 25th Maude heard from Fergusson that the East Surreys of his brigade had taken part in the assault on Hill 60 and 'had done magnificently,' but had unfortunately suffered many casualties and lost both their commanding officer and their adjutant. The knowledge that fighting of this exciting character was in progress made Maude all the more anxious to get back to France, but he had been reassured as to retaining command of the brigade provided he was back reasonably soon.

He went to Buckingham Palace on1 May to receive the C.B. from the King, and on the 3rd he returned to the front, sleeping that night in hospital at Boulogne. Next day he motored back to St Eloi, visiting General Headquarters, Corps Headquarters and Divisional Headquarters on the way, and not arriving until late to take over charge from Colonel G. Thesiger, who had been placed in temporary command of the brigade while he was away. (Colonel Thesiger was killed when commanding a division at Loos some months later.) He found himself at once in the very thick of severe fighting. The 27th and 28th Divisions on the left of the 5th Division had just been skilfully withdrawn some distance, reducing the acuteness of the Ypres salient, part of which had been rendered almost untenable as a consequence of the German attack of a few days before. The enemy on discovering this retirement had become very active, and was now inclined to press forward all round Ypres.

'Found everything just as I left it,' Maude wrote home on the 6th. 'My Devons, who had been on Hill 60 for fifteen days, having been lent to the 15th Infantry Brigade, were just coming off the hill and were relieved by the Duke of Wellington's belonging to the 18th Infantry Brigade. They had hardly left the hill four hours when the Germans turned gas on to the Duke of Wellington's © and rushed the hill, capturing it and two other trenches. So all yesterday the 138th and 15th Infantry Brigades were busy organising a counterattack to recapture the hill, which was to take place at 10 p.m. It was a magnificent sight to watch, as my headquarters are within full view and within one and a

BRIG. GENERAL F. S. MAUDE, C.B., C.M.G.
IN HOSPITAL, CARLTON HOUSE TERRACE. (APRIL 1915.)

half miles of Hill 60. For twenty minutes the artillery rained shells on to the small summit of the hill, and the bursting of the shells at fifty or sixty a minute simply lit up the countryside. The attack was successful; but the enemy counterattacked and retook the hill and they are now in possession of it and of two trenches to the north of it. The East Surreys and Devons of my brigade have done splendidly, and the Germans were not able to turn them off Hill 60 for eighteen days. Everyone says that they have been magnificent, and I am trying to get two V.C.s amongst other things for the East Surreys. The Devons also did splendidly and, when the Dorsets were badly gassed and had only about half a dozen men left standing up, pushed up their companies and by their promptitude saved the situation. Several of them have been specially mentioned for decorations also.

'Yesterday and today we have had a perfect hurricane of shells passing over our headquarters, but luckily none of them were aimed at our farm, which is fairly well concealed now that the leaf is coming out.'

There was heavy fighting on the 8th and 9th north of where 14th Brigade was posted, the 27th and 28th Divisions being assailed with great determination by formidable hostile forces; but although some ground was lost these attacks were beaten back at almost all points. The whole situation near Ypres was however causing anxiety to General and Army Headquarters, and the question of retiring the 5th Division to a rearward position was under consideration, a plan to which Maude was strongly opposed. An elaborate offensive was being carried out by the First Army further south at this time, in conjunction with some French Corps still further south; but these operations proved to be a failure for all practical purposes, the First Army suffering heavy losses without gaining any commensurate advantage, and after a few days activity was relaxed by both sides almost along the entire front. Maude had been recommended not to walk much, as his wound was not yet quite healed, but on the 10th he nevertheless made a tour round his trenches, and he was much pleased at the good work that had been done and that was being done by the D.C.L.I., Manchesters and East Surreys, who were at the time occupying them; a good deal of attention was beginning to be given to mining by both sides at this time, in which the British troops developed gratifying skill and displayed marked enterprise. In the diary and letters home there are, on the other hand, frequent references to lack of artillery ammunition and to the British being out-gunned. ' Germans have suffered enormously, and I think we have frightened them a bit; where they score is in their artillery, as their guns are heavier and they have more ammunition. But when we cross bayonets there is only one in it and our men know that well and are full of confidence .... The country is only just beginning to realise the class of war we are engaged on. We certainly are not a nation of soldiers. Everything that the Germans do is perfect from the soldiering point of view and as regards organisation, whereas we are all unorganised and haphazard about everything and muddle along as best we can.'

On the 28th the Germans attacked 28th Division with gas which, as the wind was blowing from the north, came down upon 14th Brigade, reaching Maude's headquarters where the staff were affected in spite of having on their masks. Reinforcements were hurried up to assist28th Division, and the assailants were eventually beaten off with loss; but there were many casualties on the British side and a number of men in 14th Brigade suffered from the effects of the gas. The question of retiring to a line further back was still under consideration, although the brigadiers and troops alike were entirely against such a move. 'I cannot say how strongly I feel about the policy of always looking over the shoulder,' Maude wrote in the diary on the 29th. Leave for officers, which had been closed for some weeks, was now reopened, as a period of comparative tranquillity was anticipated in high places.

'We are a truly marvellous nation,' Maude wrote on hearing this. 'Here we are in the midst of a summer campaign, where everyone ought to be straining every nerve to bring matters to a successful issue before the winter wet and cold set in again, and we simply sit down day after day and do nothing. Lack of fighting material is of course the cause; but what a terrible record of bungling and maladministration, and what needless loss of life has, and will, come of it. No doubt the guilty parties will be whitewashed in due course, as usually happens.'

On 4 June General Morland went home for a week's leave and Maude took over command of the 5th Division in his absence; but he remained at his brigade headquarters, motoring over to Divisional Headquarters daily to sign papers, et cetera June proved to be a quiet month for the 5th Division; and, as the trenches occupied by 14th Brigade were now very complete, the work for all concerned proved lighter than it had been for months. Still, in spite of the good cover now provided, the brigade continued to suffer a number of casualties from the enemy shell at times. There was also a good deal of mining activity during these weeks, and one or two scares occurred owing to reports that the enemy was about to blow trenches up; but neither side was at this time carrying out such operations to the extent and on the ambitious scale that they did on the Western Front at a somewhat later date. Maude's career in this theatre of war was however coming to an end, for on the 22nd he heard from General Lambton that he was to have command of one of the New Army divisions being organised in England, and that he was to go home at once.

'Although I am naturally delighted at my advancement in my profession,' he wrote in the diary, 'I feel sad, first at going home even for two months, although Billy tells me my division will come out then, and secondly at leaving this splendid brigade, which has been so magnificent throughout. It has been the finest command that I could ever wish for.'

On the 24th and 25th he went round bidding good-bye to his battalions in the trenches, and on the latter day learnt that he had been promoted Major General in the *Honours Gazette*. His successor, Lieutenant Colonel C. W. Compton of the Somersets, did not however arrive until the 27th. On that day he gave up command of 14th Brigade, after having been in charge of it for eight months. He went round the units that were in reserve in the afternoon, and made short speeches to each, being loudly cheered by officers and men, and he then motored to Bailleul to spend the night with General Fergusson. Next day he motored to General Headquarters and on to Boulogne, arriving in London in the evening and going on to Watford at once. On the day of his quitting his brigade he had issued the following farewell order:

> In relinquishing command of the brigade on appointment to command a division, the Major General Commanding wishes to express to his Staff, and to Commanding Officers, Warrant Officers, N.C. Officers and men, his warm appreciation of the wholehearted and loyal support which he has invariably received from all ranks during the eight months that he has been in command. It will always be to him a source of pride and pleasure to look back to his association with the five splendid regiments belonging to the brigade, which already bear historic names for gallantry on many a hard fought field, and whose reputation has been so signally enhanced during this campaign, not only by heroism in battle, but also by grit, determination and sheer hard work during the winter of exceptional severity and discomfort, and by their general smartness and efficiency in billets and bivouacs,
>
> He feels confident that the grand fighting spirit existing in the brigade will carry it triumphantly over all obstacles and enable

it to emerge at the close of the war with a record second to none, and with additional laurels entwined round the names of the five regiments composing it.

It is with a sad heart that he severs connection with his old friends, but although separated from them he will still follow their doings with the keenest interest and will wish them one and all from day to day, health, happiness and success, and ultimately a safe and victorious return to those who are near and dear to them.

During the eight months which Maude had spent at the head of 14th Brigade in the field he had acquired much valuable experience, and he had been provided with ample opportunities of proving what a resolute soldier he was. It is true that, with the exception of the critical operations about Neuve Chapelle immediately after he took up command, he had enjoyed scarcely any opportunities of handling troops actually in attack, or in conducting operations in the open field. He indeed came upon the scene as a leader almost at the very juncture when the effort on the part of the British Army under Sir J. French to turn the German right flank was brought to a standstill, and when mobile combinations on the part of the belligerents in the northern region of the Western Front gave place almost automatically to more or less stagnant trench warfare. But although his bent was ever for the offensive if the situation at all justified such an attitude, he proved himself a master of defensive action when this was imposed upon him. Moreover, even in the affair near Neuve Chapelle, he displayed a wise caution and a conspicuously well-balanced judgement under conditions when there existed exceptional temptation to run risks. Especially entrusted with the conduct of an attack almost immediately after exchanging staff duties for leadership, he nevertheless, after carefully reviewing the situation, decided that the attack must be delayed and accepted the responsibility of representing his views to be such to those set in authority over him. Maude's attitude on that occasion marked him out not merely as a good judge of perplexing tactical conditions, but also as a man of strong character.

Few brigadiers serving under Sir J. French probably paid such close and constant attention to the development of the front held by their troops as General Maude. He expected much from his battalions, it is true. He got an enormous amount of work out of his men. But as a consequence of his frequent visits to the trenches, of his sympathetic encouragement alike to regimental officers and to rank and file, and of his ready and unfailing recognition of what these accomplished from day to day, that work was always done not only willingly but even enthusiastically. He devoted every attention from the outset to the comfort and well-being of the troops under his orders, and although he was always particular on such points as tidiness and good order in the billets, his efforts to secure palliation of their hardships in so far as conditions of active service permitted made him a most popular chief amongst his men. 'We were all very sorry when he left,' remarks his old brigade-major, Lieutenant Colonel Dick-Cunyngham, 'and personally I realise that under his tuition I learned a great deal that was of immense value to me afterwards.' Writing of him in March 1919, his former chief, Lieutenant-General Sir T. Morland, pays an eloquent tribute to the value of his work as a brigadier:

> Joe Maude had charge of 14th Brigade of the 5th Division under my command from October 1914 to June 1915, and I cannot speak too highly of his services as brigade commander. He took over at a most strenuous time, and he soon impressed his personality upon the brigade. An untiring worker, he never spared himself; always a gallant fighter, he remained cheerful in the most anxious situations. A highly educated officer who was devoted to his profession, he was a strict disciplinarian and a loyal comrade, and he always looked closely after the comfort of his men by whom he was much beloved. He had all the qualities of a great leader.

As appears from some of the quotations that have been introduced into this chapter, as also from his farewell order on relinquishing command, he always took a very genuine pride in his brigade. He had fine regiments belonging to the old regular army under his orders. He had material to deal with that was plastic in his hands. The very high standard of efficiency attained by 14th Brigade while he was at their head was primarily due to the regimental officers and to the grit and valour of the rank and file, but it was also in no small measure owing to the personality, the ability, and the indefatigable efforts of the general officer who was holding the command during those strenuous months on the Western Front.

CHAPTER VIII
The Dardanelles

On reporting himself at the War Office on 29 June Maude learnt that he was to have charge of the 33rd Division of the Fourth New Army, forming in Nottinghamshire, and after a week of leave he proceeded to Mansfield and took up command. He was favourably impressed with the rank and file from the outset. 'Let me begin by saying,' he wrote on the 16th to Sir A. Murray, who was superintending at the War Office the organisation and training of the New Army divisions, 'that in practically every case the battalions consist of men of splendid physique .... They are also generally speaking a particularly smart-looking and well-behaved lot of men; these remarks apply to the R.E. and Train as well.' He was unhappy at not having his artillery with him, but was reassured on learning that he would find them on Salisbury Plain, whither the division was to move very shortly. There still remained much to be done in respect to equipment and administration, as well as in the matter of training superior officers and staffs in addition to the training of units; for Maude had been given to understand that the command would probably move over to France in September. He threw himself into the task with characteristic enthusiasm and energy.

The division proceeded to Salisbury Plain between 3 and 7 August, and Divisional Headquarters were established at Bulford; but it was to lose its new chief almost before he had made his influence felt. For, on the 15th, telegraphic instructions arrived from the War Office intimating that he was to proceed forthwith to the Dardanelles, and that all arrangements had been made for him to leave overland on the morning of the 17th. Starting by motor at a very early hour on the 16th, he was able to bid his eldest daughter Stella good-bye at Tidworth, where she happened to be staying, on his way through, and he reached Mardale early in the forenoon, proceeding from thence to the War Office, where he was made acquainted with the position of affairs in the Gallipoli Peninsula. Then, after a busy day in getting outfit for a hot climate, he motored back to Watford to spend the night, his son Eric fortunately being at home for the summer holidays. At a very early hour next morning he bid good-bye to his family for the last time and, motoring up to Victoria to catch the boat train, started off on the long trail which was eventually to lead him to beyond Baghdad.

Stirring events had been in progress on the shores of the Aegean while 33rd Division had been concentrating on Salisbury Plain. Considerable reinforcements having reached Sir I. Hamilton from home during July and the opening days of August, he had on the night of 6/7, launched his great attack upon the Sari Bair heights overlooking Anzac (see the sketch map below on p.156), simultaneously with the effecting of an entirely new descent upon the Gallipoli Peninsula in and near Suvla Bay by 10th and 11th Divisions of 9 Corps, newly arrived under his command. But after four days and nights of combat General Birdwood's efforts to secure the crest of the mountain from Anzac had been definitely defeated, even if ground had been acquired on the slopes and if the Anzac position had been much extended northwards; and this reverse was attributable to some extent to the failure of 10th and 11th Divisions to assist him as the Commander-in-Chief had intended. The delicate operation of landing the inexperienced troops of those two New Army divisions on an unknown shore in face of a certain amount of opposition had been satisfactorily carried out; but the advantage thus gained – gained in virtue of surprise had not been followed up. The Turks had been granted leisure to assemble such formidable forces facing Suvla that when, on the 9th, the newly landed contingent had at last moved forward to the attack it had been able to make no impression upon a well posted enemy, and so the hoped for cooperation between the Suvla force and Birdwood's battalions that were holding on grimly to the spurs of Sari Bair had come to nought.

In view of what had occurred, Sir Ian had asked that a commander for IX Corps should be sent to him, and also two divisional commanders. Lieutenant General Sir J. Byng had
been selected for the corps, and in the case of the two divisional commanders the choice had fallen upon Maude and upon Major-General E. A. Fanshawe, who, like Maude, was at the moment in command of one of the New Army divisions preparing in the United Kingdom for service abroad. Travelling together, Fanshawe and Maude reached Taranto near midnight on the 19th, and there they met Byng, who had proceeded thither direct from France. They sailed for the Aegean on the following day, arriving on the 22nd at Mudros, the base of the Mediterranean Expeditionary Force, where they spent the night. Next morning they continued their voyage to the island of Imbros where Sir I. Hamilton had his General Headquarters, and Maude then

learnt that he was to have command of 18th Division of the New Army at Anzac; General Shaw, who had brought it out from home, and had commanded it in the struggle for Sari Bair, had just been invalided. He proceeded thither by destroyer in the afternoon and landed on the Gallipoli Peninsula about 7 p.m., just a week after he had received his orders at Bulford for the Dardanelles.[5]

The 13th Division properly formed part of IX Corps; but it had been the earliest of the reinforcements to join Sir I. Hamilton, and, arriving in the theatre of operations about the middle of July, had in the first place been put ashore in the Helles area and had taken over trenches there so as to give the troops some experience in contact with the enemy. After a few days of this it had been transferred to Anzac and had played a prominent and highly creditable part in the furious affrays for the possession of the Sari Bair heights, fighting valiantly alongside the seasoned Australians, New Zealanders, and Ghurkas; but it had suffered very heavy losses in these encounters. Referring to them afterwards in his final despatch of 11 December 1915, Sir I. Hamilton wrote:

> The 13th Division of the New Army under Major-General Shaw had alone lost 6,000 out of a grand total of 10,500. Baldwin was gone and all his staff. Ten commanding officers, out of thirteen had disappeared from the fighting effectives. The Warwicks and the Worcesters had lost literally every single officer.

So it came about that, when Maude assumed command, he found himself at the head of three shattered brigades of infantry, the total strength of which scarcely amounted to the numbers that a single brigade is supposed to muster; the composition is given in the footnote.[6] None of its artillery was with the division, and after his experiences of close cooperation between artillery and infantry on the Western Front, of having the guns within the section held by his brigade under his own orders, and of large numbers of batteries at hand with a fair supply of

---

[5] The map 'Anzac and Suvla' illustrates the work of 13th Division up to December.
[6] 38th Brigade: 6th Royal Lancashire, 6th East Lancashire, 6th South Lancashire, and 6th North Lancashire.
39th Brigade: 9th Royal Warwick, 7th Gloucester, 9th Worcester, and 7th North Stafford.
40th Brigade: 4th South Wales Borderers, 8th Royal Welsh Fusiliers, 8th Cheshire, and 5th Wilts.
Divisional Pioneers: 8th Welsh.

ammunition, its new chief was much disturbed to find no guns under his personal command. His General Staff Officer, 1st Grade, was Colonel (now Major-General Sir W.) Gillman, R.A., who had a wide experience of staff work and had been with the division since an early date. On the morning after his arrival he pored over maps with his General Staff and examined figures with his administrative staff, and that afternoon he walked up the Chailak Dere, visited two of his brigadiers, and went round a portion of the line. Everyone but himself was in shirt sleeves owing to the heat of the weather; at a later date he adopted this same fashion for a time in the Gallipoli Peninsula, but it was noticed that he never did so in Mesopotamia. He somewhat surprised his staff by adopting the plan of writing out himself his orders and daily reports – an unusual course for a divisional general to pursue.

Two days later, he learnt that he was to move to the Suvla area in the following week, so that the whole of the IX Corps should come under General Byng's control, and the preparations for this change of position were at once put in hand. The trenches held by his infantry at Anzac were taken over between the 28th and 30th by the 54th Division from Suvla, and by 1 October Maude's own troops were settled down in the new area, his headquarters having moved by water on the night of the 31st.For the time being, 18th Division was kept in reserve about Lala Baba, and the divisional commander at once set to work to improve and to develop the trenches and dug-outs in this rearward position. The entire Suvla area was under artillery fire of the enemy from dominating positions, and that the situation was tactically extremely unsatisfactory is illustrated by the fact that on 2 September the division had from sixty to seventy casualties amongst its personnel, and 120 amongst its mules. There was moreover a deplorable lack of material for creating effective shelters, and it is clear from the entries in Maude's diary that he felt oppressed by the difference that existed between conditions on the Gallipoli Peninsula in respect to artillery, munitions and stores of all kinds, and those to which he had been accustomed to when commanding the 14th Infantry Brigade. He had left home without an aide-de-camp, but early in September he was joined by Lord Hartington and Captain Wormald of the Coldstream to act in that capacity.

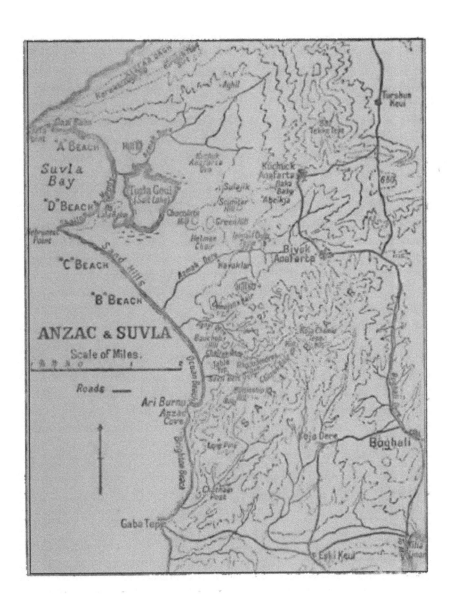

ANZAC & SUVLA

Scale of Miles.

Roads

Suvla Bay

"A" Beach

"D" Beach

"C" Beach

"B" Beach

Tuzla Gesi
(Salt Lake)

Ari Burnu
Anzac Cove

Gaba Tepe

Boghali

Turshun Keui

Kuchuck
Anafarta

Biyuk
Anafarta

'My division is still in reserve,' he wrote home on 12 September, 'cramped up in a very narrow space and mainly employed on fatigue work, building winter quarters. Not very exhilarating although the Turks wake us up most days by shelling us and causing a few casualties. But our inaction is almost comic after the speed with which we dashed out here, and meanwhile the Turks are digging hard everywhere in front of us and making themselves stronger. I suppose that shortage of reinforcements is the reason, but surely that is our fault for trying to take on more than we can do with our small army. If after a fight we have to sit down for six weeks or two months we lose all the effect of the fight. The only effective way seems to be to have reinforcements close at hand, and when you have casualties to dash them up at once, and slap at the enemy before he has had time to recover from his blow.'

The 13th Division remained some three weeks in reserve and then changed places with the 53rd, taking over the trenches on the low ground north of Chocolate Hill stretching away to about Sulajik. Lieutenant Colonel W. D. Brownrigg, who was Assistant Adjutant and Quartermaster General of 18th Division at this period and for a long time afterwards, gives an interesting account of Maude's methods and procedure in connection with his staff when he took up the command, and after he had taken their measure.

'To commence with,' he writes, 'General Maude was a difficult man to work under – as his desire for, and knowledge of, detail was almost uncanny. But gradually and kindly he instilled his methods into his staff, and was not satisfied until he had done so. In fact it was not until close intimacy with him had shown the many striking qualities under his almost querulous air of thoroughness that one learnt to love the man almost as much as one admired the soldier. From September to November 1915 was a dull, monotonous, soul-killing period. During all this time General Maude strove to raise the morale of his men after their heavy losses and privations of the August fighting.

'His daily morning staff conferences at 8 a.m. in the cliffside were in reality a parade of Staff officers and administrative heads of services and departments, to receive their orders for the day and report on their doings of the past twenty-four hours. Do not let it be supposed from this that his staff were automatons. No one was more ready than General Maude to receive, weigh and sift advice given by the most junior of his staff. He expected it and asked for it. But he always was the final adjudicator of policy .... He forgot nothing; no detail was too small for him; yet he always had time for everything and he never let the mass of detail obstruct from his vision the big idea. One of his sayings to the writer is a treasured remembrance, as it gives expression to a basic principle, 'If a man wants to go into the details of the work of his staff he must be accessible.'

'How wonderfully accessible General Maude was, no one but those who have served near him can realise. On coming into his tent or dug-out, one might find him scribbling on his knee, as was his wont, busy with one or other of the many points or problems to be considered or to be solved by a divisional commander. No matter how busy he might be, he would after finishing a sentence turn round and deal straightway with the new matter brought before him, and, when dealt with, go on with the old. Never irritable, never petulant, except when laziness or inefficiency became apparent …. Day or night, awake or asleep, he was always accessible, always ready to take advice, and always ready to give advice to those who asked for it.

'He demanded two things of his staff – energy and efficiency. The first he expected to find in a man, the second he built by his own teaching on the foundation of the first.'

At this period, and during the following three months, the Turks practically confined their activities to occasional heavy bombardments of the trenches, and Maude from the outset kept inculcating upon his subordinates the need of fostering offensive ambition amongst the troops and of keeping the enemy on the qui vive by alarms and excursions. He learnt at Corps Headquarters on the 29th that orders had come for the 10th and 53rd Divisions to leave for an unknown destination, and that his troops would take over the trenches that were at the time held by the 10th Division about Chocolate Hill.

'What a hopeless country we seem to be,' he writes on the 30th in his diary, 'always a policy of drift, and what that means when war is in the balance every soldier will appreciate. Why are we waiting here indefinitely without guns, ammunition and men, when, given those three necessaries, we could soon be in Constantinople? Troops suffering a good deal from sickness, and deteriorating generally from this sedentary life. Why cannot the policy be definitely adopted either to go on with this or to give it up? There should be no half measures – it only means further sacrifices in blood and money, which are heavy enough.'

And again on 4 October: 'Am busy trying to stimulate offensive spirit in the troops, but it is uphill work in this sedentary warfare. Still one can do something in the way of patrolling, and the 39th Infantry Brigade have started well, two young officers and having already distinguished themselves. Up at trenches each of these three days and spoke to commanding officers as well as brigadiers as to necessity of working up the dash of the troops.'[7]

Only the 10th Division left Suvla, as it turned out, proceeding to Salonika; but the consequence of its departure was to place the important Chocolate Hill position under Maude's control; the Turks were fond of making this rising ground in British possession a target for their shell fire, and this demanded special labour on the part of the troops holding the trenches in respect to repairing and perfecting cover. He entertained hopes for a time that his division would be moved to Salonika, where, he conceived, an active campaign might be contemplated; a report had got about that his old chief in Flanders, General Smith-Dorrien, had arrived there, for which as a matter-of-fact there was no foundation. An entry in his diary early in the month indicates that his request that the artillery within his section of the lines should be placed under his orders was at last complied with – he could be very persistent when he felt satisfied that he was right with regard to any point. Colonel Gillman had left the 13th Division staff to take up the appointment of commander of artillery in the corps; and it should be mentioned here that Maude's tendency to centralise staff work in himself had made the situation a little difficult at times for Gillman, although they remained always good friends and were brought together again later on in Mesopotamia. Maude indeed had wished his chief staff officer to have command of one of his infantry brigades at Suvla; but it could not be arranged.

---

[7] Maude's handwriting was not his strong point, and it had suffered owing to the injury to his shoulder at Driefontein; it is almost impossible to decipher some of the names of persons and places jotted down in pencil in his diaries. The name of one of these two officers is clear enough, but the other is illegible, and it hardly seems fair to give one without the other. There is another point in this extract to which attention may be drawn, because it is characteristic of the man. Even in his diaries, where the entries were made hurriedly and for his own use, he invariably puts the 'Infantry' Brigade. 'That is absolutely correct, as there are also artillery and cavalry brigades; but officers as a rule leave the 'infantry' out in unofficial communications, or when talking. He had accustomed himself to put the full and correct designation instinctively.

Nothing especially noteworthy happened in the Suvla area during the month of October, although a very important change took place in the Mediterranean Expeditionary Force because Sir I. Hamilton relinquished the command on the 17th, and handed over charge to General Birdwood for the time being, pending the arrival of his successor Sir C. Monro. Maude had hoped at first that the despatch of a new Commander-in-Chief might possibly synchronise with the adoption at home of a vigorous policy in respect to the Dardanelles, and with the arrival of the drafts, artillery, and stores that were needed to transform an army, which under existing conditions was helpless for offensive purposes, into a force capable of striking a resounding blow; but these hopes were doomed to be disappointed. Writing at a later date Sir I. Hamilton places his high opinion of the commander of 18th Division on record as follows:

> I always held Maude in warmest admiration. We often worked together at the War Office, and there I learnt the openness of his character, the simplicity and the charm of his manner, and his thorough-going devotion to business. But it was at Gallipoli that I first realised his outstanding qualities as a commander. Maude was the heart and soul of the Suvla Bay area, because he had the power of holding both heart and soul unmoved, serene and confident amidst much doubt and depression. Throughout, he remained a shining example of resolution unquenched by discouragement. He could never understand why we were restrained from attacking, or why the home people could not understand that we could win the war if only we were backed. Up to the bitter end his brave spirit was never defeated and never, had he had his way, would we have sailed away from the Dardanelles or yielded the half-won field.

It soon transpired that nothing was to be hoped for in the direction of reinforcements in men and munitions. As a matter-of-fact, General Monro very speedily came to the conclusion that the only course to pursue must be one of uncompromising evacuation of the Peninsula, seeing that events in the Balkans pointed to the early establishment of direct communication between the Central Powers and Constantinople, which, as matters stood, could hardly fail to render the position of the Expeditionary Force more unsatisfactory than ever, and that its difficulties must inevitably be increased by the rough seas that were to be expected in this region in winter. He telegraphed home to that effect on 3 November; but this was not known on the spot at the time, except at General Headquarters. Maude had a conversation with the new

Commander-in-Chief on 30 October, and his entry in the diary that evening gives expression to his disappointment at what he had gathered in the course of the interview:

> We are a weak-kneed nation. Why not push through and finish the business? It would not be difficult, given men, ammunition and guns. It is the dreadful policy of do nothing that is fatal.

The weather had in the meantime been growing decidedly cooler. The flies, which had caused the troops such torment during the summer months, had disappeared. Occasional rain served to lay the dust. With developing piers and jetties and with improving local communications, the situation at Suvla had become in some respects decidedly more satisfactory than it had been when Maude had brought his division thither two months before. Had there been the requisite warm clothing and had the material needed to construct suitable shelters in a region where no timber existed been available, the conditions would have been quite tolerable in spite of the unfavourable tactical position in which the troops found themselves. But important stores were wholly lacking, or else were sadly in arrears, so that, in place of officers and men being a prey to heat with its resultant ills, they were now beginning to suffer from cold and exposure. The result was that although the health of the force as a whole gave less cause of anxiety than had been the case some weeks earlier, progress in this respect was not so great as it ought to have been. Maude himself with his vigorous frame and his fine constitution suffered scarcely at all from illness; but his staff were often temporarily indisposed, and one or two of them had to be invalided from the Peninsula. His practice of, if possible, visiting some section of his trenches every afternoon, generally taking his chief staff officer, Lieutenant Colonel R. Hildyard, with him, afforded him means of getting the exercise that he always craved for, brought him into personal touch with regimental officers, and made the commanding figure and the winning smile of their chief familiar to the rank and file of 18th Division. As matters stood the Dardanelles Army, in so far as divisional commanders knew, had a winter in this bleak and exposed position to look forward to, and the lack of adequate provision for the anticipated conditions could not but cause grave anxiety to a soldier so far-sighted and so solicitous for the welfare of the troops under his control. Lord Kitchener visited the theatre of operations in the early part of November, and on the 14th spent some time at General Byng's headquarters which were at Suvla Point, but Maude did not see him.

The first intimation of an impending evacuation reached the divisional commanders of the Suvla area on the 24th, when a conference took place at Corps Headquarters, at which was shown a communication from the Commander-in-Chief suggesting the likelihood of a withdrawal from the Peninsula, directing that all surplus stores should be gradually embarked, and intimating that drafts except for the 29th, 42nd, 52nd and Royal Naval Divisions (these constituted VIII Corps and were all at Helles, except the 29th which was on the left of the 13th at Suvla) would henceforth proceed to Alexandria. In view of this intimation from Army Headquarters, Maude at once took up the question of evacuating his surplus stores as fast as possible, and also of strengthening his trenches and adapting them to the requirements of a slender garrison.

But everything, immediately afterwards, was thrown for the moment into a certain amount of confusion, and work of all kinds was greatly delayed, by a terrible storm which visited the Peninsula on the 26th and which turned into a blizzard, lasting for two days. Great suffering was caused to the troops in the Gallipoli Peninsula, especially to those stationed at Suvla, where the bivouacs and dug-outs were particularly exposed and where heavy casualties resulted in many units. Maude was then seen at his very best. Every day he with one of his staff went round the whole flooded line – or round so much of it as time and the elements would permit. His cheering presence at this time was, as one of his staff described it, worth another brigade in the trenches. The 13th Division came through the ordeal particularly well. It gained great praise from General Byng for its endurance and its resource in combating the elements, and also from General Birdwood, who was now in command of the Dardanelles Army. General Monro had delegated the duty, as he was in charge of all the troops in the Eastern Mediterranean, including Salonika which at the time was occupying much attention, while maintaining a general control.

'Went up to the 39th Infantry Brigade with Hildyard,' Maude wrote in his diary on the 28th. 'Nearly blown away getting there, and could hardly make way against head wind. Saw three commanding officers and Cayley and they were all doing splendidly. Went on to see the 40th and 38th Infantry Brigades. All very cheery in spite of desperate condition of trenches, waist high in mud and water in some places. Sent up extra fuel and rum on pack animals. Also sent troops a congratulatory message on their splendid conduct.'

There is no mention here of how highly the visits of their divisional general, staggering about through the mud and slush in the tempest, was appreciated by regimental officers and men. They felt him to be one of themselves, sharing their trials and heartening them with his cheery encouragement, for it was undoubtedly a terrible experience for all concerned. The inclement weather did not finally abate until the night of the 30th, by which time the casualties owing to exposure throughout the Suvla force had become very heavy.

'Last night after four days the gale subsided,' Maude wrote home on the 30th. 'The violence of it, added to the snow blizzard and the icy cold, have been indescribable, but the way in which the division have stuck it out has been magnificent. I have had two complimentary messages from the corps commander on the subject, and today he came over to see me and expressed himself personally. I think it would be difficult, unless you had seen it, to realise what the men have had to go through; it has been terrible for them, especially as they are not yet fitted out with warm clothing fully, nor have they material to make good shelters. We have had 1,350 sick in my division in the last three days, and I am afraid that there will be still more, and fifteen deaths from exposure; and yet I fancy that our total is about the lowest in these parts. The conditions were as bad as in Flanders as regards mud and water, but in addition there was this frightful blizzard and insufficient clothing and shelter. The water came down the gullies like rivers without warning, and some were drowned, while others had narrow escapes. The only consolation is that the Turks have had an even worse time if possible, for many dead bodies have come floating down the gullies towards us, while we could see them leaving their trenches in large numbers and we were able to fire on them accordingly. Numbers have also deserted and come over to us.'

Maude was in the meantime devoting much attention to the problem of how the withdrawal ought to be carried out, should it be ordered. Plans were prepared with the approval of General Byng for special works about Lala Baba and across the space between the Salt Lake and the shore south of Nebrunesi Point, as it had been decided that the evacuation would take place from two points and that the Suvla force would withdraw as two separate sections, the 13th Division covering the embarkation of the right or southern section. The left or northern section would embark near Suvla Point, while the right section would embark near Lala Baba and possibly also at C Beach. But no definite orders came to hand as to whether the withdrawal was to take place or not, and owing to the Government's infirmity of purpose the position was becoming an extremely anxious one. It was practically certain that the enemy would shortly receive formidable accessions to an artillery already decidedly superior to that of the forces clinging somewhat precariously to the coast of the peninsula. The stormy weather at the end of November had done great damage to the existing piers and had for a day or two cut off all communication between Suvla and the ships, affording commanders and staffs a foretaste of what they might expect if the troops remained where they were. No reinforcements were arriving nor material for constructing winter accommodation, and, to a man of Maude's temperament and instinct for looking ahead, the situation was to the last degree exasperating.

'We are truly a nation of muddlers,' he writes in his diary on 2 December. 'But surely the procrastination of the last few months and the scandal which must necessarily result must wake the Government up. First, the want of decision by which we did not arrange either to go on or to get out of here months ago. Secondly, the total lack of provision of winter clothes for the troops in adequate quantities, and the absence of material for making shelters. It is all too lamentable and has cost many valuable lives that might have been saved.'

At last, however, General Monro on the 8th received instructions from home that Suvla and Anzac were to be evacuated, and this was at once communicated to General Byng, who informed his divisional commanders.

'Hope that they have at last made up their minds,' Maude writes that day in his diary. 'Of course I would far rather have gone for the Turks and smashed them, and I think we could have; but if the Government will not let us do that the only alternative is to get out of this – and we ought to have done so long ago.'

He had a soldier's horror of half measures and could not brook indecision. We may take it that, in expressing the opinion that the Expeditionary Force could have 'smashed' the enemy, he was assuming its ranks to be filled up and its force of guns and howitzers to be greatly increased. A divisional commander would naturally not be fully acquainted with the situation in the theatre of war as a whole, nor be cognisant of the strength of the hostile forces; there is no doubt that in December 1915 the Turks had large bodies of troops in reserve about the Dardanelles as was pretty well known at Army Headquarters which could have been brought up had the Allies attempted a serious offensive. But it having at last been decided that Suvla was to be abandoned, Maude was in his element. Stagnation was at an end. Something was going to be done, even if it was something disappointing, and he vigorously entered upon the task of framing plans for an operation demanding exhaustive calculations and elaborate procedure, an operation in which perplexing tactical considerations had to be accommodated to abnormal administrative requirements, and one which could only be crowned with success if the staff work involved was to be of a high order.

Methodical in all things, Maude, alike on the Western Front and at the Dardanelles, always carefully noted down in his. diary day after day what private letters he had written and also what official communications of importance to superior authority he had despatched during the twenty-four hours; and, considering the inconvenient conditions under which correspondence had to be carried out as a rule, it is astonishing what an amount of it he got through. He never lost the opportunity of a mail going home, or of the report of such an event taking place, to despatch a number of letters to friends as well as to his family, all of them written in pencil and generally on his knee. In respect to official documents, the preparations for evacuating Suvla necessarily obliged him to communicate frequently with Corps Headquarters, and the preparation of a comparatively lengthy memorandum dealing with some subject or other would seem to have been almost a daily event with him early in December 1915. Major-General H. E. Reed, then General Byng's Chief of the General Staff, has drawn a harrowing picture of himself, cowering in a damp dug-out in the night watches with his feet in the mud, as he endeavoured by the lantern's misty light to assimilate the contents of memoranda of many paragraphs emanating from the Divisional Commander of the 13th Division, of which the purport could only gradually be ascertained by deciphering an odd word here and there. Nor wet nor cold deterred Maude from writing; and it was probably because he had not time to write concisely that he wrote often at unwelcome length, not quite realising how difficult it was for the recipient to read his communications.

The principle on which the simultaneous withdrawal from Suvla and Anzac, as also the withdrawal a month later from Helles, was carried out has often been described. The actual embarkation of stores, animals and personnel was always effected at night and every effort was made, by means of demonstrations of disembarking troops and stores by day, by the display of minor activity in front line, and by making it apparent that reliefs were being carried out as usual, to deceive the enemy as to what was in progress. Surplus animals and material, together with any men who were in doubtful health, were got away first; but as a matter-of-fact much of this work, in so far as the 13th Division was concerned, had been already completed before the definite orders to go came to hand on the 8th. Then the supplies and ammunition were cut down to a minimum consistent with means of removal, the number of guns was gradually reduced, while battalions and even brigades began to disappear as the date for final evacuation approached. The plan was that the troops left tor the last two nights, which in the case of Suvla and Anzac were provisionally fixed for those of the 18/19 and 19/20 December, should consist only of the bare minimum of combatants to make the positions reasonably safe, sustained by very modest contingents of the medical and other administrative services; half of these troops were to be withdrawn on the last night but one. On the last night the front trenches were to be held by exiguous detachments to the very end, and these detachments were at a fixed hour to steal away and to make straight for their embarking places – a decision only arrived at on the 11th after a conference between General Godley, who commanded at Anzac, and General Byng, with their divisional generals. Godley was strongly in favour of the plan, but Maude, it may be observed, felt some doubts on the subject and proved to be somewhat difficult to persuade that it was the correct course to pursue.

'This,' he wrote in his diary that night, 'is of course an attractive scheme, and one which I originally suggested, but it has the elements of a gamble. If the Turks find out we are on the move they will attack and arrive pell-mell with the troops at the ships where there will be no covering force. They may find it out by aeroplane reconnaissance noting our empty trenches during the day, by the noise of troops retiring (they are always noisy at night), or by noting the increased activity of shipping. On the other hand, if we withdraw only to some second line on first night it will decisively tell the Turks that we are off and we shall have a bit of fighting on the second night.'

Strong positions were in any case being prepared at Suvla, covering the embarking places, and Maude devoted particular attention to these works, expressing much satisfaction in his diary at the zeal and efficiency displayed by the troops in their construction. A difficulty arising from the fact that the left of the Anzac force and the right of the Suvla force would be moving off at the last in different directions, the one towards Anzac Cove three miles off and the other towards Nebrunesi Point, was overcome by an arrangement under which the troops on the extreme left in the Anzac area were to retire into Maude's section, and to come under his orders in the event of a fight. Already on the 13th his own troops had 'nearly got rid of everything worth taking away'; but he was particularly anxious that no artillery should have to be left behind and destroyed at the last moment, and he had some difficulty in inducing the corps commander to permit reducing the guns to a very low figure for the last forty-eight hours, of twelve field guns and four field howitzers, only ten pieces remained on the last day. There unquestionably was danger in this. It meant that a meagre force of infantry, charged with the responsibility of holding an extended front in close contact with the enemy, would have but frail artillery support to rely on should the enemy suddenly launch an attack or should adverse weather interrupt the process of evacuation at the last. Not all soldiers of experience would concur in Maude's view, but his attitude in the matter was typical. He recoiled from such a confession of defeat as would be proclaimed to the Turks were the wreckage of a few demolished pieces of ordnance to be left them to gloat over, and he cheerfully accepted the risk.

All this time the constantly diminishing army was being favoured by tranquil atmospheric conditions such as at that season of the year could not reasonably have been reckoned on. Night after night, personnel and animals took ship and departed, and the dumps of munitions, supplies, and ordnance stores grew smaller and smaller. General Marshall, who was in command of the 53rd Division, had been especially charged with administering the embarkation work in Maude's sector, acting in conjunction with the naval authorities. But for occasional bursts of shell fire that were directed at times on the beaches, the Turks remained apathetic, and they gave no signs of realising that their antagonists were melting away from before them. So it came about that on the morning of the 18th the programme had been carried out in full as it had been drawn up for the period preceding the final effort, and barely 20,000 invaders – less than half the numbers present at the beginning of the month – remained in the Suvla area.

Maude's left brigade, the 39th, was to withdraw under orders from General Fanshawe, who was in charge of the Suvla Point evacuation. His tactical position was that he had at command an inner fortified system consisting of well-wired lines securing the Lala Baba isthmus between the Salt Lake and Suvla Bay and the southern isthmus separating the lake from the shore to the south of Nebrunesi Point. From 13 to 24 miles in front of this inner stronghold, the front line of trenches ran north and south across the Chocolate Hill high ground and down to the junction with Anzac not far from Hill 60. The left of this line as coming under Maude's orders for evacuation was occupied by his 38th and 40th Brigades, the right part was in charge of portions of the 2nd Mounted Division. The troops from the front trenches, as also the small detachment from Anzac, were to retire by way of the isthmus south of the lake when the time came, and were to embark at and near a pier known as ' South Pier,' inside Suvla Bay between Lala Baba and Nebrunesi Point. The total numbers to be withdrawn at that point, still left on the 18th, amounted to rather less than 10,000 men with sixteen guns. Nearly half of these, with six guns, got away without difficulty on 18/19, the naval arrangements proving most satisfactory, and the operation being carried out practically without a hitch.

The Ottoman artillery was inclined to be troublesome during the 19th, and one shell in the afternoon hit the pier and did damage, which was however speedily repaired. The troops to be withdrawn during the coming night had not only the possibility of a Turkish infantry attack and pursuit to fear, but also the risk of a heavy bombardment of the area near the embarking place, of which the hostile gunners had the exact range, should the enemy become aware of what was afoot. A burst of hostile shell fire might cause serious damage to the pier and to the craft near it, which must give rise to delay and confusion. However, the enemy failed to perceive during the day what weak forces remained in the Suvla area, and then, during the night watches, allowed the detachments in the front trenches to be gradually withdrawn and the trenches finally to be left untenanted, without discovering what was in progress. Eight of the ten guns still ashore in Maude's section were run down out of their positions at dusk and removed to an embarking place near Suvla Point under special arrangements; the remaining two were withdrawn at 8 p.m. and embarked at South Pier. His other troops began to take ship in instalments, the first at 7.30 p.m., the second at 10 p.m.

'From about 11.30 onwards,' he writes in his diary, 'our front line of trenches was only held by 200 men, till 1.30 when they finally withdrew. From 11.30 onwards the Salt Lake lines were only held by 100 men and 8 machine guns, the Lala Baba defences being held by 250 men and 6 machine guns. As soon as the final party from the trenches had passed through the Salt Lake lines, we closed the gaps in the wire and withdrew everyone except the Lala Baba garrison, and embarked them, and finally we embarked the Lala Baba garrison and the 6 machine guns at 4.05 a.m.

'We got everything away and left the Turks, who seemed quite unaware of what was going on, practically nothing. At 4 a.m, we lit a huge bonfire on which we poured several thousand gallons of oil (petrol) and had a magnificent blaze. It was wicked waste and could have been avoided had more sea transport been available. No guns left behind by me, and only a few rounds which we buried. Weather simply perfect throughout and almost a flat calm, not too cold.

'I am glad to say we made a clean sweep of everything,' he wrote in a letter to General Kiggell, Sir D. Haig's Chief of the General Staff, describing the withdrawal, 'and speaking generally for my own division I do not think we left behind us £200 worth of stuff worth having. I got away all my guns and ammunition and we even destroyed the sandbags which we had to leave in the parapets by ripping them with bayonets or clasp knives to make them useless. The withdrawal was apparently a complete surprise for the Turks, for nothing happened on either night beyond the usual sniping and firing. In a way I could not help feeling a little sorry that they did not find us out, for my division had two strongly prepared lines, each with an excellent field of fire, to fall back upon, and if they had only come on we should have given them a real good dressing. But I suppose that from the broader question of the whole evacuation, it was best that it should have been a complete surprise to the Turks, as it was.' Further on he wrote: 'They are a good division and keen as mustard to get at the Turks.'

The withdrawal from Suvla without loss of a gun or an animal, with scarcely a casualty, and at the cost of very few stores of appreciable value, is acknowledged universally to have been a masterly operation of war. Once the fictions, published with the object of deceiving the public, had been abandoned by Marshal Liman von Sanders, who commanded the Ottoman forces in the Dardanelles, the Germans acquainted with the facts readily admitted the skill with which Suvla and Anzac had been vacated. There had been no precedent in modern military history for such an undertaking, and the brilliancy of its execution reflected credit alike on the commanders, on the staffs, and on the troops. The extrication of the Suvla and Anzac armies from the positions which they had occupied since August had, before the event, been looked upon by most military authorities acquainted with the situation as a dubious and dangerous undertaking. Fear that some grave disaster would result had fomented that irresolution at home which so enhanced the difficulties on the spot. The news that the thing was accomplished, virtually without any sacrifice, caused profound relief in *Entente* circles and was, rightly, hailed as a victory.

When the evacuation was completed and the morning broke, Maude with his staff were taken over to Imbros by steamer, arriving about 8 a.m., where he learnt at Army Headquarters that the division was to go to Helles. It was not known whether the Government intended to cling to Helles or not, as, although General Monro had recommended a complete abandonment of the Gallipoli Peninsula, sanction had only been received from home to evacuate Suvla and Anzac. Moreover, while some of the division was at Imbros, most of it had been shipped to Mudros, and Maude was much disappointed at the news and at the prospect of a fresh period of sedentary service; for it was obvious that if Helles were going to be retained it would be held merely as a defensive position. He however obtained permission for the division in the meantime to be concentrated at Mudros, and he proceeded thither on the following day, the 21st, having a very rough passage an experience which proved how little time the Suvla and Anzac forces had had to spare when they completed their evacuation of the peninsula some twenty-four hours earlier. At Mudros he met many friends, and he was able to discuss the present and the future with Generals Monro and Birdwood and the headquarters staff, but his stay in the island was not prolonged. For he left for Helles on the 27th with the advanced troops of his division, of which only the 39th and 40th Brigades were to accompany him, the question whether this last foothold upon Turkish soil was, or was not, to be retained not having been decided when he took his departure. Helles was under command of Lieutenant General Sir F. J. Davies, a Guardsman and old friend of Maude's, and was held at the time by the 29th, 42nd, 52nd, and Royal Naval Divisions, with some artillery left behind by the French; but the 18th were to relieve the 42nd.

The position in occupation of the Allies at the extremity of the peninsula is shown on the sketch map on p.170. It perhaps provided rather more elbow-room than there had been at Suvla, but in most respects the conditions were almost worse. The landing and embarking places were, if anything, even more exposed in case of rough weather than those within and around Suvla Bay. The Turks could shell practically the entire area from the far side of the Dardanelles, taking it in the flank. It was dominated in front by high ground which was entirely in the enemy's hands. Hostile infantry and guns, which had been tethered to Suvla and Anzac for months past, were now at liberty to succour the Ottoman divisions that had been confronting General Davies during the autumn. Successful as had been the withdrawal of Byng's and Godley's legions from the northern zone, this had made

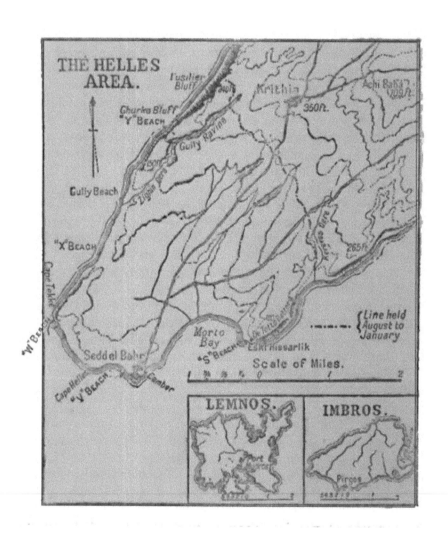

THE HELLES
AREA.

Fusilier
Bluff

Krithia

Achi Baba
709ft.

350ft.

Gurkha Bluff
"Y" BEACH

Gully Ravine

350ft.

Gully Beach

265ft.

"X" BEACH

Cape Tekke

Line held
August to
January

Morto
Bay

Eski Hissarlik

"W" BEACH

"S" BEACH

Scale of Miles.

Sedd el Bahr

Cape Helles
"V" BEACH

River Clere

½ ¼ ¼ 0   1   2

LEMNOS.

IMBROS.

Port Ierces

Piroes

170

Helles a decidedly less satisfactory position to hold than it had been before, and had made it a more awkward trap to get out of, because of the fair warning of what might peradventure be in contemplation which the enemy had received. Maude found himself and his troops planted down in new surroundings, with the prospect of his very likely having to effect a delicate retreat from his position before having settled down in it. The Home Government's delayed decision to abandon Helles did in fact reach General Davies on the 29th, at a juncture when only 39th Brigade of 13th Division had arrived. The last of 40th Brigade did not land until the 81st, and the division took over the trenches on the extreme left of the line, stretching from Fusilier Bluff for about one-fourth of the length of the front south-eastwards, relieving 42nd Division, which thereupon departed from the Peninsula. 29th Division was on the right of 13th, 52nd Division held the trenches beyond that, and the Royal Naval Division filled in the extreme right. 52nd Division was under command of Major General Hon. H. A. Lawrence, who had been in Maude's year at the Staff College; but he was placed especially in charge of the embarkation organisation, a circumstance which necessarily brought them into close contact. Maude makes special reference in his diary to how on one or two evenings he enjoyed discussing military matters in general with a friend whom he had been much associated with in Camberley days, after the points in connection with the operations they were actually engaged in at the moment had been settled.

Simultaneously with their taking up their position, Maude's infantry started work on the masses of stores which had if possible to be got down to W and V Beaches before the troops left, to be embarked by night. He was distressed at the amount of material that remained to be evacuated, as it was clear that quantities of valuable goods could not possibly be got away and would have to be destroyed, and that the operation could not consequently be conducted so cleanly as had been the case at Suvla. He refers to the point daily in his diaries between 30 December and the final evacuation; it was not merely the waste of commodities and the loss to the public that he lamented, but also the fact that abandonment of armament, stores and animals would be tantamount to a defeat of the withdrawing force in the enemy's eyes, no matter how successfully the actual troops themselves were to get away.

'Each walk that I take up to the trenches makes me feel somewhat sad,' he wrote privately to General Davies on 3 January. 'My fellows have been working like Blacks to try and get things away, but the whole place is so littered with stuff that it is difficult to collect it and bring it down to places where it can be put on carts and wagons. We are doing our level best to carry out your instructions to clear the area, and yesterday, for instance, we evacuated over thirty tons weight; but this seems only a drop in the ocean, and I am afraid that the enemy will get a considerable amount of booty when we withdraw. Still, I am telling them to keep pegging along, and I impressed this point particularly on brigadiers and commanding officers when I saw them up in the trenches this afternoon, although it seems scarcely necessary to do so as they are as keen about clearing things as I am myself.'

The night of 8/9 had been provisionally fixed for the final withdrawal, and all preliminary work was being carried out on the assumption that impedimenta must be got off before the 7th. This preliminary work was, however, a good deal interfered with by rough weather at night, although as the wind was always from the north-east the piers at W and V Beaches, on which much depended, did not suffer. It was evident that the Turks had gained accessions in strength as regards guns and shell, for their bombardments at times were vigorous, although they were mainly confined to the daytime, when interference with work on the beaches was of less consequence than at night. The two right divisions were to effect their withdrawal at V beach and the 29th Division at W Beach. Up until 5 January the design had been that a large part of 13th Division should use Gully Beach, the rest embarking at W Beach; but the plan was then modified owing to the exposure of Gully Beach to the weather, and because it had been decided that a larger force of infantry and artillery was to be retained for the last night of all than had previously been contemplated. The scheme for 18th Division that was in the end elaborated was that (except for the final detachments to quit the trenches on the last night which were to be got away from Gully Beach) the whole of it should be embarked at W Beach.

The weather was fine and calm on the morning of the 7th, and a decision was therefore arrived at to carry out the final evacuation on the night of 8/9. Soon after Maude had been made aware of this, the enemy started a violent bombardment of the general front, and especially of his sector, a cannonade which in the afternoon gave place to a formal infantry attack. As this was the first occasion on which 18th Division had been tested in serious combat since he assumed command, the account of the affair which is entered in his diary may appropriately be quoted:

> At 11.30 a.m. Turks began shelling heavily all along the front and continued till 5 p.m. Those who have been at Helles the

172

whole time say that it was the heaviest shelling that they have seen here. From 8 to 4 the shelling was intense, and at 3.45 the Turks opened heavy rifle fire. At 4 p.m. they sprung two mines near Fusilier Bluff, and at 4.15 they attacked Fifth Avenue and Fusilier Bluff resolutely. The attack was handsomely repulsed by the North Staffords, who however lost Walker, their Colonel, one of our best commanding officers. The Turks tried to attack all along our front, but the officers could not get their men forward elsewhere. Turks suffered heavily and division did splendidly, all battalions holding well to their position in spite of the fact that in many places their trenches were blown to pieces. Army Commander and Corps Commander both sent congratulatory messages. In spite of the fighting, brigades did well in getting their stuff away, including the packs which we are sending to Mudros tonight.'

There is reason to believe that this abortive offensive adventured by the Osmanlis was, from the point of view of the Helles force, a decidedly fortunate occurrence. The repulse had been unmistakable, the victory of the British at the point where a strong effort was made to break down their resistance had been complete, and the attacking side may well have deduced from their disappointing experience that the trenches confronting them were held in strong force. Marshal Liman von Sanders, the Ottoman Commander-in-Chief, undoubtedly suspected that withdrawal was in progress – that such a development was probable must indeed have been obvious to the enemy, and the hostile aviators had very likely established the fact that the dumps of stores in the Helles area were diminishing in bulk and that animals were disappearing. The Turkish staff could not, on the other hand, tell on what date the final evacuation would take place. When on the afternoon of the 7th, the vigorous bombardment of several hours' duration merged into an infantry attack which was decisively defeated, those in authority on the enemy side would seem to have come to the conclusion that, even supposing a complete withdrawal of General Davies' force to be in course of preparation, the concluding act of the drama was not actually imminent. The attitude maintained by the Osmanlis during the following thirty-six hours at all events suggested some such appreciation of the situation on the part of Liman von Sanders, for there was an almost complete cessation of shell fire from the Turkish batteries, and the Ottoman infantry remained noticeably quiet in their lines during what were perhaps the most critical hours of the Dardanelles Campaign.

The morning of 8 January broke still and fine, auguring well for the success of the formidable undertaking that was to commence at sundown. The plan decided upon was analogous to that which had been adopted with such striking success at Suvla and Anzac. Successive withdrawals were to take place during the early hours after darkness set in, and the guns, other than those which it had been decided to abandon and destroy, were to be got away as soon as possible; the depleted detachments which were to hold the front trenches to the very last were then all to withdraw simultaneously along the whole front at 12.15 a.m. So as to ac-custom the enemy to a silent period after that hour, it had been made the practice for several nights previously to cease all activity on the part of infantry patrols and of bombing operations at 11.30 p.m.; the Turks had fallen in with this arrangement and had shown scarcely any enterprise after midnight during the foregoing week. When the time came, their advanced troops entirely failed to notice that the trenches close in front of them had been vacated. For conveying the embarking troops to the transports and warships which were to take them on to Imbros and Mudros, dependence was being placed almost entirely upon the special lighters, provided with motor power, which had been extensively used since August. They were capable of carrying 500 men as a full load, although about 400 was more usual on this occasion. When it came to be a question of shipping men and guns from improvised jetties in a rising sea, they proved extremely serviceable; they had been nicknamed ' beetles' by the troops, owing to the derricks that supported their gang-boards resembling antennae. A small pier had been constructed at Gully Beach, the point from which the last detachments of the 13th Division to hold the front line trenches were to put off; the strength of these last detachments, together with divisional headquarters and some minor details, came to 645 of all ranks. Maude in his diary describes the withdrawal of his division as follows:

> Parties began assembling at Gully Beach, which I fixed as divisional headquarters, at 5 p.m., so as to send detachments of 100, 200 and 400 complete, forward to their forming-up place at W Beach, as 400 was a lighter-load. All were well up to time and numbers very accurate, which was very creditable considering yesterday's fighting and the immense amount of work which brigades have had to do cleaning up, getting orders out, et cetera. Indeed the embarkation people told me afterwards that this was the best division of the lot in getting away, and we scored consequently as we got a ship practically to ourselves for a very large part of the division. As night began to fall, the wind, which was in the south, began to freshen, and

it looked as though there might be difficulties as regards embarkation. However all went well up to the departure of the last party from W Beach, and all were embarked at 11 p.m.

By 1.15 a.m. all the last detachments from the trenches, consisting of 555 all ranks, including R.E. for closing gaps, control officers from control stations, etc., were all in at Gully Beach, and then the fun began.

First, the lighters, of which there were to be two, were half an hour late. Secondly, one, in coming alongside the pier, ran aground and had to be abandoned. Thirdly, the two steamers provided for myself and staff were late. I decided to put as many as possible on the one lighter, and we got about 500 on, leaving still 135 to embark, including headquarters, R.E., R.A.M.C., etc. Of these I had two pickets, consisting of one officer and 10 other ranks, out covering the beach. The embarkation on the lighter was very slow, and just as it was completed at 2.30 the Naval Transport Officer came to me and said that no further lighters were coming, that the sea was getting up, that the steamers could not take myself and my staff off, and that the rest of the troops and my divisional headquarters must go to W Beach to embark.

Gully Beach was a good two miles from W Beach, time was passing, with the wind rising it was obvious that getting off might prove awkward enough, and the handful of men under Maude were by this time entirely isolated, seeing that the last detachments from the trenches of the other three divisions had now been making direct for W and V Beaches for two hours, and that they had, in fact, arrived at their destination. There was moreover an uncomfortable prospect of finding the gaps through the lines, and also those through the retrenchment covering W Beach, closed up by those responsible for this service, because this belated move of a party from Gully Beach had formed no part of the programme issued to all concerned.

'I realised that it might be a rush against time,' Maude wrote to Davies next day, 'for I did not know how soon W Beach would be cleared of the last lighter and it was then after 2.30 a.m., so I pulled in my pickets covering the beach and sent off the last remaining 1,385 men with 2 staff officers, hot foot, for W Beach. This left Hildyard, the A.D.M.S. and myself and 12 men of my headquarters to dispose of. We had all the kit of headquarters with us, for which we had provided two steamboats, but as the horses had been shot and the vehicles destroyed, it was somewhat of a problem to get it along. Luckily however the A.D.M.S. remembered that there were three or four vehicle-stretchers lying handy, and these we got and loaded up. We could not go by the beach route as it was too heavy going, so we started up hill on to the plateau, and very hard work it was. We all puffed and blew like grampuses, especially as we were all warmly clad. I then sent Hildyard by the beach route to try and notify W Beach that we were going, and the A.D.M.S. and I and party pursued our weary way across the top. All went well until we came to the inner defences (except for an occasional fall in the dark), but, once there, we found that the garrison had been withdrawn and had embarked, and that the wire had been hermetically closed. One of the party however produced some wire cutters, rather like a pair of nail scissors, and after much hacking we managed to carve an opening. The Turks now began to pitch some shell about us which accelerated our movements a bit, and then we were again brought up by the Inner Defence trenches. As we could not get the stretchers over the ditch we had to abandon them and the very heavy stuff, and the men carried as much as they could over. Finally we reached W Beach, where Hildyard had obtained the last ' beetle,' in which we made our way at a slow rate and through heavy sea to Imbros, taking four and a half hours over the journey.

'Before we left the shore the bonfires had begun to blaze and the explosives were going off. It was a fine display of fireworks and we had a splendid view of them. Altogether it was an experience that I would not have missed for anything.'[8]

---

[8] The following lines were jotted down on the leaf of a notebook by one of the beach staff at W Beach in the small hours of the morning on 9 January, purporting to have been written by General Lawrence :
'Come into the lighter, Maude,
For the fuze has long been lit ;
Quick into the lighter, Maude,
And never mind your kit,
I've waited here an hour or more
The tidings that your march is o'er ;
The sea runs high; but what care I!
It's better to be sick than blown sky high.
So jump into the lighter, Maude,
The allotted time is flown ;
Come into the lighter, Maude,
I'm off on the launch alone.
I'm off on the launch alone.'

There had been considerable difficulty in carrying out the embarkations at W and V Beaches after midnight, especially at the former, and the heavy swell that was setting in had caused the naval staff considerable anxiety. This final evacuation of the Peninsula was carried out under much less favourable weather conditions than those which had attended the withdrawals from Suvla and Anzac three weeks before. Indeed, had the wind got up a very few hours earlier, the sea might have been running so high that the completion of the embarkation would have been impossible, that the piers would have carried away before the whole of the troops had reached the shore, and that a decidedly critical situation might have been created, although carefully prepared positions protecting the two beaches existed, which had been designed to meet this very contingency.

The destruction of guns, animals, vehicles, ammunition, ordnance stores, and supplies of all kinds went to Maude's heart. He deplored the waste of so much valuable material, and he grudged to the enemy such satisfaction as the Turks might derive from it. But there were larger accumulations of impedimenta in the Helles area than had been the case at Suvla and Anzac, the personnel available for the fatigue parties needed to dispose of what remained to embark was numerically considerably less in proportion to the work to be performed than had been the case in the northern zones, and, when the Home Government at last decided that the Peninsula was entirely to be evacuated, the military situation imperatively demanded as rapid a withdrawal as possible in view of a likely complete break-up of the weather. The arrangements for firing the dumps of stores and ammunition were on a most elaborate scale; they proved highly successful and gave rise to the fireworks spoken of in the letter quoted above. The spectacle of those conflagrations which rang the curtain down upon the Dardanelles Campaign apprised the Ottoman forces on the high ground overlooking the Helles area that their antagonists had slipped away from in front of them, unobserved, for a second time. Then, too late, they opened a harmless artillery fire on the beaches when the last of the troops to quit the shore were already afloat and under way for Imbros.

Maude only remained a few hours at that island, getting a passage on to Mudros in H.M.S. Chatham that same afternoon. There he found most of his division assembled. They remained until the 18th and then began embarking for Egypt, which was the destination for the time being of what had been the Dardanelles Army.

Arriving at the theatre of operations comparatively late in the day, and on a date by which serious fighting was almost at an end in the Peninsula, the commander of 18th Division had nevertheless been a particularly prominent figure during the four and a half months that were to elapse before the effort to conquer the Straits was finally abandoned. General Sir W. Birdwood, who had played so great a part in the campaign from the outset, writes as follows of Maude's services:

> General Shaw came to me in command of 18th Division, which Sir Ian Hamilton posted to my Australian and New Zealand Corps soon after the division arrived in the Gallipoli Peninsula. To my great regret, Shaw was invalided after a short time on the Peninsula, but I heartily welcomed Maude as a successor, feeling that he was just the man we wanted. He indeed proved himself to be so during his tenure of command, giving as he did a feeling of complete confidence to all who were serving under him. I am sorry to say that the division did not remain very long with my Anzac Corps, for it was shortly transferred to Byng's IX Corps at Suvla. Later on, however, on my succeeding Sir Ian in command of the Dardanelles Army, Maude again came under me, and I had an opportunity of seeing his wonderfully good work with the division at Suvla.

> Before the evacuation of Cape Helles, it was found necessary to relieve a very exhausted division there. As the troops who had formed the Suvla garrison, which had been withdrawn, were available, I decided that the best division to send to reinforce Cape Helles was that under Maude, who consequently commanded his division at the evacuation of both Suvla Bay and Cape Helles. He again showed exactly that same courage, determination and cheerfulness which he had displayed at Suvla, and he conducted the withdrawal of his division with similar success. I remember so well meeting him on the last day on the Peninsula, when I went round to see something of the troops immediately before the withdrawal. I was again much impressed by his soldierly spirit at a time of natural anxiety, which gave all complete confidence. He came to see me next day full of satisfaction and thankfulness at the success of the evacuation and of pride in his division.

> I am sorry to say that was about the last that I saw of him, except just as he passed through Egypt on his way to Mesopotamia.

It was indeed largely due to Maude's own merits as a commander that he enjoyed the good fortune of participating in both those final events which by their signal success to some extent compensated for the disappointments that had been sustained in eight months of indeterminate warfare on the Gallipoli Peninsula. He had won the full confidence of those over him as well as of those under him, and so it came about that he and his division were called upon to undertake the anxious and difficult operation of effecting a withdrawal by sea in face of the enemy twice over.

The months which he spent on the shores of the Aegean provided him with experiences very different from those which he had undergone at the head of 14th Brigade in Flanders. At Suvla his attention had been devoted rather to questions of administration and to problems of organisation than to the conduct of actual combat. The conditions of the case had obliged him to interest himself more especially with sanitation and supply and not with leadership in action. Only at the very last, on the day before the remnants of the Mediterranean Expeditionary Force finally disappeared from Turkish soil, was the division over which he had watched so vigilantly and of which he had come to be so justly proud, called upon to engage in battle under his orders. Still, if his experiences since quitting Western Europe had been in a sense disappointing to a fighter such as he was by temperament, the last weeks provided him with ample excitement and furnished him with a splendid opportunity for displaying at once that genius for methodical organisation and that strategic and tactical intuition which, in concert, were a year later completely to transform the military situation on the banks of the Tigris.

'So long as wars last,' was the dictum of a German writer when news of the evacuation of Suvla and Anzac came to hand, ' the British withdrawal from the Ari Burnu and Anafarta fronts will stand before the eyes of all strategists of retreat as a masterpiece for which there has been no precedent.'

The abandonment of Helles was in some respects an even more signal operation of war. Maude and the greater part of his division were engaged in both those critical undertakings; and they participated in the later one under conditions of special difficulty. They only appeared on the new scene of action as instructions came to leave it. Nor, amid all the innumerable stirring events which marked the progress of the great World War, did many incidents more dramatic take place than that of a group comprising a divisional general, his medical officer, and ten rank and file, the tail end of an army which a few days before had mustered many thousands of men trundling hand-carts across country, through lines of entrenchments and of wire entanglement at dead of night and in a rising storm, making for a surf-beaten beach two miles away where their arrival was impatiently awaited by sailors only too well aware that not a moment ought to be lost in sheering off and getting to sea.

For his services in the Dardanelles Campaign, Maude was mentioned in despatches both by Sir I. Hamilton and by Sir C. Monro. He was also about this time nominated a Commander of the Legion of Honour by the French Government.

CHAPTER IX
The Move From Egypt to The Front in Mesopotamia

Divisional headquarters of the 13th Division embarked on board the S.S. *Tunisian* at Mudros on 18 January and sailed next morning, proceeding in the first place to Alexandria, where the ship arrived on the 21st There Maude learnt that his division was to assemble at Port Said, and he and his staff continued the voyage thither that night, reaching their destination next morning. It had been arranged that the division should form part of the XV Corps under command of Lieutenant General H. S. (now Lord) Horne, the corps being completed by the 11th and 31st Divisions.

The ships bringing 18th Division from Mudros kept arriving during the next three or four days, and its infantry gradually took over the defences of the Canal at and near Port Said. Maude at once busied himself with training questions and selecting musketry ranges, and also with the problems of re-equipment. He was joined by most of the artillery properly belonging to his command, which had been in Egypt for some months past, and he was glad at last to have a more or less complete division under his orders. The 84th Brigade was under command of Brigadier General J. W. O. Dowda, the 89th under Brigadier General J. de S. Cayley, and the 40th under Brigadier General A. C. Lewin, all of whom retained their positions during the next six months. Several of his staff, including Lieutenant Colonel Hildyard, went home on leave on the 26th, and a few days later he was joined by two fresh aides-de-camp, Lieutenant F. P. Musgrave and Captain G. A. Ogilvie-Forbes: Lord Hartington had been invalided from Suvla in December and Captain Wormald was going home. Captain Ogilvie-Forbes gives a pleasant account of Maude's kindness and consideration on his first taking up his appointment:

> I had just arrived at Port Said and I at once made my way to the Casino Palace Hotel, which was the headquarters of 18th Division, early in the morning. Being quite a stranger and knowing nobody, I felt somewhat nervous at the prospect of

taking up duties as A.D.C. in absolutely novel and possibly somewhat critical surroundings. I waited in the hall and after a short time he came downstairs. I watched his tall figure descending the long flight, and his smile of welcome banished all misgivings as he approached me. The ice was broken, and I was perfectly happy long before he spoke to me.

We went out into the garden and he told me all about the impending departure to Mesopotamia, inquired after my regiment and division, and told me to spend the next few days in getting my kit as he would not want me immediately. So I had ample time to settle down and to get my bearings.

Even before the Dardanelles Army had been safely withdrawn from its somewhat precarious position in the Gallipoli Peninsula, an awkward situation had arisen in a theatre of war situated even further to the east. General Townshend had in November made his memorable advance up the Tigris from above Kut, which had been in British possession for some weeks past, with the object of occupying Baghdad. The story is a familiar one. After defeating the Turks at Ctesiphon, some thirty miles short of the city, he had been obliged to fall back in face of greatly superior forces and had only got back to Kut, where large accumulations of stores existed, after a most trying retreat, harassed on the way by formidable Ottoman contingents as well as by swarms of marauding Arabs. It had been agreed that he should hold the place, which was of strategic importance quite apart from the supplies that were collected there, and should send away his mounted men. On 7 December he had been invested by the enemy. The question of his relief had at once arisen, and early in January an advance had been made up the Tigris with this in view; but after some preliminary success the relieving army had been brought up short, and a second attempt made on 21 January met with a decided repulse. It speedily became apparent that if Kut was to be saved fresh troops must be hurried to this theatre of war, seeing that those on the spot had already been highly tried and had suffered heavy losses they were the same Indian divisions as Maude had met in France in October and November 1914, where they had undergone severe fighting before they were transferred to Mesopotamia. The Home Government therefore decided to move a British division from Egypt to this scene of action, and 18th Division had hardly settled down near Port Said when, on 30 January, General Horne informed Maude that he would shortly be proceeding to Mesopotamia, his command having been selected for this new undertaking by the War Office.

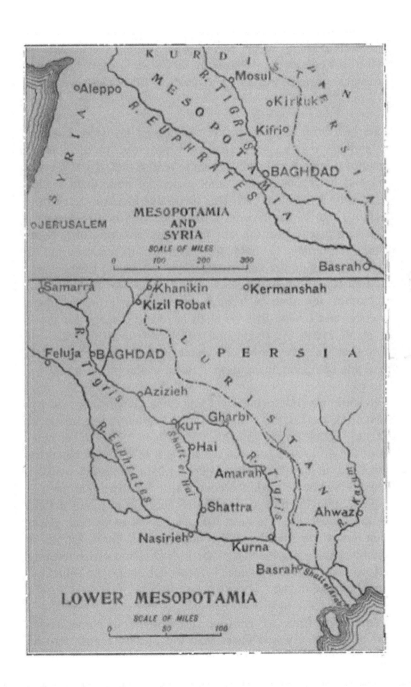

MESOPOTAMIA
AND
SYRIA

SCALE OF MILES

LOWER MESOPOTAMIA

SCALE OF MILES

Maude welcomed the news, although he fully realised that at the moment his troops were still very short of equipment, and that it would be extremely difficult to get them properly fitted out at short notice. Several of his units were furthermore far below war establishment, and the prospects of receiving adequate drafts to fill up gaps were none too rosy.

'We are still busy refitting and re-equipping,' he wrote home on the 31st, 'and are making somewhat slow progress, as there is a great shortage of things. People don't seem to realise that, if you leave things behind and burn them, you cannot expect to have them made good automatically at the other end. This waste that has been so conspicuous throughout, and the shortage of trained men, are the two factors which are delaying progress in the war more than anything else. Secret.—I was told yesterday to hold the division in readiness to go to Mesopotamia within the next two or three weeks, so I expect we shall be off almost as soon as we can be fitted out, as we shall want a lot of fresh clothes for such a tropical place. It will be an interesting experience, and I hope that we shall have more scope for movement there; at all events we ought not to get tied up in trench warfare. I suppose that we mean to make a good push there, though I have not heard of any one going in addition to this division.'

The division was inspected by Lieutenant General Sir A. Murray, commanding the troops in Egypt, on 3 February, formed up on the beach, the 'Parade State' showing 354 officers, 9,953 other ranks and 18 guns; the difference between the strength of different battalions was very marked, as the strongest mustered 1,040, while the weakest only mustered 325. Maude made the comment in his diary that 'men looked splendid, I thought, though there were necessarily many deficiencies owing to evacuations.' He must have had a strenuous time getting the division into shape after the Gallipoli campaign,' Sir A. Murray writes; 'I remember his telling me that of the 13th Division which left England, very few were serving when I inspected them; so quickly does personnel change in war.'

New equipment came to hand slowly at first; but horses and mules poured in on the division faster than the picketing gear arrived, and Maude noted in his diary that they sometimes had from 100 to 200 animals loose at a time in Port Said. In view of the situation on the Tigris, the War Office were pressing General Murray to get the division off, and on the 9th Maude was somewhat taken aback on its being proposed that his troops should begin embarking that night; but on his making representations he managed to obtain a few days' grace, during which much was accomplished. The absence of some of the staff on leave at home caused a certain amount of inconvenience, but the officers temporarily acting worked with a will and Maude was fully satisfied. Clothing, which had been very short, was satisfactorily made up, the resources of the Ordnance Department in Egypt being for the moment devoted practically entirely to the fitting out of the division. The 11th Division began taking over the Canal defences about Port Said from the 13th on 10 February, and Maude decided to start off himself in the first ship to leave on the morning of the 13th; in his diary he expressed himself as well pleased with the progress of the equipment work during the last day or two. He left Port Said late at night on the 12th with the divisional staff, arriving next morning at Suez, where he was to embark. He went on board the S.S. *Kalaya*, and his 38th Brigade began embarking during the day. The *Kalaya* sailed early on the 14th.

'This will be quite a new experience for us all, and we are looking forward to our new life immensely,' Maude wrote in a farewell letter to Sir A. Murray on the 12th. 'At all events it ought to mean fair and square fighting in the open, and manoeuvring at which we shall beat the Turks. Our refitting and re-equipping has gone well, though we still have a good many deficiencies. We ought to be more or less complete before the whole division starts, if things go on as they are doing now.'

He and his staff had gone through a particularly busy time during the previous fortnight, hard at work in dealing with innumerable administrative problems connected with fitting out the troops for the new theatre of operations, and he was very appreciative of the services performed by his immediate entourage. Lieutenant Colonel Brownrigg writes as follows of those few days of exceptional stress:

> Maude's patience and consideration for his staff during those strenuous days of reforming and re-equipping at Port Said in February 1916 will never be forgotten by me. He saw at once that the impossible had to be done, and that quickly. He saw there was no time for centralisation of details in his own hands. So he decentralised in a way that he had never done before (though the daily conferences continued), and it was a source of pride to several of his staff six weeks later at Sheikh Saad to get one of those ' pats on the back' which he was such a past master in giving, just at the right moment, straight from his heart and devoid of all fulsomeness and flattery.'

The voyage proved uneventful. Maude spent much of his time in studying such limited information as to Mesopotamia as the authorities in Egypt had been in a position to place at his disposal; he mentions in his diary that he each morning ran about a mile round the deck and did physical exercises. He was not fully acquainted with the situation in the theatre of war to which he was proceeding, and he would not seem to have been aware of the somewhat critical conditions in respect to Kut, although he fully realised that his division had hard fighting in front of it. 'I do hope that we shall carry out a business-like campaign,' he wrote; 'a definite objective, a vigorous policy, and that we shall have adequate means in the way of munitions.' News came to hand by wireless while they were crossing the Arabian Sea that the Russians were pushing down through Persia to cooperate with the British forces which were endeavouring to reach Townshend, encouraging tidings which Maude communicated to the troops on board. The *Kalaya* arrived off the bar of the Shatt-el-Arab on the 25th; but, as there was some misunderstanding about orders to proceed, she did not ultimately fetch up off Basrah until the morning of the 27th, when Maude at once proceeded ashore and reported himself to the Commander-in-Chief, Sir Percy Lake. He then learnt the state of affairs in so far as it was known at Army Headquarters.

It will be convenient at this point to discuss briefly the nature of the problem with which the Anglo-Indian forces were confronted in Mesopotamia at this juncture, and which for the moment centred on Kut and its relief; the situation is illustrated by the maps 'Lower Mesopotamia' and 'Turkish Positions, April 1916,' above.

The existence of substantial magazines of food supplies and of warlike stores, as also its site at the point where the Shattel-Hai issues out of the Tigris, had afforded strong arguments for clinging on to Kut. On the other hand, once the place had been ringed in by the Turks, that these had created their lines of circumvallation against attack from outside, and that they had occupied and had fortified positions further out which any relieving force would have to capture before it could hope to succour Townshend, geographical and topographical conditions greatly favoured them. The relieving force was on the Tigris, and for it to effect the relief it was almost imperative that it should secure possession of

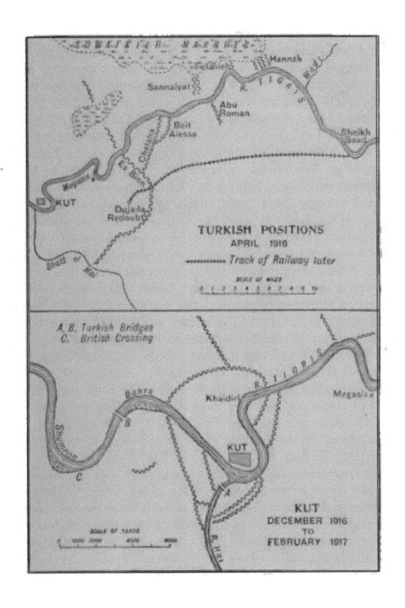

TURKISH POSITIONS
APRIL 1916
—————— Track of Railway later
SCALE OF MILES

A. B. Turkish Bridges
C. British Crossing

KUT
DECEMBER 1916
TO
FEBRUARY 1917

SCALE OF YARDS

the channel of the great waterway right up to the beleaguered city, because the river afforded the only available means of transport on any comprehensive scale. Any advance without constant use of the river meant almost insuperable difficulties in connection with supply, alike for the relieving force itself and for the beleaguered garrison after it had been relieved. It will be noticed on the sketch map above that the extensive Suwaikieh marshes approach to within a mile or two of the Tigris along a stretch of some miles of the river's course at a spot twenty-five miles or so below Kut. The consequence of the existence of this topographical feature was that nature had on the left bank of the river created a military defile which could not be turned on that bank— a defile which was to prove in some respects the main stumbling block in the way of the relieving army. As a matter-of-fact, the Turks had, after investing Townshend, moved down the river as far as Sheikh Saad. But in the January fighting they had been driven back from that point, and had again been ejected from a fresh position which they had taken up at the Wadi, although these successes had cost the Anglo-Indian forces nearly 6,000 casualties. On the other hand, when an attempt was made to force the position which they had then taken up at Hannah, at the eastern end of the defile abovementioned, the attack had failed with a loss of nearly 8,000 men. When Maude reached Basrah, the relieving army was for the most part assembled about the Wadi on the left bank of the Tigris. The enemy was holding strong lines at Hannah, had prepared another fortified position further back within the defile at Felahieh, and had moreover fortified a third position still further back at Sannaiyat - all three positions situated on the left bank of the river. They also had works on the right bank approximately abreast of Sannaiyat, and they were holding a long entrenched line extending southwards from the Tigris near Es Sinn and curling back south-westwards in the direction of the Shatt-el-Hai; its strongest point was the Dujaila Redoubt. These works barred the way for a direct advance from about Sheikh Saad on Kut. The Tigris, it should be mentioned, is apt to rise in March owing to the melting of the snows, and, although this assists navigation from the point of view of depth, the strong current impedes it from the point of view of speed. Moreover, the river is wont to overflow its banks and to flood the country, adding greatly to the difficulties of military operations. The weather in March and April is also likely to be very unsettled, rain storms usually transforming the flat alluvial plain into a morass in many places and rendering movement difficult at all points.

The War Office had taken over the general direction of the operations from the Indian Government in the middle of February, but the

Mesopotamian Field Force – D Force as it was called – continued to be supplied almost entirely under arrangements made by Simla. The army under General Lake consisted, in the first place, of the 6th Indian Division with another infantry brigade, which were shut up in Kut. The relieving force, or Tigris Army Corps, which was under General Aylmer, was composed mainly of 3rd (Lahore) and 7th (Meerut) Divisions, which had been employed on the Western Front from the late autumn of 1914, where Maude when commanding 14th Brigade had been associated with them in November, until they had arrived in Mesopotamia during December 1915 and January 1916.[9] But there were also certain other infantry units included in the army, as well as a force of cavalry. General Aylmer was very badly off for artillery, having practically only horse and field guns, and none too many of those; he was very short of field howitzers and he had no guns or howitzers of heavier calibre a serious matter when endeavouring to force a way through successions of fortified lines held by so stubborn an enemy as the Turkish infantry soldier. The Tigris Army Corps moreover was ill fitted out in respect to aircraft, and it entirely lacked certain necessary warlike stores with which the British troops operating in Europe had been equipped since a very early date in the war. The troops had suffered considerably in the January fighting and they were far short of establishment, especially the British infantry included in the force. River transport was very deficient; and although since General Lake's arrival in January the question of improving Basrah as a maritime base was being taken in hand, it still lacked most of the conveniences which a commander of Maude's experience and foresight naturally expected to find, aware as he was that Lower Mesopotamia had now been a theatre of war for more than fifteen months.

'Apparently Townshend is closely invested and is eating horse flesh,' he wrote in his diary on the 27th, after two interviews with the Commander-in-Chief. 'He has supplies to last till 15 April. Great difficulty of the campaign is that everything depends upon water transport, and steamers are quite inadequate to deal with the question.... Soon the Tigris and the Euphrates will be in flood owing to the snows melting, and then the whole of both banks of both rivers will be under water.'

---

[9] While on the Western Front these divisions had been generally designated by their territorial titles, as there were also 33rd and 7th Divisions in the British Expeditionary Force; but in Mesopotamia the numbers (which are much more convenient on service) were always employed.

He at once raised the question of drafts to fill the gaps that existed in most of his units, and he also discussed the matter of small arms ammunition, a point which caused him a good deal of anxiety. His infantry were armed with the 'short' rifle taking 'Mark VII.' ammunition, whereas the rest of the infantry in D Force were armed with the other rifle taking 'Mark VI.' Ammunition – as had been Indian troops in France, in the Gallipoli Peninsula, and in Egypt. On this point he found himself at variance with Army Headquarters, where the view was entertained that having two sorts of ammunition in the field would cause confusion. Maude pointed out that it had not caused confusion in other theatres, and that if he used the wrong ammunition the musketry of his infantry (to which he attached great importance, remembering what an asset it had proved in France a year and a half before) would for all practical purposes be little better than unaimed fire. The point was however decided against him, although no objection was raised to his using up the Mark VII ammunition that he had brought with him, if it got up the river. The division had four million rounds of this – Maude's administrative staff had a way of getting things done – the rounds reached the front, and his infantry never used any other ammunition than Mark VII.

During the next few days the ships bringing his troops from Egypt kept arriving daily, and General Lake arranged to send the 38th Brigade, the first to arrive, up the Tigris by steamer, to be followed by divisional headquarters and the 40th Brigade; the artillery were to march; in the meantime the division encamped at Basrah as it disembarked. Maude was a strict disciplinarian; but it is interesting to note in his diary for 3 March that, in the case of two young officers tried by field general court-martial for unseemly conduct and sentenced to be severely reprimanded, he commuted the sentence to a simple reprimand 'as obviously it was only a boyish prank.' Letters sent home by officers serving under him all testified to the high regard in which he was held in 18th Division. 'Our divisional general is a great fellow,' one wrote, 'and very sound. We all have the utmost faith in him.' He had not been favourably impressed with Indian staff methods during the time that he had been alongside of, and attached to, the Indian Army Corps in France, and he found much to criticise in his diary now that his division was forming part of an army organised and administered on Indian lines. But he was greatly interested in the entirely new conditions under which he found himself and in the army which he had joined, and in accordance with his usual practice he worked out more than one 'appreciation' of the situation on the Tigris, as he understood it, before proceeding to the front. 'Interesting as my experiences were in France during the first year of the war,' he wrote to Sir H. Mackinnon at the beginning of March, 'they have been still more interesting during the last six months, and I would not have missed a day of them for anything.'

The 88th Brigade began moving up river on the 4th, and Maude himself started on the 10th with his divisional headquarters, although some of the staff remained behind to superintend the moving up of later echelons. He always preferred in case of a move of this kind, where his troops in the nature of things were being transferred to their new position in driblets, to be amongst the first to arrive in the new locality. He had generally followed that course in the case of the minor changes of position of his brigade in France, he had done the same when his division was suddenly sent from the Aegean islands to Helles and when afterwards it went to Egypt, and he had embarked in the first of the vessels conveying his command from the Suez Canal to Mesopotamia. He could not understand why his brigadiers in their moves sometimes preferred to adopt the opposite course, and waited to see everything off from the point of departure before proceeding themselves. Lord Wolseley in the Nile Expedition adopted the same plan as that favoured by Maude, proceeding practically in advance of his army first to Dongola and later to Korti; but his action was criticised in some quarters. It is one of those points that admit of difference of opinion.

Two days before Maude quitted Basrah, General Aylmer had after six weeks' pause undertaken an offensive against the Turkish position about the Dujaila Redoubt, which, had all gone well, might have achieved a success of immense importance. Previous attacks had taken place on the left bank of the Tigris. On this occasion the commander of the Tigris Army Corps endeavoured to break the enemy's front on the right bank, and he proposed to effect his purpose by surprise. A night march was carried out by practically the whole force from the right bank near the Wadi, with the idea of assaulting the hostile entrenchments at dawn. Even on paper there was little margin left in the matter of time for reaching the objective during the dark hours, and, as it turned out, the march had not been completed by the whole of the force at daybreak. Whether success ought not to have been achieved even so has been the subject of a good deal of controversy; but what actually occurred was that an attack was not delivered at once with the troops which had arrived, that the operation proved unsuccessful when the attack was delivered, and that the relieving army suffered a somewhat serious reverse.

Steaming up the Tigris on the 11th, Maude passed many boat-loads of wounded coming down – casualties in this unfortunate engagement, which, besides causing somewhat heavy losses, was not calculated to stimulate the morale of troops who had already experienced mortifying rebuffs. A strong headwind checked the speed of the steamer going up stream, so that he only arrived at corps headquarters at the Wadi on the morning of the 13th. He then found that General Gorringe, previously General Aylmer's Chief of Staff, had assumed command at the front, and he learnt that he ought to have stopped at Sheikh Saad, as that was the place where his division was to assemble. Before turning down stream he was however able to discuss matters with Gorringe, to post himself up with regard to the general situation at the front, and to hear particulars as to the unsuccessful combat of the 8th. He found some of the 38th Brigade already in camp at Sheikh Saad.

'Gorringe had a long talk with me about things,' he wrote in his diary on the 13th, 'and told me that he meant to leave us at Sheikh Saad till about the 25th, when he would use us to attack the Hannah position on the left bank of the river, unless he was able to burst the bunds[10] with shell fire and flood the Turks out. This would be the first step towards relieving Townshend and, after that, we repeat the attempted coup of the 8th against the Sinn position.'

He was delighted to find an excellent training ground about Sheikh Saad, and he at once started to make the most of the little time that would be available for the instruction of his troops as they arrived at the front, in anticipation of the effort to be made very shortly. Hearing that a good supply of hand grenades had arrived at the base, he pressed for the early despatch of a class of weapon of which he had learnt the value in France, at Suvla and at Helles, and he started grenade training. The members of his staff who had gone home on leave from Egypt rejoined him on the 17th. The river was rising, and exercises were occasionally interrupted by the need of hurrying off large working parties to fill gaps torn in the bunds by the flood, which threatened the camps. Sir P. Lake arrived at the front on the 21st to discuss matters and returned to the base on the following day; and by the 23rd the 40th and 39th Brigades, the artillery and practically the whole of the 13th Division, had arrived at Sheikh Saad and were preparing for the anticipated offensive, which had been put off for a few days. Maude when in the field was at all

---

[10] Although Maude had only become associated with an Anglo-Indian Army a fortnight before, he was already picking up Anglo-Indian expressions; 'bund' is Hindustani for dyke.

times most anxious to receive his letters from home, and he was a good deal put out at this juncture by the unaccountable delays in receiving his mails. Writing on the 30th he mentioned that he had only received one set of letters from Mardale within the past two months. But in this same letter he also refers to another point, which attracted attention then and at a later time in this country, which is indirectly suggested in the report of the Mesopotamia Commission, and which is animadverted upon very freely by Mr Candler in The Long Road to Baghdad. Seeing that he had already served during the war in France, in the Gallipoli Peninsula and in Egypt, and was at a later date to assume a paramount responsibility for the conduct of the operations in this theatre of war, Maude's views, as bluntly expressed on a subject of general military interest, are worthy of note.

'What makes us all very angry however,' he wrote, 'is the rigorous censorship that exists here, coming as we do from France and the Dardanelles, where the censorship was reasonably strict, but not excessively so. For instance, a short time ago we were told that no reference to any operation in Mesopotamia was allowed. I wrote suggesting that this must be a mistake, and that only reference to present or future operations, but not to past operations, was meant, but I have had a reply to the effect that even past operations must not be mentioned. The War Office instructions on the point are quite clear and include no such instructions, and it is difficult to see what harm can be done now by saying that such and such a unit or individual, for instance, did well or badly at Ctesiphon, or even in more recent fighting, or that we have killed, wounded or taken prisoner so many hundred Turks. However there it is, and consequently there is little left to write about; in fact, I may say, nothing, for, apart from the fighting, one's daily life is uneventful and the country baffles description, it is so uninteresting. Censorship is of course of inestimable value in preventing useful information reaching the enemy, but throughout this war we have sadly overstepped the mark as to what is necessary in this respect, although in England the public have long since awakened to this fact and demanded that undue secrecy should cease....

'I have letters from Jack Cowans and Willingdon[11] asking me how things are going (amongst many others), but of course I am precluded from answering them, and shall only be able to explain at the end of the war the reason for my silence. It certainly seems strange that a general officer cannot be trusted to use his discretion as to what he says and

---

[11] Governor of Bombay.

does not say, and, even if he is silly enough to say the wrong thing, the censor can still cut it out, without his being prohibited to mention the war as it affects him.' (The envelope containing this letter is marked 'Passed by the censor.')

The ruling, without any qualification, that past operations must not be mentioned was somewhat unfortunate, seeing that these operations had latterly been unsuccessful and that hospital arrangements had broken down. It is possible that, had this restriction not been in force, the deplorable condition of affairs in the Mesopotamian theatre of war would have been realised both at Simla and in England at an earlier date than it came to be, it is possible that steps to place matters on a proper footing would have been taken sooner than they eventually were, and it is even possible that a relieving army, more effectively fitted out for the undertaking and stronger in numbers, might have pushed up the Tigris and have carried out successfully the task of saving Kut. As will be seen, Sir P. Lake, who had not been long in command and who was carrying on a system that was in force when he arrived, relaxed the rules shortly after this.

CHAPTER X
The Effort to Relieve Kut

Maude was busy during the closing days of March making all preparations for the important operation which his division was about to undertake, and General Gorringe had accepted his proposals with regard to the method by which the attack on the Hannah entrenchments was to be carried out. The 7th (Meerut) Division under General Younghusband, it should be mentioned, was at this time on the left bank of the Tigris and was holding trenches facing Hannah, while the 3rd (Lahore) Division under General Keary was on the other side of the river. Maude had gone all round 7th Division's trenches on the 23rd with Younghusband, and had asked that they should be advanced nearer to the enemy's lines, a task which Younghusband promised to have carried out. He had also carefully reconnoitred the enemy's position from the right bank of the river, and he had framed his plans well in advance. His 38th Brigade had moved to Wadi from Sheikh Saad on the 20th, and by the end of the month the whole division except the 39th Brigade and divisional headquarters was in the forward position.

The 38th and 40th Brigades relieved 7th Division in their trenches on the night of 1 April, and that same night the 89th Brigade marched from Sheikh Saad to Wadi. Maude himself, with his staff, went up by steamer on the 1st, and after a consultation with General Gorringe at corps headquarters, they proceeded to the trenches and settled down in them in heavy rain.

'This rain continued all the evening,' he wrote in his diary of that day, 'and we were sitting soon in a bog. Got my tent pitched in the trench and with difficulty managed to get a shovel, with which I worked for one and a quarter hours, and finally drained and made tent so habitable that I was able to take in three of my staff. Wretched cold and wet night lying in the mud, but rain stopped and it will probably be fine and hot in the morning. Went round part of the trenches on arrival and saw to many things. Cold dinner and not very much of it. Corps operation orders for assault issued and reached me following morning.'

The weather off and on had been very bad for some days past; the Tigris was already in flood, and its swollen waters had caused much inconvenience at Sheikh Saad, bursting the dykes and inundating portions of the camping grounds. The attempt to force the awkward defile on the left bank of the river was in fact about to be undertaken under most unfavourable weather conditions, as there was always the risk of this flat, low-lying isthmus being flooded from either flank. Although this in a measure affected both sides, the Turks had made preparations against such an eventuality, while their assailants were not in a position to do so in advance, in the event of their not securing the different hostile positions and of their having to dig in in front. The actual Hannah position consisted of five lines of entrenchments, at a point where the defile was only about 1,000 yards wide. About four miles further through the defile, at a point where a bend in the river narrowed it to about 1,000 yards, was a second position – that of Felahieh – which was not so elaborately prepared. Two miles further on was the third position of Sannaiyat, a strongly entrenched line at the locality where, going westwards, the defile widens out to about 1500 yards; the Turks placed their main dependence upon this third set of defences. The assault on Hannah was originally to have taken place on the 3rd; but it was put off till the 4th, and eventually it was postponed till the morning of the 5th.

It ought to be mentioned here, because it is a fact that is not generally known in connection with the final effort of the forces on the Tigris to relieve Kut, that Sir P. Lake was running considerable risks in undertaking offensive operations at all. Owing to the difficulties caused by the lack of river transport there was an alarming deficiency of supplies at the front. The short campaign, Maude's share in which is about to be related, was fought with only three days reserve of supplies in the area occupied by General Gorringe's Corps. The communications were no doubt fairly safe, and they were afforded useful protection on the left bank of the river by the extensive Suwaikieh marshes, which would have obliged the enemy to make a wide detour to get at the rear of the Anglo-Indian Army on that side. But could the Turks have managed to get a gun down to below Sheikh Saad and sunk a few of the river craft plying in the channel, the troops at the front might have starved. The truth was that, although experience was to prove that the relieving force was not strong enough to effect its purpose, it was in reality too strong for its own communications; these were not fully equal to feeding three divisions, with the cavalry and attendant troops.

Maude was very appreciative of the work which 7th Division had carried out since 23 March, and he was also quite satisfied with what had been effected by the artillery in respect to cutting the wire entanglements in front of the Hannah lines. The plan was that the assault was to be delivered at 4.55 a.m., without artillery preparation, the guns only opening fire on the rear trenches as the assault on the front ones took place. The 39th Brigade had gone into the trenches during the night of 2/3 April, and all the orders for the attack were issued on the 3rd. Maude mentions in his diary that on the afternoon of the 4th he went round the trenches and talked to some of the men in most of his battalions. 'They were all full of fight and keenness,' he remarks. All ranks indeed realised that much depended upon them, and that much was expected of them. The arrival of an entirely British division at the front had given great encouragement to the Tigris Army Corps, and officers and men belonging to it could not but feel that the force which was trying to relieve Kut was looking to them for a lead. They had come upon the scene in Mesopotamia, bringing with them a high reputation earned on the slopes of the Sari Bair mountain and during the successful evacuations of Suvla and Helles. They knew that their division had been specially selected from amongst several others to proceed to a theatre of war where all was not going well. 'They were a cool, hard, determined-looking breed,' Mr Candler writes, 'well seasoned now, and burnt to the complexion of Ghurkas.' They had confidence in themselves, confidence in their brigadiers, unbounded confidence in their divisional commander, and during the next few hours they were to show that the confidence was not misplaced. The story of the fighting of the 5th may well be told in Maude's own words, as jotted down in his diary:

> 5.4.16. Up at 3 a.m. and had breakfast at 4.15. Attack went in at 4.55 and was entirely successful. Took the three lines one after the other and pushed on at once, driving the Turks before us. We gained ground steadily till about midday, when we came up against the trenches at the Felahieh bend.
>
> I had arranged for an attack at 1 p.m., preceded by an artillery bombardment at noon till 1, but corps commander came up to see me about noon and suggested waiting till dark. Had already pushed my headquarters forward twice and was now within about 1,500 yards of the firing line. Here Forbes, one of my A.D.C.'s, was hit.

Made all my plans for the attack in the evening and issued the orders. Told corps commander that I feared that 7.45 would be too late, by means of a message sent by one of his staff. Bombardment began at 7, by which time it was almost dark, and at 7.45 the assault went in and the position was captured. Everything went splendidly. There were the usual lot of panic-mongers who came in and spoke of every one having been killed, but nothing could have been better than the work of the division and indeed throughout the day.

Machine guns very busy, especially during the last attack, and it was a pity that the assault was made in pitch darkness, as it does not do for half-trained troops. Weather fine and quite hot. 7th Division came through us and relieved us for the night, and we withdrew to bivouacs near the river.'

The casualties suffered by the division in this day of battle came to a total of 1,796. General Gorringe commended Maude and all under him for their preliminary success at Hannah, and he was still more generous with his eulogies for what had been accomplished in the second phase of the struggle. 'The highest praise is due to General Maude and his brigade commanders and all under their command for this successful night attack, a difficult operation at all times, requiring dash and good leadership as well as personal bravery among the junior commissioned and non-commissioned ranks.' Sir P. Lake in his despatch of 12 August 1916 wrote that 'the 38th Infantry Brigade and the Warwicks and Worcesters of the 39th Infantry Brigade did particularly well in this assault. High praise is due to Major-General Maude, his brigade commanders, and all under them for this successful night attack.' The capture of the Turkish first line had in reality been a simple business enough, for the enemy had offered no stubborn resistance to the assault, to the disappointment of the troops who had been most anxious to show their mettle. The attack upon the Felahieh works had been a much higher trial. There the Ottoman troops had defended themselves stoutly, and the infantry had been obliged to fight their way through without artillery support and in the dark. Colonel Brownrigg describes the operations as follows:

His [Maude's] operation orders for the attack on the Hannah trenches are a model of thoroughness and are a wonderful example of his own axiom for orders and instructions – that they should be 'clear, concise and complete.' As it happened, the Turk got wind of the impending move against him and, having become aware of the presence of an 'all British' division in the trenches opposite, had made himself scarce prior to the attack, which spent itself on almost thin air. This was unfortunate, as the preparations were so complete that success was assured – as far as could be humanly seen –even if the Turks had held the Hannah position in full force. The evening following the capture of the Hannah position, however, Maude decisively beat the Turk in an encounter battle; and in one day he, at the head of his division, had covered six miles of the distance separating us from Kut. The troops rested on the ground won –but not so Maude, who spent nearly the whole night visiting and cheering the wounded and dying, and getting his first glimpse of those insufficient medical arrangements which his own powers of organisation were so soon to put on a happier footing.

The offensive on the left bank of the Tigris which had opened so auspiciously was not destined, however, to accomplish its purpose. Within a few hours of the 13th Division's triumph at Felahieh, the force endeavouring to succour Kut met with a serious reverse close at hand; for 7th Division, after relieving the 18th during the night of 5/6, advanced and were repulsed in their attack upon the third Turkish set of entrenchments, that at Sannaiyat, but under circumstances that assuredly reflected no discredit on the troops. The position had not been reconnoitred effectually. The assaulting columns had to find their way through 18th Division in the dark, and they were also greatly hampered during their advance by numerous and deep cross-trenches. The result was that, instead of their being ready to make their rush at dawn as had been intended, the battalions were still more than a mile from their objectives when it became light. The ground to be traversed was flat and it was destitute of cover. No preparation by artillery had been arranged for, as the attack was to have been delivered on the same lines as Maude's on Hannah on the previous morning. In spite of the delays, the attempt to storm the formidable hostile lines was actually made; but the troops could not get within some hundreds of yards of the enemy front, and they eventually had to fall back and to dig in. The situation was made the more untoward by the Tigris overflowing its banks and by a strong wind from the north causing a flood to break over portions of the ground from the side of the Suwaikieh marsh. 7th Division, however, held on grimly in spite of the reverse, and the troops even tried to get forward gradually on the 7th. They did manage to make some progress that night.

In the combats which took place at the time of the attempted relief of Kut, and during most of the fighting indeed that occurred in Mesopotamia below Baghdad, one of the principal difficulties which commanders and subordinate leaders of troops had to contend with was that, owing to the flatness of the ground and to the total absence of trees almost everywhere, there were no points to march on. There was nothing but a dead level with no topographical features of any kind to help. Particularly did this happen to be the case about Sannaiyat where, to secure direction, the expedient was to some extent resorted to of sticking up posts in rear of troops as they advanced, enabling guides to keep direction by looking backwards from time to time. Even in broad daylight, free use had to be made of the compass for making a move over a comparatively short distance. Such conditions undoubtedly favour the defending side during the progress of tactical operations, and they accentuated the obstacles to victory with which the Anglo-Indian troops were constantly confronted during their unsuccessful conflicts of April 1916.

There had been an idea of delivering a fresh attack upon Sannaiyat, 7th Division advancing on the right and the 13th on the left; but it was ultimately decided to employ only the 13th for the projected undertaking. Gorringe regarded this portion of the Turkish lines that had been constructed to cover the siege of Kut as the key of the situation, and, seeing that it coincided with the widening out of the defile on the left bank of the Tigris, its capture must inevitably have exerted a great influence over the campaign for the relief of General Townshend. It was arranged that Maude should make the attempt at dawn on the 9th. 3rd Division, which was on the right bank of the river, had contrived to push forward some distance on the 7th, and this enabled him to reconnoitre the trenches about to be attacked from the flank and from their right rear, his brigadiers accompanying him. All the plans for the advance were drawn up with the utmost care. A bridge was completed over the Tigris at Felahieh on the 8th, which may have helped to mislead the Turks, inducing them to anticipate a transfer of the bulk of the relieving force from the left to the right bank; but ample enemy forces remained in the Sannaiyat lines. The attack of 18th Division took place at dawn on the 9th, as intended, and the story of the combat may be told in Maude's words as recorded in his diary:

> Division moved as soon as it was dark. 40th Infantry Brigade to be at 7th Division headquarters at 8.30, 38th at 9.30, and 39th at 10.30. My disposition as follows: Troops to deploy in line 600 yards from enemy's front, 38th on right, 40th on left, 39th in

second line. Line deployed quite successfully, no noise, and everything with utmost regularity. Had staff officers out to superintend and had front line pegged out with pickets. Also had a member from each battalion to mark its left. At 4.20 a.m. the line moved forward to assault, orders being to rush the first three lines. Two leading ranks of platoons to carry and consolidate first line, two rear ranks of platoons to carry and consolidate second line, 39th Brigade to carry and consolidate third line. Line advanced steadily and noiselessly till 4.28 when leading line was within 100 yards of position.

Then Turks sent up a flare from their left which made our left lose direction slightly (our compass bearing was 260 degrees true). About half a minute after, another flare went up from the enemy's right, followed by heavy outburst of machinegun and rifle fire. Second line lay down while first line pushed on. Consequently first line, which did splendidly, got into Turk's trenches in a good many places, North Lancs, King's Own, Welsh Fusiliers, and Wilts especially. But being unsupported by second line had to give way. Officers most gallant in trying to rally second line, but were unable to get men forward more than a few yards, and subsequently second line recoiled carrying in a great measure lines in rear with it. Men quite surprised by flares.

We held on tenaciously where we were all day, the troops scratching holes in the ground and digging themselves in as best they could, and at night we withdrew into the trenches we started from in the morning. Division required a good deal of sorting, so got permission to send in the 89th Infantry Brigade to Felahieh.

The casualties suffered by 18th Division in this unsuccessful engagement amounted to 1,792 of all ranks, and the result was a grievous disappointment to Maude and to the whole relief force. The reverse foreshadowed the final failure of Sir P. Lake to save Kut, and its gravity was apparent to all concerned, following as it did upon the failure of 7th Division to force a way through three days before. Whether this formidable Sannaiyat position would have been reduced had Maude's second line performed its share in the original rush intended to win a way through the three lines of entrenchments, it is impossible to say; but 18th Division had undoubtedly been set a formidable task. It is clear that the enemy was fully prepared for an assault, and the Turks had enjoyed three clear days for perfecting their defences since being ejected from the Felahieh line and since beating off the onset of 7th Division on the morning of the 6th.

'In this attack the division was badly shattered,' writes Colonel Brownrigg, 'and it was perhaps on this occasion, more than any other, that General Maude proved his greatness of spirit and bigness of heart.

'Divisional H.Q. was well up behind the fire trenches from which the attack was to be delivered next morning, and all night General Maude sat in a chair in a shallow recess, wrapped up in a coat (for it was bitterly cold) receiving news of the troops arriving in position, and now and again referring to a map. His staff lay huddled together in a trench beside him. There was no overhead cover for any one and there were no blankets.

'Shortly before dawn the final advance was made, the attack was delivered – and failed. Then the big man showed himself with a cheerful face and a smile for everyone. He accepted the inevitable. Kut was not yet to be reached. His staff were gloomy, but not so Maude. As soon as the position of the troops was more or less understood, he proceeded to go round the whole front line, smiling and whistling, and cheering the wounded. He never showed for one moment, not even to his staff, the bitter disappointment which must have been weighing on his heart.'

Maude mentions in his diary that he was so exhausted on the night of 10/11, after being awake all the previous night and after the busy day that he had spent on the 9th, that he 'did not wake up, although lying in water the greater part of the night.'

'In the waterlogged trenches of El Hannah,' writes Captain Ogilvie-Forbes, 'he gave what he jokingly used to refer to as his 'house-party', when he invited those who had no shelter from the torrential rain to share the hospitality of his little tent. He always kept open house, especially when the hardships were at their worst, for any casual visitor be he ever so junior. 'Ask him to dinner,' 'ask him to lunch,' were amongst his most frequent orders.'

The Tigris Corps was not merely struggling with antagonists who were holding skilfully designed entrenchments in strong force, during its gallant efforts to bring succour to the stricken garrison of Kut. It was also struggling against nature, and it was struggling against time. On the one hand, the inundation of much of the country, coupled with the mud that was created everywhere by temporary overflows from the Tigris and by the occasional torrents of rain, forbade any attempt to turn the formidable hostile positions, and it at the same time rendered advance preparatory to attacking them frontally most difficult. On the other hand, the sands were running out fast, and every day, even every hour, that was lost, rendered the situation of Kut more desperate. Supported by such very inadequate artillery power as Gorringe had at command, a mere local victory at any point necessarily ranked as a fine feat of arms under the existing conditions. But only a succession of such victories would achieve the purpose that the Tigris Army Corps had in view. Some doubt had existed as to the exact date up to which Townshend would, on the reduced rations that he was now issuing, be able to hold out; but it was now known that if the relief was to be effected it would have to be effected by the 25th.

Sir P. Lake decided after a consultation with Gorringe that a fresh effort to penetrate the Turkish lines must be made, but on the right bank of the Tigris where, as already mentioned, the 3rd Division had made good some ground while 13th and 7th Divisions had been trying to break through on the further side of the river. It was arranged that 7th Division should remain in the trenches facing Sannaiyat, and that 13th Division should be transferred to the southern bank and should cooperate with 3rd Division. This move of Maude's troops was carried out on different dates between 12th and 16th, his infantry taking up positions at Abu Roman some distance in rear of 3rd Division. He records in his diary that he had been very busy during these days writing letters to the relatives of the numerous officers under his command who had fallen in the conflicts at Hannah, Felahieh and Sannaiyat.

The operations on the right bank were to start with an attack by the 3rd Division upon the end of the Turkish lines next the river at a locality named Beit Aiessa. This was situated about a mile and a half upstream from the end of the Sannaiyat lines on the further bank; and there were important dykes here, which gave the Turks power to inundate considerable areas of ground when they thought fit. The 3rd Division had gained a footing in some of the forward trenches on the 15th; its attack delivered on the morning of the 17th was most successful, for practically the whole of the trenches that formed the objective were taken.

It was arranged that its infantry brigades should be relieved by those of 18th Division after dusk; but at about 7 p.m., before the relief had actually commenced, the Turks suddenly assumed the offensive in strong force and with great determination. A desperate affray ensued in the dark. The Ottoman assailants recaptured some guns and machine guns which they had lost in the morning, and they threw portions of the 3rd Division into confusion. Called upon urgently for aid, Maude hurried up five of his battalions, and these played an important part in restoring the situation at some points where the 3rd Division had been compelled to give way. But there would seem in the first instance to have been some delay in the arrival of the whole of the troops of 18th Division, who were supposed to be ready to take the lines over; for they should have been on the spot almost immediately after the Turkish counterattack was delivered. Maude himself was not altogether satisfied. 'Reinforcements from 18th Division were already moving forward,' Sir P. Lake wrote in his despatch of 12th August, 'but owing to the darkness and boggy ground they were delayed and some hours elapsed before they arrived.' The results of this nocturnal combat were undoubtedly most unfortunate for the relieving force, as valuable ground which had been well won in the morning, and possession of which would have greatly aided further advance towards Es Sinn, passed back into Turkish hands.

Those battalions of 18th Division which were thrust into the fray did admirably, and, had some additional ones reached the fighting front, the enemy might perhaps have been beaten off at all points and a very important victory might have been gained, Maude would seem to have disposed all but five of them in second line after a time; but the accounts of this combat are somewhat conflicting, and his own view clearly was that upon the whole his command had done well. 'Division behaved magnificently during the fight last night,' he wrote in his diary next day; 'Worcesters, East Lancs, South Wales Borderers and Wilts did especially well.' He was delighted with their performance under exceptionally trying conditions. The Turks had succeeded in retaking some of the trenches closest to the river, and in recovering the guns and machine guns they had lost in the morning; but they lost very heavily in the combat, and victory on the whole rested with the relieving force. In his despatch of 12 August Sir P. Lake estimated their casualties at from 4,000 to 5,000. Maude issued the following complimentary order in connection with this affray:

> The G.O.C. wishes to express his appreciation of the excellent work done by the division on the night of 17/18, when the 3rd

Division was heavily attacked by the enemy and in a position of some danger.

The readiness with which the reinforcing battalions moved forward, and the steadiness which they subsequently displayed, undoubtedly saved the situation and were mainly instrumental in inflicting on the Turks the huge casualties which they suffered on that occasion.

The gallantry of the division and its: splendid tenacity have received the commendation of the corps commander when conversing with the G.O.C.

In a letter of thanks to General O'Dowda, commanding the 38th Brigade, General Keary remarked: 'It is hardly possible that my worn-out troops could have held on without the assistance so loyally accorded by your troops.'

18th Division relieved the 3rd Division in the Beit Aiessa position on the 18th. On the following morning the 39th Brigade attempted to recapture the trenches close to the Tigris, which had been taken forty-eight hours before and had been won back by the Osmanlis on the occasion of their counterattack by night, but the operation failed. 'Want of officers chief cause,' Maude wrote in his diary; 'casualties not too heavy though we have lost up to tonight some 800 killed and wounded in three days.' The troops on this occasion were greatly hampered by flooded ground, some of the men being drowned.

Kut could only hold out for about another week. In view of the strength of the enemy lines in rear of Beit Aiessa which had still to be reduced if the offensive was to continue on the right bank of the Tigris, and also of the fact that Sannaiyat closed the river to steamers a mile and a half below Beit Aiessa – a point of considerable importance from the aspect of trying as a forlorn hope to run a vessel with supplies through to the starving garrison – Sir P. Lake resolved that there must be yet another attempt to break through on the left bank. 7th Division were to be employed for the undertaking; but they were to be helped as far as possible by fire from the right bank. The Sannaiyat entrenchments could be taken in enfilade, and to a certain extent in reverse, from below Beit Aiessa. This plan was communicated to Maude, who at once started selecting positions for his machine guns and his artillery so that they should play their part effectively in the contemplated operation. The attack was to have been delivered on the 20th; but owing to a sudden inundation from the side of the Suwaikieh marsh it had to be postponed until the 22nd. Maude's guns violently bombarded Sannaiyat on the 20th and 21st. On both those days his infantry also made some progress in front of Beit Aiessa, although not without encountering sturdy opposition; the bombing parties were particularly successful, and he was much pleased with their performances.

'Casualties especially heavy in officers, and we are having bad luck in this respect,' he wrote in his diary on the 21st; 'some of the battalions have only five or six, including the Colonel and Adjutant, left. Some drafts are however arriving, but not in sufficient numbers to keep pace with casualties. We lost about 8,500 at Hannah, Felahieh and Sannaiyat, and about 1,000 since we have been at Abu Roman. On the other hand, we have punished the Turks, especially during the night attack of 17/18, when they are reported to have lost very heavily, and in front of our trenches and quite close to them are at least 1,000 bodies. Attack on Sannaiyat position by 7th Division postponed till tomorrow. Meantime I have a battery of thirty-five machine guns in position just across the river ready to rake their line.

'22.38.16. Up and breakfasted early. Had bombardment of the enemy in my front by my artillery early to mislead the enemy. For attack on Sannaiyat position registration began at 6 a.m., slow bombardment at 6.20 a.m., and intense bombardment at 7 a.m. Infantry 7th Division attacked at 7 a.m. They got a footing in the Turkish trenches, but could not hold on, and after fierce fighting were compelled to give way. My guns and machine guns got good targets and did great execution among the Turks.'

Mr Candler (who witnessed this final effort to force the Turkish entrenchments on the left bank of the Tigris from the same side of the river as Maude) gives a graphic description of the action. 'The 7th Division went very near to achieving success. They were however terribly handicapped by floods and mud, and, in spite of the heroism of troops who had forced their way well home into the hostile position and of the effective assistance that they were receiving from the opposite side of the river, they could not maintain what had been won at the outset. It does not follow that, even if they had secured possession of the whole position, their victory would necessarily have ensured the saving of Kut. But for practical purposes their failure meant that the prolonged attempt to relieve the place had come to an end, although neither the Commander-in-Chief nor Maude even then gave up all hope.'

Maude had from the outset been of opinion that the real offensive ought to be conducted on the right bank of the Tigris, as there was elbow-room there. His appreciation of the situation was that the extensive Beit Aiessa-Es Sinn lines covering the approaches to Kut on that side of the river ought to have been made the objective, the main attack being delivered on the right or southern part of the enemy front which practically had an eastern and a southern face. He would have kept the Turks busy on the eastern face by local attacks and bombardments, and would have occupied their attention on the left bank of the Tigris by a show of force, while all the time intending to break through the southern face and to roll up the line. He had a discussion with Sir P. Lake on the 23rd, and even at this late date there seems to have been an idea of carrying out an operation somewhat on these lines; because the 3rd Division, which had been in reserve since the 18th, was sent off to the left on the morning of the 24th, when it pressed forward and dug in about two miles from the Es Sinn position; a brigade of 7th Division was also brought across the river and placed in reserve. Nothing however came of these preliminary movements. That night the Julnar made its intrepid essay to run the gauntlet of the Tigris defences and to convey food to Kut. Maude, who knew of the enterprise, had his machine guns and artillery sweeping the further river bank after dark, and he mentions in his diary that she passed his advanced troops at Beit Aiessa at 9.15 p.m. 'without incident.' She got as far up as the river bend at Megasis, and was there brought up short by a wire rope across the channel and captured. This was ascertained by aeroplane reconnaissance next morning.

Gorringe made Maude aware on the 26th of the instructions which had been sent to General Townshend with regard to his getting into communication with the Ottoman commander and trying to secure the most favourable terms possible. Kut still had supplies enough to hold out until 30th, and the Corps Commander asked Maude for his opinion as to whether a relief before that date could any longer be regarded as a feasible proposition. Reluctantly, Maude gave it as his view that, in consequence of the condition of the force (especially in respect to officers), of the shortness of the time available, and of the situation as a whole, the thing was impracticable. 'In such fighting as this,' he wrote in his diary, 'the officer is all-important, and right well he does it. But without him even the Regulars will not go on, and when it comes to partially trained troops such as the New Army divisions the position is quite impossible.' Two days later, on 28 April, Kut surrendered after its garrison had made a glorious defence of five months, and after 24,000 troops had been killed, wounded and taken prisoner in trying to bring it aid. Of the 24,000 casualties 10,000 had occurred since 4 April, the day before 13th Division was first engaged.

'You will have read in the papers,' Maude wrote a few days later to Colonel J. Magill, 'the full narrative of our failure to relieve Kut. Its fall has been very disappointing, but I do not think that the fault lies with the soldiers, although no doubt an attempt will be made to saddle them with the responsibility. The local difficulties, the long line of communications, the water transport (or rather the lack of it), the menace from floods and rains, the barrenness of the country – all these factors rendered the most careful organisation and liberal expenditure necessary as a preliminary to success. The obstacles in our way were enormous, hampered as we were by floods and restricted as our movements were by being tied to the river – but we did our best, as I think will be admitted when the story is known.' Then, after a brief résumé of the various actions up to the repulse of the Turkish counterattack on the night of 17/18 April, he goes on: 'During the next few days the division distinguished itself by some very good grenade work, during which we inflicted many casualties on the Turks and drove them back, and then on the 22nd 7th Division failed once more in an attack upon the Sannaiyat position. After this it was adjudged that we could not continue our attempt to relieve Kut, and here we are, holding on to the position we held previously. Kut has fallen, Townshend, I understand, having previously destroyed his guns and munitions. An attempt to re-provision him by running a ship through failed, the stream being too strong and the ship too noisy. It was a good attempt however.

'We were beat by want of time to clear away the remaining obstacles in our way, and by want of drafts to replace our casualties and especially those amongst officers.'

Maude goes on to refer to a point that he also mentions more than once in his diaries, and which would seem to be deserving of note in summing-up the causes of Sir P. Lake's failure. The importance of the relieving force knowing the exact date up to which the besieged place of arms could hold out would not seem to have been quite sufficiently realised within the place itself. It may be observed that it is not unusual for some doubt to exist upon this point under similar conditions, and that beleaguered garrisons have on many – occasions in the past held out a few days longer than had been expected. They have even been succoured at a later date than that laid down as the date beyond which defence was impossible. When Maude attacked Sannaiyat on the 9 April, with troops who had gained very substantial successes three days before and who were full of confidence, he was under the impression that Kut could only hold out till the 18th – that only four days in fact remained for the garrison to be saved. As it turned out, the garrison could have held out, and did hold out, for nearly another three weeks. Had the commander of 18th Division known this he would have proposed to sap up much nearer to the position to be attacked before delivering his assault upon it; and, as General Gorringe had readily agreed to his proposals hitherto, Maude would no doubt have been granted the additional time that he asked for. Whether an attack by 18th Division under such conditions would have proved successful is a matter of conjecture. But its leader was a master of the art of thorough preparation for an enterprise, when given facilities for making such preparation, and he seems to have thought himself that two or three days' grace might have changed the result.

'I need not enlarge upon the bitter disappointment felt by all ranks on the Tigris line at the failure of their effort to relieve their comrades in Kut,' Sir P. Lake wrote in his despatch of 12 August. Maude shared in this feeling of disappointment to the full; but he never showed it. Nor in his diary nor yet in his letters does he offer any criticisms or complaints with regard to the handling of the force, except on quite minor points, although the plan of operations actually adopted in April was not in accordance with his own appreciation of the situation. It may be mentioned here that the diary, as it has come to hand, closes on 1 May 1916, practically synchronising with the fall of Kut. He had kept it carefully ever since the outbreak of the Great War, and he continued to do so. But the portions of it subsequent to May 1916 were in his room when he died in November 1917, and they had to be destroyed for fear of infection. The Army Commander had fortunately taken off the embargo which had previously been placed upon references to past events in Mesopotamia, and consequently Maude's letters, which during the previous weeks had been uninformative, became full of interest again from about the date of the fall of Kut onwards.

CHAPTER XI
From Divisional to Army Commander

The weeks immediately subsequent to the surrender of General Townshend's force constituted a particularly trying and tragic period for the Tigris Army Corps. All ranks were to a greater or less extent depressed by the sense of failure. The troops had suffered hardships of no common order, buoyed up by the hope that they would, somehow, succeed in bringing succour to comrades in sore distress. The losses suffered since January had been very heavy. The yawning gaps in the ranks were but slowly being filled up. Exhausting operations had been carried out by an army, beset by inundations, struggling through sticky mud, drenched at times by violent rainstorms, and carrying out an almost impossible task on rations that were barely sufficient. Officers and men could not but be aware that, although the medical arrangements had been ameliorated within the past two or three months, they still fell short of what soldiers have a right to expect when campaigning in a theatre of war where hostilities have already been for a considerable time in progress. The fall of Kut moreover occurred just at that season of the year when the hot weather sets in with intensity in Mesopotamia, and when the troops necessarily began to experience the trials which sojourn in encampments or bivouacs in summer in desolate tropical lands carries with it.

When an army on field service in a hot country settles down to a condition of comparative quiet after having been engaged on extremely active operations, sickness almost invariably sets in. Maude had experienced this fifteen years before when he joined up with the Coldstream on the Modder during the lull between Lord Methuen's vigorous effort to relieve Kimberley and the commencement of Lord Roberts' great forward movement into the enemy's territory. It is a question of reaction. There was however bound to be disease in May and June on the Tigris even had the army been on the move, even had it been furnished with ample supplies and comforts of all kinds, and even had perfect hospital arrangements been the order of the day. As the floods dry up under the rays of a burning sun, the climate naturally becomes unhealthy. Strong winds, which incidentally create almost suffocating dust storms, distribute the germs that are bound to be created in camping grounds no matter how carefully sanitation is attended to. The heat is intense. Flies, insects and creeping things become a torment, and in the case of General Lake's forces these untoward conditions were confronting a soldiery who were already somewhat debilitated, who were suffering from a not unnatural despondency, and who were therefore particularly liable to contract any ailments that are common in Irak. Maude's division was, it is true, somewhat better situated than those alongside of it in this respect, seeing that his troops had enjoyed a fair amount of rest and much change of scene on their travels from the Helles beaches to the plain of Sheikh Saad; but no one would realise more clearly than he did how imperative it was to look after the well-being of his men under the circumstances, to watch with jealousy all matters connected with the sanitation of his encampments, and to stimulate by precept and encouragement the morale of troops of whom he was the trusted chief.

There had already on 24 April been some suspicious cases of cholera in the 13th Division; these foreshadowed an epidemic which however happily did not prove very serious. Maude records in his diary that on the 28th there were twenty to thirty cases daily and five to eight deaths' cause obscure, some people say water, some that it comes from the Wadi, probably the latter. All manner of precautions were taken, and the outbreak was kept well in hand; Maude insisted on visiting the cholera camps from time to time, against the wishes of the medical officers. His troops were still in the early part of May holding the line about Beit Aiessa in the right of the front south of the Tigris, with 3rd Division on their left; the 35th Brigade of 7th Division (which remained on the other bank of the river) was temporarily under his orders. Those of his troops not actually in the trenches were inspected by Sir P. Lake early on 1 May in their various encampments, and Maude mentions in his diary that, after going round the trenches a little later on that day, he was badly sniped on the way back. 'A frightful sand-storm all day, blinding every one and smothering things with dust; rain in the evening. Decided to move our camp tomorrow,' so runs the last entry in this particular booklet of the diary and closes a most valuable personal record. Little of special importance occurred for some three weeks subsequently, but that Maude had lost none of his enthusiasm for action and that he found plenty to occupy him, is shown by what he wrote to Colonel Magill on 10 May, in the letter of which part has already been quoted above.

Now I am busy reorganising my division, and only hoping that an advance by the Russians will bring about a corresponding advance on our side, for one would dearly love to enter at least Kut – if not Baghdad – so as to settle matters with the Turks. However we shall see how matters develop. The weather gets hotter day by day, but the nights though somewhat stuffy are not yet unpleasantly so. But by night every creeping thing imaginable appears, flying bugs and quaint animals of sundry descriptions, including sand-flies, many of which bite badly. The flies too in the daytime are rather a plague. However none of these things will matter if we can get a move on; it is inaction that I dread, and we seem in danger of relapsing into trench warfare, which, in this country at all events, ought to be unnecessary. The wastage in my staff has already begun again, and I have one sick and one (an A.D.C.) wounded within the last month. Duststorms are trying, and I hardly like to estimate the amount of sand that I swallowed going round the trenches the day before yesterday. At all events one came back black as a nigger minstrel.

At this time Maude was still living in a single-fly tent in spite of the heat. 'Shorts' and shirt-sleeves had come to be the recognised parade costume for officers; but he himself never appeared outside his tent without a jacket. Every Sunday, if he possibly could, he visited every tent in his three field ambulances and he saw, if he did not actually speak to, every patient – and there were by this time generally large numbers of patients. He was greatly pleased one day to see in a newspaper arriving by the mail that his son Eric had passed into Woolwich from Lancing. A few days after this circumstances suddenly arose calling for prompt action, in which he showed that neither heat, nor the discouragement so generally felt throughout the force, had affected his vigour as a leader and his capacity for correctly appreciating a military situation at short notice.

As will be seen from the sketch map on page 217 above, the Tigris between the Megasis bend and Beit Aiessa runs north-eastwards. The general direction taken by the enemy trenches from where they quitted the river bank in front of Beit Aiessa was southerly, down to a point about three miles east of the Megasis bend and some way north of the Dujaila Redoubt. The Turks had always looked for a British advance along the river bank, and their main Es Sinn position, designed to meet such a move, faced almost northwards and at right angles to their general line. The enemy front between the right of the Es Sinn position and where this met the Tigris facing Beit Aiessa was known by the name of the Chehala lines. Supposing Maude's division to advance, it would first have to force the northern end of these Chehala lines, and would then in the nature of things make a left wheel and push almost in a southerly direction towards the Es Sinn position, with its right following the Tigris bank.

Early in the morning of the 19th a message came to hand from the 40th Brigade trenches that the enemy had disappeared from in front of them, information which was speedily found to be correct by patrols. Maude at once ordered two battalions to press forward without delay, and by 9 a.m. they had occupied the part of the Chehala lines facing his division, while patrols were already on their way towards Es Sinn. This was reported to be vacated both by the patrols and also by aeroplanes, and he was anxious to advance forthwith to take possession of the position and to hurry up guns into it, so as to bear upon the retreating enemy. But the Corps Commander was unfortunately away at Sheikh Saad, and an opportunity of harassing the Turks, and of showing them that there was plenty of fight left in the army opposed to them, was lost. The Turks had a bridge over the Tigris between the Megasis loop and Kut, and this they removed during the night. Next morning the cavalry made a wide sweep south of the Dujaila Redoubt, and reached the vicinity of the Tigris and of the Hai near Kut, while 3rd Division, after making a detour involving an exhausting march, occupied the Es Sinn position without opposition. The enemy, in so far as the right bank of the Tigris was concerned, had quietly retired to fresh ground close to Kut, a withdrawal on the part of the Osmanli forces which appreciably altered the general situation on the Mesopotamian front. In consequence thereof, General Lake was now in a position to push forward his advanced line on that side of the river as far as the Megasis loop, to within about five miles of the position where General Townshend had maintained himself so long.

The Sultan's troops were however maintaining their grip upon the Sannaiyat entrenchments on the further side of the great waterway; so that the retreat of the Turks on the right bank did not, under the conditions existing at the moment, in reality benefit the British very much. So long as Khalil Pasha's forces had been in the position of besiegers of the stronghold, they had been obliged to maintain a line of defence at a distance of several miles from Kut, so as to keep the relieving army at arm's length. Now, however, that the place had fallen and was in their hands, it was in many respects of advantage to the Turks to shorten their front on the right bank of the Tigris and retire in that quarter – so long as they held Sannaiyat. Supposing their opponents to follow such retirement up, as they were almost obliged to do, the immediate result was automatically to lengthen their opponents' land communications – for British vessels could not pass Sannaiyat and the abandonment of a few square miles of barren country was a matter of small moment to the Turks. The Ottoman retreat did, on the other hand, bring a certain amount of encouragement to the Tigris Army Corps at a moment when this stood much in need of some such stimulus.

There had been several references in Maude's diary since the beginning of the World War to the unsatisfactory character of the staff methods in vogue, and comments of the same kind had also appeared in the diary which he kept in South Africa. This was a subject which he thoroughly understood and which he had closely studied, and he was (perhaps more than the majority of British officers of experience) convinced of the vital importance of regularity and system in the conduct of such transactions. His own abnormal acquaintance with detail enabled him to detect failures in this respect more readily than would be the case with most soldiers of authority and standing, and it undoubtedly made him a somewhat exacting critic. Alike on the Western Front, in the Gallipoli Peninsula and during the short time that his division spent in Egypt, he had found grounds for complaint. In Mesopotamia matters appeared to him to be even more unsatisfactory. 'Staff work,' he observed in a letter written home on 22 May from near Beit Aiessa, 'has been a shortcoming throughout this war. Our number of trained staff officers was even at first scarcely adequate, but now, with our large army, it is dreadful. I speak with some knowledge, having been in eight different army corps during the war, and the 2nd, 3rd and 9th were the best in this respect. It is one of the chief points towards which we shall have to turn our attention at the end of the war, this training of the staff. The broad principles are in many cases unknown.'

He was much interested in riding over the ground which the enemy had abandoned, noting the character and the details of the Ottoman trenches, and he mentioned in a letter home that at this time he was keeping all the three horses which he had busy. A 14th Division had been constituted at Sheikh Saad on the 12th, and it was in contemplation that this should shortly relieve the 13th at the front. The Arabs had latterly been becoming somewhat aggressive against convoys and isolated parties, and the question of dealing with the marauders was exercising the various staffs. The 40th Brigade, the first portion of 18th Division to move back from the front, started for Wadi on the 29th. An interesting event had taken place in the middle of the month, which deserves

214

mention although Maude was in no way directly concerned – a Cossack *sotnia* had ridden through from Persia to Ali Gharbi, on the line of communications below Sheikh Saad, and it remained with the Mesopotamia Army until 4 June, when the visitors rode back to rejoin the Russian general, Baratoff, beyond the Turko-Persian frontier. By 18 June the whole of 18th Division was back about Sheikh Saad and Wadi.

'Life is very uneventful and supremely uninteresting,' Maude wrote home on the 28th. 'It is certainly not the country to select for campaigning, for in summer you cannot move owing to the heat and sickness, and in the winter you are beset with cold and floods. All the offices close from 12 to 4, some of them from 10 to 4, and consequently everything gets blocked. As you will realise, this is little to my taste, and the thing that would really amuse me would be to see someone like' (a very well-known and dashing commander) 'wrestling under such conditions! Of course one must keep the men under cover during the heat of the day or they would go down like ninepins; but I find no difficulty in working from 8.15 till 5, with short intervals for meals, and I do my riding in the early morning and late in the evening.

'What a lot there will be to talk about when the war is over! I only wish that we were not so far away and that visitors could run out here and tell us, and get, all the news. Heat is intense – 117 degrees and 118 degrees under cover and little wind, but the nights are cool or comparatively so. We are fairly free from flies now as the heat has killed them off, but mosquitoes and sand-flies abound and are troublesome. Arabs are fairly active and truculent; they are the most accomplished thieves you ever saw, and will get into your tent and steal your things without thinking twice about it. They have not paid me a visit yet, but my people have been robbed of rifles, clothing, stores, horses, etc. Told me that he had lost most of his things.

'I shall be glad to get back to an active and vigorous life. As I told them at the War Office the other day, although I have been steadily at it from the start of the war, I feel as ready as ever to take on anything reasonable, and long for a sustained offensive. I would have loved to join those Cossacks who came down to see us the other day and to join them in their roving life about the country, travelling light and covering the ground quickly. We understand the science of mobility so little.'

The day after this letter was written an event which was to exercise a considerable influence over the operations in this theatre in future, and under Maude's own control, took place.

This was the beginning of a railway from the left river bank opposite Sheikh Saad, which was to lead in the direction of the Dujaila Redoubt, and which would in due course overcome much of the difficulty that was at present felt in respect to supplying the troops that were pushed forward south of the river owing to the use of the river itself being closed by the Sannaiyat position above Felahieh. It may be remarked here that the effect of general control of the operations having been taken over by the War Office was making itself felt at last in many directions, and that it was about this date that the Mesopotamian campaign came to be managed practically entirely from Whitehall, although supplies and stores continued to be very largely provided from India. Sir W. Robertson, the Chief of the Imperial General Staff, fully realised that if the forces under Sir P. Lake were to retrieve the disaster that had occurred at Kut, means of transport of all kinds, whether by river, or in the form of railways, or in the matter of motor lorries and animals, must be provided on a generous scale; and steps had been, and still were being, taken to fit out the army operating in this region with the means of acting on the offensive when at a later period of the year the climate would permit of active movements. Considerable reinforcements in respect to artillery of comparatively heavy type also had already arrived in the country and had reached the front. Much was, however, still lacking in the matter of material, especially in respect to that which was needed for the long line of communications.

At Sheikh Saad, Maude was in a position to attend closely to the comfort of his troops, and he was constantly being seen by them in the mornings and evenings as he rode about the encampments and watched them at their work and at their various exercises. It was to a certain extent a period of rest for 13th Division, although rest under most trying climatic conditions. The Arabs occasionally caused some excitement, however, quite apart from their nocturnal depredations. The War Diary of the Tigris Army Corps records that, to try and put a stop to the nuisance at night, General Gorringe on 4 July issued an order that sentries were to fire first and to challenge afterwards, but that Maude pointed out that in the case of his division and of their system of patrols this would be too dangerous.

His career as a divisional commander was however drawing unexpectedly to a close. 'One day at the beginning of July,' writes

Colonel Brownrigg (it apparently was on the 10th),'he summoned an early morning conference of all brigadiers, commanding officers, senior chaplains, and heads of services and departments. At this conference he told us that he was leaving us to assume command of the Tigris Corps. One was stunned by the suddenness of it. He was nearly the junior major general in Mesopotamia, and some people felt that the division could never be quite the same without him. His personality had permeated into every corner of its organisation, and he had been such a real 'commander' in every sense of the word.' He had received a cipher telegram on the 9th, which he was told to decipher personally. This informed him that he was to take up command of the army corps. He proceeded up the Tigris to corps headquarters, which were near the river on its right bank in the bend opposite Felahieh, on the following day, arriving at noon. His intimate connection with 18th Division, which had lasted for ten and a half months, thus came to an end, although the division was within a very few months to win fresh laurels under him as Commander-in-Chief. Brigadier General Cayley, who had been in charge of the 39th Brigade from the outset, took over command, and was confirmed as leader of the division in due course.

It should be mentioned here that the K.C.B. was conferred upon Maude at a somewhat later period, but antedated 8 June 1916, and this honour therefore represented a recognition of his services as divisional commander.

Of the many distinguished British officers who led divisions during the World War, few perhaps were so completely identified with the troops under their control while divisional commander as was Maude. With the precious gift of a singularly attractive personality were combined in him a fine physique and an inexhaustible energy that enabled him to keep touch with those under his orders to an extent which not all men of his age would have found possible. 'The hardest and most efficient worker I have ever met,' was General O'Dowda's description of him in a letter home. When officers and rank and file learnt that he had left them for a higher sphere they hardly knew whether to be glad or sorry. For while they deeply regretted losing him as their divisional chief, they had such a belief in him that they knew that his rise in the hierarchy of command in Mesopotamia vastly improved the prospects of British arms in that region henceforward. Many sympathetic appreciations of Maude have been written by subordinates of his in the division which he loved so well and for which he did so much; but of these the following must suffice:

In a letter to his mother (written on the day after the death of the famous soldier at Baghdad) an engineer officer expressed the affectionate remembrance he entertained of his former divisional chief very happily: 'From the day he first took over command of us at Anzac he has been universally respected and admired. In Gallipoli, Egypt and Mesopotamia everyone has felt that in command he had a friend – a strong man who has done his best for the soldier and for the country's good. I shall never forget his kindness to me on three occasions. Once at Suvla during the deluge, when he went 200 yards out of his way through the most appalling water and mud to thank my company for what we had done under somewhat trying conditions. Again when he asked four of us to dinner to celebrate 4 June last year; and then this year on 5 June he asked again those who had dined with him last year. On each occasion he was charming –most cordial and quite unassuming. As a commander he was cheerful and would never entertain any suggestion that we were not a hundred times better than the enemy, and yet he was by no means foolhardy and always took the very greatest pains to see after the soldier's welfare …. I believe no commander in this war would have been followed further or with more trust and confidence by his men. T. Atkins as a rule does not know or think much about those in high authority. But in General Maude's case it was different. In this division at any rate every man had the highest regard for him and confidence in him.'

'From a staff officer's point of view,' writes Brigadier General R. Hildyard, who was the principal General Staff Officer of the 13th Division most of the time that the subject of this Memoir was in command, 'what appeared to me to be General Maude's most outstanding characteristics were his devotion to duty, his method, his profound knowledge of detail and his thoroughness. He mapped out his day so that he never had an idle moment. I never knew him to take five minutes off to read a paper or a book which did not deal with military matters. He rose before dawn, then went through all the messages and correspondence of the previous day, bringing out any points at a conference of all his divisional staff. He then spent six or seven hours visiting the frontline trenches, which he did every day except Sunday, when he inspected hospitals.

'This routine he never varied while his troops were in the trenches, and every regimental officer when speaking of Maude always mentions the way he came up in the mud and cold to visit them when the big blizzard of November 1915 raged for four days in Gallipoli, causing 2,000 casualties to the division and obliterating the trenches.

'His knowledge of detail was wonderful. Nothing was too trivial for him to examine and to give orders about. As well as being a commander, he was his own staff officer, dictating his own orders. This procedure may not, from his staff officer's point of view, have been altogether pleasant; but the service gained, as his orders were models of lucidity and conciseness.'

'I knew him first when I was assistant to the Principal Chaplain in Gallipoli and he was in command of 18th Division,' writes the Rev. A. C. E. Jarvis, Principal Chaplain. 'No G.O.C. ever took a greater interest in the chaplain's work than he. As a matter-of-fact, as divisional commander, he arranged their weekly duties personally. He had a high ideal of the possibilities of a chaplain's work, not only as a spiritual and moral influence but as a corporate factor of real military value. He held strongly that the chaplain's department was a vital part of the army organism.'

Sir W. Gillman, in an appreciation of Maude as a divisional commander, pronounces him to have been 'an indefatigable worker. No day was too long for him and his powers of endurance were remarkable. He was furthermore as brave as he was indefatigable, and he possessed the highest sense of honour based on strong religious convictions. Revelling in hard work himself, he expected others to do the same. His rare powers of application had given him as thorough an insight into General Staff duties as into those connected with the administration of an army, and no one was more fully qualified than he was to criticise details of schemes submitted to him by his subordinates. He aimed at a policy of perfection, and expected those under him to be imbued with the same lofty sentiments.'

'He has been criticised as a centraliser,' General Gillman goes on to say, 'and no doubt with justification. He insisted on keeping his hand on the reins, and considered it essential for himself not only to direct but also to watch how his directions were carried out. His habit of centralising did not imply that he did not trust his subordinates; rather was it second nature with him to look into the details of everything. If the work was not being done to his satisfaction, he took over the guiding himself. As G.O.C. of a division in Gallipoli and Mesopotamia he was easily able to keep all the reins in his own hand, and did so with markedly good results. He took over 18th Division just after it had been shot to pieces, and he worked it up in six months to a pitch of perfection that made it second to none.'

Maude assumed command of the Tigris Corps at noon on 11 July, which automatically gave him the temporary rank and position of a Lieutenant General. It will be convenient before proceeding with the narrative of his services as a corps commander to indicate the composition and the general distribution of the troops which had come under his orders.

The force which in reality represented more than an army corps – although it was known as the III Army Corps or Tigris Corps – comprised the 6th Indian Cavalry Brigade; the 3rd Division under General Keary; 7th Division under Major General A. S. Cobbe (he had recently taken charge in place of General Younghusband who had been invalided some weeks before); 13th Division, now under General Cayley; 14th Division under Major General R. C. Egerton; corps artillery, which included two brigades of field howitzers, a brigade of 60-pounders, some other heavy pieces and anti-aircraft guns; various departmental units. 14th Division was in front line on the right bank of the Tigris, about the old Es Sinn position, the Dujaila Redoubt and Megasis. 7th Division was on the left bank, in the narrow strip stretching from the trenches facing the Sannaiyat position eastwards to Hannah. 3rd Division was distributed so as to act as a reserve to 14th Division on the right bank of the river. 18th Division was back about Sheikh Saad. The cavalry and corps artillery were distributed throughout the area in occupation of the corps. It should be added that the light railway was now under construction all the way to Es Sinn and that railhead was temporarily established about five miles out from Sheikh Saad. There was one bridge over the Tigris at Sheikh Saad and another a little above Hannah. The Turks were holding Sannaiyat, and they occupied some newly constructed lines near Kut on the right bank of the Tigris; but south of the river the opposing lines were not in the same close contact as was the case at Sannaiyat.

With his usual energy, and in no way deterred by the intense heat, the new Corps Commander set to work at once to make himself thoroughly acquainted with the situation within his extensive and important area of command. He devoted special attention to the question of utilising the newly arrived Stokes mortars to the best advantage. After a discussion which he had with General Cobbe with regard to position and possibilities in the zone on the left bank of the Tigris, that general arranged for a special reconnaissance to be carried out on the night of 13/14 to ascertain whether an operation through the rapidly drying Suwaikieh marsh could be regarded as a practical proposition; the result was discouraging. On the 14th, Maude moved out to Es Sinn and spent the following day there, examining the defences of that advanced front. He decided that the defences required strengthening, and particularly wished those that were pushed furthest forward to receive attention; two existing posts were to be substantially strengthened and a section of 60-pounders was to be placed in either of them, when completed. The guns were not to be fired (except in case of emergency) without leave from corps headquarters; from so forward a position these powerful weapons could sweep most portions of the Kut defences, and Maude contemplated giving the Turks an unpleasant surprise with them should a favourable occasion present itself. On the 18th he went downstream to Sheikh Saad to meet the Army Commander who was coming up to pay a visit of inspection.

Sir P. Lake, it may be observed here, had already spent some years in India before taking up, at an inauspicious moment some seven months earlier, the very serious responsibilities of commanding D Force, the Army in Mesopotamia. Townshend had then already been invested for six weeks, the relieving force had met with a decided check at Hannah, there was a serious lack of everything that an army requires for conducting an active campaign, and the task to be performed was in any case one of extraordinary difficulty. To the last, during the desperate efforts made to save Kut, he had kept in good heart – Maude in his diary pays a signal tribute to his chief's resolution at the very end – but he had seen those efforts fail. Senior by some years to his principal lieutenant and not fitted out with the same iron constitution, the trying climate was telling upon Lake, and Maude, realising that the Commander-in-Chief was by no means in robust health, did what he could to lighten the fatigue that was inseparable from the carrying out of inspection duties under the existing conditions.

'Sir Percy has been up here for the last few days, and so I have been pretty busy,' he wrote home on the 23rd. 'I have taken him round and shown him as much as possible, but he is not too strong, and naturally one must be careful to see that he does not overdo things. Our longest journey was out to the Dujaila Redoubt, and the fact that it gets hot so early increased the difficulty. Moreover he did not want to stay a day out there, so we came straight back which made it longer. I generally send tents out on these sort of occasions and stay 24 or 48 hours; then one can see and do more, But it is a big command to get about over, and especially so when communications are so difficult. Some people motor, but I find riding best, as the bumping on the motor cars is far worse than Ireland at its worst.'

The Commander-in-Chief paid especial attention to the light railway; this was making excellent progress, railhead at the time being roughly half way between Sheikh Saad and Dujaila. He finished up his visit by seeing the 13th Division at Sheikh Saad, and he left for Basrah on the 26th. Maude had been able to discuss a number of matters with him and was taking several important questions of organisation in hand, notably in respect to machinegun companies and artillery distribution. The Arabs were continuing to provide local excitement; their depredations were not sufficiently important, however, to give grounds for any real anxiety, and they kept the troops on the alert without throwing an undue strain upon the soldiery.

In a letter to Colonel Magill, dated 4 August, Maude, after speaking of his good fortune in finding himself a corps commander, goes on: 'But it is such an absorbingly interesting command. First and foremost it has such a large proportion of Indian troops, and it is strange that I, who have never been in India, should be commanding them. Secondly, it is so much bigger than most corps, comprising as it does four divisions and a cavalry brigade. And finally it is a campaign so full of difficulties and complications as can hardly be realised at home. Again, I was only the third senior divisional commander here, and so I was lucky to be selected.

'It is all a big business. First, the expedition wants organising – not only the fighting troops, but also the line of communications; and with difficulties as to river transport, supplies, intense heat and sickness to contend with, it is far more difficult a matter than the armchair critics think. Still everyone from the Commander-in-Chief downward is working with a will, and good results are sure to follow. I only hope that I shall do my part all right – it certainly will not be for want of trying.

'The last two months have been intensely hot – up to 126 degrees under cover sometimes, and generally over 120 degrees. So we have stewed pretty well, and all work has to be done before 8 and after 6; and even after 7 a.m. it is almost too hot for white men to stir.

'We have a headquarters camp on the river within 4,000 yards of the Turks' first line, and they occasionally shell us but do little damage. I get a bathe (just a dip) at 4 a.m. daily, which freshens one up, and I don't stay in long enough to get slack. Most people turn in in the middle of the day, but I prefer to go to bed at 8.30 p.m., and my daily programme is work 5.80 to 7.80, then breakfast, work till luncheon, work till 4, tea, ride 5 to 7, dinner 7.30. Of course this is often varied by inspections of ground and positions. For instance, the night before last I shifted my camp and spent the whole of yesterday going round one of my divisions.

'I have a most palatial dug-out, built by my predecessor, of mud and very airy, so I am not to be pitied. Flies are all dead long since from excessive heat, and so we are spared that trouble. Also most of the flying bugs, etc., that used to annoy us at dinner have disappeared.'

Although he would have been more than human had he not felt gratified at having so large a body of troops under his immediate orders, and at controlling so extensive and so important an area of country, Maude was too accomplished an organiser not to realise that he was responsible for an unwieldy charge, and that it would be desirable to assimilate the organisation more closely to that generally accepted as the right one in the British Army. His experiences gained in command were of great use to him when, shortly afterwards, he found himself transferred to an even higher sphere, enabling him to decide upon a number of improvements in the order of battle of the forces on the Tigris front, which a practical acquaintance with their requirements had shown him to be necessary.

An interesting correspondence that took place early in August between corps headquarters and the 14th Division, which was holding the advanced position about and beyond Es Sinn, illustrates his theory as to how the campaign on the Tigris ought to be conducted. The division was disposed to regard the works which it had been constructing purely from the defensive point of view. A memorandum, signed by Maude's chief staff officer, but bearing unmistakable signs of being virtually his own handiwork, begins: 'The notes as to the position at Es Sinn by your C.R.E. seem to be drawn up under a misconception of the policy which is to be followed. The line now held by your division is to be held offensively, not defensively; that is to say, it has been secured as a jumping-off place for further aggressive operations as the opportunity offers.' Further on, referring to three strongpoints, which had been developed and which were to have appreciable garrisons, the memorandum observes: 'As regards the suggestion made that the Pentagon, Imaal Mansur and Dujaila Redoubt might become miniature 'Kuts,' this is a situation that we should earnestly wish for. Kut, it must be remembered, had no relieving force at hand; here we have ample forces to strike instantly, and the plight of the Turks who had the temerity to attempt such a move would be a pitiable one.' The memorandum concludes: 'If your division were attacked, it would not be so much a question of sending up another division to reinforce it, as of a force being sent up to counterattack the Turks vigorously from such direction as would be most likely to give the most favourable results.'

'Like all, I think, who had to do with Maude during his service, I formed a high opinion of his military capacity during the time when he was serving under me in Mesopotamia,' writes Sir P. Lake, 'and particularly after he had succeeded to the command of the Tigris Army Corps.

'His work at this time was especially valuable, for his close touch with his subordinates, and his knowledge of his men and their wants, did much to maintain morale under the trying conditions of a prolonged hot season in a treeless country, of unavoidable sickness, and of an almost entire absence, due to shortage of river transport, of creature comforts.

'He was a gallant soldier and an inspiring leader, for his cheerfulness, optimism and energy gave him a remarkable influence over those whom he commanded, while his careful and thorough working out of his plans went far to ensure the intelligent cooperation of all ranks. For his personal character we all had the highest respect. He was a true gentleman and Christian.'

Maude was wrapped up in the work connected with his corps, and he was particularly interested in the question of utilising the river transport to the best advantage, consequent upon a request from the Army Command for his views on the subject; he had also expressed his agreement with a proposal from Basrah that 18th Division should be moved back to Amarah so as to relieve pressure in respect to supplies at the front and so as to liberate some of the daily arriving stores for the purpose of building up a reserve. But on 21 August he received a cipher message directing him to hand over command of the Tigris Corps to General Cobbe, and to proceed to Basrah to take over command of the army from Sir P. Lake. He consequently went down by steamer to Sheikh Saad on the 22nd. There he had a three hours' conference with his successor, who met him by arrangement, and he then continued his voyage down to the Shatt-el-Arab.

The War Council at home had for some time been watching the course of events in the Asiatic theatre of operations with growing solicitude.

Since the War Office had begun to take general charge of the campaign, much had been done to ameliorate the position of D Force in respect to war material and means of transportation, even if the effect of this could hardly yet be fully felt. But reports coming to hand from various sources were all pointing to the morale of the troops having gravely suffered, as a result of the Kut disaster and of the defeat of all their efforts to relieve General 'Townshend's gallant garrison. It was realised that climatic conditions in the summer time in this torrid region were not calculated to invigorate, mentally or physically, a military personnel which was suffering from depression and which was weakened in health. The condition of the army in August, immobile on the Tigris and the Euphrates, was not such as to promise its embarking on an active and effective campaign as soon as the cold weather should approach. The revelations that had been made in connection with the prosecution of this undertaking in its earlier stages had aroused in the minds of many members of the Home Government a certain distrust of India and of matters Indian. There had also been a tendency latterly to entrust high command in the various theatres where our forces were carrying on operations against the enemy, to men somewhat junior in years to those upon whom at the outbreak of the Great War these heavy responsibilities had almost automatically been placed. The War Council had therefore come to the conclusion that the chief command of the Army in Mesopotamia ought to be entrusted to a man younger than the distinguished officer who had been holding that arduous and responsible position since the beginning of the year, and to one whom recent experience had kept thoroughly in touch with the War Office and the home forces.

It was a stroke of good fortune for the country under these circumstances that Sir W. Robertson, the Chief of the Imperial General Staff, had been closely associated with Maude just before the outbreak of hostilities in August 1914, and had then enjoyed opportunities for gauging the capabilities as an organiser and administrator as also for estimating the character of a soldier who, since that date, had proved himself a doughty commander of men in the field. Maude was on the spot. He was nine years younger than Sir P. Lake, he was known to possess a strong constitution, and he never seemed to be sick or sorry. Although he was the junior in respect to permanent military rank of every divisional general in Mesopotamia except General Cobbe, although his standing in the military forces was considerably lower than that of many officers who had proved their capacity for high command on the Western Front and who could easily have been sent out to Basrah, although he had never been in India in his life and D Force was composed largely of Indian troops, Sir W. Robertson accepted the responsibility of recommending that Maude should take over the charge of the Asiatic campaign, and Sir P. Lake received instructions to hand over command to him and to proceed to England. The War Council at the same time ordered that charge of the Tigris Corps should be assumed by General Cobbe in place of Maude, although he was junior in grading to the other divisional commanders and was considerably younger in years than any of them. Steps were at the same time taken to procure the services of certain staff officers and directors of departments from other theatres of war.

Maude arrived at Basrah on 24 August, and he then enjoyed the advantage of spending some days in consultation with Sir P. Lake before that general sailed for England on the 28th. There was a bond of sympathy and a complete understanding between the outgoing chief and his successor; for no one realised better than Maude what difficulties had been contended with and in many instances overcome during the past eight months under most trying conditions by the responsible head in Mesopotamia. 'I am more sorry than I can say for him,' Maude wrote home when announcing to his family the advancement to the chief command, 'and have a great admiration for him; for he has battled splendidly against ill-health practically all through.' This feeling was common throughout the forces. One of General Cobble's first acts on assuming control of the Tigris Corps was to despatch a gracefully worded message of farewell on behalf of all ranks under his orders to the departing Commander-in-Chief, which was cordially acknowledged. Then a page was turned over in the history of the Empire, as the vessel with Sir P. Lake on board cast off and steamed down the Shatt-el-Arab.

CHAPTER XII
Preparations for an Offensive Campaign

The new Army Commander of the Anglo-Indian forces in Mesopotamia had brought his two aides-de-camp, Captains Ogilvie-Forbes and Musgrave, with him. Apart from them, he took over the headquarters staff as this had been constituted under his predecessor; this included the Assistant Military Secretary, Lieutenant Colonel L. G. Williams, who with the two A.D.C.s henceforward constituted his personal staff. The two principal members of the staff at Army Headquarters were Major General A. W. Money, Chief of the General Staff, and Major General M. Cowper, D.A. and Q.M.G., who being an officer of the Indian Army was fully acquainted with the conditions of service, and so forth, of the native troops under Maude's command. The important post of Inspector General of Communications was in the hands of Major General G. F. MacMunn, with whom Maude had had frequent dealings while in the Gallipoli Peninsula and while in Egypt, as he had then held a high position on the line of communications in the Eastern Mediterranean. There is also always a 'Political Officer' in Asiatic campaigns which are being carried out under the orders of the Indian Government; this appointment had been held by Sir P. Cox for some considerable time in Mesopotamia, and he retained it under the new order of things, acting under the instructions of the Army Commander.

In so far as the distribution of the forces is concerned, the situation in respect to the Tigris Corps (which represented the bulk of the fighting forces) has been indicated in the last chapter; it had already been arranged before the change took place in the command of the corps that 18th Division should be withdrawn from it and be stationed at Amarah temporarily, and that it should come direct under the orders of Army Headquarters for the time being. Still, these troops up the Tigris did not

227

represent the whole of Maude's army. There was also the 15th Indian Division, under Major General H. T. Brooking (who had passed out of Sandhurst at the same time as Maude and had gone into the Indian Army), which was situated on the Euphrates and was assembled for the most part about Nasirieh. There was furthermore a body of troops who were distributed along the line of the Karun River, and who were particularly charged with the defence of the important oilfields in that region. A detachment stationed at Bushire down the Persian Gulf was also under the orders of Army Headquarters. Finally, and in some respects by far the most important of all, there were the numerous important base establishments at Basrah itself upon which almost everything depended, together with the garrisons of the links on the chain of communications.

On the way downstream from Sheikh Saad to take over his new responsibilities, Maude had written a very interesting letter to Colonel Magill, which deserves to be quoted in full as it serves to illustrate his point of view at the time of his assuming chief command, as also to indicate his plans for the immediate future. These had to be modified in some respects, for he found it necessary to remain somewhat longer at the base than he had originally contemplated.

'No doubt you will have heard before this reaches you,' he wrote, 'of my appointment to command the army in Mesopotamia, as following quickly on my previous appointment last month to command the Tigris Corps. It is a great advancement for me and I look upon myself as being exceptionally lucky. It is of course a great responsibility.

'The conduct of any expedition naturally must be this, but here there are such peculiar difficulties in connection with the campaign that it makes this far from easy to control. There is the long and vulnerable line of communications, shortage of river transport, the absence of roads and railways, the intense heat, the floods, the non-existence of local supplies, and the time which it takes at this distance to get our supplies and war stores here. These all complicate matters tremendously, and constitute an interesting though a stiff problem.

'However, here we are, and the only thing is to get at it, heart and soul, for difficulties exist only to be overcome, and I cannot help feeling that with vigour and determination we may bring the campaign to a fairly speedy and successful conclusion. But we shall have to work hard, and the delays, the lethargy and the apathy apparent now in some quarters must cease once and for all. The political questions, of which there are many too in connection with Persia and Arabistan, will be peculiarly interesting, and with them I shall have to deal very largely.

'I propose to put in two or three weeks at Basrah so as to talk over matters very thoroughly with the I.G.C., let him know my plans, see how he proposes to carry them out, give him clear instructions, and then leave him to settle the details himself. Then I hope to get a bit nearer the front, for although there are columns under my command in various directions, still the place where a decision will be sought is on the Tigris, and it is there that, being in chief command, I should be. Basrah is far too distant for the commander's headquarters, for down there one would know little or nothing of what is going on. The heat is diminishing gradually and we have cooler mornings, evenings and nights – although the middle of the day is still hot enough for any one. Next month I understand it gets cooler, and almost cold in October. Organisation is what we want more than anything at present, and, that once obtained and our supplies and transport put on sound lines, it will then be possible to set to and tackle the enemy.'

The last paragraph of this letter is especially noteworthy, and is to some extent very typical of Maude. It displays that same determination to be well up to the front which was noticeable in his actions right through the Great War, whether as a general staff officer repining at the withdrawal of his corps commander from a headquarters that was a shell trap to a locality slightly further back from the firing line, or as a brigadier, when ordered by superior authority to move it on account of its exposed position, shifting his headquarters forward instead of backward as was intended, or as a divisional commander ever going on in advance of his division on the occasion of any move of the force under his control. It serves to show moreover that, at all events in theory, he was in favour of decentralisation. His forecast however was, as will be seen, too sanguine on the subject of the period that would suffice for him to revolutionise the conditions at the base, and of the date when he would be able to quit Basrah and move his Army Headquarters nearer to the fighting front. Finally, the letter indicates his firm intention, even before he had taken up his charge, to institute vertebrate offensive operations against the Ottoman forces as soon as he had satisfied himself that all was ready.

Ever since he had arrived in this theatre of war, Maude had been taking careful note of the general situation from the point of view of supply, in so far as he could judge of such matters as a subordinate commander. During his short stay at Basrah before. going to the front in March he had taken stock of many points which appeared to him to call for modification or improvement. Much had as a matter-of-fact been done since that date to accelerate the unloading of ships, to develop store accommodation, to improve the hospitals, and to raise the river port more nearly to the level of what was required in the case of a locality which was serving as the base for a great military force. But even before he returned to the Shatt-el-Arab and revisited this focus of the fighting organisation of which he was now taking up charge, he was fully persuaded that any prospect which there might be of undertaking an offensive campaign against the Turks as soon as the great heats of summer came to an end, must hinge absolutely upon a substantial development of the establishments at Basrah taking place, on a generous expansion of means of transport in all its forms being secured, and upon the accomplishment of a thorough-going development of the whole administrative system behind those divisions and brigades with which he hoped, when the time came, to transform the situation in the theatre of war. On his way downstream from Sheikh Saad, and during the few days before Sir P. Lake left, he made up his mind to devote himself personally to setting the house in order in rear of the army in the immediate future. But he desired also to impress his views as to the need of preparing for an early offensive upon commanders at the front, and, before recording his labours as an administrator and organiser at Basrah and on the communications, a memorandum ought to be mentioned which he issued on 1 September, three days after taking up the office of Commander-in-Chief.

This document, while referring to the difficulties in respect to communications which the army had been suffering from during the summer season, intimated that there was good prospect of these matters being placed on a satisfactory basis within a couple of months. It enjoined on commanding officers the importance of utilising every available moment in developing the offensive spirit amongst the troops, and in training them for active operations in the field by day and by night. Sannaiyat and Es Sinn were to be held defensively for the time being; but this was not to prevent local offensive movements should a favourable opportunity present itself. All possible information of the area which might be traversed in case of an advance was to be obtained; but the work was. to be carried out by aeroplane in preference to reconnaissance on the part of mounted troops, for fear of putting the enemy on the alert. The memorandum advocated minor local offensive operations in the form of patrolling, laying ambushes, and throwing hand grenades, with a view to inculcating dash and enterprise amongst the soldiery; but it deprecated undertakings such as the destruction of bridges, and any enterprises of that kind that would be of a purely temporary nature and which would be more usefully associated with a definite scheme of operations. Maude in fact was anxious by every means to raise the morale of the troops and to prepare for an offensive campaign; but he did not wish any steps to be taken which might indicate to the enemy that the apparent stagnation behind the outposts of his legions was shortly to give place to a very pronounced and purposeful activity.

The climate of Basrah in September is not an invigorating one, many of the staff at the base were feeling the effects of the summer temperature, and a certain air of lassitude hung about the place for which there was a good deal of excuse. The new Commander-in-Chief perceived at once that it was imperative to infuse energy into the aggregate of personnel working in close contact with Army Headquarters, to improve methods in most directions, to divide up certain branches of administration and to create certain new ones; but he introduced such changes as he considered necessary, tactfully, and he stimulated his subordinates to display alacrity and animation by force of example rather than by injunction. To poke a stick into the heap and start all the ants tearing about frantically was not his way. But it was wonderful how speedily he made the presence of his vigorous personality felt, and how the stir which it almost imperceptibly created at Basrah vibrated in all directions throughout that portion of the theatre of war which was under control of the British forces. He was joined at the end of the month by Brigadier General F. F. Ready as D.A.G., Brigadier General H. O. Knoxas D.Q.M.G., and Brigadier General G. L. Holdsworth as head of his Remount Department.

The inadequacy of the river transport had admittedly been one of the main causes contributing to the ill-success of the military operations ever since General Townshend had been compelled to fall back from Ctesiphon after having been committed to an enterprise for which no adequate preparations had been made. Much had been done by General Lake to develop this, and valuable accessions in river craft arrived just at this time. But very much still remained to be done, and Maude at once went into the whole question and was not long in deciding what further material must be asked for. Some of the difficulty experienced in this respect at an earlier date had been removed by the construction of a light railway from Kurna to Amarah, which to a considerable extent eliminated a particularly awkward stretch of the Tigris, but the total absence of stone made the construction of permanent way very difficult. This railway was being transformed into a metre gauge line;

Maude saw to it that the work should be actively proceeded with, and that there should be an adequate staff to ensure full use being made of the line when completed.

Although operations in Mesopotamia had commenced in the latter part of 1914, scarcely anything had been done to improve the wharves, to create new jetties, or to supply floating landing-stages until General Lake took this all-important question up after arriving in January. Still, a metamorphosis could not be effected in a matter of such magnitude as this in a day. Much still remained to be done before the original programme would be completed, and the contemplated developments did not in all respects go so far as Maude deemed to be absolutely necessary. There had been grievous delays in getting the ocean-going ships discharged at the base and at Kurna during the spring and the summer, ships which were bringing the war material and the food supplies upon which the army depended. Big vessels sometimes remained for weeks moored in the Shatt-el-Arab waiting to unload –this at a time when the available tonnage was insufficient to meet the requirements of the Empire. So, calling in expert advisers to his aid, Maude set himself to think out what further developments of a practical nature the situation called for, and to decide how these could most rapidly be carried into effect. Then again, a deplorable deficiency of labour was hampering operations at the base; the Army Commander perceived that it would be necessary to import personnel to overcome part of this want, but he also perceived that a certain amount of quite appropriate local personnel existed, and that this only stood in need of organisation to bring it into play.

Moreover, while speedily making up his mind on the subject of the material requirements, the supply of which appeared to him to be indispensable for prosecuting the operations which he was already visualising in outline, Maude also satisfied himself on the subject of to some extent remodelling the existing staff organisation on the line of communications and at the base. Some entirely new branches, he came to the conclusion, must be set on foot. Certain existing branches, he determined, should be split up and their duties decentralised.

Already, before his predecessor quitted Basrah, he had drawn up a long telegram to Sir W. Robertson, indicating a number of requirements that he wished to have met and enumerating a list of articles of war material that he desired to have despatched to him as soon as possible, and no sooner had the ship with Sir P. Lake on board dropped down the reach than he saw to it that this message was promptly despatched. Besides

Sir W. Robertson, another former chief of Maude's was installed in high office in Whitehall, for Sir J. Cowans, who had been Director General of the Territorial Forces in succession to Sir H. Mackinnon, was Quartermaster General. From the time that Maude assumed the chief command, a complete understanding was established between General Headquarters at Basrah and the War Office, to the great advantage of the Anglo-Indian Army that was campaigning in Mesopotamia. What he asked for he got, if it could possibly be provided; and the friendly consideration with which his demands were treated by the military authorities in England he was the first to acknowledge himself.

'Whenever I telegraph for anything, and this I do most days, I almost invariably, unless there is a good reason to the contrary, get a reply promising supply,' he wrote home on 9 September. 'I cannot, of course, for obvious reasons, mention the various items that I have demanded during the bare fortnight that I have been in command, but almost without exception I have received an instant reply saying that they will be sent .... So I am very hopeful that when we have had a little time to get things running and to collect ourselves for our spring, we may be able to tackle the Turks to some effect. But this of course will depend on the instructions which I shall receive from time to time as to the general policy of the Government.

'I am busy all day seeing my directors of the various departments, my staff and the senior officers responsible on the lines of communications, speeding up things, making suggestions as to possibilities and trying to see our way through difficulties. The fall of the river is hampering us a good deal, but it is only one of many difficulties which have to be got over. Everyone is working with a will, and as things improve from day to day we are bound to feel the machine moving with increased speed.

'In the evenings I ride, or go by launch on the river, to visit anything that wants looking into. I am at this moment on my way back from the Anglo-Persian Oil Company's works, where we have a dockyard for putting our barges and boats together as they arrive. The delay and chaos there in the past have been stupendous, but we are now shoving along with increased speed daily, and I have some really capable men in charge. Other nights recently I have been through the Ordnance Stores, Supply Depots, Hospitals, Red Cross Department, Remount Depots, Aircraft Park, along the railway to railhead, and to visit numerous outlying detachments. There is always something to be done, and I keep my horses busy, though I have not got the full number (six) that I am entitled to yet.'

Amongst the new directorates that were set on foot was that of Inland Water Transport, a department which as soon as it had been properly constituted effected something in the nature of a transformation in connection with the management of the multifarious river craft plying on the waterways, and which succeeded in utilising to the best advantage the important reinforcements of material which were now coming to hand. Maude also recognised at once that considerable additions were required to the available skilled personnel in respect to the administration of the Works Department, to the railways (with the progress of which he was not wholly satisfied), to the Ordnance Department, and to the central control of the Supply and Transport services. He had no hesitation in putting forward requests for expansion of the existing administrative staff regulating these matters, and, within a very few weeks of his taking up the chief command, important accessions of experts had landed at Basrah to aid him in reorganisation. The whole subject of hospital accommodation was also carefully reviewed, and although immense improvements had been introduced in respect to this under Sir P. Lake's regime, a further expansion of establishments was deemed to be expedient and was carried out. The Remount organisation was overhauled and placed on an improved footing, and the Veterinary branch was to a certain extent reconstituted.

Thanks to the amplitude of his acquaintance with the administrative requirements of an army, Maude was in a position to go very closely into the minutiae of the majority of these problems himself, and most of the modifications that were introduced bore the stamp of his own hand. No detail was too insignificant for him to concern himself with; he indeed centralised control in himself to an extent that might have been mischievous, but for his indefatigable energy and his abnormal powers of getting through work. In respect to matters of which he possessed no knowledge, such as dockyard operations, wharfage questions and troubles in connection with the unloading of ships, he contrived to select the very best men available to act as his advisers and to control the operations.

It is true that under the conditions that he found existing at the base and on the line of communications, he was perhaps to some extent hampered by his own warm-heartedness and kindliness of disposition. Mr Candler hints at this when he says that the Commander-in-Chief was 'more ready to make allowances than most disciplinarians.' The very last man to tolerate sloth or procrastination for a moment on the part of any individual under his orders, Maude would hesitate to rid himself of a subordinate who was doing his best, but who was not intellectually equal to the task. He would in fact be disposed to do the work himself rather than to take the more drastic course which many soldiers similarly placed would adopt without hesitation and as a matter of course. Mediocrity was distasteful to him; and yet be would put up with mediocrity at times in preference to hurting another man's feelings.

He very soon discovered that his original hope of being able to push Army Headquarters forward well in advance of Basrah within two or three weeks of his assuming the chief command, was doomed to disappointment. Resolved not to commence serious operation in the field until all was absolutely ready, until the establishments in rear of the fighting front were in perfect order, until ample reserves of supplies, ammunition and stores had been accumulated within reach of the troops who were to carry out the active campaign, and until the organisation on the line of communications could be thoroughly relied on, he found it impossible to quit the base so soon as he had originally contemplated. He remained at and about the port on the Shatt-el-Arab during the whole of September, and he was still there in the third week of October when Sir C. Monro, the newly appointed Commander-in-Chief in India, arrived on a visit of inspection on his way out from home to take up his appointment.

This visit of General Monro's was a most opportune incident, and was welcomed by Maude. Not only did it afford the incoming Commander-in-Chief in India the opportunity of acquainting himself at first hand with the situation in Mesopotamia and of discussing questions in connection with it on the spot with the commander of the forces operating there, but it also gave no small encouragement to the army as a whole. The troops were already beginning to realise the driving power penetrating through the ramifications of the rearward services from Basrah almost to the very trenches, a driving power which emanated from Maude. General Monro's appearance amongst them, of which all ranks speedily became aware, served to assure them that the Mesopotamian Field Force was no longer a Cinderella, apparently looked upon with comparative indifference by Government Departments in Simla and in Whitehall. After the fall of Kut, and during the torrid summer that was now over, the morale of the army had suffered to some extent. It was already improving rapidly, just as its health was improving with the gradual setting in of cooler weather, and

Sir C. Monro's visit put a finishing touch to the amelioration that was being affected.

Maude accompanied him up the Tigris to the Front, and the inspection served to some extent as one by himself, as all the superior commanders and the principal staff officers were seen by General Monro and also some of the troops. One point that particularly struck Maude was the marked advance which had taken place in the appearance of the rank and file within the two months that had passed since he had last seen much of them. Then they had been, as he expressed it, all parched and dried up by the sun,' now they looked healthy and were evidently in good heart. The trip upstream was made under fairly pleasant conditions in a new steamer, which nevertheless was not altogether comfortable in the middle of the day when the sun was in full force. General Monro had unfortunately met with an accident some time before which somewhat, interfered with his activity; but he went out to Es Sinn by railway, and he saw something of all the divisions and cavalry brigades under General Cobbe's orders. On the way back a halt was made at Amarah, where Maude's old Division, the 18th, was inspected. Sir C. Monro altogether spent about a fortnight in the country, and he managed to see a great deal, even if he was unable to visit Nasirieh or the Karun River line. 'What impressed him more than anything, I think,' Maude wrote home, 'was the magnitude of the undertaking: in fact, he said to me that this would be reckoned in history as about the biggest expedition of its kind that England had ever sent out.'

Two or three days after General Monro's departure for India on 26 October, Maude started on a visit to the Karun line and the Anglo-Persian Oilfields. He had been somewhat unwell, and on the 27th Colonel Willcox, consulting physician to the force, saw him and found him suffering from sand-fly fever.

'His only care then was,' writes Colonel Willcox, 'for the important duties that he was engaged on, and after hearing what his illness was and the treatment necessary, his anxiety was that his work should be interfered with as little as possible. Removal to hospital was not necessary, and part of the time required for rest was occupied in his journey up the Karun River to visit the oilfields area. General Maude made a complete and rapid recovery from this illness, which to most patients means a week or more in hospital, but to him was two days' rest in bed, after which he was able to resume his duties with certain restrictions as regards over-exertion.'

The Army Commander's own account of the river trip hardly conveys the impression that it represented a period of repose. He proceeded on the 29th by steamer up the Karun as far as Ahwaz, where he inspected the troops and defences, and he then went on to the oilfields.

> First we motored some fifty miles over the desert, crossing three rivers, and then we had a light luncheon and got into some American buck-boards, in which we drove through the mountains – thirty-five miles over roads which only exist in name. It was a wild journey, and we only reached the oilfields after dark, having in the course of our drive crossed one river, which zigzagged continuously, no less than thirty-nine times. We stayed the night at the oilfields. I should have liked to have stayed several days and to have investigated the oilfields, not only from a military but also from a business point of view; but time pressed, so, after a cursory look round in the morning, we were off at 5.45 a.m., driving five miles in American buck-boards and then riding sixteen miles through the mountain passes. We then had lunch and drove another nine miles in American buck-boards, after which we motored about a hundred miles to rejoin our ship, which had gone some distance down the Karun.
>
> Of course you understand the reason of my visit to this quarter. It is because my responsibilities extend not only over the Tigris and Euphrates fronts, but also right into Persia as far as a line drawn north and south through Ispahan, where we get into touch with the Russians. So I felt that I ought to make myself acquainted as far as possible with all this neighbourhood.

On the day after getting back to Basrah he started for Nasirieh, going by train as far as the railway was completed, ninety miles, and then motoring on the remaining forty-five miles. Next day he inspected the troops there under General Brooking, rode through the remains of Ur of the Chaldees, and afterwards went by gunboat some distance up the Euphrates. Next day, 2 November, after inspecting the troops at another station near Nasirieh, he returned to Basrah, spent the afternoon there interviewing heads of departments and other officials, and at night proceeded up the Tigris to Amarah, on the way up to the front where he now proposed to fix Army Headquarters. He was satisfied that the arrangements at the base and on the line of communications were sufficiently advanced to admit of his quitting Basrah for good. He had indeed been very well pleased latterly with the progress that had been made, and he was confident that he could now rely upon the services in rear of his fighting army keeping this supplied regularly with all that it was likely to need. It should be mentioned that during a stay of a few hours at Amarah he performed a service which gave him great pleasure.

> I had a parade of my old division for the purpose of presenting the ribbon of the Victoria Cross to four members of the division who earned it in the fighting last April. The parade was a fine one and the division looked magnificent. It is extraordinary how the men have picked up during the last few weeks, and they looked not only clean and smart, but they stepped briskly and looked healthy. It was a red-letter day for the division, for I fancy that there are not many – if any – divisions that can say they have had four V.C.s presented on the same day.

During the weeks when he had been so constantly busy with the development of the base and the line of communications during September and October, Maude had not overlooked the desirability of effecting certain changes in the order of battle of the troops on the Tigris line. The arrangement under which all of these, from Sheikh Saad forward to the advanced trenches, constituted one single Army corps was not a satisfactory one on paper, and he had experienced its inconveniences in practice himself, both as a divisional general and as the Corps Commander. Soon after reaching Basrah he had requested Sir W. Robertson to send him an additional corps commander with the requisite staff, and the choice had fallen in London on General Marshall, who was commanding the division in Egypt which had been under him at the Dardanelles, and with whom Maude had been associated closely at the time of the evacuation of Suvla. A reorganisation was carried out on 15 November under which the Tigris Corps (with the 138th Division which was to move up from Amarah) was split into two army corps, while the cavalry brigades became independent of the corps organisation and were formed into a division. The title 'Tigris Corps' was finally dropped; a I Indian Army Corps, consisting of 3rd and 7th Divisions with corps troops, was constituted under General Cobbe; a third Indian Army Corps, consisting of 138th and 14th Divisions with corps troops, was constituted under General Marshall. As regards general distribution, I Corps was to be on the right on both sides of the river, with III Corps on its left, the latter taking over some of the ground previously held by troops of I Corps as soon as the 13th Division came up to the front from Amarah. These changes were brought fully into force during the second half of November.

Maude was delighted to be at the front again and was much pleased with the appearance of the troops and with the general outlook. As regards supplies, the situation was now improving from day to day, the light railway was completed to Es Sinn and beyond, railhead being close up to the most advanced trenches, and although the days were getting shorter the weather had now become suitable in all respects for campaigning. He felt that the era of preparation was nearly at an end, and that the hour for action was approaching.

The varied nature of the questions with which at this time he occasionally had to deal is illustrated by the following extract from a letter of his to his family:

> My chief political officer, Sir Percy Cox, has been off touring with a Potentate who lives some two hundred miles west from here, and whom we are anxious to get to help us in that direction. He has been presenting him with K.C.S.I.'s and things like that, and now he is bringing him to Basrah where we have got up a great programme for him. He is to have salutes fired for him (which those sort of people love), an aeroplane display, an artillery display, a tour to see the development of the Port of Basrah, etc., so that I think he will be impressed. I have sent him a personal message regretting my absence, and Cox wired yesterday to know whether he might present him with a jewelled sword from me, to which I replied 'Certainly, provided that I do not have to pay for it.' Such a funny thing to be able to produce at a few minutes' notice on active service; but I suppose that political officers are rather like the professional ladies who make long journeys on liners, and who produce the most elaborate fancy dresses for dances on board.

By the early days of December the protracted period of preparation was virtually at an end, although a few finishing touches to the organisation as a whole still remained to be added. A steady stream of reinforcements had been moving up the Tigris for some weeks, and a generous supply of drafts which the War Office and the military authorities in India had taken care to despatch betimes, were filling up the gaps in the units at the front and were providing depots for rapidly making good the wastage to be expected during the fights which Maude contemplated. The troops were in good health, partly owing to improved food arrangements and partly owing to the arrival of the cool weather, and they were now full of confidence and looked forward eagerly to trying conclusions afresh with the Turks. The training camps which had been formed at Amarah had been broken up, and the units that had been stationed there for some time past were now in their places at and beyond Sheikh Saad. The general concentration was in fact completed, and the accumulation of supplies and war material in advanced position was in a very forward condition. The army commander felt sure that, with General MacMunn as Inspector General of Communications and with ample reserves of everything actually in the country, the flow of personnel and material from the base up to the front, as required, was assured.

Lieutenant General Sir A. Cobbe, who played so prominent a part in the campaign now about to be launched, writes of Maude's share in preparing for the operations which led to the conquest of all Lower Mesopotamia within the next few months that 'he took over command of the force at a time when the country was aroused by the misfortunes of Kut. He thus enjoyed the advantage, as he himself said, of drawing to the full on the resources of the Empire. But it is one thing to have the power and it is another thing to have the capacity enabling that power to be effectively used, and it is here that his remarkable military knowledge and foresight were displayed. From guns and ammunition, river and land transport, to rations and clothing for his men and the thousand other details required in war, he personally worked out the requirements for his future operations; the results gained are the most convincing proofs of his prescience.'

The three and a half months which had passed since Maude had taken up his highly responsible position at the head of the forces of the Empire in the Asiatic theatre of war had produced nothing to interest the outside world, and, except in Irak itself and amongst the few in England and India who were behind the scenes, the situation on the banks of the Tigris and Euphrates appeared to be one of unprofitable stagnation. But a dramatic change was about to take place. Great events were at hand.

CHAPTER XIII
The Campaign of Baghdad

The Turkish Army on the Tigris front occupied the same positions in the early part of December as they had been occupying ever since their withdrawal from the Es Sinn position in the previous May. On the left bank of the river they were still holding the Sannaiyat position; but, during the months that had intervened since the last attack made by General Gorringe's forces upon those formidable entrenchments, the Ottoman defence system in that area had been much developed, a series of elaborately fortified positions now extended right back to Kut, and the river bank between Kut and Sannaiyat was effectively secured by earthworks and armament. On the other bank of the Tigris (as shown on the map 'Kut, December 1916 to February 1917' on page 188) new lines had been taken up in May, which extended from a point on the river three miles north-west of Kut in a south-westerly direction across the Khaidiri Bend to the Shatt-el-Hai, and then turned north-west on the further bank of that stream. Within their entrenched position the Turks had a pontoon bridge across the Hai near its exit from the Tigris; and the enemy also possessed another pontoon bridge on the eastern side of the Shumran Peninsula, which afforded access across the main river. Ottoman and Arab posts moreover extended for some miles down the Hai, to the south of the entrenched bridgehead.

On the left bank of the Tigris, Maude's advanced troops were disposed in trenches within 120 yards of the Sannaiyat defences. On the other bank his foremost detachments were situated eleven miles upstream from Sannaiyat, and there also were advanced posts within a couple of miles of the Ottoman lines across the Khaidiri Bend and within about five miles of the enemy position on the Hai. Strategically, as Maude pointed out in his despatch of 10 April 1917, the Turks were in a somewhat uncomfortable position; because their line of communications to Sannaiyat ran more or less parallel to the British front facing the Tigris from the south-east. The danger represented by this was fairly obvious, and the Ottoman commander had prepared against it by the very elaborate system of entrenchments in rear of the Sannaiyat position to which reference has been made above. Any

241

British advance across the Hai necessarily threatened the enemy's communications on the left bank of the Tigris in sectors still further back from Sannaiyat, whereas the extensive Suwaikieh marshes provided a natural protection to Maude's communications against any effort that the Turks might make
to strike at Sheikh Saad or the Tigris line of communications lower down. His plan, as indicated in his despatch, was designed to make the most of this significant strategic situation. It was: 'First to secure possession of the Hai; secondly, to clear the Turkish trench systems still remaining on the right bank of the Tigris; thirdly, to sap the enemy's strength by constant attacks and give him no rest; fourthly, to compel him to give up the Sannaiyat position, or in default of that to extend his attenuated forces more and more to counter our strokes against his communications; and lastly, to cross the Tigris at the weakest part of his line as far west as possible, and to sever his communications.'

All being ready for the offensive, General Cobbe's artillery opened a heavy bombardment of the Sannaiyat position on 13 December to convey the impression to the enemy that this was about to be assailed. Then, after dark, the Cavalry Division, and III Corps under General Marshall, made a night march from about Es Sinn and to the south, heading for the Hai, and they effected a complete surprise although the river itself proved to be a somewhat awkward obstacle to get across.

'Yesterday morning,' Maude wrote home on the 15th, 'after a night march, very creditably carried out by the Cavalry Division and III Corps, we threw our left forward to the River Hai and obtained a footing there. This I was most anxious to do as it gives us control of the Hai waterway, stops the Turks from drawing supplies from Hai Town, gives additional security to Nasirieh, separates the Turks from the turbulent Arabs about Shattra, who will now become more peaceably disposed towards us, and incidentally places us in a more satisfactory position. While the ground which we had secured was being consolidated, III Corps swung northwards and cleared the left bank of the Hai of hostile troops to within three miles of Kut, while the cavalry moving with great dash got within 700 yards of their bridge over the Tigris and shelled the Turks fairly heavily. These movements, which were made against the Turkish right, had been preceded by a strong feint extending over some thirty-six hours which I made with I Corps against the Turkish left at Sannaiyat, so as to try to mislead him and draw his attention away. In this we had a great measure of success, for he reinforced his left at the expense of his right.

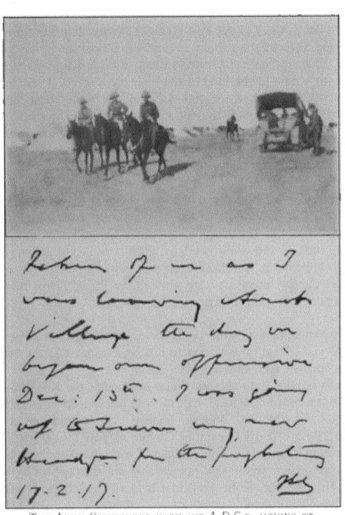

THE ARMY COMMANDER WITH HIS A.D.C.s. MOVING TO
ADVANCED G.H.Q., 13th DEC. 1916.

(With facsimile of his note sent to Lady Maude with snapshot.)

'During last night one of our aeroplanes paid three visits to Kut and found the Turks trying to tow their bridge upstream. The pilot dropped bombs on each occasion and the pontoons were cut adrift and are now all over the river. They are consequently without bridges over the Tigris or the Hai now.

'During today, while I Corps still continue bombarding the Sannaiyat position and attracting a certain amount of Turkish attention in that direction, III Corps gained further ground towards Kut, and are now within about a mile of the loop of the river on which Kut stands. The cavalry have also worked forward well, and have given the Turks a busy time. Consequently we are well satisfied with our two days' work. We have also had to deal with a certain number of marauding Arabs, but we have managed to keep them at a respectful distance and to give them more than they bargained for.

'The weather has been beautiful and most suitable for operations nice and cool even in the middle of the day, although perhaps the nights have been too cold for the troops bivouacking. But still one cannot have everything, and on the whole we have been very lucky, and supplies, transport, ammunition, etc., have been excellent. The troops have done splendidly, and the reconnaissance work of the Flying Corps has been quite first rate and most useful to us.'

Pressure was maintained on the Turks during the next two or three days, and by the end of that time a position had been secured on the bank of the Tigris opposite Kut, although the
enemy held on grimly to the entrenchments across the Khaidiri Bend and also to the Hai bridgehead. Maude now determined to consolidate his position on the Hai and to improve communications before developing fresh offensive operations, while keeping the opposing side busy by means of raids and bombardments, and while the light railway was being pushed on to the Hai. Some delay was then caused by heavy rains towards the end of the year, and by a sudden rise of the Tigris which caused considerable areas of the country to be flooded and damaged the permanent-way of the light railway, so that it was 5 January before resolute active operations could be resumed. These in the first place took the form of a prolonged attack by portions of General Cobbe's I Corps upon the elaborately constructed system of defence works stretching across the Khaidiri Bend, which secured to the Turks a footing on the right bank of the Tigris below Kut. This undertaking brought about a period of almost continuous trench combats and bombardments, which lasted a fortnight and in the course

of which the enemy displayed a most unyielding spirit, frequently counter-attacking with vigour and intrepidity and suffering heavily in the process. But the Ottoman power of resistance was gradually sapped, line after line was wrested out of hostile hands, and on the night of 18/19 the Turks finally abandoned the position and retired across the river.

'We have had some very strenuous fighting during the last ten days,' Maude wrote home on the 21st with reference to these operations, 'but it has all been eminently successful, and we have driven the Turks from the whole of their trench system on the right bank of the Tigris north-east of Kut, back across the river. The 3rd Division did most of the fighting and did it splendidly. As you know, the Turks are very stubborn fighters, especially in trenches; but our men fairly beat them at their own game, and with bomb and bayonet drove them steadily back, foot by foot, till by the morning of the 20th they were all pushed across the river .... The men are tremendously pleased with themselves as well they may be, for their conduct has been splendid.'

Already before this set of operations had been brought to its triumphant conclusion, General Marshall was getting to work against the hostile entrenchments that stretched athwart the Hai River and formed the bridgehead in the enemy's hands on the right bank of the Tigris to the south and south-west of Kut. This offensive likewise gave rise to protracted and bitter affrays, in which somewhat heavy casualties were suffered by both sides. But Maude's heart never failed him on such occasions. Although the progress of the assailants was checked from time to time at some particular section of the defensive line, and although the Turks would occasionally deliver some resolute counter-stroke which would win a patch of ground back for them temporarily, progress was for all practical purposes continuous, so that by 4 February the enemy had been forced to quit the whole of the lines east of the Hai. The whole of the right bank of the Tigris from opposite Sannaiyat up to the point where the Hai flows out of the main waterway, had thus been brought under Maude's control. He was more than satisfied with what his troops were accomplishing, and he was particularly pleased one day when a brigade of his old division picked up 348 dead Turks in the trenches which it had captured with the loss of only 224 casualties altogether. The hospital arrangements also were working most satisfactorily, for whereas in the previous April it had taken three days to evacuate wounded personnel from about Beit Aiessa back to Sheikh Saad, the injured now were within a few hours on board very specially fitted up ships which conveyed them from Sheikh Saad to Amarah. The whole journey sometimes took less than thirty-six hours.

No pause took place in the offensive. General Marshall proceeded to extend his left, with a view to ultimately enclosing the Dahra Bend, and a fresh set of offensive operations thus developed which led ultimately to the whole of the enemy's forces within that segment of a circle being destroyed, or surrendering, or fleeing across the river. By the 13th the Turks had been definitely enclosed within the bend, and were fighting with their backs to the Tigris. Then on the 15th a general assault was delivered on the inner position which the enemy had gradually been forced back upon, and it became apparent during the course of the battle that the Ottoman power of resistance in this quarter was virtually broken.

'Today we have had a very heavy fight,' Maude wrote on the 15th. 'We had previously ringed in the Turks into the Dahra Bend on the right bank of the Tigris, and this morning, after a heavy bombardment against their left centre, we attacked their right centre and immediately established ourselves in our objective, and consolidated it, the whole assault being carried out under a heavy bombardment. Artillery work went on for some hours after this, and then we launched a second attack against the enemy's left centre, which was also completely successful. We of course have not got the details yet, for the fight is still progressing, and I do not wish to exaggerate; but I think that I can safely say that we have taken a thousand prisoners; and General Marshall who commands III Corps which has been engaged, assures me that it will be nearer two thousand. Still we shall see, and of course there will be many dead and wounded Turks as well, besides masses of arms and equipment, and possibly machine guns, etc. So this is a very heavy blow for them, coming as it does on the top of two months of continuous fighting with scarcely any success. I fancy too that the Turks are getting short of food and ammunition, while we have plenty of both, and that all helps to make people feel happy and confident.

'They are wonderful stickers, those Turks, and there are few troops that would fight like they do. I think that they are bound to crack before long; but till they do we shall keep hammering at them, and I have already planned some more operations to keep them on the move which we shall carry out with the least possible delay.

'The weather has been wonderfully mild lately and we have no complaints on that score; but the rain is a nuisance, today it is raining heavily the result of a thunderstorm. It does not matter to me personally as I have a little tent, but I am sorry for the troops, most of whom have to be out in the open; besides, it complicates our movements. The Turks have cut the bund upstream of Kut and have flooded the country westwards, so that it makes it difficult for us to operate. But I must not complain, for we have been extraordinarily lucky taking all into consideration. Things could not have gone better for us than they have done.'

The victory of the 15th proved to be as complete as General Marshall had promised the Army Commander. By nightfall all resistance had ceased except along a short stretch close to the river bank at a point where the remnants of the Turks were trying to escape across the channel. This was to have been dealt with by a combined operation during the night, but two Ghurka companies forestalled the contemplated movement by delivering an assault on their own initiative, which was completely successful. The total number of prisoners taken on the 15th and 16th in the Dahra Bend amounted to 2,005; many rifles, five machine guns and great quantities of ammunition, hand grenades and other war material were also captured. In his despatch of the 10 April Maude gave warm praise to the infantry and artillery for an operation 'brilliantly carried out,' which had had the effect of driving the Turks finally from the right bank of the Tigris in the neighbourhood of Kut.

The first three phases of the Commander-in-Chief's plan of campaign, as explained in his own words in the passage quoted above, had now been brought to a successful conclusion. Although the fighting had been very severe at times and although casualties had on some occasions been regrettably heavy, the Anglo-Indian forces, even if occasionally temporarily brought to a standstill, had invariably been completely victorious in the end, and Maude had good reason for feeling gratified at the fine spirit that had been displayed by the soldiers fighting under his orders. 'The troops are on the top of their toes now,' he wrote, 'and one can hardly hold them in, they are so keen to get at the Turks.' Moreover, everything had proceeded smoothly in rear of the fighting front as a result of the carefully thought out preparations in the elaboration of which he had borne so prominent a part. There had at no time been any anxiety on the score of supplies. The river transport was working admirably, and it was as a matter-of-fact also gaining valuable accessions of tonnage; the railways were pulling their full weight; and the animal transport, although at times sorely hampered by the mud following the occasionally heavy rains, was performing what was required of it. The administrative personnel had worked wholeheartedly throughout, and its enthusiastic cooperation with the actual combatants had played, and was playing, a dominating part in breaking Ottoman fighting power in Mesopotamia. Even the fact of the enemy cutting the bunds some distance further up the Tigris than where the advanced portions of the Anglo-Indian Army was awaiting the next move, in reality proved to be a blessing in disguise, seeing that it enabled the Cavalry Division to find water where there otherwise would have been none. Moreover, although the Osmanli troops in the Dahra Bend had undoubtedly been highly tried by artillery fire on the 15th and were battling under perilous and discouraging conditions, their readiness to yield themselves up on that day suggested that the enemy's morale was deteriorating.

The further operations which Maude had in mind and to which he referred in his letter of the 15th, quoted above, consisted of an attack upon Sannaiyat by troops of I Corps, and of the passage of the Tigris at a point above the Dahra Bend by a portion of General Marshall's command. As will be seen from the sketch map, there is a very well defined loop in the river's course immediately above Dahra which came to be known as the Shumran Bend. The Commander-in-Chief's design was to force a way across the river channel at about the southern end of this loop, and preparations for embarking on this daring venture were set on foot as soon as the Dahra Bend had been cleared of the enemy. In the meantime the Army Commander published the following Order of the Day, in recognition of what his army had already accomplished, and as an encouragement in view of what it was still to be called upon to perform;

> After a period of severe and strenuous fighting, extending with only short pauses over a period of two months, I wish to express to the Navy, to Lieutenant Generals Marshall and Cobbe, to the divisional and brigade commanders, to the staffs, including my own, and to all ranks of the fighting troops, my warmest thanks for their splendid work, and my congratulations on their brilliant successes. To the regimental officers, non-commissioned officers and men a special word is due for their matchless heroism and fighting spirit, and for their grit and determination so fully in accord with the best traditions of British and Indian regiments. While regretting deeply the casualties necessarily incurred in the attainment of our object, the series of stinging blows dealt to the enemy, his severe losses which are out of all proportion to the size of his force, and his

obviously falling spirits, afford ample proof to all ranks that their sacrifices have not been made in vain.

My thanks too are due to Major General MacMunn, to the directors and their assistants, and to all ranks of the Administrative Services and Departments, both in the field and on the lines of communication, who, in the face of unexampled difficulties, have by sterling work and energy risen superior to them and have regularly met the needs of the fighting troops with ample supplies, stores and munitions, without which the loss of life would have been considerably increased and success rendered impossible, and have been the means of providing every comfort attainable for the sick and wounded.

To each and every member of the Navy and Army, and to those who though not belonging to either of the Services have helped to bring about the results achieved, I tender my warmest thanks for their wholehearted and magnificent support. The end is not yet; but with such absolute cooperation and vigour animating all, continuance of our success is assured.

F. S. Maung, Lieutenant-General,
Commanding Indian Expeditionary Force D
15th February 1917.

General Cobbe had been keeping the enemy on the qui vive in the Sannaiyat lines while the Dahra Bend operations were in progress, helping to distract the attention of the Turks, and Maude now issued instructions that the formidable position on the left bank of the great river, which three times over had proved too strong to reduce in the previous April, was to be assailed on the 17th. The attack proved a failure. Heavy rains on the previous day had converted the approaches into a quagmire, and although the two front series of entrenchments were captured in gallant style, a determined counterattack on the part of the defenders led to the ground which had been so secured passing back into Ottoman hands again. The waterlogged condition of the country and a sudden rise of the Tigris then put a period to further efforts for five days, although an almost incessant bombardment was kept up with the object of deceiving the enemy as to when a fresh attack might be expected.

'On Sunday, the 18th, I did duty with the advanced section,' writes the Rev. A. Jarvis. 'Before returning to Sheikh Saad on the Monday the army commander told me that he particularly wanted a celebration on the Wednesday morning; all the preparations for the advance on Kut and Baghdad had been kept a profound secret. On the morning of the 21st, a cold, dark, glimmering dawn with a hoar frost on the ground, the guard tent was prepared and our simple altar erected, and there we gathered for the Holy Mysteries. After the service he remained for a long time in silent prayer. There were perhaps a dozen of us present; some of the General Staff knew what the day meant for the campaign.

'After breakfast I saw him walking alone to a nullah overlooking Sannaiyat, and almost immediately afterwards the artillery opened an overwhelming fire. The advance to Baghdad had begun, and it never stopped until we were beyond the city. That historic event will always be associated in my mind with the solitary figure kneeling before the lighted altar in the presence of his God in the grey light of a winter morn, and I have often wondered how much those silent moments contributed to the great achievement with which Maude's name will ever be associated.'

The final attack on Sannaiyat was delivered on the 22nd. The two front lines were not only captured on this day but were also effectively consolidated in preparation for a further bound forward towards Kut. Feints of crossing the Tigris near Megasis and at Kut from the right bank of the river were also carried out on this date, while the finishing touches were being quietly put to the paramount design that of forcing a way across the great obstacle at the apex of the Shumran Bend.

Winning a passage over the mighty stream when almost at its highest, in defiance of an enemy sustained by a formidable assemblage of guns, was a project recalling Wellington's forcing of the Douro and of the Bidassoa during the Peninsular War. In his The Long Road to Baghdad, Mr Candler, an eyewitness of this memorable operation of war, provides us with a stirring description of the adventures met with by the parties which enjoyed precedence in the adventure. Maude makes clear in his despatch how great were the difficulties which had to be overcome, and he at the same time indicates how far-reaching was the success that attended the efforts of those who led the way. The scene opened just before dawn on the 23rd with the ferrying of detachments of infantry across the channel at three points, downstream from the spot where the bridge was to be thrown. All three advanced parties made good a footing; but owing to the very heavy fire brought by the Turks to bear upon the water, the two lower ferries were speedily abandoned and all the remaining troops were put across at the point highest up.

Gradually the leaders pressed forward within the loop of the river, and the construction of the bridge was promptly taken in hand.

At 4.30 p.m. this was completed, and reinforcements thereupon began to pour across. 'By nightfall,' Maude wrote in his despatch, 'as a result of the day's operations, our troops had by their unconquerable valour and determination forced a passage across a river in flood, 340 yards wide, in face of strong opposition, and had secured a position 2,000 yards in depth covering the bridgehead, while ahead of this line our patrols were acting vigorously against the enemy's advanced detachments, who had suffered heavy losses, including about 700 prisoners taken in all. The infantry of one division were across and another division was ready to follow.' Nor were the triumphs of that day of victory confined to the stirring events on the extreme left of the Anglo-Indian Army, for General Cobbe's troops followed up their success of the 22nd by securing possession of the third, fourth and fifth lines at Sannalyat, so that by the evening they had placed themselves in a dominating position on the extreme right of Maude's far-flung front.

General Marshall's forces were in considerable strength on the left bank of the Tigris by the morning of the 24th, and they continued their pressure on the enemy within and beyond the Shumran Bend the whole day long, gradually overcoming all resistance other than what was offered by a stalwart Turkish rearguard, as the enemy retired in disorder up the river. 1650 prisoners, 5 guns and 8 machine guns were included in the day's booty. General Cobbe simultaneously gained possession of the last line of trenches at Sannaiyat, whereupon his troops moved forward rapidly, almost unopposed, through the successive defensive systems which the enemy had constructed between Sannaiyat and Kut, his advanced guard reaching the vicinity of the latter place before dark. The Turks, it may be remarked, had regarded Sannaiyat as impregnable, and, taking into consideration the comparatively weak support in respect to heavy artillery which I Corps had at its disposal, it seems doubtful whether the position could have been captured, even in spite of the valour of the assailants, had it not been for the influence exerted upon the defenders of the lines by events in the Dahra Bend and at Shumran. Even so, the garrison of Sannaiyat had manifested a rare tenacity and fortitude, as was evidenced by the very heavy losses which they had endured. 'Many trenches were choked with corpses,' Maude wrote, 'and the open ground where counter-attacks had taken place was strewn with them.' When darkness closed in on the 24th, what was left of the Ottoman forces was in full flight from the scene of their triumphs of a few months before, and that night the British gunboats, pushing up from Felahich, moored off Kut.

Maude was the very last man to rest on his laurels and to allow a discomfited antagonist breathing space to recover from defeat. The events of 22–24 February may nevertheless fairly be said to have placed the coping-stone on the series of offensive operations which had commenced a little more than two months before, when he of a sudden pushed forward his left and secured the passages over the Hai. The lines of entrenchments on which the Turks had expended infinite labour on both sides of the Tigris, defences which converted the environs of Kut into one huge stronghold, were now all in the hands of his troops. The enemy, almost bereft of armament and war material, was in full retreat. The Tigris was open as a line of communications for supplies to be brought up abreast of the leading troops of the Anglo-Indian Army, and armed river craft could now be depended upon to take a prominent part in such further offensive operations as Maude might contemplate. The disaster which had befallen General Townshend's force ten months before, and the succession of reverses which the troops under Aylmer and Gorringe had met with when engaged on an almost impossible task, were amply avenged. Not often in the history of war has so dramatic a transformation been recorded in the relative positions of opposing belligerents.

It is difficult to pick a hole either in the conception or in the execution of this two and a half months' campaign, which entirely revolutionised the military situation in Mesopotamia. If the plan was a bold one, it was also at the same time a reasonably safe one, and every fresh undertaking in connection with its execution had been thought out in advance. It might be suggested that the attack delivered upon Sannaiyat (which in the first instance was unsuccessful) was unnecessary, seeing that the enemy was bound to abandon that formidable position should the passage of the Tigris at Shumran prove successful. But that forcing of the river was in reality by far the most hazardous undertaking of all the various enterprises comprised in the scheme of operations as a whole, the realisation of the plan in full hinged upon its success, and to facilitate the crossing by every means that Maude had at his disposal was imperative. The attack on Sannaiyat on the 17th chained large Ottoman forces to the spot on that day as also on the following days, infantry and artillery, and it automatically diminished the resistance that was bound to be encountered at Shumran; moreover the Turks as a matter-of-fact lost the more heavily of the two contending sides on that day, even if they repulsed General Cobbe's troops. One of Maude's outstanding merits as a commander in the field indeed was that, in spite of his constant solicitude for the comfort and well-being of the troops serving under his orders, he never shrank from losing men when there was a definite strategic or tactical object to be gained by doing so. A success at Sannaiyat on the 17th would naturally have been preferable to a set-back; but whether the result of the operations at that point was to be a success or to be a set-back meant a matter of secondary consideration. The point of real importance was that the Turks should be kept fully occupied opposite Maude's extreme right at the moment when he was striking the decisive blow with his extreme left.

Messages of congratulation poured in upon the Army Commander after the news of his triumphs became known; for the recovery of Kut, although the place was of no importance in itself, appealed warmly to the imagination of the people all over the Empire. Maude received cablegrams from the King, from the War Office, from the Commander-in-Chief in India, from Sir Douglas Haig, and from Sir A. Murray; these were published, with his replies, in an Order of the Day for the information of his troops. But the completeness of his success was hardly known even to himself until two or three days later. For even on the 25th, when General Marshall pressed on vigorously after the retreating enemy on the left bank of the Tigris, with cavalry pushing forward on his right and the gunboats steaming upstream on his left, he was met with some stubborn opposition after advancing some eight miles; and he had to deploy his guns and infantry and to deliver an attack before the Turks gave way. During that night however the Ottoman forces became utterly demoralised in the course of a hurried retreat, and this retreat developed into a veritable rout on the following day, as a result of daring action on the part of the Royal Navy and of relentless pressure by the mounted troops.

For the three gunboats, relieved to some extent of fear of heavy artillery fire from guns concealed in pits, pushed boldly ahead of the army, and they became completely separated from it for a time owing to the sinuosity of the river channel. Although strongly opposed at one point by rifle and gun fire from the banks, the little fleet steamed hard against the current, and in the afternoon came up with the heterogeneous Turkish flotilla of fighting craft, transports and barges. This armament was attacked at once. The hostile crews fought their vessels gallantly enough; but the British gunboats proved very much more than a match for the enemy armada and gained a complete victory, capturing or destroying the entire flotilla but for a couple of patrol boats which managed to escape upstream. The flying Ottoman army had in the meantime entirely outstripped Marshall's infantry; but the British and Indian cavalry kept well up with the fugitives, accelerating their movements, making imposing captures, and pressing so close on the heels of the fugitive foe that on the evening of the 27th the foremost echelons of the mounted troops reached Azizieh, half way from Kut to Baghdad. 'At the commencement of operations,' writes Sir A. Cobbe, 'the army Commander was hampered by the necessity of avoiding losses a policy which so often defeats its own ends and leads to extravagance in this direction owing to effecting nothing. When given a freer hand he framed his plans with the intention of defeating the enemy's forces before they could be reinforced, and of inflicting such blows on the Turks that their morale would be lowered for the future. This could only be attained by hard fighting, seeing that his opponents were flushed with their successes at Kut, and were confident that their own fighting powers far surpassed ours. Having made his plans, Maude carried them through without a falter. Unaffected by temporary set-backs, always eager for action, chafing at inaction though suffering it when necessary (such as during the halt in pursuit to Baghdad in order to let rations come forward and keep pace with his rapid advance), he inspired those under him with the same spirit. He filled them with confidence that they would be backed up in what they undertook and that the services behind them would not fail.'

'I fancy that in my last letter I told you all about the crossing of the Tigris, and the magnificent way in which the troops accomplished it,' Maude wrote home on the 28th. 'Nothing could have been finer, and, as Sir Charles Monro said in his telegram to me, it will take a very high place in the records of the British Army.

'Since then we have been pushing on merrily. First the whole army was in pursuit, and then, as the infantry became less and less able to keep up with the flying enemy, the gunboats and Cavalry Division took it up, and they are still at it now. The enemy is absolutely demoralised and streaming away towards Baghdad in confusion, leaving guns, trench mortars, machine guns, rifles, ammunition, equipment, tents and stores of all kinds scattered along the road, while they have burnt and buried a certain amount. Then, on the river, the gunboats have captured quite a lot of shipping four ships (including one of our gunboats which we lost in the retirement from Ctesiphon), launches, barges, mahalas, pontoons and a considerable amount of bridging material. The Turks have thrown some guns into the river, and altogether it is a complete rout. Since we started operations in December we have taken something like 7,500

prisoners, including over 2,500 yesterday, and this, added to the dead whom we have actually counted and buried, and allowing for a reasonable proportion of wounded, means – placing it at a low figure that we have accounted for over three-quarters of the Turkish Army which was opposed to us. Naturally the troops are delighted at their excellent performance, as they may well be.

'I have called a halt temporarily just to pull things together and to reorganise our communications, which have unavoidably become somewhat dislocated by the transfer from our former system back to the river line only. It is a great thing to have got control of the Tigris once more, and it will help us enormously in our future operations which I trust that the Government will allow me to undertake. We have again had some more rain, but luckily only for a short time, and the strong north wind which came soon dried up things generally.

'As soon as we got the navigation of the river again I came right forward, and it is interesting to see closely much of the ground over which the fighting had been near the river, such as the Khaidiri Fort Bend, the Dahra Bend, and the actual place where the passage was forced. Looking at the ground, it scarcely seems feasible that a force should have crossed as we did, first in loose pontoons and then by a bridge, in face of an enemy entrenched and holding the far bank with infantry, machine guns, and artillery. But we managed to help matters by having a semi-circle of artillery and machine guns right round the bend on the day in question, and their fire simply smothered the Turks. Still, even with that, it was a great performance and one that those who took part in it ought to remember for the rest of their lives.

'I did not think much of Kut as we passed it, and did not stop to go into it. It has been badly shelled and the minaret had been knocked over by our artillery, and it really possesses no interest except from the sentimental point of view. I am now living once more on a river steamer, and shall probably do so for the present, as one has to be constantly on the move and it is the easiest method of getting over the ground; but as soon as we can get more or less settled down I shall get ashore again.'

The Army Commander was intent upon giving the enemy no rest, but, as mentioned in the letter quoted above, he had been compelled to stay the forward movement for fear of entirely outrunning his supplies. The staff had found some difficulty in persuading him of the need for this pause; but the arrival of General MacMunn with a flotilla of vessels crammed with food and stores as soon as navigation was safe, and his representations as to the imperative need of getting these forward before a fresh rush to the front was undertaken, decided the matter. The Inspector General of Communications went aboard the steamer on which Maude with Army Headquarters was on the point of moving upstream. The staff feared that further advance was for the moment premature, and they urged General MacMunn to make representations.

'I was literally pushed into his curtained-off space,' is General MacMunn's account of what followed. 'He said, 'How are supplies?' I said, 'Coming on well, but it is two miles of river for every one mile by land, and I can't feed you and supply ammunition if you move another yard yet.' He looked at me quizzically and asked, 'When may they start?' So I said, 'Not before the 5th,' when all he remarked was 'Right.' By that time we had the show in hand. You see, I had received no warning of his proposed push for Baghdad.'

From 28 February to 4 March the movements of combatant units consisted in the main of a general closing up towards the front at Azizieh, where the mounted troops had come to a standstill, having outrun their supplies. I Corps was pressing up in rear of III Corps, and a satisfactory concentration of force was effected within the week in anticipation of a fresh advance. Very heavy administrative work had to be got through during those few days, ending in a triumph of organisation; for when the pause came to an end everything was ready for a final move on Baghdad. Amongst other things it had suddenly become necessary to transfer some of the great accumulations of goods assembled at the terminus of the light railway between Sheikh Saad and the Hai, from that locality to the river, partly by employing motor and animal transport across the space between the terminus and the Tigris by Kut, and partly by evacuating the stores back by rail to Sheikh Saad.

'Sinn railway station,' as Mr Candler puts it in his compelling picture of how the communications of the army were transformed, 'which had seemed the centre of our universe, was left out of the scheme of things. The S. and T. staff who were needed for the advance were locked up in the depots as caretakers, or to evacuate supplies down, not up the line. Three or four thousand tons of ammunition and R.E. stores had to be cleared, and local transport was necessary to collect it and get it away. Thirty train-loads of empty shell cases and empty boxes alone were removed, and the Arabs were kept off while the gleaning was going on.

'But the abandonment of the main artery at Sinn was merely a temporary dislocation; the river was the permanent and compensating gain. Not that it was all plain sailing. Every division had so many ships allotted to it. But some were slower than others; some ran against mud banks; the channel had changed its course many times since Ctesiphon, and the pilots did not know the way; in some cases coal gave out, and there were knavish units on the banks commandeering other people's food. Often at first we looked anxiously for the smoke of the supply steamers. Once or twice emergency rations were consumed. But soon anxiety was forgotten. 'Q' never failed us. When a day's rations went wrong, a camel convoy would emerge out of the blue, or a leisurely cortege of Ford's vans would traverse the Biblical plain. During the whole pursuit only one division was on half rations, and that only for one day. How it was done Providence alone knows, and Providence was 'Q'.'

The reference to the Arabs above suggests mention of their operations directed against the fugitive Osmanlis during their hurried retirement from Kut to beyond Azizieh. The beaten army had not been harried during its retreat by the speedy gunboats and the eager horse alone. They had also experienced extremely rough treatment at the hands of the Arabs, who, as is not unusual in the case of warriors of that predatory character, swarmed on the flanks and the rear of the beaten side, cutting off and murdering stragglers, increasing the panic and the rout, and appropriating any booty that was sufficiently light to be carried off. It may moreover be mentioned here that the continuous victories of Maude's forces had latterly been exercising a most pacifying influence over the nomads and villagers dwelling in the area of Mesopotamia lying below Kut. This gratifying state of things held good both along the line of the Tigris and also in the region to the south along the Hai and the lower Euphrates, where General Brooking and the 15th Division were with some impatience awaiting orders to push forward.

By 4 March the administrative situation was completely restored, and Maude had received a guarded approval from home for his continuing the advance on Baghdad. It is in this connection a matter of regret that the Commander-in-Chief's diaries during the last eighteen months of his life had to be destroyed afterwards; because in his numerous letters to his family and to many soldier friends during the long period of preparations that led up to his starting his offensive in December 1916, as also during the succession of combats around Kut, he would never appear to have mentioned any intention of pressing on to the City of the

Caliphs. He does in his letter of the 28th, which has been quoted above, it is true, speak of further operations for which he hoped to get Government consent; but even at that late date, and after so much of the programme had been carried out, he does not name Baghdad. Still, Mr Candler is probably right when, in a fine appreciation of the army commander after his death, he puts it thus: 'And yet, I believe, General Maude saw Baghdad in his grasp all the while, his own personal objective, for he had no orders from home in which the city was written large as a definite goal.' The truth indeed is that, had Maude, before he commenced his offensive campaign in the Kut region, suggested to the War Council that he proposed or even that he merely hoped to gain possession of the capital of Mesopotamia, that body would, after their untoward experiences at the Dardanelles and in connection with General Townshend's force, have had some justification for placing a curb on the activities of so enterprising a commander and for tying him down very tightly to the achievement of some strictly limited object.

His theory and practice of making war was to bide his time until all was properly in train for an effort, and then to move rapidly and to strike hard. All being ready at nightfall on 4 March, the mounted troops, with General Marshall following and I Corps bringing up the rear, surged forward on the left bank of the Tigris on the morning of the 5th, and during that afternoon the cavalry came upon the enemy in position at a place called Lajj, some twenty-five miles from Azizieh.[12] At the expense of somewhat heavy losses to themselves, the 13th Hussars by their intrepid action here helped very materially to dislodge the Turks, and to constrain them, in face of the arrival of further troops from the south, to effect a precipitate retreat during the night. Next day the mounted troops, still pushing ahead at speed, found a carefully prepared position near the famous arch of Ctesiphon evacuated by the Turks, and that night the horsemen were close to the Diala River, the channel of which created a very formidable obstacle barring the road which led along that bank of the Tigris to Baghdad. In a letter home, written on the 8th, Maude gives a concise and graphic description of the course of events on the first four days of the advance from Azizieh:

> We were off on the morning of the 5th towards Baghdad. We did twenty miles on that day to Zeur, and the cavalry got a bit beyond that and had a stiffish fight with the 51st Division, which was the only one remaining intact, in the neighbourhood

---

[12] The operations in Mesopotamia subsequent to the advance from Azizieh are illustrated by the map 'Environs of Baghdad' on page 297.

of Lajj. However during the night the Turks withdrew, and pretty fast at that for we found it difficult to catch them next day, although we got a number of prisoners who were straggling. Next day we pursued our course to Bustan, and on the 7th we got to the line of the Diala, where the enemy though not in strength managed to hold us up on the river, mainly by a few guns and a number of machine guns. During the night we tried to force a passage at one or two places, but the machine guns in the moonlight were too much for us without incurring heavy casualties, which hardly seemed justified.

Meantime I Corps was coming up steadily behind III Corps. I had taken the precaution of ordering a bridging train and a half forward in case of need, and so it seemed to me that the best way would be to turn the line of the Diala by moving up the right bank of the Tigris. I therefore ordered a bridge to be thrown at Bawi. This was completed in four hours this morning (8th), and the Cavalry Division are now across, and I Corps leading division are following them. Their instructions are to press on to Baghdad, which is twenty-one miles from where they are at present, while I have given full instructions to III Corps which I trust will ensure the passage of the Diala being forced during the night.

Yesterday we passed Ctesiphon, and though the Turks had prepared a very strong position almost a fortress they went straight through it, and I think that the rapidity of our advance had something to do with their not stopping. All the work there was new and very well designed and strong. Yesterday afternoon there was a series of explosions in Baghdad, and today fires are burning fiercely in many directions. We hear stories of reinforcements coming from various directions, but I fancy that the Turks will clear if we can only press them sufficiently strongly.

Our great difficulty now will be the floods, which will be a serious problem to tackle; but if we can get into Baghdad within the next few days we shall get to work determinedly to combat this disability, and no doubt we shall find a way out of it. I have been busy drafting proclamations, orders, etc., to come into effect when we get to Baghdad; but I think that we have broken the back of it now. Supplies are coming up well, and it is quite an imposing fleet to see on the river. It is a terribly long line of communications, and so I hope when we get into Baghdad we may be able to organise a good supply system there locally. The country seems very fruitful up here – large vegetable gardens and any amount of live stock – so it all looks promising. All is quiet on other fronts.

The troops throughout have done magnificently, and the number of regiments which have specially distinguished themselves is very large, both British and Indian. The men are at the top of their form, and although tired after their recent marches, owing to the fact that they have done so much trench life and because of the gale of wind and dust that we have had, they are most cheery.

The actual occupation of the capital of Mesopotamia was not to be effected without some severe fighting, in which the enemy was greatly aided by the topographical difficulties which the lie and the nature of the country placed in the way of Maude's forces, and in which the enemy was in particular aided by the existence of the Diala, a river 120 yards wide, with houses and walled gardens on both sides of the channel favouring defence while opposing obstacles to the bringing up of pontoons. There could be no question of surprise here as there had been at Shumran. The bold attempt of portions of 18th Division to force a crossing on the night of the 7/8 had failed completely and with loss. A fresh effort made the following night and preceded by a bombardment, only succeeded in very limited degree and almost by a miracle, in spite of devoted gallantry on the part of the troops concerned. Some of the Loyal North Lancashire did manage to gain a footing on the further bank, and they not only gained a footing but they maintained their grip upon a small loop in the river embankment, unsupported except by fire from the other side, for nearly twenty-four hours in spite of every effort of the enemy to dislodge them. Early on the morning of the 10th the passage was really effectively forced; other troops of the 13th Division were ferried over at two points and they joined hands with the Loyal North Lancashiremen. More infantry followed, a bridge was thrown and completed by noon, and then General Marshall pressed forward in the afternoon up to near a position which the enemy had taken up barring the way to Baghdad. 'The passage of the Tigris and the Diala in face of an enemy in position,' Maude wrote to Lord Dundonald a few days later, 'stand out as episodes which will take some beating.'

Sir Arthur Lawley, who was superintending the working of the Red Cross, had been invited by the Army Commander to come up the river in view of the expected taking of Baghdad. ' Yesterday morning at breakfast-time we passed close to the great Ctesiphon Arch, and an hour later we anchored just south of the bridge of boats which carried over the Tigris all the troops operating southwest and west of Baghdad, to the right bank of the river,' he wrote home on the 10th. 'There was a ceaseless flow of traffic until about 3 o'clock, when they opened the bridge to let through our ship and a good many others that were eager to get forward. The next bend of the river brought us within sight of *H.P.53*, which is the boat in which General Maude and all his headquarters staff are established. We anchored just astern of them and then pitched our tents on the bank just opposite *H.P.53*.

'We found Joe Maude in great spirits and full of confidence, as indeed he well may be, in spite of a temporary check at the Diala River – a very strong position occupied by the Turks. The night before last about 100 men of the East Lancashire's got over the river and hung on all day under cover of our guns, and a bad time they must have had; but they stuck it out, and last night a lot more of our men got over.

'I hear that there were about 600 wounded in this force yesterday on the right bank, so there must have been some sharp fighting. The cavalry are there, and they have had a great time since the operations in December began; since the Sannaiyat and Shumran actions they have had an opportunity which has not been given to a British Cavalry Division for the last hundred years. The move has been amazingly rapid, which shows how admirably thought out and laid down were the preliminary preparations.

'The strain on every department has been tremendous; but each one has stood the strain, and when you realise that Joe Maude has gone into every detail of every department himself, and is personally responsible for the setting up and working of the whole machine, you will see that he has proved himself a great administrator as well as a great soldier.'

While the operations for the forcing of the Diala were in progress, the cavalry and I Corps on the right bank of the Tigris had been much impeded by dry watercourses, and there was moreover a complete lack of water away from the river bank. They were however within about seven miles of the city by the evening of the 9th, and their advance was continued on the morrow in spite of a blinding dust-storm, meeting with opposition sometimes fitful and sometimes determined, and delayed almost as much by physical difficulties as by the efforts of the Turks; but at nightfall the advanced troops were very near to Baghdad. That night the Turks gave up the idea of trying to stay the advance of the conquering army, and drew off to the north, so that the city was occupied by troops especially detailed for the purpose early on the 11th, the Black Watch, on the right bank, having the honour of being first in the place and of seizing the railway terminus of the line leading to Samarra, a section of the contemplated German Baghdad Railway.

'We were now within close range of the city,' Maude wrote home of the night of 10/11, 'and I think the Turks saw the game was up; for during the night they fell back all along the line and made off as fast as they could along both banks of the Tigris, the remnants of the 4th, 51st and 52nd Divisions by the right bank, and the remnants of the 14th and 45th Divisions by the left bank. Our patrols were in close touch with them all night, and as soon as we found that there was movement going on we followed up, though the difficulty of moving as fast as they did with our imperfect knowledge of the ground was almost insuperable. However by daybreak the Black Watch had occupied the railway station and Baghdad fell into our hands shortly after that. The cavalry followed in pursuit; but the exhaustion of the troops after their severe fighting and unavoidable shortage of water lessened the vigour of the pursuit. The cavalry however occupied Khadimain and got over 100 prisoners and four aeroplanes. The gunboats joined in the chase as soon as possible, and at dusk the enemy were reported to be entrenching in a new position fifteen miles north of Baghdad, covering the entrainment of their troops. More prisoners were captured by III Corps, and they also got large quantities of arms, ammunition, and equipment.'

As for the Army Commander himself, his steamer proceeded up the river comparatively early in the morning and, it being known that the troops which had been told off to enter the city and to keep order had taken up their stations, the vessel quietly brought up alongside the building which had been the British Residency in peace days, and which the Turks had been using as a hospital, at 3.30 p.m. Maude stepped ashore accompanied by his personal staff. It was somewhat characteristic of the conqueror of Baghdad that he should have made his entry into the ancient seat of the Caliphs in this undemonstrative fashion; and some even think it was a mistake. The Oriental believes in display. Impressed by pomp and circumstance in placid times of peace, the spectacle of a victorious commander entering a captured city almost like an ordinary traveller arriving to make a stay, amounts in his eyes to something like an anachronism. But the citizens of Baghdad had here to do with a conqueror who would never take credit to himself for what he had accomplished, but who always gave the credit to those under him who had cooperated in the achievement. What Maude no doubt above all things wished to avoid was to convey the impression, by making a formal entry into the city at the head of his troops, that this climax to a campaign, as well as the signal successes which had preceded it, were as they undoubtedly were primarily his own handiwork. It is interesting to contrast the details of his entry into Baghdad with those of his entry into another capital, Pretoria, sixteen years before.

'As we steamed up into the city with the gunboats escorting us on the 11th, the day we got the town,' he wrote home a few days later, 'the banks were lined on both sides by crowds of inhabitants, who applauded vociferously at intervals, and altogether ninety percent of the population seemed delighted that we had arrived. The city was in rather a turmoil, for directly the Turks went out at 2 o'clock in the morning, Kurds and Arabs began looting everywhere, and although we got into the city by about 6 a.m. there was time for them to do a considerable amount of damage. Still we soon reduced them to order.'

The actual occupation of Baghdad by no means connoted an immediate cessation of active operations. Maude was much too far-seeing and resolute a soldier to check the advance of his troops for one moment, so long as the enemy displayed the slightest symptoms of recovering from the shocks sustained, or while any strategic points of importance situated within the immediate zone of campaigning remained in hostile hands. Already on the 12th, portions of III Corps were on the move, pressing forward on the left bank of the Tigris to secure possession of certain important embankments upstream which, were they to be cut by the Turks, would cause disastrous floods lower down. By the 14th, the troops had fixed their grip upon these bunds nearly thirty miles above the city, after encountering but feeble opposition on the way.

But the enemy at first displayed a much more unyielding disposition on the opposite side of the river. In that direction the Turks were moreover in more formidable force. A considerable body of Ottoman troops of all arms were found to have taken up a strong position near Mushaidieh on that bank of the Tigris, some twenty miles or so north of Baghdad. There General Cobbe attacked them on the 14th. After a prolonged and at times well-contested engagement, in which all arms of the Anglo-Indian forces cooperated to admiration and the gunboats on the river played an effective part, the Turks were completely rolled up. They were kept on the move all night by Cobbe's eager infantry and dispersed so rapidly towards morning that all touch with them was practically lost next day. Then the town of Bakuba, which is situated in a productive district on the left bank of the Diala, was taken on the morning of the 18th, after a surprise crossing of the stream during the night; and the very next day Feluja on the Euphrates, on the opposite flank of the arena of operations to Bakuba, was occupied with little difficulty. Reports to the effect that the Turks had started breaching the bunds of the great western waterway and were flooding the country had caused Maude anxiety; but the stories proved to be exaggerated, and the prompt action taken prevented much harm being done. Thus, by following up his victories below Baghdad immediately and relentlessly, the Army Commander had, within ten days of his securing possession of the city, virtually occupied all the surrounding country, had got the river embankments absolutely under his control, and had secured for the use of his army the abounding produce of a considerable tract of fertile and thickly populated country.

The second phase of the campaign for the conquest of Baghdad hardly calls for lengthy comment. It nevertheless illustrates Maude's methods of making war to the full as effectively, as do his victorious operations around Kut. Preparations for an active campaign had been so complete beforehand, that elaborate additional administrative processes were not necessary to enable him to make a fresh rapid advance from Azizieh. But he took care not to move forward from that half way house between Kut and the Mesopotamian capital until all was absolutely ready for the delivery of a decisive stroke, and, in spite of the temptation to push on the leading portions of his army in hot pursuit of the retreating enemy, he paused for a week to ensure his supply system and to enable the whole of his troops to take part in the final move. The consequence was that, within a fortnight of his pushing forward from Azizieh, the programme was complete and the Turks were scattered. Most commanders would probably have done as he did in respect to throwing a bridge across the Tigris below the junction of the Diala with the main river. But not all commanders, having done so, would have kept practically half their force on the left bank of the Tigris and have accepted the risks involved in forcing a passage across the tributary stream, when the enemy's front along it would virtually be turned by the troops who were advancing up the right bank of the main river. Maude however meant to inflict an absolutely crushing defeat upon his antagonists. It was no part of his theory of operations that the enemy should be manoeuvred out of a position and be allowed time to withdraw northwards at leisure. By attacking the Diala line, while at the same time moving up the further bank of the Tigris, he pinned down the Turks who were on the one bank, while part of his army was pressing forward to attack those who were on the other bank, and in consequence

265

he signally defeated both hostile forces in actual encounter. By the procedure adopted he won a total victory instead of only a partial one.

Nor would his victory have been so complete as it was, but for the decision and ruthlessness with which the enemy was followed up immediately after the occupation of Baghdad. The taking of the place was in itself such a triumph, and the moral effect of its fall was bound to be so great that, seeing what a strain had already been put upon the successful troops, a good excuse undoubtedly existed for sanctioning a temporary relaxation of effort, but that was not Maude's way. Like Nelson, he would not be satisfied with any but the utmost results. 'Had ten ships been taken and the eleventh escaped, we being able to get at her, I should never consider it well done,' was the great admiral's doctrine, and Maude conducted operations on land in that same spirit.

Tidings of the capture of Baghdad aroused enthusiasm, not only throughout the confines of the British Empire, but also in all the Allied countries. It was the first conspicuous and dramatic triumph that had been achieved by *Entente* forces on land since the Battle of the Marne, and the likelihood of its exercising a far-reaching effect over the whole course of the war in Eastern regions was manifest. A message of hearty congratulation was received from the King, and telegrams also came to hand, amongst others, from the Viceroy of India, from the Grand Duke Nicholas of Russia, from the Secretary of State for War, from the Commander-in-Chief in India, from Admiral Sir David Beatty on behalf of himself and the Grand Fleet, from the commanders of the British armies in all the other theatres of war, and from the Lord Mayor of London. Vice Admiral Sir Rosslyn Wemyss, the Naval Commander-in-Chief in the East Indies, expressed particular gratification that the Royal Navy had been able to cooperate with the troops in their triumph. Nor did the Home Government fail to give their recognition of what the Army Commander in Mesopotamia had accomplished in practical form, for Maude was definitely promoted to the rank of lieutenant general.

CHAPTER XIV
Consolidating the Conquest

If the capture of Baghdad and the subjection of the immediately surrounding district in some respects changed the character of Maude's preoccupations, these highly important events rather increased his labours and responsibilities than diminished them. In the first place, the great Oriental city itself required to be organised, although this work was rendered the easier by the fact that the inhabitants in general were delighted to be relieved of the presence of the Turk. Marauders and similar evil-disposed persons had to be laid by the heels. A military administration had to be set up, and correct relations had to be established with such remnants of the former civil power as it seemed desirable to retain. The question of sanitation in particular was promptly and energetically grappled with. Then again, communications had to be improved, and the matter of throwing bridges had straightway to be taken in hand; a boat bridge over the Tigris had already been completed by 17 March. A house-to-house search for arms was instituted, and this proved highly productive even if the weapons secured were of a varied character. Hospitals were fitted up in suitable buildings, and even at this early date arrangements for the comfort and the housing of the troops during the coming summer were already being devised.

Then there was also the question of developing and making full use of the produce of the fertile tracts around Baghdad, so as to relieve some of the strain on the very long line of communications which reached back to the Shatt-el-Arab. Maude was well aware that this region contained considerable resources of grain, of fodder, of meat, and of fruits and vegetables, as also of fuel (a commodity of great importance to the army owing to the extent to which the river transport depended on its supply), and he was determined to get value out of what could be made available. He had therefore arranged to have a Local Produce Controller on his staff, and this official, Colonel E. K. Dickson, lost no time in setting to work on duties which were to prove of great assistance to the maintenance of the army and to the prosecution of its subsequent operations in the field. The Army Commander was much impressed with what he noted as regards the fertility of the country during his first few days near and in Baghdad, and in his letters home he made comparisons between the agricultural wealth of the region where the bulk of his troops now found themselves, and the arid tracts where they had undergone such extremes of fortune during the preceding fifteen months.

It should also be mentioned that the moral effect which the triumphant advance of the Anglo-Indian forces from Es Sinn to the City of the Caliphs was exerting all over Lower Mesopotamia had become distinct and pronounced. This relieved Maude of a certain amount of anxiety concerning his rear. Arab sheikhs kept coming in to pay their respects at local posts all along the line. The tribesmen were displaying less and less bent for turbulence. Even marauding was on the decline. Certain exiguous Turkish detachments which had been disposed in posts along the lower Euphrates had withdrawn up that river as the invaders from the sea swept forward up the Tigris, and, gathering as one body at Feluja, they had represented the garrison of that place which was so summarily ejected on 19 March. The situation on the Karun and between Kurna and Kut was quite satisfactory, and at
Nasirieh much had been done by energetic measures of administration to develop and to settle the surrounding region.

All the time that Maude had been busy elaborating his plans for a far-reaching offensive campaign, which was to make him virtually master of all Lower Mesopotamia and its capital, and had been carrying them out, the question of Russian cooperation from the side of Persia had been a subject of inter-communication between London and Petrograd. It had indeed been at one time hoped that the Anglo-Indian Army would receive very substantial assistance from this quarter, even before it had penetrated beyond Kut. The Tsar's forces were in occupation of all northern Persia, with bodies of advanced troops pushed forward generally to about Kermanshah, and it had been fairly obvious that any progress on their part directed in a westerly or south-westerly direction must automatically threaten the communications with Mosul and Aleppo of such Turks as happened to be operating in regions to the south-east of Baghdad. Strategically speaking, the situation had in fact appeared to be full of promising possibilities. But the Russian forces available for action were not large, they were opposed by the Turkish XIII Corps, they were hampered by having to rely upon lengthy and indifferent communications with their own home territory, and they were not, as a matter-of-fact, handled with any remarkable enterprise during the early stages of Maude's offensive campaign at the time, that is to say, when they appeared to be offered somewhat tempting opportunities for delivering an effective stroke. Now, however, that Baghdad was in his hands and that news from Persia pointed to the Ottoman XIII Corps being in full retreat from the region about Khanikin, east of the upper Diala River, the Army Commander was particularly anxious to arrange for effective conjunct operations between portions of his own forces and such troops as the Russians might be able to push forward from the direction of Kermanshah. He was anxious to prevent the junction of the enemy XIII Corps (14th and 45th Divisions), which had retired northwards from Bakuba after that place had been occupied, with the enemy XVIII Corps (4th, 51st and 52nd Divisions) part of which had crossed the Tigris from the right to the left bank, and to complete the overthrow of the latter. There appeared to be a good prospect of dealing the Turks a heavy blow if the Russians would press forward strenuously. So Maude obtained leave from London to make all arrangements direct with General Baratoff, who was in command of the Russian forces.

Information as to the actual position of affairs as between the Russians and the Turkish XIII Corps was however somewhat defective. The Ottoman force was entitled to more respect than was believed to be the case and General Baratoff's troops were advancing under considerable difficulties and without any compelling impulse. Maude constituted a 'Khanikin Column' under charge of General Keary, which pressed north from Bakuba on 20 March; but it found itself strongly opposed by the XVIII Corps in hilly ground on the 23rd, and a vigorous attack was delivered that proved unsuccessful. This enabled XVIII Turkish Corps to cross the Diala about Kizil Robat and to get touch with XVIII Corps, so that Maude had to push forward additional troops to help the 'Khanikin Column.' Several encounters took place during the closing days of the month, in which the enemy suffered heavily. But the Russians failed to come up, no decisive success was achieved by the Anglo-Indian forces, and the results of the operations were indeed less far-reaching than had appeared probable when the scheme was being drawn up.

It was not until 2 April that direct touch was at last gained between the British and Russian patrols about Kizil Robat. By that time the strategic advantages of the situation had disappeared, for the Turks had succeeded in withdrawing more or less intact to the general line of the Shatt-el-Adhaim. It moreover had become apparent that the Russian forces were in no condition for prosecuting an active campaign, and that they could therefore hardly be relied upon to afford any really effective aid, although arrangements had been made to afford them substantial assistance in respect to supplies and transport.

'We have been busy again out here,' Maude wrote home on 31 March, 'and on the 25th we had a big fight with the Turks coming down from Persia. Although we were not able to turn them out of their positions which are very strong we hung on to them tenaciously, and that is what I wanted to do, so as to prevent their getting away before the Russians come along. We know that the Russians have very few troops in front of them, because we have identified nearly all the regiments in front of us; but I suppose that they have difficulties with transport and supplies, and the things that have happened recently in Russia do not I expect help them much. However I hope that they will come along soon.

'In the meantime we are keeping the Turks busy, and the day before yesterday my old division attacked the 51st and 52nd Turkish Divisions and gave them a good beating, driving them back across the river which they had advanced from, and inflicting very severe losses upon them, besides taking many prisoners. It was a capital performance, and as the 14th Division is also retreating towards Kifri, this has rid us of three of the five Turkish divisions opposed to us. The other two I should very much like to keep here till the Russians arrive, if they ever do; but we can hear little or nothing of them, and although we send out aeroplanes constantly to look for them they are not to be found anywhere, The weather still continues fine, and the river is wonderfully low for the time of the year; but I expect that we shall be having floods before very long now, as the thaw must have begun up in the Caucasus.'

So long as the situation on the left bank of the Tigris had not been satisfactorily cleared up, Maude had not been prepared to push his troops forward on the right bank so as to secure the terminus of the railway at Samarra. But as soon as the Turks fell back on the left bank behind the Shatt-el-Adhaim, 7th Division pressed forward from Mushaidieh, the scene of General Cobbe's victory of 14 March, and after overcoming some stubborn opposition it advanced to beyond Beled, capturing useful rolling stock on the line. Then it found itself strongly opposed. As it had now advanced further forward along the Tigris on its right bank than the line of the Shatt-el-Adhaim (on the left bank) which the Turks were holding, the situation obliged the Army Commander to call a halt.

The position on 10 April on the left bank of the Tigris was that the bulk of XVIII Turkish Corps was holding the line of the Shatt-el-Adhaim near the junction of that stream with the main river, while XVIII Turkish Corps was for the most part disposed in the stretch of the Jebel Hamrin which extends between the Diala and the Shattel-Adhaim, threatening any Anglo-Indian forces in flank that might advance with the idea of forcing a passage across the latter stream and of defeating XVIII Turkish Corps. It had been intended that General Marshall should attack the line of the Shatt-el-Adhaim on the night of 10/11 with his 3 Corps; but the enemy XVIII Corps suddenly came down on the 10th from the Jebel Hamrin on Marshall's flank. This Turkish move gave rise to some lively encounters which lasted over two days, but which by the 14th had terminated in a notable triumph for III Corps, the enemy drawing off northwards through the defiles of the Jebel Hamrin. Having thus settled XIII Corps for the moment, Marshall now turned his attention afresh to the Shatt-el-Adhaim, and his troops forced the passage of that river in brilliant style on the night of 17/18.

This success made an advance on the right bank of the Tigris at last justifiable, and the force on that side of the river at once moved forward. The Turks had created defensive lines barring the way, and the troops had severe fighting before they made railhead opposite Samarra good. But this was taken on the 23rd, and the victory achieved on this occasion was very complete: for over 700 prisoners were secured, 15 guns were taken, and a large quantity of rolling stock, of which only part had been seriously damaged by the Turks before they beat a retreat, fell into the hands of 7th Division which had carried the operation out. The division had been appreciably assisted by artillery fire from the other bank of the Tigris during the fighting.

The Turkish XIII Corps, which throughout the weeks immediately following the British occupation of Baghdad was handled by its commander with creditable enterprise, had been moving down the right bank of the Shatt-el-Adhaim with the intention of trying to save Samarra, a circumstance which afforded General Marshall a welcome opportunity for dealing this hostile force a crushing blow. The position held by one of its two divisions was captured by a surprise attack at night on 24 April, and the corps thereupon retreated hastily up the right bank of the river. Marshall followed the enemy up with vigour, in spite of heat and transport difficulties, and attacked the defeated corps again by surprise on the 30th at a point some thirty miles from the Tigris. The result was a complete victory. The Turks were rolled up and driven north in disarray, and this gratifying success may be said practically to have closed the prolonged series of operations on a large scale on the part of Maude's army which had been in progress since the previous December.

'Altogether I do not think that they [the Turks] can have been pleased with their experiences during the last month,' Maude wrote home on 4 May, 'as XVIII Corps have been beaten five times, and XIII Corps three times. They have lost very heavily in casualties, while we have taken 17 guns, close on 3,000 prisoners, and masses of other things, including a large amount of rolling stock and some barges. All this time the Russians have been quite inactive, which has been a thousand pities; because they might have done a lot while we were engaging both corps, for there was little or nothing left for them to fight. But I suppose that they are all at sixes and sevens, and cannot get anything done properly. Still, it is to be regretted, as we ought by now to have got them well established on the Tigris above us, and that would have simplified the situation tremendously for the next autumn, when we begin fighting again.'

He had had a visit from two Russian generals at the end of April and had arrived at a certain understanding with his allies; but he realised himself that the results of the Revolution of the previous month were bound to exercise a disastrous influence over their military dispositions and their military efficiency in the future, even if he could hardly yet foresee the total collapse that was to supervene before long. Russian forces still practically dominated Armenia, and the Army Commander no doubt at this time, when already beginning according to his custom to look forward to what the strategic situation was likely to be some months later, pictured to himself that this promising condition of things would still exist when the season arrived for starting offensive operations in the autumn. In the meantime, however, the time had come to effect a redistribution of his forces, seeing that the hot weather had practically set in.

While the strenuous operations beyond Baghdad, of which a brief account has been given above, were being carried out under the general direction of the Army Commander in the latter part of March and throughout April, he had been devoting close attention to the question of ensuring general security during the period of comparative inactivity that would ensue in the hot weather, and he had also been concerned with arranging for the welfare of his troops during that trying time. Tents were brought up from the rear. Encampments were laid out on carefully selected sites. Well-organised canteens were provided.

Supplies of comforts were distributed. Provision for the recreation of men and officers was not forgotten. Arrangements had moreover been made for laying a metre gauge railway from Kut to Baghdad, so as to relieve the strain on the water transport to some extent, in view of the coming season of low water. Orders had furthermore been sent for the infantry of the 15th Division to move up from Nasirieh to the front so as to increase the strength of the forces in immediate contact with the Turks – this although the Arabs had been displaying a good deal of effervescence at the time when the Sheikh Saad-Es Sinn railway was being pulled up and removed. The Tigris, it should be mentioned, had given less trouble than had been anticipated in respect to inundations; the River had kept particularly low this year, and in this respect the army enjoyed better luck in 1917 than had been the case twelve months before when Maude's division was participating in the endeavour to relieve Kut; anxiety on this score was indeed virtually at an end by the beginning of May.

The question of local supplies had already been placed on a sound footing, and the situation in this respect was improving from day to day as better relations were established with the Arab producers. Maude's genius for organisation and his forethought at this time were almost as valuable to his army as was the influence of his personality over the course of the warlike combinations which were being carried out by Generals Marshall and Cobbe. Much of his time, moreover, was taken up with political and administrative questions in connection with the territory which he had conquered.

'I have some quaint interviews from day to day,' he wrote on 14 April, 'and I have been obliged to limit them considerably, as they take up so much of my time. One of my recent ones was with a Chaldean priest who came on Easter Sunday to give me his blessing. He had asked previously if he might do so, and I said 'Certainly.' When he came in he proceeded to give me his blessing, and said that he hailed me as the first Christian conqueror of Baghdad, so I immediately interjected 'How do you know I am a Christian?' This seemed rather to upset him. However he started again and finished off without interruption. He is a very nice old thing, and he did a lot of good work for our prisoners... I forget whether I told you that we have got a most comfortable house which used to belong to Khalil, and we have settled down very happily in it. Everything is most comfortable, and we have even got electric light now and double doors to keep the mosquitoes out, so we are not to be pitied.

'We are doing a lot in the town. We have practically remade the streets, which were full of holes and indeed full of chasms. We have also organised a military and civil police, and we have got a system of night watchmen for night work. The people are all delighted to see us, and whenever I ride out in the evening one is met with smiling faces and salutations everywhere. I have only been twice assaulted so far, once by a man and once by a woman, who rushed out from the crowd and insisted on kissing my boots, which I hope they liked. All round outside, too, our troops are received in a most friendly manner, though of course, as you know, the Arab character is a treacherous one. Still, whenever we occupy places which the Turks have been holding previously, they cheer our arrival.

'Everything is pretty quiet elsewhere, and the country seems to be settling down well. I have had the Chief of the Indian General Staff, General Kirkpatrick, who was with me at the Staff College, here recently and he has seen as much as possible in the time at his disposal.'

By the end of April the heat was getting severe, and during the closing stages of their offensive the troops suffered considerably from it, the water difficulty also presenting itself from time to time. Maude was therefore very glad to be able to call something in the nature of a halt, so as to give the troops that rest which they had so fully earned after five months of very strenuous fighting. The Mesopotamian Comforts Fund,[13] in the organisation of which Lady Maude and her daughters had taken a prominent part, was beginning to bear fruit even up at the front, luxuries of various kinds coming to hand for the troops. Bands were arriving in the country. The Army Commander knew well that there would be a risk of sickness spreading as soon as the rank and file became sedentary for the summer after their exertions, and he was determined that plenty of recreation should be provided for them. The health of the force was however still most satisfactory, and, as it turned out, it remained satisfactory upon the whole throughout the hot weather.

'Personally I look forward to a busy summer,' Maude wrote to Sir W. Lambton on 17 May, 'as there is much to do. Future operations, restless Arab tribes all round, reorganisation of civil and military administration of Baghdad and surrounding country, reconstruction of our

---

[13] It may be mentioned that in the middle of October 1917 the receipts of this fund amounted to nearly £57,000; over £18,000 was collected on 'Flag Days.' At the end of the campaign there was a balance of some £9,000 left over, and this sum is being set apart to endow a 'Stanley Maude Ward' in the Endell Street Hospital for Tropical Diseases.

communications, development of local supplies, new railway lines, the proximity of the Russians, political questions, and a thousand and one other items give one plenty to do and to think about. But we are all in tearing spirits, and shall be quite ready for the Turks when they feel like trying conclusions again.'

Actually, the whole of the troops could not even yet settle comfortably because some punitive work had to be undertaken against the Arabs. In the middle of May the Russians moreover suddenly proposed to undertake an offensive from where they were drawn up east of the Diala, towards Kifri, and they asked for cooperation by Anglo-Indian troops. This was prepared in haste and a couple of columns moved out; but the Russians were incontinently hustled back again after crossing the Diala, and the undertaking thereupon collapsed. Maude was sufficiently satisfied with the progress of the various matters that he had been occupying himself with at Baghdad towards the end of the month, to admit of his paying a visit to Samarra, going out by train on 18th and returning next day. On the way back a quantity of sand had been blown on to the line at one place, the engine was derailed and the first five trucks were telescoped, four men unfortunately being killed and seven injured. A few days later he paid a visit to the front about Deltawa and Bakuba, and he would have liked to take a run down to the base and to see how matters were progressing at Basrah, Nasirieh and Ahwaz; but he could not find the time to do so, as such a trip would have taken several days. By the end of May matters had settled down for the summer, June proving a very quiet month except for an important punitive operation against the Arabs in the Diala valley, in which 14,000 sheep, 240 camels and large quantities of grain were captured; 80 of the tribesmen moreover were killed. A number of officers, including General Money, Chief of the General Staff, had gone away on leave at the end of April, but these began returning in the latter part of June.

'We held a most successful 4 June dinner,' Maude wrote home on the 8th. 'About twenty-eight were present and I made General Holdsworth take the chair, as he was senior to me at Eton. He and I used to have great races there; he beat me in the Mile and I beat him in the Steeplechase, and I won the Mile next year. We had dinner at the Hotel Maude, and every one enjoyed themselves immensely. I left about half-past ten, but I believe that the others stayed till nearly one o'clock and played football, etc., in the courtyard of the hotel.'

'I ride most evenings and occasionally go by launch,' he wrote on the 27th, 'but always to inspect something as there are such numbers of things to look into. Last night I was down at the Expeditionary Force canteen – we have got eight canteens running at different places about here now. I saw one man buying a number of things there, and I asked him whether he was hungry, and he said 'Yes.' So I said, 'That means that you do not get enough to eat?' And he said that he had never been so well fed in his life, but that he liked a few extras to go with it. That is just the advantage that the canteen gives us, as it enables the troops to get little luxuries to supplement their already substantial rations. .

'Things are going along very satisfactorily in every direction. My only worries are the Russians and political questions, but I do not let them worry me too much. I just say what I think and leave it at that...

'I had a capital flight by aeroplane the day before yesterday. 7th Division were very anxious that I should present their Football Cup to the winning team after the final match, but the train would have taken eight hours each way to Samarra and back. So we flew there in an hour and fifty minutes, and came back in fifty minutes – eighty miles each way. It took us a long time to get there as there was a strong Shamal blowing, which made us rock unpleasantly at times. I went out in daylight and flew back by moonlight, so that I had the experience of day and night flying.'

The action of the Army Commander in paying this aerial visit to Samarra was very highly appreciated by all ranks. It appealed to their sporting instincts, and it demonstrated to 7th Division what a lively interest Maude took in their welfare and in their occupations. Sir C. Monro in India was somewhat concerned on learning that the Commander-in-Chief in Mesopotamia had taken to making flying trips, and he conveyed a hint to Baghdad on the subject. 'The answer seems to be that you can lose your life walking down stairs,' was Maude's comment when mentioning the matter in a letter home; but that same answer might, after all, be made to a remonstrance with regard to any reckless act. Although he could not keep so closely in touch with regimental officers and rank and file, now that he was in control of a great army distributed over a wide area of country, as had been possible for him when at the head of 18th Division, he never missed an opportunity of going among the troops when one offered, and he made a point of presenting ribbons of decorations personally after having awarded them, if it could be managed. The consequence was that his army not merely entertained a feeling of profound confidence in his soldiership, but that British and Indian troops alike also felt a genuine affection for this chief, whose manner and bearing were ever so sympathetic and who was so prompt with his commendation when any good work had been performed. The story of his frequent visits to the station hospitals, and of his kindly inquiries when making his rounds on these occasions, was carried out to the distant camps by convalescents. All hands moreover fully realised how much the vastly improved conditions in which they were living, as compared to earlier experiences, were attributable to initiative and drive at the very top.

'Few could visit an hospital as he did,' writes the Rev. A. C. E. Jarvis, Principal Chaplain. 'No one knows better than a chaplain how difficult this gracious ministry is, but he possessed the gift in a rare degree. Entering a ward he took possession of it; rank made no difference, he was equally at ease with all always saying and doing the right thing, always apparently knowing something about everybody, and always cheerful. His presence radiated confidence and hope.'

The Army Commander had been supplied with a singular craft known as a 'glisseur' or 'scooter', driven by a powerful motor engine, which skimmed along the surface of the water at a great rate and making a fearsome noise. This contrivance enabled him to travel at speed about the waterways immediately round Baghdad, and it assisted him considerably in respect to carrying out inspections and visits by adding to the time at his disposal. Amongst his many duties was that of conducting interviews with local notabilities, and he was also ex officio charged with exercising general control over the administration of the country. How effectively he performed this service is shown by the fact that Mesopotamia has perhaps been the most peaceful region in British occupation during the months following the Armistice. Colonel Willcox gives an interesting description of Maude's work in connection with the medical arrangements and of the care of the sick during the summer months:

> It was frequently my privilege to meet General Maude, and to discuss with him matters relating to the prevention of illness amongst the troops, and any practical suggestions always received his utmost support. He took the greatest interest in the prevention of scurvy, which had been a great scourge to the Indian troops, and he gave instructions to Colonel Dickson that at all costs fresh vegetables and supplies were to be issued up to the fullest medical requirements. These instructions were

faithfully carried out and as a consequence scurvy speedily disappeared from the force.

After the occupation of Baghdad General Maude took the keenest interest in every detail of the medical arrangements, and it was largely due to his active support that so very high a degree of efficiency was attained. The hospitals at Baghdad and the medical arrangements generally were as satisfactory in every way, as regards medical care, nursing and equipment, as any hospitals in London or in any theatre of war. He personally visited the hospitals at least twice a week, and by his kindly interest did a very great deal to alleviate the sufferings of the patients and to encourage them in their progress towards recovery. He took a special interest in the Indian patients, and as an example of his thoughtfulness and sympathy he learnt Hindustani in order to be able to converse with them on his visits to the Indian hospitals. It is impossible to exaggerate the great help and sympathy which the Medical Service in Mesopotamia received from him during the whole time of his service as G.O.C. His personal interest and great sympathy were the prime causes of the perfection of the medical arrangements in the hospitals and in the field.'

Maude had always, alike as a brigade commander, as a divisional commander and as a corps commander, kept a watchful eye over the chaplain's department, and had interested himself particularly in its work, forming close relations with its personnel. The Rev. A. C. E. Jarvis writes as follows of his work in this connection when Army Commander in Mesopotamia:

I met him officially for the first time when I was sent by the War Office to Mesopotamia to report on the Chaplain's Department on its transfer from the Indian Ecclesiastical Department. He gave me all facilities and a free hand. He told me that he was seriously understaffed, and at once stated the total number of all denominations he required, a figure which I found, after careful investigation, to be absolutely correct. Having made up his mind he never rested until he got his men.

The Army Council appointed me Principal Chaplain to the force, and I took over in January 1917, and it was then that I was brought into close personal touch with him. Persistent in inquiry, unfailing in solicitude in all that concerned the

Department and the spiritual and moral welfare of the men, he always stood by me. 'My chaplains,' as he always referred to us, meant as much to him as did any other branch of the service.

The year 1917 was one of climatic extremes in Mesopotamia. The heat during the month of July was intense, the temperature rising considerably higher than it had done during either of the previous summers passed by Anglo-Indian troops in this tropical part of the world. Thanks, however, to the excellent arrangements which had been made in the matter of tentage accommodation, the health of the troops gave rise to little real anxiety, even if there were an undesirable number of cases of heatstroke. One operation undertaken during this torrid period did not prove successful, and what occurred rather suggested that active work in the field ought to be avoided until the weather grew a little cooler. News had come to hand that the Turkish garrison of Ramadi, their furthest advanced post on the Euphrates above Feluja, was scanty in numbers. So Maude gave directions for a portion of I Corps to fall upon the place. The enterprise took place on the night of 10/11 July; but the result was disappointing, the failure being largely due to a very severe dust-storm – a form of atmospheric disturbance that was very common during the summer months. The losses sustained in the affair were chiefly owing to the temperature, and as a matter-of-fact a number of Turks from Ramadi came in afterwards and voluntarily surrendered, which indicated that the garrison had been roughly handled even if the attack had been unsuccessful.

General Money, who had been in indifferent health ever since Maude had taken up the chief command, had to be invalided soon after his return from leave, and it is worth mentioning that when referring to this in a letter home the Army Commander remarked that he 'did most of the General Staff work himself,' an admission of his system of centralisation. Colonel H. R. Hopwood became Chief of the General Staff. Suggestions had been made to Maude that he should himself take short leave of absence to India; but, although he fully realised that men who had severely felt the strain of the campaign or whose health was suffering ought to be allowed a change, he would not hear of it. 'The cases I cannot understand,' he wrote, 'are those that are well and strong and have nothing the matter with them. Surely it is a time when every day and every hour should be utilised to the full by everybody to try and bring this war to a successful conclusion.' That life in Baghdad was none too pleasant at this time is shown by the following extract from a letter of his of 20 July:

279

My house at night is literally like an oven, for the sun bakes the bricks in the walls and the tiles on the floor throughout the day, and they give off the heat all night. I wish that I could get out under canvas; but there is too much to be done, although as soon as all the reorganisation and preparation is finished I mean to get back to tent life as early as possible. It is so much more satisfactory being right up with the troops and seeing and hearing all that is going on at first hand; and although some people do not like losing their little comforts it is unquestionably in my opinion the right place to be.

The railway from Kut to Baghdad was completed before the end of the month; this proved a great boon, for the Tigris was now getting very low, and navigation along some of its stretches was becoming liable to interruption. The two lengths of railway Kurna-Amarah and Kut-Baghdad avoided the shallowest portion of the waterway, upon the uninterrupted navigation of which the very existence of the army would otherwise have depended, and within a month half a dozen trains a day were conveying war material and food supplies up to the advanced base. It was becoming more and more apparent to Maude as the summer wore on that no reliance could be placed upon Russian assistance from the side of Persia, and that the situation in Armenia was coming to be such that he must be prepared for considerable bodies of Turkish troops being liberated from that mountainous region for action against himself. That the fall of Baghdad had aroused consternation in Berlin as well as in Constantinople was well known. Everything pointed to the Anglo-Indian Army in Mesopotamia being called upon during the coming cold season to withstand determined efforts on the part of the enemy to recover possession of the city and the territory which had been wrested out of the hands of the Osmanlis.

It was understood that General Allenby, who had just assumed command of the British forces on the borders of Palestine, would shortly commence active operations in that quarter; but, even allowing for the effect of an offensive from the side of Egypt, the position of Maude's army around Baghdad, dependent on its long line of communications, was not wholly without anxiety. Report at one time declared that the very successful German commander, Mackensen, was about to take charge of hostile operations in Northern Mesopotamia.

This story proved to be incorrect; but it transpired, on the other hand, that general superintendence over the Ottoman operations was going to be exercised by another distinguished German soldier, Von Falkenhayn. The Army Commander at Baghdad had therefore to be prepared for an active offensive campaign on the part of the enemy, conducted under skilled leadership, when the cooler weather set in. But he was nowise dismayed. He indeed looked forward with calm confidence to the future, well aware of the adequacy of his own arrangements and placing the fullest reliance on his troops.

The earlier days of August were signalised by no occurrences of importance, although the great heat was beginning to pass away and the health of the army remained satisfactory. A memorandum was issued on the 7th urging upon subordinate commanders the importance of getting all ranks fit for rapid marching and entrenching, and by the middle of the month Maude had decided that a beginning of active operations might now be made. Sharaban, twenty-five miles north-east of Bakuba, was occupied on the 20th and fortified, the Army Commander paying a visit of inspection to the place at the end of the month. Orders were also issued for more or less continuous reconnaissance work to be carried out by the Air Force, which had received substantial additions to its strength in personnel and material, with the object of locating and of harassing the enemy.

About this time Maude was a good deal disappointed at only seeing a précis of his despatch of 10 April appearing, in which he had recorded the results of his campaign of conquest up to the end of the previous March.

'I see that they have only published a résumé of my despatch,' he wrote home, 'which of course is very different from the real article; a paraphrase such as this will convey little or nothing to the troops for whom, so far as I am concerned, it was primarily intended. So I am having it printed in full and will distribute copies throughout the army, so that they may see at least how much their work is appreciated.

'I realise of course that paper is getting scarce in England, and if they were simply to publish my next despatch in an abbreviated form I would have nothing to say. But it seems to me that a place like Baghdad is not captured every day, and this fact might have justified a little more extravagance, so that everyone might know exactly what had happened.'

He would, however, appear to have been under a misapprehension in this matter. The despatch was published in full in the *London Gazette* of

10 July. It was a long communication, however, so the various newspapers only made extracts from it, or published it in the form of a summary. The same thing happened to many other despatches sent into the War Office by commanders-in-chief during the progress of the Great War. The mistake in such cases seems to be – and it is one especially to be avoided where operations are being carried out in lands far away from home like Mesopotamia or East Africa – that a liberal consignment of copies of the Gazette is not sent out to the scene of operations as a matter of course by the War Office. Despatches sent in by a victorious general (that institution should remember) serve a twofold purpose. They furnish the Government and the country with information. They also acquaint the army concerned that its leader has brought to the notice of the Government and the country what his troops have done, and that he has given them the credit that they deserve for the trials they have undergone uncomplainingly and for the resolution and hardihood they have displayed when at grips with the foe.

While quietly making preparations for the offensive campaign which he had been planning, Maude was also continuing to devote attention to the innumerable questions that arose in connection with the comfort and contentment of the troops under his command. He was particularly pleased with the development of the hospital arrangements in Baghdad and with the results obtained by the Local Produce Control which he had set up on first arrival at the city. The place was indeed assuming many of the characteristics of an Indian cantonment of old standing.

'I am sending you the programme of the races which we had last week,' he wrote home on 6 September, 'they were a great success and will, I hope, be the beginning of a succession of meetings in years to come. The new club is being laid out with polo ground, racing tracks, lawn tennis courts, cricket and football grounds, golf course, and arrangements are being made for aquatics in connection with it. We are also starting an Officers' Club in the city, and it ought to be open in two or three days' time. I went over it yesterday and it ought to be a first rate institution.

'A few nights ago the nursing sisters here gave a moonlight party to which they asked me, and it really was very well done. They have a nice house on the river bank about one and a half miles above Baghdad. They prevailed on me to play a game of musical chairs, for which about twenty or thirty people started, and finally I won the competition, although not without a struggle. Later on in the evening suggested that they should have two or three dances, which all the nurses loved, although there were some very black looks amongst the matrons and senior medical officers who seemed to think that there was something very dreadful in dancing. I never can follow the thoughts of such people; for dancing in itself is quite harmless, and considering the splendid way in which these young girls have worked throughout the intense heat all this summer I think that they deserve any reasonable relaxation one can give them.

'I get so impatient sometimes because things do not go as quickly as I could wish, but one is apt to forget the difficulties of our communications and the length of the river line. It is indeed wonderful how things are coming along, and the work of the railways and inland water transport is quite magnificent especially the latter, as the river is down at its very lowest, and yet groundings are few and far between. We have got simply masses of men, munitions, and supplies coming along, and everything looks most prosperous.'

'The general was strict, but not unreasonably so,' Captain Musgrave, Maude's aide-de-camp, writes of him, 'if he gave an order for a thing to be done at a certain hour he expected it to be done at the hour named. Those who knew him always had sufficient trust in him to feel sure that he would not attempt to carry out impossible projects. His great power of inspiring confidence in those under him was perhaps one of his most remarkable characteristics; this went through the whole of the force – right down to the private soldiers.

'Very precise in respect to punctuality, I never knew him to be late for anything. Nor was he ever before his time. A favourite saying of his was that every officer ought to have written up over his shaving glass in order to be perpetually reminded of it, 'In war, time is everything.'

'When at home in his own house with his personal staff he would at meals and such times put business away from him as far as possible, and the conversation would carry one far away from Mesopotamia. But if an important message or telegram arrived he would attend to it at once and dictate the reply.'

During the closing days of September two important operations were carried out with a view partly to extending the area under control of the Anglo-Indian forces, and partly to depriving the enemy of valuable sources of supply. The first was the occupation of Mendali on the Persian frontier about fifty miles east of Bakuba, which was effected on the 29th by a cavalry force after a sharp skirmish. The second, a much

283

more serious enterprise, was a carefully prepared attack by General Brooking with his 15th Division upon Ramadi on the Euphrates above Feluja, where a Turkish force had been in position all the summer. This undertaking proved a signal success. The place was surrounded on the 28th after a night march and its main defences were captured, and then, when the attack was resumed next morning, the Turks surrendered almost to a man: 3,500 prisoners, 18 guns and 10 machine guns fell into the hands of the victors, besides launches, barges and armaments of various kinds, a most satisfactory opening to the autumn campaign. The capture of the few river craft was especially useful in connection with establishing a water transport service on the Euphrates. Major Generals R. Stuart Wortley and W. Gillman (who had been Maude's G.S.O.1. in 18th Division when he first joined it in Gallipoli) arrived during the month, Stuart Wortley becoming Deputy Quartermaster General and Gillman being appointed to take command of the 17th Division which was to be formed at Baghdad.

Having rendered the position on the Euphrates secure, Maude now turned his attention to his right flank beyond Sharaban, and in the middle of October a number of columns operating in concert succeeded in occupying the whole of the section of the Jebel Hamrin range of hills which is situated to the west of the Diala, and also portions of the range to the east of that river. This was accomplished without encountering much opposition. The weather was now very pleasant and was even cold at night. Maude wrote home in excellent spirits, delighted at the prospect of active operations and at the success which was attending their opening stage.

'I forget whether I told you that I flew out to Ramadi in an aeroplane shortly after the fight,' he mentioned in a letter home, 'starting at 6 a.m. and getting there soon after 7 o'clock. I then rode round the battlefield and saw everything in detail, and later inspected the captured. In the afternoon I went out and planned the new defences for the place with the general in command there, and in the evening I flew back, taking just an hour to do so. It was much the best way of getting there as I could not well spare much time, and if I had motored it would have meant seven and a half hours each way at least, and the jolting and jerking would have been dreadful. In fact it was this question of bad communications which required so much careful preparation before we attacked Ramadi, and although things are much better in this respect they are still very bad. But we are hard at work on them and matters are improving.'

The Army Commander always had twenty-four orderlies about him, who had been especially chosen from his old division, four being on duty at a time. His immediate entourage, as also the military police authorities in Baghdad, were anxious about his safety. There was some reason to believe that fanatical elements were plotting against his life, and a report reached Headquarters one time in the autumn that an attempt would actually be made against him. Although rather disposed to pooh-pooh such stories, he allowed himself to be persuaded that special preventive steps were called for, and he agreed to the guards over his personal quarters in the house where he resided being doubled. His rides and motor drives through the streets caused those in charge of the police considerable apprehension at times, and special precautions were taken if it was known beforehand what route he was going to follow and where he was going to.

The caravan route that for centuries has led from Baghdad to Mosul does not coincide with the line of the Tigris. It skirts the foothills that project outwards from the upland regions of Kurdistan and Luristan into the great plain of Babylon and Chaldea. In his plans for prosecuting further offensive operations against the Ottoman forces, Maude had ever kept his eye fixed on Kifri and Kirkuk as a next objective, and in the early days of summer, before the utter collapse of fighting potentialities in the Russian hosts consequent upon the Revolution became apparent, he had always contemplated joint combinations by the Allies in this region. Although any aid worthy of serious consideration from the side of Persia could be regarded as at an end by the autumn of 1917, and although this circumstance, coupled with the disquieting situation in Armenia, necessarily added to the difficulties of any advance northwards from the Jebel Hamrin, the Army Commander had evidently proposed to act in this direction in due course during the cold weather that was now setting in. The operations of October had indeed made a good commencement for such a plan of campaign. But before committing any large portion of his army to offensive operations on an ambitious scale directed towards Kirkuk, the Commander-in-Chief deemed it necessary to dispose effectually of the Turkish contingents which all the summer had been assembled on the Tigris to the north of Samarra.

The enemy, as it happened, made the first move in this quarter, advancing somewhat unexpectedly but in tentative fashion down both banks of the river towards the end of October. General Cobbe from Samarra prepared to fall upon this hostile armament, but it drew back. Maude thereupon sent orders that it was to be dealt with where it had halted, about midway between Samarra and Tikrit. The enemy position on the right bank of the Tigris was in consequence attacked and taken on 2 November, and Cobbe followed this up three days later by a successful onset upon the hostile forces gathered at Tikrit, the fruits of the victory being a number of prisoners and some valuable booty in war material and river craft, while the discomfited Turks retreated precipitately up the Tigris. This very satisfactory encounter proved to be the last triumph on the battlefield to be placed to the account of the ever victorious army that had grown out of D Force, while it served under the orders of Sir Stanley Maude. The fight has therefore a tragic significance of its own. For a very few days later, the British and Indian detachments that were spread out over a wide stretch of country fanwise round Baghdad, and that were holding the chains of communications that led back from the city to the Persian Gulf, learnt with profound grief, and at first with consternation, that they had lost their beloved chief.

But there were no grounds for consternation. The conqueror had consolidated his conquest. If his task was not in a military sense completed, such substantial progress had been accomplished towards its completion, so surely had the foundations been laid, that the Anglo-Indian Army had now no grounds for fearing a reverse of fortune in Mesopotamia, nor for anticipating that yet further triumphs would not fall to its lot under the guiding hand of the distinguished soldier who took Maude's place.

In this and in preceding chapters references have been made to the mutual confidence that sprang up between Maude and those serving under him in the field, as he passed upwards through the various stages of Brigade commander, Divisional commander and Corps commander up to that of Army commander. But he possessed the precious gift of inspiring trust in those set over him as well as in subordinates of all degrees, and this was one of the secrets of his achievements at the head of formidable legions. From the time that he had assumed supreme control in Mesopotamia he had enjoyed, and had been sustained by, the full confidence of his military superiors at home and in India. The extent to which this mutual reliance held good, and the benefit which it conferred upon the State and upon the forces engaged in an arduous campaign, is expressed by Sir W. Robertson, to whose unvarying practical support and moral support Maude and his men owed so much, in the following tribute to the memory of the conqueror of Baghdad:

I saw much of Maude and his work for some years before the war, especially when he was one of my chief assistants in the Directorate of Military Training in 1914, and was greatly impressed, not only with his professional attainments and his love for the army, but also with his sincerity of purpose and his high standard of honour and justice. In my opinion these are amongst the first qualifications required in a leader of men, and without them no man is fit to lead. Therefore, when it became necessary in August 1916 to appoint a new commander to our forces in Mesopotamia, I had not a moment's hesitation in recommending Maude for the place.

It was very important that no mistake should be made in the selection, for the campaign had hitherto been a series of dismal failures and disappointments, and had entailed great hardships and suffering upon the troops. Further, Maude was then practically an unknown man to the War Cabinet, while there were not a few other officers, some of whom were known to the War Cabinet, whose fitness for the post could not be overlooked. I consequently realised that I was taking upon myself a great responsibility in recommending Maude, and him alone; but it sat lightly upon me, because I always felt satisfied that he would do everything that was humanly possible to retrieve the situation. How well he retrieved it is one of the finest pages in the history of the war, and from first to last our relations were of the most cordial and mutually helpful kind.

This was the more remarkable seeing that we could communicate with each other only by telegraph, and, as everybody knows, it is always difficult in these circumstances to convey one's real meaning. But I cannot recall a single instance of misunderstanding arising between us as to our respective wishes and intentions, and this satisfactory result could not have been achieved but for Maude's clear military vision and his single-minded devotion to duty. Throughout the war I was fortunate in having to deal with commanders in the different theatres of operations whose one desire was loyally to play the game and, ignoring self, to advance the general cause. No one was more conspicuous in these endeavours than was Maude. He was a gentleman and a soldier in the best sense of the word, beloved by all who had the privilege of knowing and of working with him.

What might be called the combatant side of the role enacted by the Anglo-Indian forces in the Mesopotamian theatre from April to November, furnishes convincing testimony as to the understanding which existed between the Army Commander and those, high and low, who were serving under his orders. The operations of April and early May, which rendered the position around Baghdad absolutely safe from real danger, and which during the summer months caused the troops to be virtually immune from molestation even in minor degree, were carried out under no inconsiderable conditions of difficulty. They called for rapid movements and exhausting marches effected in great heat by troops who had already gone through a strenuous campaign, troops who had passed through the wilderness, who had reached the Promised Land, and who might reasonably hope for a respite. But even if their chief could not from the nature of the case be up and amongst them in those trying days, his unconquerable spirit animated them all. The nomadic events on the Shatt-el-Adhaim, the dramatic capture of Samarra, the dash across the desert to Feluja on the Euphrates, all in their way threw a heavy strain for the time being upon the personnel of the forces entrusted with the tasks; but officers and men made light of this. Every undertaking of those few weeks moreover, with the exception of some of the earlier work on the Diala that went partly awry owing to the fully expected cooperation of the Russians failing to materialise, was wholly triumphant; moreover, even there, the balance of success was, in the end, emphatically on the side of the Anglo-Indian forces engaged. 'I hope always to cherish his memory as I saw him in Baghdad on the occasion of my visit,' General Kirkpatrick wrote of Maude at that particular time; 'calm, cool, determined to pursue his success to the utmost of his means, and enjoying the confidence of all. He has indeed left the heritage of a great name.'

The following appreciation by his distinguished subordinate, Sir A. Cobbe, serves to indicate how the conqueror of Baghdad was regarded by an experienced soldier, who enjoyed the privilege of commanding one of his army corps and of contributing to, and sharing in, his anxieties and his triumphs:

> Maude's greatest weakness perhaps was that he undertook too much himself, so that his staff were apt to feel themselves in the position of confidential clerks. Methodical to a degree and punctual to a minute, his day was mapped out from the time when he rose until he went to bed. Engrossed in his work, a slave-driver of himself perhaps more than of those under him, he gave one the impression of a cold, calculating nature, which

was almost repellent at times. That this was not his real nature was shown by his impetuosity in the hour of victory, by his humanity, by his care and thought for those under him, and also as I can testify by his large-hearted and very human acceptance of sharp differences of opinion with his subordinate commanders. As he once said to me in reply to an apology for a somewhat heated conversation over the telephone, 'I never remember those things. I know that it is only keenness.'

His standard of duty and self-sacrifice was a high one. He rewarded those who came up to it generously. He was coldly just to those who in his eyes fell short of full performance of their military duty. He possessed most of the attributes of a big commander. His plans were always laid with the larger possibility in view, while he was meticulous in working out the details for the initial stroke. He was a past master of that systematic staff work which is so necessary when conducting a campaign. A little apt to be impatient by nature, he could nevertheless keep himself in check owing to the self-control he always exercised.

If ever a man gave all his thoughts and his life to his country it was Maude. He died in the hour of victory, a victory secured in a distant and minor theatre of operations, but one which undoubtedly exercised its effect upon the general fortunes of the Great War. He lived and he died a very gallant English gentleman.

Sir George MacMunn, who had played so important a part in rendering possible the brilliant campaign carried out by the Army Commander and who assumed command on the return home of Sir W. Marshall, sends the following account, dated 17 July 1919, of the relations that existed between them, and of what Maude accomplished during his period of service in Mesopotamia.

I write this note on our late chief from his quarters in Baghdad (where died also Von der Goltz), and from the room in which he died, in which I work in some hope that his hand may rest on my shoulder.

I first met Maude at the War Office in those strenuous years of preparation before the war. We next met in Gallipoli where I had official dealings with him as commander of 18th Division.

But we first came really together when, one of the last to leave Suvla Bay, he landed on peaceful Imbros to find his tired men drawing hot Maconochie rations as they stepped off their lighters. That gift of the old officer, care and thought for his men, lay very deep within him.

In Egypt I helped to equip his division for Mesopotamia, following him thither shortly afterwards as Inspector General of Communications. In May 1916, just after the fall of Kut, I found him at Sheikh Saad on the Tigris, once again reforming that division that had so often been battle-swept; and we talked far into the night of how to maintain the army in health and efficiency in an undeveloped land of great extremes. It was not however until September 1916, when he had succeeded to the command of the army and I was constantly thrown with him, that I came to appreciate and to understand the determination, the vision, and the knowledge of principle and detail that animated him.

Few knew how anxious were his days from the advance beyond Kut to the last days in 1917. The army hung by a thread and the enemy attempts to expel us were considerable; but maintenance was his chief anxiety in my interviews with him during and after the advance, and at times he would wire to me twice or thrice a day. It was this strain on mind and body, continued through a long and abnormally hot summer that left him little strength when the trial came. Efficiency and thoroughness had been his watchword, and he died at the height of his achievement.

One great difficulty which Maude unavoidably laboured under in Mesopotamia, at all events during the earlier days of his occupying high command in that theatre of war, was the fact of his never having served east of the Red Sea before 1916, with the result that he necessarily at first was wholly unacquainted with the language and the customs of a considerable proportion of the soldiers under his orders. Until he took over charge of the Tigris Corps in July 1916 he had never been closely associated with Indian units. He had seen something of native troops at Suakin and at Tofrek for a few weeks as a youngster, and he had met them again from time to time on the Western Front; but for all practical purposes he had had nothing to do with them. Of the five divisions with which he carried out his victorious operations of advance and consolidation for eleven months in the Cradle of the World, four, however, were on Indian establishment, with three-quarters of their infantry composed of native troops, as were also his cavalry.

But he set himself to get over this difficulty by studying the habits of the Indian portion of his army as far as time permitted, and by learning Hindustani. With the aid of officers of the Indian Army on his staff he contrived to ascertain a great deal about the peculiarities of those warriors who were recruited in the great British Dependency in Asia and on its borderland, and whom he led to victory. They discovered this and appreciated it, and so, by force of his sympathetic personality and as a result of his continuous success, he won the confidence of Punjabis and Sikhs and Rajputs as fully as he did that of Englishmen and Scots. In all questions connected with these troops he was moreover aided by the very close understanding secured between himself and the military authorities at Simla, by whom, under the impulse given by the newly arrived Commander-in-Chief, the existing resources in personnel and material of all parts of Hindustan were developed and turned to account to a wonderful extent during the months when Maude was Army Commander in Irak. The following appreciation of him, written by Sir C. Monro, is proof of the mutual trust which existed between two of the foremost soldiers produced in the critical days of the four years' war.

> Maude was a typical Guardsman thorough in every sense. He had the invaluable gift of inspiring those under him to great efforts at critical moments. His rare military instinct and judgement, combined with his infinite capacity for attention to detail, made him a commander who, but for his untimely death, would have achieved even greater successes in war than the defeat of the Turks in Mesopotamia. His sad end, coming as it did at the height of his achievements, was an irreparable loss to the Empire, for it is to the skill and tenacity of such men as Maude that we owe in a large measure our successes in the Great War.

> His was no light task in Mesopotamia. He assumed command of the Force at a critical time and under difficult conditions. After long-sustained and unsuccessful efforts, suffering from heat, privation and sickness, the Force over which he assumed command was well-nigh exhausted. But the morale was there. The tradition of the unbeaten 6th Division of Kut fame still remained, and within three months Maude infused fresh determination into his troops, who in their unbounded confidence in their great leader were prepared to respond to any

call, however arduous, that he made upon them. His brilliant advance, including the capture of Kut, Baghdad and Samarra, constituted the most glorious stage of the Mesopotamian Campaign which, commencing with the capture of Basrah by the 6th Division, terminated in the destruction of the Turkish Army near Mosul.

During the heats of a particularly torrid summer season there was probably no single man between the Jebel Hamrin Hills and the Persian Gulf who worked so hard and so continuously as did the Army Commander. Purposeful, methodical and untiring, his reserves of energy astonished all who were brought into contact with him; and of the results of his labours it might, when the cold weather at last arrived, with justice have been said, *st monumentum quaeris, circumspice.* Baghdad was a transformed city. A railway connected the place with Kut. Agricultural pursuits were flourishing in the surrounding country, as they had not flourished since the setting up of Osmani power in this historic region centuries before. The troops abode in comfort, in so far as comfort was obtainable in what is one of the hottest regions on the face of the globe. The magnetism of his personality had brought it about that all heads of departments and services, together with their subordinates, vied with himself in their enthusiasm for furthering the common cause, and delighted to carry into execution any suggestion with regard to their labours which he might happen to make. In so far as the medical side of the administration arrangements in connection with the army was concerned, their efficiency manifested itself in the admirable state of health in which the rank and file, both British and Indian, found themselves when the season approached for resuming active operations. Speaking of the labours of Colonel Willcox, his consulting physician, to Colonel Dickson, the Controller of Local Produce, one day, Maude said, 'I consider his work in improving the health of my forces equal to two divisions. Whatever it costs in work and money you must see that the country provides everything that Willcox thinks necessary.' Nor did the Commander-in-Chief confine his attention in respect to the well-being of his men to matters concerning their comfort and their health. The ample provision made for their recreation bore the mark of encouragement, of foresight and of incessant driving power exercised at the top.

THE ARMY COMMANDER RIDING IN BAGHDAD.

293

'It is true he centralised,' Maude's Deputy Adjutant General, General Ready, writes of him, 'but his general military knowledge both of principles and of details was so great that this, combined with his wonderful energy and unique capacity for work, surmounted all difficulties. His power of concentration was remarkable. Even during operations when the closest attention to the situation was necessary, he was able to discuss questions of minor administrative work with enthusiasm.

'In disciplinary cases he gave full warning as to how he would deal with serious offences, but he always took a 'human' view of what might be called errors of judgement or offences due to excitement or impetuosity. Slackness he would never tolerate. Nothing could submerge his sense of humour. It was his invariable habit before operations commenced to review the arrangements made for the transport and care of the wounded. His solicitude for those in hospital was evident to all who knew his daily life.

'He often spoke to me even early in 1917 of the acute shortage of man-power, which would arise from the prolongation of the war, and the necessity of continually making efforts to ensure that every available fighting man should be with the units in the field. He was a deeply religious man; few, if any, Sundays passed that he did not attend an early celebration of the Holy Communion.'

'As his successes increased,' writes Sir W. Gillman, who was appointed Chief of the General Staff to Sir W. Marshall shortly after Maude's death, 'so did the area over which he had charge. But his hand remained ever the guiding one. The control of one brain over troops fighting astride the Tigris, as well as of the initial supervision of the measures for pacifying the newly conquered Irak, brought about decisive success and at the same time ensured a continuity of policy that proved of the utmost value later. When he died, the pulse of the army stopped for quite an appreciable time. The guiding hand had gone, and as he seldom confided his plans to others, the blank caused by his death took a long time to fill up.'

It has been said of him that he did too much himself, that he left too little initiative to his subordinates, that he centralised staff work to an undesirable extent, and that by doing so he created a dangerous system of undue dependence on one single man. The proof of the pudding is after all in the eating. His campaign in Mesopotamia, lasting from August 1916 to November 1917, stands for one of the most uniformly successful sets of military operations recorded in the annals of war, and when he was of a sudden struck down and disappeared from the scene of his triumphs, no serious collapse of organisation of any kind occurred and after a pause the army carried on. In his despatch of 29 August 1918, Sir W. Marshall summed up the services of his predecessor in a paragraph which the whole of that army will have warmly endorsed, except the reference to Maude's loss being irreparable in the theatre of war. The foundations had been too surely laid for that by the chief who was gone.

'General Maude,' he wrote, 'whose genius had altered the whole face of affairs in Mesopotamia, was an almost irreparable loss. He had taken over an army whose morale had been severely tried by the failure of their efforts to relieve Kut, whose health had been sapped by a very trying climate, and he consequently had a very difficult task in restoring its fighting efficiency. But in a few months, by his hard work and his great gifts of organisation, clear sightedness, determination, and above all by his sympathy with and love of his soldiers, a very different state of affairs had come into being. Strongly backed by His Excellency the Viceroy and the Government of India, and by the War Office, he thoroughly reorganised the transport services, and the troops were as well fed and made as comfortable as circumstances permitted, though training and discipline were never relaxed. When he considered that all was ready, and not till then, he moved, and from that time the force never looked back. When therefore I had the honour of being appointed his successor the army was magnificent, while organisation and training had reached a high state of efficiency.'

Moreover, even granting that Maude was disposed when in chief command in Mesopotamia to centralise staff work and administration in himself to a somewhat unusual extent, as
had been his practice when at the head of 14th Brigade and of 18th Division and also when holding certain appointments in peace time, no soldier in high position was ever more generously emphatic in giving the credit for all that was accomplished under his orders to his subordinates, and in refusing to take any to himself. Just as he would never admit that his own foresight and the impulse given by him to a successful operation influenced the result, so also was it according to him the skill, the resource and the organising ability of his various directors and their staffs, not of himself, that made it possible for a great army, amply supplied with war material of all kinds, to conduct a brilliant campaign in a theatre of war where nature was a more formidable and a more insidious enemy than was the opposing host.

CHAPTER XV
The Death of Maude

Although he had never spared himself and had worked incessantly, with no alleviation other than that provided by the evening rides to which he always looked forward or by visits of inspection, during weeks of broiling sunshine followed by nights of suffocating heat, Maude had kept in fairly sound health all the summer, while others amongst his entourage, even when not seriously ill, were often somewhat out of sorts. Thanks, no doubt, to the possession of a vigorous constitution and exceptional strength of will, thanks also perhaps to his custom since boyhood of always keeping himself more or less in training by regular habits and by exercise in so far as circumstances permitted, he withstood the trying climate of Mesopotamia in the hot weather better than the majority of the British personnel at Baghdad and of the army under his command. His devoted personal staff always tried their utmost to make things easy for him. But they received scanty encouragement if they ever suggested that he should slacken the strain that he was constantly placing on himself, or that he should take better care of his own health while ever solicitous as to the health of others.

A charming host, determined to make the stay of such visitors as came to put up in his house, the house in which Von der Goltz had died pleasant for them, his letters home nevertheless indicate that he did not always welcome the presence of outsiders at his personal headquarters. They inevitably trenched to some extent upon his time. It so happened however that a proposal emanating from Lord Willingdon, the Governor of Bombay, who was an old friend of his, came to hand in Baghdad to the effect that a lady, Mrs Egan, who represented an important syndicate of American newspapers, should be permitted to proceed to Mesopotamia and to the headquarters of the Anglo-Indian Army. The proposal had the approval of Simla and also of Sir W. Robertson. The United States were now associated with the Entente in the contest with the Central Powers, although Washington was not at war with the Sublime Porte, and from the political point of view there was much to be said for making the public in the Western Hemisphere acquainted with the position of affairs in the one theatre of war where fighting forces on the side of the Allies had unquestionably gained the upper hand. So Maude consented, and Mrs Egan duly arrived on 11 November to stay with the Army Commander.

All that was possible was done for the visitor's comfort. Maude interested himself personally in ensuring that she should see all that was worth seeing in and around Baghdad, and in her book The War in the Cradle of the World, she provides us with a sympathetic and animated description of the Army Commander's mode of life and of his bearing as it appeared to her. He was anxious that she should be made acquainted with the condition of life in the great Oriental city under British governance, and he arranged to take her one night to a singular variety and theatrical entertainment got up by a Jewish school, which (as it turned out, although he was unaware of it beforehand) had been arranged especially in his honour. Of this she gives a vivacious account, as also of the elaborate precautions for guarding the route that she noted. In the course of the proceedings coffee was brought for Mrs Egan and her host. He took milk with it and she did not.

Two days later, on Friday 16 November, Maude when he went to the office at Army Headquarters as usual in the morning felt and looked unwell, and at 7.45 a.m, he sent for the Staff Surgeon, Lieutenant Moloney, I.M.S., who prescribed quiet with milk diet. After returning home at lunch time the Army Commander remained in his room during the afternoon, although he did some work, dictating correspondence to his confidential clerk. The Staff Surgeon brought Colonel Willcox, the Consulting Physician to the Forces, with him when he called in to see the patient at six o'clock, and Colonel Willcox then firmly vetoed Maude's proposal to fulfil an engagement to dine that evening with Colonel Dickson, although at that time no serious symptoms were present. But when the Staff Surgeon called in again a little later he noted with concern that a change for the worse had taken place in the condition of the sick general, and Colonel Willcox was summoned afresh. They took a serious view of the case, and the malady was definitely diagnosed to be cholera in a virulent form. Maude had refused to let himself be inoculated against this fell disease, although insisting on his staff submitting to the process; Mrs Egan had on arrival been inoculated at his express wish, but it may be observed that this would afford no protection for fourteen days; his excuse as regards himself always was that a man of his age was immune. The medical assumption is that the Army Commander was infected by the milk that he had taken with the coffee at the Jewish school entertainment.

Colonel Willcox gives the following account of the course of the illness:

> About 7.45 p.m. an acute attack of cholera commenced with great suddenness, and in a few minutes a state of extreme collapse occurred. Without delay immediate treatment was adopted, and everything possible was done to combat the acute symptoms. Lieutenant Moloney and myself as consulting physician remained with General Maude throughout his illness. Colonel Legg, A.M.S., and Colonel Hugo, I.M.S., consulting surgeons to the force, were called into consultation and remained in attendance during the illness. Miss Walker, the matron of No.31 British Stationary Hospital, and four specially selected nurses carried out with the greatest care and devotion their nursing duties.
>
> A slight improvement followed and some of the acute symptoms were alleviated, but the condition of extreme cardiac weakness remained throughout, and there was little if any hope of recovery from the very onset of the symptoms of cholera. No permanent improvement followed on the intravenous saline treatment, which was carried out without delay from the onset of the acute symptoms.
>
> General Maude retained his mental activity in spite of his great weakness until two hours before the end. He instinctively knew after the onset of the acute symptoms that he was suffering from cholera, and his first request was that none of his staff should run any risk of infection. During his illness his constant thought was the army under his command; he anxiously inquired as to certain recommendations for awards to his men which he had made, and it was necessary for him to be assured that these had been forwarded. Within a few hours of his death he received a telegram from Lady Maude and dictated an encouraging reply.
>
> At 4.30 p.m. on Sunday, 18 November 1917, unconsciousness supervened, and he passed peacefully away at 6.25 p.m. The cause of death was cardiac failure consequent on the toxaemia of a very severe cholera injection.

Some rumours occurred in Baghdad, and I believe in England, as to the possibility of General Maude's illness being due to poison. I would like most emphatically to contradict the possibility of this having been the case. Throughout the illness most careful bacteriological examinations were made at the Central Laboratory, Baghdad, and most definite evidence was obtained of the presence of a very virulent infection of cholera, thus confirming entirely the clinical diagnosis. As regards the date of infection, it seems very probable that this was contracted on Wednesday evening, 14 November 1917. At the performance he partook of some light refreshment and had coffee with which he took some milk. In that area of the city at that time it would be very likely that the milk would be infected with cholera organisms, and it seems very probable that the actual infection occurred in this way. There is no reason to suspect that the infection of the milk was otherwise than an accidental infection from the water of the area, which was known to be under great suspicion at the time, cholera being present in that part of the city.

'I was with him during the last hours of his life,' writes the Rev. A. C. E. Jarvis. 'Of some of these things I cannot write; but what follows should be placed on record, for the passing of the first Christian conqueror of Baghdad was a triumphal entry into the presence of his Lord and Master. He died as he had lived. The simplicity of his life was reflected in everything about him, the ordinary camp bed, the army blankets he never carried more than the normal officer's kit allowance. For physical reasons he could not partake of the elements of the Sacrament; but, delirious and semi-delirious as he was for the greater part of the time, he
knew that he was in the presence of the Reserved Sacrament; he joined in all the prayers and, suffering as he did, the calm joyous peace light which irradiated his face betokened that, while temporal shadows were receding, the glory of the spiritual world was already becoming more real.

'At the end it was all very beautiful. His immediate personal staff, the doctors, nurses and orderly stood round the bed. Outside the measured tread of the Ghurka guard. A peaceful calm filled the room. I began the service of commendation at five minutes past six, and at twenty-five minutes past, just as I was uttering the words :
      Rest Eternal grant to him, O Lord,
      And let Light Everlasting shine upon him

he peacefully entered Paradise. Thus our beloved commander left us, victor, as always, over the last great enemy.'

The news of this sudden and tragic termination to a great career aroused profound concern throughout the Empire. Maude's continuous record of success in the field had sounded a trumpet call of encouragement at a juncture when the Allies' prospects of final victory in the world contest had been affected most adversely by the disastrous consequences of the Russian Revolution. The transformation which had taken place in a theatre of operations where British arms had been signally worsted with deplorable results to the troops concerned, had fired the imagination of his countrymen. Sheaves of letters, scrawled in pencil by officers and rank and file amid dust storms and downpours in a distant land, had been testifying for months past to the extent to which the triumphs in Irak were the direct and immediate handiwork of the Commander-in-Chief himself. In his message to Sir W. Marshall, who had been summoned in haste to Army Headquarters as senior lieutenant general on the spot, the King voiced not only his own sentiments, but also those of the nation at large:

> November 19. I have just heard with the deepest regret of the death under such sad and tragic circumstances of General Maude, who has rendered incalculable services to India, the Empire and the Allies. I join with my Army in Mesopotamia in mourning the loss of their gallant and beloved commander, but I am confident that his memory will ever be an incentive to the completion of the work for which he laboured and died. GEORGE, R.I.

General Marshall issued the following Special Order of the Day:

> It is with feelings of the deepest regret and sorrow that I announce the sad death from cholera on the afternoon of the 18th November, 1917, of Lieutenant General Sir F. S. Maude, K.C.B., C.M.G., D.S.O., General Officer Commanding-in-Chief, of this Force.

> Lieutenant General Sir F. S. Maude gave nearly thirty-four years of distinguished service to the State, and it is due to his remarkable ability, unwearying energy and admirable example that the Army in Mesopotamia gained its successes in the past

and is today so grandly upholding the traditional glories of our Empire.

He will be mourned by the nation, the Army and by all ranks in Mesopotamia, as a great soldier, who rendered valuable and devoted service both in the Army and the State.

W. R. Marshall, Lieutenant General,
Commanding-in-Chief
Mesopotamian Expeditionary Force,
General Headquarters, Baghdad,
19th November 1917.

Lady Maude received telegrams and letters of sympathy from all quarters of the Empire, from the King and Queen, from the Government of India, from the Army Council, from many public bodies, and from numberless private individuals, and two of these messages may perhaps be quoted. The Under Secretary of State for India wrote:

> In pursuance of a resolution passed today by the Council of India, I am requested to state that the Council have received with the profoundest regret intelligence of the sudden and lamentable death of your gallant and distinguished husband, Sir F. S. Maude, K.C.B., C.M.G., D.S.O., and that they desire respectfully to express their deep sympathy with you in your great bereavement. The Council have followed with the liveliest interest the achievements in Mesopotamia of the army under his leadership, and the series of brilliant victories which have restored the fame of British arms in that region. They have frequently noted with pleasure the tributes which at various times he paid to the valour and endurance of the Indian troops serving under him, and they feel assured that the Indian Army deeply deplores the loss of a wise and skilful commander who ever had their fullest confidence and affection.

The Premier of Canada cabled:

> My colleagues and I desire to express to you on our own behalf and that of all Canadian people the deep sorrow felt universally throughout the Dominion at the untimely death of your gallant husband, whose career has been so splendid and whose service to the Empire has been so conspicuous.

A special memorial service was held on 4 December at St Paul's, under arrangements made by the Order of St Michael and St George, of which

Maude was a Commander. It was attended by representatives of the King and Queen and of Queen Alexandra, by the Duke of Connaught and a special contingent of officers and men of the Guards, by the War Cabinet, by the Lord Mayor and Sheriffs in state, and by numbers of officers and public men of note. The musical portion of the service was provided by the Coldstream Guards.

But if grief at the death of an eminent public servant was general in the United Kingdom, in India, in the British Dominions and Colonies beyond the seas, and in the theatres of war in France, in Egypt and at Salonika, where Maude's fellow soldiers had been following the course of events on the Tigris with interest and admiration, the distress was incomparably more pervading and deep-seated amongst the troops who had actually lost their own immediate leader and chief. The evil tidings of the Army Commander's grave condition had travelled fast through the encampments on the Saturday and Sunday; the news that all was over gave rise to an outburst of emotion. For in some indefinable way Maude had come to be regarded even amongst the lowest grades of the thousands who obeyed his behests, and who looked up to him trustfully for guidance, as a friend. While the numberless letters received by Lady Maude from Mesopotamia a few weeks later, many if not most of them emanating from soldiers and others with whom she was unacquainted, contained eloquent tributes to what he had accomplished, they almost without exception sounded the prevailing note of personal loss. To make a selection from them or to quote extracts would be out of place. Suffice it to say that they represent in themselves a not unworthy memorial to the commander who was gone.

The proposal that the country should make a special grant to the widow and family of Sir Stanley Maude afforded representative statesmen an opportunity, a few months later, for paying striking tributes to the memory of the victorious general who had one day steamed quietly up to a wharf on the riverside of the City of the Caliphs, and had stepped out without ceremony to take possession on behalf of his country of one of the most important places in all Asia.

'The services which Sir Stanley Maude rendered to the Empire, notably in Mesopotamia,' said Mr Lloyd George as Prime Minister in the House of Commons, 'were distinguished, far-reaching and permanent in their effect. He found British prestige at a very low ebb in a quarter of the globe where prestige counts for much. The British Army in the East had suffered a series of severe reverses. One great enterprise on which a good deal of the strength of the Empire had been concentrated had to be abandoned. One British Army had surrendered to the Turkish forces, after another British Army had been defeated in a series of attempts to relieve it. In Egypt we had a large force sheltering behind the desert and the Canal from an inferior Turkish Army. This tale of discomfiture and humiliation spread throughout every bazaar in the East, and, like a tree, grew as it spread. Before it ran into irreparable mischief for the Empire the genius of Sir Stanley Maude had changed and restored the position. I know well how much of this success was due to the reorganisation of the transport service by Sir John Cowans and his able staff, the reorganisation of the medical service by Sir Alfred Keogh and his assistants, and the reinforcements brought in by Sir William Robertson and Sir Charles Monro. But the enemy also had time to reinforce, and to strengthen his forces. The ground lent itself to entrenchments. Those entrenchments were constructed under the advice and direction of German engineers. The Turk was fighting at his best in a climate which suited him and did not suit us. But against all these obstacles the leadership of Sir Stanley Maude and the valour of his army triumphed.

'The highest proof of generalship is not so much in the winning of a victory as in its exploitation. No general ever made better or wiser use of his victory than did Sir Stanley Maude. The relentless pursuit of the defeated army, which ultimately destroyed it, and ended in the dramatic capture of Baghdad, sounded throughout the East. These were amongst the finest feats in military history, and they had a magical effect on the fame and position of Britain throughout the whole of the East. The Germans realised it. Sir Stanley Maude's achievements had destroyed their cherished dream. They sent one of their ablest generals there to effect a reconquest, and I do not think it is too much to say that their abandonment of that enterprise was due very largely to their appreciation of the fact, when they came there, that they were confronted by a leader of exceptional resource and power.

'But Sir Stanley Maude's real greatness was displayed in the use which he made of the victory after it had been obtained. He showed as much wisdom as an administrator as he displayed skill as a general. Every great general has a strain of statesmanship, and Sir Stanley Maude exhibited great gifts of statesmanship in his administration of that difficult country. While ruling with a firm hand, he won the esteem and affection of that gifted but suspicious race, not merely by the equity of his rule, but by the intelligent sympathy which he displayed. He possessed that rare tact which is a blend of gentleness and understanding, and the article that appeared in an Arab paper after his death, and which was, I think, reproduced in the British Press last week, is the highest tribute that could have been paid to his great qualities as a governor and a man....

'Sir Stanley Maude will always be remembered as one of the great figures of this War, not merely for what he achieved, but for what he was. I know not what destiny may have in store for the famed land which he conquered, but of two things I am certain. The first is, that the whole course of its history will be changed for the better as a result of the victory and the rule of Sir Stanley Maude; and the second is, that his name will always be cherished by the inhabitants of that land as that of the gentlest conqueror who ever entered the gates of Baghdad.'

'In 1916,' said Earl Curzon of Kedleston, the Lord President of the Council, in the House of Lords, 'General Maude was sent with his division to Mesopotamia, and there he took part in the arduous operations that were then in course of being carried out for the relief of the beleaguered garrison of Kut. As your Lordships will remember, that place fell after an heroic defence by General Townshend and his brave men; and in August of that year General Maude succeeded Sir Percy Lake as Commander-in-Chief of the British Expeditionary Force in Mesopotamia. It was a dark moment in the history of the war. It was a critical moment in the fortunes of Great Britain in the East. The issues of the conflict themselves trembled in the balance, and the prestige of the British Empire may be described not unfairly as having been at stake. General Maude had to deal with an enemy flushed with victory, entrenched in a position of exceptional strength, provided with all the scientific military resources which he had received from his European ally. The advance upon Baghdad in the month of December 1916, the dramatic crossing of the Tigris, the forced evacuation of Kut by the Turks, the disorderly retreat of the fleeing enemy upon Baghdad, the rapid pursuit by General Maude and his men, constituted a military achievement of no mean order.

'But General Maude was by no means content with his initial victory; he was not the kind of man to rest upon his laurels. Following the Turks with great speed up the Diala River in one direction, up the Tigris in another, and, at a later date, up the waters of the Euphrates, he inflicted upon them a series of crushing defeats which rendered them incapable of any further sustained military effort. He lifted the danger which overhung the Persian border, and which might, unless arrested, have reacted, through Persia, upon Afghanistan and upon India itself, and he occupied the whole of the Baghdad Vilayet. And be it remembered that he carried out the series of operations which I have described, labouring under a sense of bitter disappointment at the failure of our Russian Allies, who were at that time in the north-western part of Persia, to extend to him the support which he had reason to expect.

'The last few months of General Maude's life were devoted to the task of organising and administering the territories which he had won; and there in November 1917, in an act of unthinking courtesy, he contracted that fatal pestilence which always broods behind the atmosphere of the East, and in a few hours had passed away. Thus in a few months of time it was given to General Maude to achieve what many military commanders do not attain in a lifetime. He retrieved a great disaster; he won a resounding victory; he recovered a province almost a country once one of the gardens of the East, which had mouldered for centuries under the blight of Turkish misrule. Nay, more. By a single stroke, or series of strokes, he may be said to have altered the history of the world. It is surely inconceivable that the inhabitants of those fair regions can ever be thrust back into the servitude from which
General Maude and his forces succeeded in emancipating them. And then in the hour of his triumph the General was stricken down, not, indeed, on the battlefield, but, as I have pointed out, by a death not less honourable and infinitely more pathetic.

'My Lords, if we turn from the contemplation of the soldier to that of the man, there is a consensus of opinion among those who knew General Maude well of whom, unfortunately, I was not one that not merely did he possess the genius of a military commander, but that he had many of those qualities of personal character which endeared him to all those with whom he was associated. The soul of chivalry, he was not less strict in the discipline that he applied to himself than he was in that which he applied to others. A non-smoker, almost a total abstainer, he set an example of conscientious abnegation and self-control which profoundly affected the conduct of those whom he either commanded or who served under him. At the same time, he was kind and thoughtful to a degree of his soldiers, and, as abundant testimony confirms, he was exceptionally considerate to the native inhabitants of the countries that had passed under his sway. Thus I think we may say of the departed general that in manifold respects he fulfilled the ideal of the Happy Warrior which was drawn for us in such moving terms by one of the greatest of our poets more than a century ago.'

'My Lords, this motion is so sure of receiving the universal assent of your Lordships' House, said the Marquess of Crewe, 'that it is really more for my own satisfaction as a very old friend of General Maude –

having known him in the days when he was a subaltern in the Coldstream Guards – that I rise to say a word in its support, although, indeed, that is not necessary after the eloquent statement which has been made by the noble Earl who leads the House.

'General Maude was a man who was always greatly regarded and beloved by his friends. He was a quiet and dignified man even in his younger days. He had the reputation of being a most excellent regimental officer, and he also became a careful student at the Staff College. I know very well that the senior officers of that day always looked upon him as a man who, if the time of test came, would prove himself to be in all respects an admirable soldier. How the test would come, and how severe it would be, of course nobody in those days could foretell; but that it was met not merely with the gallantry which everybody would have expected
of General Maude, but also with a degree of military skill which was to a great degree the reward of the hard work that he had exercised in his younger days, will not be denied by anybody.

'As the noble Earl has stated, the circumstances of General Maude's death were singularly pathetic. He knew, of course, the admiration which his conduct and that of his troops had won from his fellow-countrymen, but he was not spared to receive at home those tributes of respect and affection which would have been lavished on him had he returned here. We all, I am certain, feel that this small tribute is the least that the country can pay to his memory.'

The burial took place on the afternoon of the 19th in the desert cemetery beyond the North Gate. Every officer and man who could be present was there to pay a last tribute of respect and affection to their departed chief; the pall-bearers were commanders who had over and over again led their men to victory under his supreme control, a special contingent of officers from his old division, far away, contrived to arrive in time, the people of the city assembled in great numbers to do honour to their liberator and patron. 'Coming generations,' says Mr Candler, 'will perhaps class General Maude as a great leader with Alexander and Julian, who conquered the ungrateful soil and became its victims. He fixed a memorable link in the continuity of history when he entered Baghdad; and one may safely predict that his name will be associated with a more lasting and beneficent change in the fortunes of the country than can be credited to Roman, Persian, or Greek. But at the moment, the men who helped him to make history were not concerned with posterity. The thought that troubled them, recurring at all hours, was that of the two or three new graves in the British cemetery, one covered the bones of the man they least could spare, of the commander whose quiet and confident smile was an assurance that no sacrifice that he demanded of them would be in vain.'

The following lines written by Lieutenant J. G. Fairfax, serving in the army which expelled the Osmanlis from Mesopotamia, are proof of the respect and affection in which its commander was held:

AVE ATQUE VALE
F. S. M.
Hail and farewell, across the clash of swords!
Hail and farewell, all laurels to the dust,
So soon returned, so bitterly; farewell!
The dark clouds, Sisters to the solemn hour,
Wait on thy passing, and the heavy air
Bears, as we bear our sorrow silently,
The leaden burden, and there is no voice -
Mute, with bent heads, before the open grave,
We stand, and each one feels his pulses ache,
And his throat parches, and the unspoken grief
Closes an iron hand upon his heart.
Three times the volley strikes the solemn vault
Of that imprisoning arch, and piercing clear
The bugles cry upon the dead. 'Arise!'
The scarlet and blue pennants droop; the night
Draws darkly on, and dawn, when dawn shall come,
Throws a drear light upon the Eastern sky,
And Dome and Minaret wake ghostly grey,
And in the trees a little wind will sigh.
Hail and farewell! the laurels with the dust
Are levelled, but thou hast thy sure crown,
Peace and immortal calm, the victory won.
Somewhere serene thy watchful power inspires;
Thou art a living purpose, being dead,
Fruitful of nobleness in lesser lives,
A guardian and a guide; Hail and farewell!

A simple cross marks the spot where Maude of Baghdad lies, surrounded by the last resting-places of soldiers whom he loved and who loved him. Monuments to his memory may take, and have taken, various forms. A statue of their famous chief is to be set up in the capital of Mesopotamia by the army which he led. Roads especially laid out beyond the North Gate and an arch, the cost defrayed by subscriptions of its citizens, are a tribute of the chief place in Irak to the man who freed the city from the Turkish yoke. Hospitals and schools, erected by the inhabitants of other towns within the liberated territory, commemorate what he achieved and stand for tokens of gratitude to a benefactor and a friend. An obelisk erected by 13th Division towers amongst the rocky fastnesses of the Jebel Hamrin, coupling Maude's name with the names of all ranks belonging to the division who laid down their lives for their country in the far-off land of the Two Rivers. Yet the finest memorial perhaps to the conqueror is to be found in a redeemed region and a contented people, which have taken the place of territories that he found waste and desolate and of races who had been for ages victims of oppression and misrule.

CHAPTER XVI
An Appreciation

When endeavouring to sum up the salient features in the character, the qualifications and the methods of Sir Stanley Maude as soldier and man, the biographer enjoys this great advantage: the achievements of the subject of this Memoir were so conspicuous, his popularity amongst those who came into close contact with him was so unquestionable, and his nature was so unselfish, that there is no temptation to gloss over such minor shortcomings as ought in the interests of truth and of example to be touched upon. Where assets are so rich and overflowing, there is no excuse for concealing a few liabilities. Maude's fellow-countrymen will ever regard him primarily as a soldier, and it is in his capacity of soldier that he will in the first instance be discussed here. Nor can an examination of his attributes as an officer be more appropriately initiated than by indicating certain points in his disposition and in his normal procedure which lay him open to some tempered disparagement. Reference has already been made to them in passages scattered through earlier chapters of this volume.

By nature Maude was exceedingly tenacious, an invaluable trait for a soldier to possess in many situations. As one of his warmest friends indeed says of him: 'When he did speak he put the pros and cons clearly and concisely and gave a decided opinion, from which nothing would turn him.' Fixity of purpose was one of his most valid professional resources, because he was generally right. But no man can always be right, and if Maude by any chance happened to be wrong, this characteristic of his lost its merits as is illustrated by an incident which occurred when he was serving as a regimental subaltern in the Coldstream Guards.

One day during the progress of some field operations that were being carried out with other troops, Maude was in command of his company; it was engaged alongside another company of his battalion under charge of a captain, an officer senior to himself and admittedly an extremely capable soldier. A tactical situation arose in the course of the proceedings which suggested to this captain that it would be well for Maude's company to do a certain thing, so, neither the commanding officer nor the second in command happening to be about, he expressed a wish that Maude should carry out the movement. Maude however demurred. The captain pressed the matter. Maude remained obdurate. Finally the captain formally ordered Maude to execute the movement, and Maude, equally formally, refused. Now, the senior may perhaps have acted a little tactlessly in the first instance, and it is conceivable that impartial observers would have ruled that in the existing situation on the field of manoeuvre the senior's project was militarily unsound. But in deliberately refusing to obey an order given under such circumstances by a superior officer, Maude put himself entirely in the wrong, disciplinarian as he was. Some commanding officers holding rigid views on the subject of military subservience would be disposed to take a very serious view of an episode of this kind when it was reported to them – as this episode of course was.

Instances of what practically amounted to obstinacy on Maude's part have cropped up occasionally in the narrative of his career recorded in foregoing chapters. Thus he could not be induced to remain on the sick list so long as his medical advisers prescribed after the accident that befell him at Driefontein, and the result was that his shoulder gave him serious trouble during several subsequent months of strenuous work in the field, when he needed to be at his best; it indeed never wholly recovered from the injury. The fact would seem to be that he regarded sickness as a sign of weakness which would be overcome by the individual exercise of will-power. At the same time, if medical advice was forcibly put and was clearly based on grounds of reason, he accepted it readily. For instance, he allowed himself to be persuaded not to undertake a journey by 'glisseur' from Baghdad to Basrah in the heat of summer, on Colonel Willcox urging that he would run great risk of heat stroke were he to venture on such an expedition.

When at the head of 14th Brigade, he turned a deaf ear to the friendly suggestions of his divisional commander and his corps commander concerning the undue exposure of his headquarters near Neuve Eglise; and when he was at last ordered to move them, he moved them nearer to the enemy instead of further away as had been intended. When the arrangements with regard to the evacuation of Anzac and Helles were being debated, he was almost the only one of the generals concerned who advocated retiring to an inner line; and it proved hard to persuade him that the course actually adopted was the right one, although when the question had been decided against him he executed the alternative plan to admiration. But it must be remembered that it was this same obstinacy to repeat a somewhat disagreeable word which was at the root of Maude's confidence in himself and in his plans, and that it was this confidence in himself and in his plans which kept him undisturbed and of good cheer when the temporary discomfitures, the heavy losses, and the untoward conditions of weather which chequered the course of the conflicts to the south of Kut, might have caused a less resolute commander than him to hold his hand.

Accounts practically all agree that paperwork took up much of his time and that he was always thoroughly at home in the labours of an office. As adjutant, and later as brigade-major, he developed a propensity for issuing numerous and somewhat lengthy memoranda, and (although opinions are not unanimous on this point) his orders in the field which while a brigade commander and a divisional commander he generally prepared himself, contrary to the normal practice would seem to have inclined towards prolixity at times. All those who were associated with him while he was holding staff appointments testify to his rare powers of work, and enlarge on the long hours that he was in the habit of passing at his desk; but there are indications that his indefatigable efforts in this field of endeavour may not invariably have been profitable efforts, and that he may even occasionally have made work as many soldiers proficient in office pursuits have a tendency to do. Seeing that he was by bias the very reverse of an indoors man, the amount of time that he was in the habit of spending in his bureau during these periods is at all events evidence of a single-minded devotion to duty; but military men of experience will not perhaps be quite so favourably impressed with this particular feature in his mode of life as outsiders have been.

The truth is that, if Maude had not been a most earnest student of his profession in all its branches, had he not been a particularly keen and effective exponent of tactical procedure out in the open, had he not been an enthusiastic trainer of troops and ever ready to take part in exercises and manoeuvres, finally, had he not proved himself to be a rare leader of men when his opportunity came, he would have run considerable risk of being set down as an 'office man' by brother-soldiers. But this tendency had the result that when he was on active service he was tireless in writing letters, not only to his family and to friends but also to military authorities to whom the letters were as useful as they were interesting. Constant practice had given him a facility of expressing himself clearly and to the point, and, considering the difficulties and discomfort under which his correspondence was carried out in France, at Suvla and during the earlier part of his time in Mesopotamia, his letters from the front must be acknowledged to be extremely informative documents. Nor should it be forgotten that, while he was in command of a brigade and of a division in presence of the enemy, Maude never failed to communicate his regret and his sympathy to the relatives of any officer under his command who had died for his country, and unhappily he had only too many of such letters to write.

But the characteristic of Maude which was the most strongly marked and was the most open to objection from the soldier's point of view was his tendency to centralise, his almost irrepressible instinct for doing whatever had to be done himself, his plan of keeping everything in his own hands. That this was his habit is notorious and is acknowledged by those who knew him best and who admired him most. 'If he had a fault,' writes Sir W. Lambton, 'it was that of centralising and of attempting too much himself.' All who came into contact with him officially vouch for his abnormal diligence, and depose to the protracted hours which he spent on his military duties; but if you do everybody's work as well as your own you must labour abundantly or the machine will come to a standstill. Special mention must be made of this, and the objections to such procedure when practised by a staff officer or a commander pointed out, because the very greatness of Maude's triumphs in the field might induce the idea that his methods in this respect were methods to be imitated. The fact that gratifying results have been arrived at in spite of a thing having been done the wrong way does not make the wrong way right.

This bent for absorbing control and administration in himself displayed itself constantly during his military career, and it manifested itself in connection with almost every form of question with which he had officially to deal. In Canada his duties were scarcely of a military nature; but he kept all details in connection with the Governor-General's tours and entertainments and public observances in his own grip. When holding high appointment on the War Office staff, his subordinates were deprived of the initiative and of the responsibility usually permitted to individuals occupying their positions. It was the same when he was in command of a brigade and of a division on active service. It was to a great extent the same when he was at the head of a mighty host fitted out with all the impedimenta found necessary by a modern army when on the warpath. But what was perhaps most remarkable about this feature in Maude's character and disposition was that the centralisation which he practised was not the outcome of any

desire for self-advancement. It was wholly disinterested and altruistic. Having done what it was a subordinate's business to do, he gave all the credit to the
subordinate and he took none for himself. His abnegation, his modesty, and his ready and chivalrous recognition of the services of those working under him, sugared the pill, and induced capable and self-reliant officers under his orders, who at the outset were disposed to resent his system, to accept it loyally in the long run and to prove themselves his compliant assistants.

The objections to the practice of centralisation are a matter of common, knowledge. Some of them are indeed obvious. The commander, or the superior staff officer as the case may
be, who keeps all the strings in his own hands is subject just as others are to the ills that flesh is heir to, and he may break down temporarily or permanently at some critical juncture. He may, again, happen to be absent on some special duty just at the moment when a vital problem unexpectedly arises which, owing to his system, cannot be solved without his presence. Undue dependence upon any individual is in the nature of things unsound, and it may become a grave peril. Centralisation moreover inevitably discourages the efficient subordinate, while it is apt to serve as a cloak concealing the unfitness of an incompetent underling. It in reality sets at defiance the fundamental principles upon which command and administration in the military world are supposed to be conducted. It is an obstacle in the path of the junior officer who desires to learn his work and who hopes to qualify himself for rising to higher grades, and on this point Maude by his methods was, without perhaps realising it himself, contravening his own theories.

For he always took the utmost interest in the training of the staff in peace time, and in promoting its efficiency for purposes of war. His standard of efficiency was moreover a very high one. In his diaries kept during the South African Campaign and during the Great War, frequent entries occur condemning the staff work, as its practice on active service came to his notice. Even in the early days of the operations of the British Expeditionary Force in France in 1914, at a juncture when the highly trained and specially selected staff with the troops was probably as competent as the staff of any army in the field in existence, he finds grounds for disapprobation at times – and, no doubt, reasonably, seeing that there is no such thing as perfection in such matters. But unless there be judicious decentralisation, unless the various individuals who form the aggregate of the staff in brigades, or

divisions, or army corps, or armies, are allowed to perform the duties which they are supposed to perform, and are trusted by those set over them until found wanting, the staff as a whole does
not enjoy the practice nor does it acquire the experience, in the absence of which that body cannot be expected adequately to fulfil its functions.

Situations will arise in war, it is true, and they may sometimes even arise in time of peace, where it is expedient and where it may even be imperative for a superior officer to take the entire control of matters into his own hands and to transform his subordinates for the time being into virtual ciphers. When Maude was called upon to assume supreme control over the operations in Mesopotamia, the machine as a whole was running none too smoothly, some of its parts were the worse for the wear, certain new devices had to be introduced, nor was the available driving power being effectually exercised throughout the whole of the complicated works. A man in sound health and of inexhaustible energy, a man immune from the lassitude which a debilitating climate is apt to induce, a man fitted out with ample knowledge concerning the bulk of the questions that called for investigation and settlement, and fortified by a clear conception of what objects the army could and should fulfil in the early future, was needed; and the newly appointed Army Commander was most fully justified in going himself thoroughly into every detail of organisation and administration before he committed his troops to an offensive campaign. Whether it was indispensable for him
to retain the close control that he did over the administration at a later date, when all was in working order and proceeding satisfactorily, seems open to question. But in the first instance,
centralisation would appear not only to have been permissible, but to have been in the highest degree appropriate.

There is also this to be said. Centralisation is in principle fundamentally unsound. It to all intents and purposes sets army regulations at defiance. In the case of an officer who has passed through the mill of staff training its practice ignores precepts that have always been strongly inculcated at Camberley. Nevertheless Maude's custom of doing himself so much that ought properly to have been done by his subordinates does afford convincing testimony of his having been equipped with other precious and engaging qualifications. The fact that in spite of suffering from this drawback he should have accomplished such great things, serves to prove how deft an organiser, what an ardent worker, and what a competent master of the art of war he must have been. The way that he managed to get the best out of capable men holding positions of responsibility under him who found themselves in a manner thrust on one side, is clear indication of the confidence which he inspired, of the knowledge of his profession that made itself apparent to all who were associated with him, and of his own magnetic charm. It may be observed here that in many eulogistic references to him that appeared when he was carrying all before him on the Tigris, and in those which saw the light after untimely death at Baghdad had robbed his country of his services, reference is constantly and with justice made to the fact that no detail was too small for him to interest himself in. This is a most valuable quality in an administrator and in a commander, always provided that it is, as in his case, combined with a sense of proportion. He never allowed his concern for questions of second and third rate importance to stand in the way of attention to matters of major moment. Nor must vigilance in respect to detail be confused with centralisation. By making inspections take the most searching form possible, a superior officer ensures that duties are being correctly carried out in all their various branches. Suggestions from a high quarter in connection with even trivial points act as a tonic. Maude's heedfulness and solicitude in connection with inconsiderable questions was combined with a very thorough knowledge of military requirements and of the best method of meeting them, which was the result of years of study, of constant application to professional pursuits, and of the possession of an exceptionally retentive memory. He indeed to a strange extent resembled in some vital respects the greatest of all modern soldiers.

Widely as they differed in general character and in their outlook upon life, Maude in his military capacity had much in common with Napoleon. Both of them were signalised by an almost uncanny familiarity with the details of the requirements of an army, both were pertinacious students of the principles and practice of prosecuting hostilities, both were gifted with unusual powers of concentration on the thing in hand, both could lay claim to abnormal memories, both were by instinct and by habit centralisers, both had mastered the closeness of the connection which exists between adequate preparation for operations in the field and their effective execution, neither of them shrank from incurring reasonable losses if by incurring those losses gains might be achieved, neither of them hesitated to run risks when the occasion called for it, both must be classed as egregiously sedulous workers, both from dissimilar causes and as a result of different methods contrived to win and to retain in exceptional measure the confidence and the affection of the men whom they led, and both were absolute masters of the art of controlling hosts to good purpose in a theatre of war.

In one notable respect however Maude was almost the antithesis of the illustrious Corsican. He was business-like to a degree, and punctuality with him amounted almost to a religion. Napoleon, on the other hand, although his mind acted systematically, was the very reverse of methodical in his dealings with others, and was so irregular – and even so irresponsible in regard to his hours for meals and his hours for work as often to cause his staff and his suite grave perplexity. That combination of instinctive orderliness with brilliant gifts of leadership, which was one of Maude's characteristics, is indeed somewhat unusual in a Great Captain.

To compare Maude to Napoleon as a tactician, to contrast them as handlers of legions actually on the field of battle, would be absurd. The whole aspect of combat has been transformed since the days of Austerlitz and Jena. Progress in armament has created conditions which deprive the superior commander as a rule of openings for disclosing genius in this connection. No opportunity for his manifesting tactical aptitude of a high order ever presented itself to Maude while a simple brigadier. His masterly withdrawals from Suvlaand and from Helles were the result of forethought and of effectual administration, and no affrays took place during their critical stages. Even on the occasion when, at Felahieh, he was suddenly faced with a situation for which no elaborate preparation had been, or could be, made and his division gained so gratifying a victory, the Turks who were opposed to him were not in truculent mood and they offered no very spirited resistance to his troops. During the course of that triumphant series of operations which carried his army from Es Sinn to Baghdad, actual tactical direction was in the hands of subordinates even if he was giving the impulse to the combinations.

A staff officer whom Mr Candler quotes sums up Maude's qualifications as a commander in the field very aptly: 'There are three things necessary for carrying on a campaign. You want the fighting man whose genius is strategy and tactics, and you want the man who understands everything about staff work; but these may be wasted without the brain for organisation and the interior economy of the army. I don't think that I had ever struck a man who combined two of these qualities, certainly not three, until I met Maude.' But the staff officer omitted two other attributes, to both of which Maude could lay claim and which are almost as valuable to a commander in the field as those indicated – sympathy with those commanded, and serenity of air in the hour of adversity.

316

A successful commander will always enjoy a certain popularity amongst those serving under his orders, no matter what his personality may be. Unsympathetic as he was by nature, despising sentiment, a stern disciplinarian who was economical of praise and who troubled himself little concerning the comfort of his troops, Wellington, although not exactly beloved, was nevertheless looked up to by his men in the Peninsula and could always get the very best out of them so long as fighting was actually in progress. Napoleon, on the other hand, not merely fired the enthusiasm of the soldiers with whom he overran Europe by the splendour of his victories, but he lost no opportunity of appealing to the emotional side of the Gallic character; his custom was ever to pose as chief and to be the central figure in skilfully staged pageants; but he combined this with the display of keen interest – which may or may not have been feigned – in the welfare of his men, and he won them by his camaraderie and apt chaff when he moved about unceremoniously amongst the bivouac fires or rode alongside columns on the line of march. Maude's personality exercised its influence after another fashion, and he had acquired the confidence of those under him before he had made his mark as a leader in the field. No triumph was registered by 14th Brigade while he was their brigadier; nor, until its tailmost echelons had slipped quietly away by night from Suvla Bay, had 18th Division accomplished anything especially noteworthy under his command; and yet the brigade and the division, alike, elected to put their trust in him, one had almost said, on sight.

He no doubt enjoyed certain natural advantages in possessing a tough frame, a strong constitution and a commanding figure. But his inexhaustible energy and his frequent appearances amongst them made him also familiar to the troops under his orders. His unaffected solicitude concerning their food, their clothing and the alleviation in so far as this was practicable of their ordeals, won the hearts of the rank and file, both British and Indian. His practice of always getting his own way impressed those who saw him at close quarters. His sanguine disposition infected others with his own confidence. His insensibility to danger and his wont of frequently visiting the most advanced trenches and of traversing the most exposed approaches when he was a brigadier and a divisional commander, were warmly appreciated by those under him, even if they caused some apprehension in those over him. That absence of pose which came natural to him fitted in with the temper of British troops, just as Napoleon's histrionic procedure suited the French. While his devotion to duty, his ability and his exhaustive knowledge of his profession aroused the admiration of his staff and of those senior officers with whom questions of importance had to be discussed, his sympathetic bearing and his cheery greetings delighted non-commissioned officers and men whom accident brought momentarily into close relations with him, and these spread the tidings far and wide.

His letters are evidence of the genuine affection that he felt for the regimental officers and the rank and file serving under him in the field, and of his eager appreciation of their work. A commander always gives credit to his troops in his official despatches for any success that may have been achieved. That goes without saying. Most commanders perhaps will do so even in their private letters. But Maude was constantly expressing his warm admiration of his troops, not only to outsiders but also to himself, i.e. in his diaries. There never was any pretence or make-believe about it, he wrote down just what he felt. On the one occasion when his men, or some of them, undoubtedly failed him, it is noteworthy that he would seem to have been unwilling to fully admit this even to himself; the passage is quoted above. Officers and rank and file soon came to realise his feeling towards them and to reciprocate it, because although by nature undemonstrative he had a particularly happy way with him when proposing to show friendliness to subordinates, especially when off duty.

An inherent buoyancy of temperament in Maude assumed the form of an unconquerable spirit when dangers gathered thick. His attitude at the moment when the attack of 18th Division on the Sannaiyat lines miscarried is a striking example of that. Unruffled demeanour in the chieftain is the first step towards repairing defeat when fortune has been unkind in war, and his habitual self-possession and his fortitude were priceless assets during the dark days of April 1916 on the Tigris. Although they could not change the aspect of affairs even in respect to his own division, his troops noted and remembered them; and other divisions which had met with discomfiture like unto his heard tell of this general whom his men all swore by. So, when the Tigris Army Corps learnt that Maude was their commander, and when it became known a few weeks later that he was supreme chief in Mesopotamia, the Anglo-Indian forces welcomed with enthusiasm the appointment of a leader whom most of them had never seen and whom many of them four months before had never even heard of. His personality had already put new life into the army before the influence of his reforming activities and of his energetic administration had made themselves felt outside of Army Headquarters on the Shatt-el-Arab.

In the estimation of posterity, Maude will inevitably be judged by the campaign which virtually gave him Mesopotamia. That campaign was a masterpiece. Its salient features have been discussed in previous chapters, and they need not be dealt with further. Suffice it to say that, recognising from the outset how neither skill nor valour in the absence of effective organisation will command success, the Army Commander invariably made strategy and administration move hand in hand throughout its progress. The plan was bold; some of its details – the crossing of the Tigris at Shumran, for instance – might be characterised as audacious. But it was as comprehensive as it was bold, and its designer ever had the destruction of the foe for objective rather than mere winning of territory or the achieving of some local triumph. Victory, until hostile resistance had been beaten down, was not victory to him. The Turks were appalled by the relentless energy of this formidable antagonist, who was as vehement in treading a fugitive enemy underfoot as he had been calculating in his preparations for putting the antagonist to flight. Maude was as thorough as a conqueror as he had been thorough in elaborating his scheme for making himself master in the theatre of war, and this, more perhaps than anything else, singles him out as one of the foremost soldiers of his time.

But it was not only when the enemy was actually in the gate that Maude gave indications of an instinct for war. Frequent references have occurred in foregoing pages to his zeal for military study; but that he also closely followed the progress of international events and that he foresaw clearly whither they were leading, is made evident by quotations from his diary and from his conversations which have been given. That talk of his with Doctor Peatling one evening at Carshalton which is mentioned earlier, his insistence that the Territorials ought to be warned that they would all be needed for war work overseas when the national emergency arose, point unmistakably to his conviction that a great European war was impending; and they prove furthermore that he entertained no illusions as to the immensity of the struggle's scope when it should come. Moreover even at an earlier date, during those years immediately after his return from Canada, somewhat lean and discouraging years in so far as his professional prospects were concerned, a prophetic instinct seems to have moved him at times to foresee that one day he might play a great part in the affairs of his country. Most thinking officers in the United Kingdom no doubt perceived what was looming ahead, and deplored the inadequacy of the Government's preparations for meeting the storm. Few of them, however, visualised the situation which was to arise quite so clearly as did Maude.

But we have not here to consider him only in his capacity as a soldier and commander in the field. He was a type of man bound to make his mark in any walk of life as a consequence of natural ability, of exceptional application, and of being governed by a lofty sense of duty. The sense of duty in him was moreover fostered by strong religious convictions, to which Mr Vaux of Carshalton has paid a remarkable tribute (see above). Maude's diaries bear indirect testimony to this. Even during the most strenuous days of his experiences in the field from 1914 onwards, he scarcely ever missed attendance at the early celebration of a Sunday morning, and he always made a point of joining in at least one other service if it could possibly be managed. Although it was impossible to make the Sunday a day of rest when in presence of the enemy, Maude tried to preserve it as a day set apart by devoting his spare hours to visiting the sick and wounded when a brigadier; and at a later date when he came to occupy higher military positions he made it his day for going round hospitals. He gave every possible encouragement to the army chaplains who were at different times serving under his orders, as also to others with whom he happened to come into contact, frequently mentioning them by name in his diaries. In no department indeed did he take a warmer and more practical interest than in that which is devoted to the spiritual welfare of the troops. His principal chaplain in Mesopotamia, the Rev. A. C. E. Jarvis, who was with Maude at his death, writes of the Army Commander in eloquent terms:

> For many months I acted as Church of England Chaplain at General Headquarters. It was during this period that, outside of official intercourse, the veil was lifted and that I got to know more of the man. He was very reserved, the innermost was not revealed, and it was thus that some misunderstood him. To me he was great, and great because he was good. He was an essentially good man. He was not ashamed of his religion; he did not make a parade of it, but it formed a vital part of a wholly disciplined life, always simple, always devout. He never missed a communion, not once, and he was a very busy man, while frequent celebrations were the rule in Mesopotamia.
>
> In an indefinable way he differed from any man I have ever known. Of him it may truly be said that he possessed a distinctive and unique personality. At the memorial service held at Baghdad the week after his death, in trying to find one word to express it, I chose the word 'intense.' His virility, his

simplicity, the thoroughness with which he did everything, are all summed up in that word – intensity of thought, intensity of insight, intensity of action. He was a strong man, quiet, self-effacing, but it was the strength of the great flood which, moving, seems asleep. Carelessness and slackness he abhorred, and he had no mercy on offenders; yet he was essentially generous and kind. In thousands of lives at home, in India and in the East, he lives enshrined for ever a great soldier, a keen sportsman, a typical English gentleman, a good man.

'His splendid abilities as a soldier,' Maude's old chief of Home District days, Lord Methuen, wrote of him after his death to Lady Maude, 'were apparent to all from the time when he was the best of adjutants. But there are other men who have risen to height in the Army, but yet have not succeeded in gaining the love of all as he did. No one ever grudged him his glory. There are some like him I wish there were more who never seek their own interests, who play the game, and in whose minds jealousy finds no place. As Burke puts it, 'to bring dispositions that are lovely in private life into the service and conduct of the commonwealth; so to be patriots as not to forget we are gentlemen.' This is why so many feel they have lost a friend that cannot be replaced, and why we feel so much for you and yours in your grief. Having been closely associated with him all his life, I think that the cause of his success was his thoroughness in whatever he undertook,' is the view of his old friend Sir W. Lambton; 'whether it was soldiering or sport he threw his whole heart and energy into what was on hand. No detail was too small for his notice, and no trouble too great, and that he achieved so much was due to the charm of his character as well as to his driving power. He had an intense love for his old school, Eton, and for his Regiment, and however great might be the stress of work at any time he always managed to keep touch with his old comrades.'

It was those who knew him the most intimately who respected him the most highly and who liked him best. His old schoolfellows remember him as ever intent upon whatever he happened to be engaged in and yet a bright and merry lad withal. The sunny side of his disposition came to be less apparent to those who met him casually or to mere acquaintances, as he grew older; but it was there all the time, although cloaked by a form of reserve and held in check by absorption in official duties and in the cares of life. As a man he required knowing; and yet no one who came into contact with him could fail to be struck by his courtesy, his accessibility and his readiness to enter with interest into any matter put before him. He liked to take the measure of any new acquaintances before granting his confidence or acquiescing in intimacy; but amongst those admitted to his friendship he unbent entirely and proved to be a most attractive companion. His quiet sense of humour came to his aid alike with acquaintances and with friends; it was turned to account to smooth over difficulties in the one case, and it made association with him all the more agreeable in the other case.

His addiction to sport of all kinds commended him alike to equals and to inferiors, and he was moreover of the class of sportsmen who prefer performing even performing indifferently to looking on. Running with him was a natural gift; but he made the most of the gift by his abstemiousness, and this self-denial also aided him in his feats on the river as a young man and in later days. Although he played most outdoor games he had no special aptitude for those demanding skill; he was, however, a good shot, considering that he was too intent on his military duties from the time of his leaving Sandhurst to devote much time to this form of sport. Owing to his weight and to the expense involved he only hunted occasionally, but when he did he went well to hounds. Most mounted officers got falls during the South African War owing to the treacherous nature of the ground, but were little the worse; the fact that Maude met with two accidents and suffered considerable damage each time, viz. at Driefontein and on the day before Diamond Hill, suggests that he was a somewhat reckless horseman, as he had excellent sight. Thorough in all things, he was also thorough in respect to sport so long as he was actually engaged in it whether he was playing lawn tennis, or was following the beagles, or was taking part in a sculling match at Maidenhead and he always inculcated this same wholeheartedness in others.

An appreciation of this distinguished public servant would be incomplete without some brief reference to his home life. He was one of those men whom brains, character and the force of circumstances thrust into the limelight; but who nevertheless are happiest in the domestic circle, for he was wrapped up in his family. That they were ever in his thoughts is made manifest by his diaries. In moments of stress and worry in the field he would remember that it was the birthday of one of his children and would note it down. If a mail arrived at the Dardanelles or in Mesopotamia which, owing to those accidents that are ever occurring in postal arrangements on field service, brought him no letter from Mardale, he was much put out. Devotion to his military duties never prevented his settling down in the temporary homes that he occupied and, glad as he was on service grounds to quit Plymouth and to exchange Carshalton for the Curragh, he hated leaving his retreat on the shores of the Stonehouse creek and shrank from bidding good-bye to his garden at 'Greengates.' He ever loved to be with those nearest to him, sharing alike their pleasures and their troubles.

Take him for all in all, soldier, student, thinker, sportsman, gentleman, friend, Maude was an arresting and in many respects a fascinating figure. He proved himself a man of war. He left no stone unturned to ensure his mastery of any subject which he felt he ought to fathom. He took the long view in questions which the statesman too often hesitates to grapple with. He played the game through life as he had played it as a fag in Cornish's House at Eton. He won the regard and admiration of those who saw most of him and were best fitted to appraise his merits, and only those who enjoyed the privilege of his friendship realised how great that privilege was. Few men of the day have set a more shining example for the rising generation to follow, have consecrated themselves more wholeheartedly to the service of their country without thought of self, and have left a deeper and a more enduring footprint on the sands of time.